The Compact Reader

SHORT ESSAYS BY
METHOD AND THEME

Seventh Edition

The Compact Reader

SHORT ESSAYS BY METHOD AND THEME

Jane E. Aaron

Assisted by Kim Sanabria

Eugenio María de Hostos Community College
City University of New York

BEDFORD / ST. MARTIN'S
Boston ◆ *New York*

For Bedford/St. Martin's

Developmental Editors: Genevieve Hamilton and Maura Shea
Production Editor: Stasia Zomkowski
Marketing Manager: Brian Wheel
Editorial Assistant: Karin Halbert
Copyeditor: Mary Lou Wilshaw-Watts
Cover Design: Donna Dennison
Cover Art: Ocean Park #105, 1978. Richard Diebenkorn. Oil and charcoal on canvas. Collection of the Modern Art Museum of Forth Worth, Museum Purchase, Sid W. Richardson Foundation Endowment Fund and The Burnett Foundation.
Composition: Pine Tree Composition, Inc.
Printing and Binding: Haddon Craftsmen, Inc.

President: Joan E. Feinberg
Editor in Chief: Karen S. Henry
Director of Marketing: Karen Melton
Director of Editing, Design, and Production: Marcia Cohen
Managing Editor: Elizabeth M. Schaaf

Library of Congress Control Number: 2002102533

For information, write: Bedford/St. Martin's, 75 Arlington Street, Boston, MA 02116 (617-399-4000).

ISBN-10: 0–312–39225–7
ISBN-13: 978–0–312–39225–3

Acknowledgments

Barbara Lazear Ascher. "The Box Man." From Playing After Dark by Barbara Lazear Ascher. Copyright © 1982, 1983, 1984, 1986 by Barbara Lazear Ascher. Used by permission of Doubleday, a division of Random House, Inc.

Acknowledgments and copyrights are continued at the back of the book on pages 379–80, which constitute an extension of the copyright page. It is a violation of the law to reproduce these selections by any means whatsoever without the written permission of the copyright holder.

Preface

The seventh edition of *The Compact Reader,* like its predecessors, combines three texts in one brief volume: a rhetorical reader, a thematic reader, and a short-essay reader. As before, three introductory chapters guide students through the process of critical reading, writing, and revising. Then eleven chapters focus on the rhetorical methods of development, with each chapter's brief selections both illustrating a method and centering on a common theme. This edition adds substantial prereading activities, sixteen new essays, and other features designed to make *The Compact Reader* stimulating and helpful for both students and instructors.

Three Readers in One

The core of *The Compact Reader* remains its selections. Thirty-four essays and twenty paragraphs provide interesting reading that will enliven class discussion and spark good writing. The selections represent both emerging writers — including a student in every chapter — and established writers such as Joan Didion, Langston Hughes, Anne Lamott, and Russell Baker. Sixteen essays and nine paragraphs are new to this edition.

The Compact Reader's unique structure suits courses that take a rhetorical or a thematic approach and call for brief essays:

- In Chapters 4–13, three essays and two annotated paragraphs illustrate each rhetorical method, such as narration, comparison, and argument. Above all, the essays offer clear models, but they also show the methods at work in varied styles for varied purposes. Then Chapter 14 includes two annotated essays that demonstrate how writers combine methods to achieve their purposes.
- Each rhetorical chapter also has an overlapping thematic focus that shows the method developing the same general subject and

provides diverse perspectives to stimulate students' critical thinking, discussion, and writing. Five themes are new to this edition.

1. Description	Sensing the natural world
2. Narration	Recalling childhood
3. Example	Using language
4. Division or analysis	Looking at popular culture
5. Classification	Sorting thoughts and behaviors
6. Process analysis	Examining writing practices (new)
7. Comparison and contrast	Distinguishing ourselves from others (new)
8. Definition	Clarifying gender roles (new)
9. Cause-and-effect analysis	Exploring the influence of cultural identity (new)
10. Argument and persuasion	Debating current issues (new)
11. Combining methods of development	Articulating a vision

• The essays in *The Compact Reader* average just two to four pages apiece so that students can read them quickly, analyze them thoroughly, and emulate them successfully. A few longer essays, such as Russell Baker's "Gumption," help students make the transition to more challenging material.

An Introduction to Reading and Writing

An introduction to critical reading and the writing process appears in the first three chapters:

• Chapter 1 demonstrates the reading process, showing a student's annotations on a sample passage and providing detailed analysis of a professional essay, Barbara Lazear Ascher's "The Box Man."
• Chapter 2 covers the initial stages of composing, from assessing the writing situation through drafting, following the student's response to Ascher's essay and first draft. New material in this chapter discusses prereading, such as responding to the quotations and journal prompt now preceding each selection in the book.
• Chapter 3 then discusses revising and editing, from rethinking the thesis through reshaping paragraphs to reworking sentences and changing words. The chapter includes boxed checklists for revision and editing as well as revised and final drafts by the student responding to Ascher's essay.

The Compact Reader's emphasis on the union of reading and writing carries through the entire book:

- Complementing Chapter 3, the introduction to each rhetorical method features a "Focus" box that covers an element of writing especially relevant to that method, such as verbs in narration, paragraph coherence in comparison and contrast, and tone in argument and persuasion. Each box falls within a revision and editing checklist that extends Chapter 3's more general checklists to the particular method.
- To help students find what they need in the book, a guide to the elements of writing appears inside the book's back cover. This index covers Chapters 2 and 3 as well as all the rhetorical introductions.

Unique Editorial Apparatus

In addition to the features already mentioned, *The Compact Reader* offers numerous aids for students and teachers:

- A detailed, practical introduction to each of the ten rhetorical methods discusses basic concepts, offers two sample paragraphs illustrating the method, and suggests strategies for starting, organizing, drafting, revising, and editing an essay using the method. The introductions draw connections among purpose, subject, and method, helping students analyze and respond to any writing situation. A final "Note on Thematic Connections" explains how the chapter's paragraphs and essays relate to one another.
- New to this edition, quotations and a journal prompt precede every essay. These prereading materials will get students thinking and writing about the essay's topic, forming and expressing their own ideas, before they read the essay itself.
- Headnotes about the author and the essay place every selection in a context that helps focus students' reading.
- Detailed questions after each essay guide students' analysis of meaning, purpose and audience, method and structure, and language. A question labeled "Other Methods" highlights the author's use of combined methods.
- At least four writing topics after each selection give students specific direction for their own work. A "Journal to Essay" topic helps students build their journal writing into a finished essay. A "Cultural Considerations" topic leads students to consider

similarities and differences between cultures. And a "Connections" topic encourages students to make thematic or rhetorical links to other selections in the book.

*   Additional writing topics appear at the end of chapters. "Using the Method" lists ideas for applying the chapter's method of development, and "Writing About the Theme" includes ideas for drawing on the chapter's resources to explore its topic.
*   A glossary at the end of the book defines and illustrates more than a hundred terms, with specific cross-references to longer discussions in the text.

Helpful Instructor's Manual and Web Site

Resources for Teaching THE COMPACT READER, bound into the instructor's edition of the book, aims to help teachers integrate the text into their courses and use it in class. It includes an overview of the book's organization and chapters, ideas for combining the reader with other course materials, and varied resources for each selection: teaching tips, a content quiz, a vocabulary quiz, and detailed answers to all questions. The manual also reprints one essay from each rhetorical chapter with annotations that highlight the author's thesis and methods.

Students have access to a range of helpful resources at *The Compact Reader*'s companion Web site (*www.bedfordstmartins.com/compactreader*). Annotated links for each of the book's themes direct students to further reading. And direct links lead to two Bedford/St. Martin's sites — *The English Research Room* and *Research and Documentation Online* — that provide advice on research writing and documentation, practice tutorials, and to Internet research sources.

Acknowledgments

Many instructors helped to shape this edition of *The Compact Reader*, offering insights from their experience and suggestions for improvement. Special thanks to Louise Ackley, Boise State University; Brent E. Adrian, Central Community College; Bill Bennett, Wayne Community College; Kathryn N. Benzel, University of Nebraska, Kearney; Devan Cook, Boise State University; Leslie Dennen, University of San Francisco; James Kosmicki, Central Community College; Patricia A. Kramer, Rock Valley College; Lisa K. Miller, Phoenix

College; Michael Minassian, Broward Community College; Rebecca P. Mooney, Bakersfield College; Diane Nowicki, Portland Community College; David L. Pulling, Louisiana State University, Eunice; Jonah Rice, Southeastern Illinois College; Linda Schmidt, Iowa Western Community College; Nancy J. Schneider, University of Maine, Augusta; Donna Smith, Odessa College; Jacqueline Stark, Los Angeles Valley College; Michael W. White, Odessa College; Ted Wise, Porterville College.

Kim Sanabria, Hostos Community College, was an invaluable collaborator on this edition of *The Compact Reader*. She drew on her experience with the book to propose ideas for new features, suggest specific revisions, and provide extensive help with new selections and new apparatus.

The people at Bedford/St. Martin's once again contributed greatly to this project. Charles Christensen, Joan Feinberg, and Karen Henry provided encouraging and supportive leadership. Genevieve Hamilton and Maura Shea, assisted by Karin Halbert, helped to conceive the book's features and managed myriad details. And Stasia Zomkowski deftly shepherded the manuscript through production. Deep and happy thanks to all.

Contents

3	**WRITING** **Revising and Editing**	33

6	**EXAMPLE** *Using Language*	**118**

7	DIVISION OR ANALYSIS *Looking at Popular Culture*	146

10   COMPARISON AND CONTRAST   230
Distinguishing Ourselves from Others

---

11   **DEFINITION**   267
Clarifying Gender Roles

| **14** | **COMBINING METHODS OF DEVELOPMENT** *Articulating a Vision* | 368 |

Chapter 1

READING

This collection of essays has one purpose: to help you become a more proficient reader and writer. It combines examples of good writing with explanations of the writers' methods, questions to guide your reading, and ideas for your own writing. In doing so, it shows how you can adapt the processes and techniques of others as you learn to communicate clearly and effectively on paper.

Writing well is not an inborn skill but an acquired one: you will become proficient only by writing and rewriting, experimenting with different strategies, listening to the responses of readers. How, then, can it help to read the work of other writers?

- Reading others' ideas can introduce you to new information and give you new perspectives on your own experience. Many of the essays collected here demonstrate that personal experience is a rich and powerful source of material for writing. But the knowledge gained from reading can help pinpoint just what is remarkable in your experience. And by introducing varieties of behavior and ways of thinking that would otherwise remain unknown to you, reading can also help you understand where you fit in the scheme of things. Such insight not only reveals subjects for writing but also improves your ability to communicate with others whose experiences naturally differ from your own.

- Reading exposes you to a broad range of strategies and styles. Just seeing that these vary as much as the writers themselves should assure you that there is no fixed standard of writing, while it should also encourage you to find your own strategies and style. At the same time, you will see that writers do make choices to suit their subjects, their purposes, and especially their readers. Writing is rarely easy, even for the pros; but the more options you have to choose from, the more likely you are to succeed at it.

- Reading makes you sensitive to the role of audience in writing. As you become adept at reading the work of other writers critically, discovering intentions and analyzing choices, you will see how a writer's decisions affect you as audience. Training yourself to read consciously and critically is a first step to becoming a more objective reader of your own writing.

USING THIS BOOK FOR READING

The rest of this chapter offers strategies for making the most of your reading in this book and elsewhere. But first you should understand this book's overall organization. Most of the essays appear in Chapters 4–13, which introduce ten methods of developing a piece of writing:

description	process analysis
narration	comparison and contrast
example	definition
division or analysis	cause-and-effect analysis
classification	argument and persuasion

These methods correspond to basic and familiar patterns of thought and expression, common in our daily musings and conversations as well as in writing for all sorts of purposes and audiences: college term papers, lab reports, and examinations; business memos and reports; letters to the editors of newspapers; articles in popular magazines.

As writers we draw on the methods, sometimes unconsciously, to give order to our ideas and even to find ideas. For instance, a writer narrates, or tells, a story of her experiences to understand and convey the feeling of living her life. As readers, in turn, we have expectations for these familiar methods. When we read a narrative of someone's experiences, for instance, we expect enough details to understand what happened, we anticipate that events will be told primarily in the order they occurred, and we want the story to have a point—a reason for its being told and for our bothering to read it.

Making such expectations conscious can sharpen your skills as a critical reader and as a writer. The next chapter discusses all the methods in a bit more detail, and a full chapter on each one explains how it works, shows it at work in paragraphs, and gives advice for using it to develop your own essays. The three essays in each chapter provide clear examples that you can analyze and learn from (with the help of specific questions) and can refer to while writing (with the help of specific writing suggestions). In Chapter 14, two additional essays illustrate how writers combine the methods of development to suit their subjects and purposes.

To make your reading more interesting and also to stimulate your writing, the sample paragraphs and essays in Chapters 4–13 all focus on a common subject, such as childhood, popular culture, or gender roles. You'll see how flexible the methods are when they help five writers produce five unique pieces on the same theme. You'll also have a springboard for producing your own unique pieces, whether you take up some of the book's writing suggestions or take off with your own topics.

READING CRITICALLY

When we look for something to watch on television or listen to on the radio, we often tune in one station after another, pausing just long enough each time to catch the program or music being broadcast before settling on one choice. Much of the reading we do is similar: we skim a newspaper, magazine, or online document, noting headings and scanning paragraphs to get the gist of the content. But such skimming is not really reading, for it neither involves us deeply in the subject nor engages us in interaction with the writer.

To get the most out of reading, we must invest something of ourselves in the process, applying our own ideas and emotions and attending not just to the substance but to the writer's interpretation of it. This kind of reading is **critical** because it looks beneath the surface of a piece of writing. (The common meaning of *critical* as "negative" doesn't apply here: critical reading may result in positive, negative, or even neutral reactions.)

Critical reading can be enormously rewarding, but of course it takes care and time. A good method for developing your own skill in critical reading is to prepare yourself beforehand and then read the work at least twice to uncover what it has to offer.

Preparing

Preparing to read need involve no more than a few minutes as you form some ideas about the author, the work, and your likely response to the work:

- What is the author's background, what qualifications does he or she bring to the subject, and what approach is he or she likely to take? The biographical information provided before each essay in this book should help answer these questions; and many periodicals and books include similar information on their authors.
- What does the title convey about the subject and the author's attitude toward it? Note, for instance, the quite different attitudes conveyed by these three titles on the same subject: "Safe Hunting," "In Touch with Ancient Spirits," and "Killing Animals for Fun and Profit."
- What can you predict about your own response to the work? What might you already know about the author's subject? Based on the title and other clues, are you likely to agree or disagree with the author's views? *The Compact Reader* helps ready you for reading by providing two features before each selection. First, quotations from varied writers comment on the selection's core theme to give you a range of views. And second, a prompt labeled "Journal Response" encourages you to write about your existing views on or experiences with the author's subject before you see what the author has to say. By giving you a head start in considering the author's ideas and approach, writing *before* reading encourages you to read more actively and critically.

Reading Actively

After developing some expectations about the piece of writing, read it through carefully to acquaint yourself with the subject, the author's reason for writing about it, and the way the author presents it. (Each essay in this book is short enough to be read at one sitting.) Try not to read passively, letting the words wash over you, but instead interact directly with the work to discover its meaning, the author's intentions, and your own responses.

One of the best aids to active reading is to make notes on separate sheets of paper or, preferably (if you own the book), on the pages themselves. As you practice making notes, you will probably develop a personal code meaningful only to you. As a start, however, try this system:

- Underline or bracket passages that you find particularly effective or that seem especially important to the author's purpose.
- Circle words you don't understand so that you can look them up when you finish.
- Put question marks in the margins next to unclear passages.
- Jot down associations that occur to you, such as examples from your own experience, disagreements with the author's assumptions, or links to other works you've read.

When you have finished such an active reading, your annotations might look like those below. (The paragraph is from the end of the essay reprinted on pp. 7–11.)

The first half of our lives is spent stubbornly denying it. As children we acquire language to make ourselves understood and soon learn from the blank stares in response to our babblings that even these, our saviors, our parents, are strangers. In adolescence when we replay earlier dramas with peers in the place of parents, we begin the quest for the best friend, that person who will receive all thoughts as if they were her own. Later we assert that true love will find the way. True love finds many ways, but no escape from exile. The shores are littered with us, Annas and Ophelias, Emmas and Juliets, all outcasts from the dream of perfect understanding. We might as well draw the night around us and find solace there and a friend in our own voice.

true?

What about his own? Audience = women?

Ophelia + Juliet from Shakespeare. Others also?

In other words, just give up?

Before leaving the essay after such an initial reading, try to answer your own questions by looking up unfamiliar words and figuring out the meaning of unclear passages. Then let the essay rest in your mind for at least an hour or two before approaching it again.

Rereading

When rereading the essay, write a one- or two-sentence summary of each paragraph—in your own words—to increase your mastery of the material. Aim to answer the following questions:

- Why did the author write about this subject?
- What impression did the author wish to make on readers?
- How do the many parts of the work—for instance, the sequencing of information, the tone, the evidence—contribute to the author's purpose?
- How effective is the essay, and why?

A procedure for such an analysis—and the insights to be gained from it—can best be illustrated by examining an actual essay.

READING A SAMPLE ESSAY

The paragraph on page 5 comes from "The Box Man" by Barbara Lazear Ascher. The entire essay is reprinted here in the same format as other selections in the book, with quotations from other writers to get you thinking about the essay's subject, a suggestion for exploring your attitudes further in your journal, a note on the author, and a note on the essay.

Be it ever so humble, there is no place like home. —John Howard Payne

People who are homeless are not social inadequates. They are people without homes. —Sheila McKechnie

How does it feel / To be without a home / Like a complete unknown / Like a rolling stone? —Bob Dylan

Journal Response In your journal write briefly about how you typically feel when you encounter a person who appears to be homeless. Are you sympathetic? disgusted? something in between?

———— *Barbara Lazear Ascher* ————

Born in 1946, American writer Barbara Lazear Ascher is known for her insightful, inspiring essays. She obtained a B.A. from Bennington College in 1968 and a J.D. from Cardozo School of Law in 1979. After practicing law for two years, Ascher turned to writing full-time. Her essays have appeared in a diverse assortment of periodicals, including the New York Times, Vogue, The Yale Review, Redbook, *and* National Geographic Traveler. *Ascher has also published a memoir of her brother, who died of AIDS,* Landscape Without Gravity: A Memoir of Grief *(1993), and several collections of essays:* Playing After Dark *(1986),* The Habit of Loving *(1989), and* Dancing in the Dark: Romance, Yearning, and the Search for the Sublime *(1999).*

The Box Man

In this essay from Playing After Dark, *the evening ritual of a homeless man prompts Ascher's reflection on the nature of solitude. By describing the Box Man alongside two other solitary people, Ascher distinguishes between chosen and unchosen loneliness.*

The Box Man was at it again. It was his lucky night.   1

The first stroke of good fortune occurred as darkness fell and the   2
night watchman at 220 East Forty-fifth Street neglected to close the
door as he slipped out for a cup of coffee. I saw them before the Box
Man did. Just inside the entrance, cardboard cartons, clean and with

their top flaps intact. With the silent fervor of a mute at a horse race, I willed him toward them.

It was slow going. His collar was pulled so high that he appeared 3 headless as he shuffled across the street like a man who must feel Earth with his toes to know that he walks there.

Standing unselfconsciously in the white glare of an over- 4 head light, he began to sort through the boxes, picking them up, one by one, inspecting tops, insides, flaps. Three were tossed aside. They looked perfectly good to me, but then, who knows what the Box Man knows? When he found the one that suited his purpose, he dragged it up the block and dropped it in a doorway.

Then, as if dogged by luck, he set out again and discovered, be- 5 hind the sign at the parking garage, a plastic Dellwood box, strong and clean, once used to deliver milk. Back in the doorway the grand design was revealed as he pushed the Dellwood box against the door and set its cardboard cousin two feet in front—the usual distance between coffee table and couch. Six full shopping bags were distributed evenly on either side.

He eased himself with slow care onto the stronger box, reached 6 into one of the bags, pulled out a *Daily News,* and snapped it open against his cardboard table. All done with the ease of IRT Express passengers whose white-tipped, fair-haired fingers reach into attaché cases as if radar-directed to the *Wall Street Journal.* They know how to fold it. They know how to stare at the print, not at the girl who stares at them.

That's just what the Box Man did, except that he touched his 7 tongue to his fingers before turning each page, something grandmothers do.

One could live like this. Gathering boxes to organize a life. Wan- 8 dering through the night collecting comforts to fill a doorway.

When I was a child, my favorite book was *The Boxcar Children.* 9 If I remember correctly, the young protagonists were orphaned, and rather than live with cruel relatives, they ran away to the woods to live life on their own terms. An abandoned boxcar was turned into a home, a bubbling brook became an icebox. Wild berries provided abundant desserts and days were spent in the happy, adultless pursuit of joy. The children never worried where the next meal would come from or what February's chill might bring. They had unquestioning faith that berries would ripen and streams run cold and clear. And unlike Thoreau,[1] whose deliberate living was self-conscious and purposeful, theirs had the ease of children at play.

Even now, when life seems complicated and reason slips, I long to live like a Boxcar Child, to have enough open space and freedom of movement to arrange my surroundings according to what I find. To turn streams into iceboxes. To be ingenious with simple things. To let the imagination hold sway.

Who is to say that the Box Man does not feel as Thoreau did in his doorway, not "crowded or confined in the least," with "pasture enough for [. . .] imagination." Who is to say that his dawns don't bring back heroic ages? That he doesn't imagine a goddess trailing her garments across his blistered legs?

His is a life of the mind, such as it is, and voices only he can hear. Although it would appear to be a life of misery, judging from the bandages and chill of night, it is of his choosing. He will ignore you if you offer an alternative. Last winter, Mayor Koch[2] tried, coaxing him with promises and the persuasive tones reserved for rabid dogs. The Box Man backed away, keeping a car and paranoia between them.

He is not to be confused with the lonely ones. You'll find them everywhere. The lady who comes into our local coffee shop each evening at five-thirty, orders a bowl of soup and extra Saltines. She drags it out as long as possible, breaking the crackers into smaller and smaller pieces, first in halves and then halves of halves and so on until the last pieces burst into salty splinters and fall from dry fingers onto the soup's shimmering surface. By 6 P.M., it's all over. What will she do with the rest of the night?

You can tell by the vacancy of expression that no memories linger there. She does not wear a gold charm bracelet with silhouettes of boys and girls bearing grandchildren's birthdates and a chip of the appropriate birthstone. When she opens her black purse to pay, there is only a crumpled Kleenex and a wallet inside, no photographs spill onto her lap. Her children, if there are any, live far away and prefer not to visit. If she worked as a secretary for forty years in a downtown office, she was given a retirement party, a cake, a reproduction

---

[1] Henry David Thoreau (1817–62) was an American essayist and poet who for two years lived a solitary and simple life in the woods. He wrote of his experiences in *Walden* (1854). [Editor's note.]

[2] Edward Koch was the mayor of New York City from 1978 through 1989. [Editor's note.]

of an antique perfume atomizer and sent on her way. Old colleagues—those who traded knitting patterns and brownie recipes
over the water cooler, who discussed the weather, health, and office
scandal while applying lipstick and blush before the ladies' room mirror—they are lost to time and the new young employees who take
their places in the typing pool.

Each year she gets a Christmas card from her ex-boss. The enve- 15
lope is canceled in the office mailroom and addressed by memory
typewriter. Within is a family in black and white against a wooded
Connecticut landscape. The boss, his wife, who wears her hair in a
gray page boy, the three blond daughters, two with tall husbands and
an occasional additional grandchild. All assembled before a worn
stone wall.

Does she watch game shows? Talk to a parakeet, feed him cuttle- 16
bone, and call him Pete? When she rides the buses on her Senior Citizen pass, does she go anywhere or wait for something to happen?
Does she have a niece like the one in Cynthia Ozick's story "Rosa,"
who sends enough money to keep her aunt at a distance?

There's a lady across the way whose lights and television stay on 17
all night. A crystal chandelier in the dining room and matching Chinese lamps on Regency end tables in the living room. She has six cats,
some Siamese, others Angora and Abyssinian. She pets them and waters her plethora of plants—African violets, a ficus tree, a palm, and
geraniums in season. Not necessarily a lonely life except that 3 A.M.
lights and television seem to proclaim it so.

The Box Man welcomes the night, opens to it like a lover. He 18
moves in darkness and prefers it that way. He's not waiting for the
phone to ring or an engraved invitation to arrive in the mail. Not for
him a P.O. number. Not for him the overcrowded jollity of office
parties, the hot anticipation of a singles' bar. Not even for him a holiday handout. People have tried and he shuffled away.

The Box Man knows that loneliness chosen loses its sting and 19
claims no victims. He declares what we all know in the secret
passages of our own nights, that although we long for perfect har-
mony, communion, and blending with another soul, this is a solo
voyage.

The first half of our lives is spent stubbornly denying it. As chil- 20
dren we acquire language to make ourselves understood and soon
learn from the blank stares in response to our babblings that even
these, our saviors, our parents, are strangers. In adolescence when we
replay earlier dramas with peers in the place of parents, we begin the

quest for the best friend, that person who will receive all thoughts as if they were her own. Later we assert that true love will find the way. True love finds many ways, but no escape from exile. The shores are littered with us, Annas and Ophelias, Emmas and Juliets,[3] all outcasts from the dream of perfect understanding. We might as well draw the night around us and find solace there and a friend in our own voice.

One could do worse than be a collector of boxes.   *21*

Even read quickly, Ascher's essay would not be difficult to comprehend: the author draws on examples of three people to make a point at the end about solitude. In fact, a quick reading might give the impression that Ascher produced the essay effortlessly, artlessly. But close, critical reading reveals a carefully conceived work whose parts work independently and together to achieve the author's purpose.

One way to uncover underlying intentions and relations like those in Ascher's essay is to work through a series of questions about the work. The following questions proceed from the general to the specific—from overall meaning through purpose and method to word choices—and they parallel the more specific questions after the essays in this book. Here the questions come with possible answers for Ascher's essay. (The paragraph numbers can help you locate the appropriate passages in Ascher's essay as you follow the analysis.)

Meaning

What is the main idea of the essay—the chief point the writer makes about the subject, to which all other ideas and details relate? What are the subordinate ideas that contribute to the main idea?

Ascher states her main idea (or thesis) near the end of her essay: in choosing solitude, the Box Man confirms the essential aloneness of human beings (paragraph 19) but also demonstrates that we can "find solace" within ourselves (20). (Writers sometimes postpone

---

[3] These are all doomed heroines of literature. Anna is the title character of Leo Tolstoy's novel *Anna Karenina* (1876). Emma is the title character of Gustave Flaubert's novel *Madame Bovary* (1856). Ophelia and Juliet are in Shakespeare's plays—the lovers, respectively, of Hamlet and Romeo. [Editor's note.]

stating their main idea, as Ascher does here. Perhaps more often, they state it near the beginning of the essay. See pp. 18–19.) Ascher leads up to and supports her idea with three examples—the Box Man (paragraphs 1–7, 11–12) and, in contrast, two women whose loneliness seems unchosen (13–16, 17). These examples are developed with specific details from Ascher's observations (such as the nearly empty purse, 14) and from the imagined lives these observations suggest (such as the remote, perhaps nonexistent children, 14).

Occasionally, you may need to puzzle over some of the author's words before you can fully understand his or her meaning. Try to guess the word's meaning from its context first, and then check your guess in a dictionary. (To help master the word so that you know it next time and can draw on it yourself, use it in a sentence or more of your own.)

Purpose and Audience

Why did the author write the essay? What did the author hope readers would gain from it? What did the author assume about the knowledge and interests of readers, and how are these assumptions reflected in the essay?

Ascher seems to have written her essay for two interlocking reasons: to show and thus explain that solitude need not always be lonely and to argue gently for defeating loneliness by becoming one's own friend. In choosing the Box Man as her main example, she reveals perhaps a third purpose as well—to convince readers that a homeless person can have dignity and may achieve a measure of self-satisfaction lacking in some people who do have homes.

Ascher seems to assume that her readers, like her, are people with homes, people to whom the Box Man and his life might seem completely foreign: she comments on the Box Man's slow shuffle (paragraph 3), his mysterious discrimination among boxes (4), his "blistered legs" (11), how miserable his life looks (12), his bandages (12), the cold night he inhabits (12), the fearful or condescending approaches of strangers (12, 18). Building from this assumption that her readers will find the Box Man strange, Ascher takes pains to show the dignity of the Box Man—his "grand design" for furniture (5), his resemblance to commuters (6), his grandmotherly finger licking (7), his refusal of handouts (18).

Several other apparent assumptions about her audience also influence Ascher's selection of details, if less significantly. First, she assumes some familiarity with literature—at least with the writings of Thoreau (9, 11) and the characters named in paragraph 20. Second, Ascher seems to address women: in paragraph 20 she speaks of each person confiding in "her" friend, and she chooses only female figures from literature to illustrate "us, [. . .] all outcasts from the dream of perfect understanding." Finally, Ascher seems to address people who are familiar with, if not actually residents of, New York City: she refers to a New York street address (2); alludes to a New York newspaper, the *Daily News,* and a New York subway line, the IRT Express (6); and mentions the city's mayor (12). However, readers who do not know the literature Ascher cites, who are not women, and who do not know New York City are still likely to understand and appreciate Ascher's main point.

Method and Structure

What method or methods does the author use to develop the main idea, and how do the methods serve the author's subject and purpose? How does the organization serve the author's subject and purpose?

Ascher's primary support for her idea consists of three examples (Chapter 6)—specific instances of solitary people. The method of example especially suits Ascher's subject and purpose because it allows her to show contrasting responses to solitude: one person who seems to choose it and two people who don't.

As writers often do, Ascher relies on more than a single method, more than just example. She develops her examples with description (Chapter 4), vividly portraying the Box Man and the two women, as in paragraphs 6–7, so that we see them clearly. Paragraphs 1–7 in the portrayal of the Box Man involve retelling, or narrating (Chapter 5), his activities. Ascher uses division or analysis (Chapter 7) to tease apart the elements of her three characters' lives. And she relies on comparison and contrast (Chapter 10) to show the differences between the Box Man and the other two in paragraphs 13 and 17–18.

While using many methods to develop her idea, Ascher keeps her organization fairly simple. She does not begin with a formal introduction or a statement of her idea but instead starts right off with her main example, the inspiration for her idea. In the first seven paragraphs she narrates and describes the Box Man's activities. Then, in paragraphs 8–12, she explains what appeals to her about circumstances like the Box Man's and she applies those thoughts to what she imagines are his thoughts. Still delaying a statement of her main idea, Ascher contrasts the Box Man and two other solitary people, whose lives she sees as different from his (13–17). Finally, she returns to the Box Man (18–19) and zeroes in on her main idea (19–20). Though she has withheld this idea until the end, we see that everything in the essay has been controlled by it and directed toward it.

Language

How are the author's main idea and purpose revealed at the level of sentences and words? How does the author use language to convey his or her attitudes toward the subject and to make meaning clear and vivid?

One reason Ascher's essay works is that she uses specific language to portray her three examples—she *shows* them to us—and to let us know what she thinks about them. For instance, the language changes markedly from the depiction of the Box Man to the next-to-last paragraph on solitude. The Box Man comes to life in warm terms: Ascher watches him with "silent fervor" (paragraph 2); he seems "dogged by luck" (5); he sits with "slow care" and opens the newspaper with "ease" (6); his page turning reminds Ascher of "grandmothers" (7); it is conceivable that, in Thoreau's word, the Box Man's imagination has "pasture" to roam, that he dreams of "heroic ages" and a "goddess trailing her garments" (11). In contrast, isolation comes across as a desperate state in paragraph 20, where Ascher uses such words as "blank stares," "strangers," "exile," "littered," and "outcasts." The contrast in language helps to emphasize Ascher's point about the individual's ability to find comfort in solitude.

In describing the two other solitary people—those who evidently have not found comfort in aloneness—Ascher uses words that emphasize the heaviness of time and the sterility of existence. The first woman "drags" her meal out and crumbles crackers between "dry fingers" (13), a "vacancy of expression" on her face (14). She lacks even the trinkets of attachment—a "gold charm bracelet" with pictures of grandchildren (14). A vividly imagined photograph of her ex-boss and his family (15)—the wife with "her hair in a gray page boy," "the three blond daughters"—emphasizes the probable absence of such scenes in the woman's own life.

Ascher occasionally uses incomplete sentences (or sentence fragments) to stress the accumulation of details or the quickness of her impressions. For example, in paragraph 10 the incomplete sentences beginning "To" sketch Ascher's dream. And in paragraph 18 the incomplete sentences beginning "Not" emphasize the Box Man's withdrawal. Both of these sets of incomplete sentences gain emphasis from **parallelism**, the use of similar grammatical form for ideas of equal importance. (See p. 50) The parallelism begins in the complete sentence preceding each set of incomplete sentences—for example, "[. . .] I long to live like a Boxcar Child, to have enough open space and freedom of movement [. . .]. To turn streams into iceboxes. To be ingenious with simple things. To let the imagination hold sway." Although incomplete sentences can be unclear, these and the others in Ascher's essay are clear: she uses them deliberately and carefully, for a purpose. (Inexperienced writers often find it safer to avoid any incomplete sentences until they have mastered the complete sentence.)

These notes on Ascher's essay show how one can arrive at a deeper, more personal understanding of a piece of writing by attentive, thoughtful analysis. Guided by the questions at the end of each essay and by your own sense of what works and why, you'll find similar lessons and pleasures in all of this book's readings.

Chapter 2

WRITING

GETTING STARTED
THROUGH DRAFTING

Analyzing a text in the way shown in the preceding chapter is valuable in itself: it can be fun, and the process helps you better understand and appreciate whatever you read. But it can make you a better
writer, too, by showing you how to read your own work critically,
increasing the strategies available to you, and suggesting topics for
you to write about.

USING THIS BOOK FOR WRITING

Though it is mainly a collection of essays, *The Compact Reader* also
contains a range of material designed to help you use your reading to
write effectively.

   The first element consists of this chapter and the next, on writing;
you may want to refer to these chapters again and again as your writing skills develop. (See the inside back cover for a guide to the topics
covered.) Offering specific ways to strengthen and clarify your work,

the chapters also include a student's essay-in-progress from idea through final draft.

These two chapters follow the stages of the **writing process:** getting started, organizing, drafting, revising, and editing. Most writers experience such stages on their way to a finished piece of writing, and each stage tends to have a dominant activity, such as discovering ideas or shaping ideas or making corrections. But actually, the stages are quite arbitrary because writers rarely move in straight lines through fixed steps, like locomotives over tracks. Instead, just as they do when thinking, writers continually circle back over covered territory, each time picking up more information or seeing new relationships, until their meaning is clear to themselves and can be made clear to readers. No two writers proceed in exactly the same way, either, so that your writing process may differ considerably from your classmates'. Still, viewing the process in stages does help sort out its many activities so that you can develop the process or processes that work best for you.

Complementing this and the next chapter's overview of writing are the more specific introductions to the methods of development in Chapters 4–13—narration, comparison and contrast, definition, and so on. These method introductions follow the pattern set here by also proceeding from beginning to end of the writing process, but they take up particular concerns of the method, such as organizing a narrative or clarifying a definition.

Besides its advice on writing, *The Compact Reader* also contains scores of suggestions for what to write about. At least four writing topics follow each essay: some call for your analysis of the essay; others lead you to examine your own experiences or other sources in light of the essay's ideas. Two additional sets of topics fall at the end of each chapter: one group provides a range of subjects for using the chapter's method of development; the other encourages you to focus on thematic connections in the chapter.

GETTING STARTED

Every writing situation involves several elements: you communicate an *idea* about a subject to an *audience* of readers for a particular *purpose.* At first you may not be sure of your idea or your purpose. You may not know how you want to approach your readers, even when you know who they are. Your job in getting started, then, is to explore options and make choices.

Considering Your Subject and Purpose

A subject for writing may arise from any source, including your own experience or reading, a suggestion in this book, or an assignment from your instructor. In the previous chapter, Barbara Ascher's essay on a homeless man demonstrates how an excellent subject can be found from observing one's surroundings. Whatever its source, the subject should be something you care enough about to probe deeply and to stamp with your own perspective.

This personal stamp comprises both your main idea, the central point you want to make about the subject, and your **purpose**, your reason for writing. The purpose may be one of the following:

- To explain the subject so that readers understand it or see it in a new light.
- To persuade readers to accept or reject an opinion or to take a certain action.
- To entertain readers with a humorous or exciting story.
- To express the thoughts and emotions triggered by a revealing or instructive experience.

A single essay may sometimes have more than one purpose: for instance, a writer might both explain what it's like to be disabled and try to persuade readers to respect special parking zones for the disabled. Your purpose and your main idea may occur to you early on, arising out of the subject and its significance for you. But you may need to explore your subject for a while—even to the point of writing a draft—before it becomes clear to you.

Considering Your Thesis

How many times have you read a work of nonfiction and wondered, "What's the point?" Whether consciously or not, we expect a writer to *have* a point, a central idea that he or she wants readers to take away from the work. We expect that idea to determine the content of the work—so that everything relates to it—and we expect the content in turn to demonstrate or prove the idea.

Arriving at a main idea, or **thesis,** is thus an essential part of the writing process. Sometimes it will occur to you at the moment you hit on your subject—for instance, if you think of writing about the new grading policy because you want to make a point about its unfairness. At other times you may struggle through a draft or more to pin down just what you have to say. Even if your thesis will evolve, however, you'll probably benefit from focusing on it early so that it can help you generate ideas, seek information, organize your thoughts, and so on.

The best way to focus on your thesis is to write it out in a **thesis sentence** or sentences, an assertion about the subject. In these two sentences from the end of "The Box Man" (p. 11), Barbara Ascher asserts the point of her essay:

> [We are] all outcasts from the dream of perfect understanding. We might as well draw the night around us and find solace there and a friend in our own voice.

Because your thesis itself may change over the course of the writing process, your thesis sentence may also change, sometimes considerably. The following thesis sentences show how one writer shifted his opinion and moved from an explanatory to a persuasive purpose between the early stages of the writing process and the final draft.

> TENTATIVE   With persistence, adopted children can often locate information about their birth parents.
>
> FINAL   Adopted children are unfairly hampered in seeking information about their birth parents.

The final sentence makes a definite assertion ("Adopted children are unfairly hampered") and clearly conveys the persuasive purpose of the essay to come. Thus the sentence lets readers know what to expect: an argument that adopted children should be treated more fairly when they seek information about their birth parents. Readers will also expect some discussion of what hampers an adoptee's search, what is "unfair" and "fair" in this situation, and what changes the author proposes.

Most commonly, the thesis sentence comes near the beginning of an essay, sometimes in the first paragraph, where it serves as a promise to examine a particular subject from a particular perspective. But as Ascher demonstrates by stating her thesis at the end, the thesis sentence may come elsewhere as long as it controls the whole essay. The thesis may even go unstated, as other essays in this book illustrate, but it still must govern every element of the work as if it were announced.

Considering Your Audience

Either very early, when you first begin exploring your subject, or later, as a check on what you have generated, you may want to make a few notes on your anticipated audience. The notes are optional, but thinking about audience definitely is not. Your purpose and thesis as well as supporting ideas, details and examples, organization, style, tone, and language—all should reflect your answers to the following questions:

- What impression do you want to make on readers?
- What do readers already know about your subject? What do they need to know?
- What are readers' likely expectations and assumptions about your subject?
- How can you build on readers' previous knowledge, expectations, and assumptions to bring them around to your view?

These considerations are obviously crucial to achieve the fundamental purpose of all public writing: communication. Accordingly, they come up again and again in the chapter introductions and the questions after each essay.

Discovering Ideas

Ideas for your writing—whether your subject or your thesis or the many smaller ideas and details that build your thesis—may come to you in a rush, or you may need to search for them. Writers use a variety of searching techniques, from jotting down thoughts while they pursue other activities to writing concentratedly for a set period. Here are a few techniques you might try.

Journal Writing

Many writers keep a **journal,** a record of thoughts and observations. Whether in a notebook or in a computer file, journal entries give you an opportunity to explore ideas just for yourself, free of concerns about readers who will judge what you say or how you say it. Regular journal entries can also make you more comfortable with the act of writing and build your confidence. Indeed, writing teachers often require their students to keep journals for these reasons.

In a journal you can write about whatever interests, puzzles, or disturbs you. Here are just a few possible uses:

- Record your responses to your reading in this book and other sources.
- Prepare for a class by summarizing the week's reading or the previous class's discussion.
- Analyze a relationship that's causing you problems.
- Imitate a writer you admire, such as a poet or songwriter.
- Explore your reactions to a movie or a music album.
- Confide your dreams and fears.

Any of this material could provide a seed for a writing assignment, but you can also use a journal deliberately to develop ideas for assignments. One approach is built into this book: before every essay you will find several quotations and a suggestion for journal writing—all centering on the topic of the essay. In responding to the quotations and journal prompt preceding Barbara Ascher's "The Box Man" (p. 7), you might explore your feelings about homeless people or recount a particular encounter with a homeless person. One student, Grace Patterson, wrote this journal entry in response to the material preceding Ascher's essay:

> It seems that nothing works to solve the problem of
> homeless people. My first reaction is fear--especially
> if the person is really dirty or rambling on about
> something, I just walk away as fast as I can. Can't say
> I'm proud of myself though--there's always guilt--I
> should be helping. But how? I like what Bob Dylan
> says--a home is important, so how must it feel to be
> without one?

Writing for herself, Patterson felt free to explore what was on her mind, without worrying about correctness and without trying to make it clear to external readers what she meant by such words as *fear* and *guilt*. By articulating her mixed reactions to homelessness, Patterson established a personal context in which to read Ascher's essay, and that context made her a more engaged, more critical reader.

Patterson used journal writing for another purpose as well: to respond to Ascher's essay *after* she read it.

```
Ascher gives an odd view of homelessness--hadn't
really occurred to me that the homeless man on the
street might want to be there. Always assumed that no
one would want to live in filthy clothes, without a
roof. What is a home anyway -- shelter? decor? a
clothes closet? Can your body and few "possessions" =
home?
```

As this entry's final question makes clear, Patterson didn't come to any conclusions about homelessness or about Ascher's essay. She did, however, begin to work out ideas that would serve as the foundation for a more considered critical response later on. (Further stages of Patterson's writing process appear throughout the rest of this chapter.)

Freewriting

To discover ideas for a particular assignment, you may find it useful to try **freewriting,** or writing without stopping for a set amount of time, usually ten to fifteen minutes. In freewriting you push yourself to keep writing, following ideas wherever they lead, paying no attention to completeness or correctness or even sense. When she began composing an essay response to Barbara Ascher's "The Box Man," Grace Patterson produced this freewriting:

```
Something in Ascher's essay keeps nagging at me. Almost
ticks me off. What she says about the Box Man is based
on certain assumptions. Like she knows what he's been
through, how he feels. Can he be as content as she
says? What bothers me is, how much choice does the guy
really have? Just cuz he manages to put a little
dignity into his life on the street and refuses
handouts--does that mean he chooses homelessness? Life
in a shelter might be worse than life on the street.
```

Notice that this freewriting is rough: the tone is very informal, as if Patterson were speaking to herself; some thoughts are left dangling; some sentences are shapeless or incomplete; a word is misspelled (*cuz* for *because*). But none of this matters because the freewriting is just exploratory. Writing fluently, without halting to rethink or edit, actually pulled insights out of Patterson. She moved from being vaguely uneasy with Ascher's essay to conceiving an argument against it. Then, with a more definite focus, she could begin drafting in earnest.

If you have difficulty writing without correcting and you compose on a word processor, you might try **invisible writing:** turn the computer's monitor off while you freewrite, so that you can't see what you're producing. When your time is up, turn the monitor back on to work with the material.

Brainstorming

Another discovery technique that helps to pull ideas from you is **brainstorming,** listing ideas without stopping to censor or change them. As in freewriting, write without stopping for ten or fifteen minutes, jotting down everything that seems even remotely related to your subject. Don't stop to reread and rethink what you have written; just keep pulling and recording ideas, no matter how silly or dull or irrelevant they seem. When your time is up, look over the list to find the promising ideas and discard the rest. Depending on *how* promising the remaining ideas are, you can resume brainstorming, try freewriting about them, or begin a draft.

Considering Your Method of Development

The ten methods of development discussed in Chapters 4–13 can help you continue to expand your thinking or begin to focus and shape your ideas. You can use the methods singly, with one method dominating in an essay, or in combination, with different methods providing varied perspectives on your subject.

The following sections begin with questions suggested by each method. Asking these questions about your subject can open up approaches you may not have considered. Then the sections show how each method also provides a direction that may help you achieve your particular purpose for writing.

Description (Chapter 4)

How does the subject look, sound, smell, taste, and feel?

We use description to depict objects, places, people, and emotions through the evidence of our senses. It will come into play if you want to express your feelings about playing a sport, portray a friend, report on a laboratory procedure in biology or an observation session in psychology, file an insurance claim after a car accident, or show a denuded mountain as a way of arguing against clear-cutting forests.

Narration (Chapter 5)

What is the story in the subject? How did it happen?

Narration is storytelling, either fictional (as in novels) or nonfictional (as in recounting an experience you had). You can use narration to entertain readers by retelling an amusing or scary experience, to explain the sequence of events in a chemistry experiment, to summarize actions in a letter complaining about a product, to explain what went wrong in a ball game, or to persuade readers by means of several stories that the forestry industry is sincere about restoring clear-cut forests.

Example (Chapter 6)

How can the subject be illustrated? What are instances of it?

An example is evidence for a general statement, a particular instance of what the statement claims. We use examples constantly to clarify and support our general claims. You might use the method to entertain readers with the idea that you're accident prone, to demonstrate why your school should reduce maximum class size, to counter a prevailing view about your city, or to show by citing another company's policy how recycling could work in your company.

Division or Analysis (Chapter 7)

What are the subject's parts, and what is their relationship or significance?

Division or analysis (alternative names for the same process) is the method of taking apart and reassembling. With division or analysis, we peer into the insides of an object, institution, work of art, policy, or any other whole: we identify the parts, see how the parts relate, and draw on that vision to form conclusions about the whole. You can use division or analysis to write critically about a movie, poem, or journal article, to identify the flaws in a theory of schizophrenia, to explain a company's organization after a merger, to determine whether the company is now a good investment, or to argue that television talk shows do more good than harm.

Classification (Chapter 8)

What groups or categories can the subject be sorted into?

Classification takes many items that share at least one characteristic — writing students, tax laws, motorcycles — and arranges them into groups based on their similarities. You could draw on classification if you wanted to explain four styles of communicating by e-mail, argue that one type of campaign contribution is more corrupting than the others, propose new categories of nonsalaried employees, or explain the types of health-insurance policies.

Process Analysis (Chapter 9)

How does the subject work, or how does one do it?

Process analysis explains *how* a sequence of actions leads to an expected result: sending and receiving e-mail, manufacturing a car, training to be a registered nurse. Use process analysis when you want readers to understand how something works — for instance, in explaining how an electric car can save energy, how a congressional committee can shape legislation, or how a new kind of junction box can prevent household electrical fires. Also use process analysis when you want to tell readers how to do something, such as how to design a Web page, how to get the most from managed health care, or how to follow a new office procedure.

Comparison and Contrast (Chapter 10)

How is the subject similar to or different from something else?

A dual method, comparison and contrast allows us to explain or evaluate subjects by putting them side by side, showing how they are alike and different. You'll find the method useful if you want to explain that computer hackers are not like their popular image, to explain how nursing has changed in the past ten years, or to explain the likenesses between American football and rugby. Comparison and contrast is also useful for evaluating two or more subjects and perhaps arguing the superiority of one of them — for instance, two detective novels, three options for company health benefits, or two ways of routing traffic downtown.

Definition (Chapter 11)

What are the subject's characteristics and boundaries?

With definition we specify what something is and what it is not. We use definition often in sentences or paragraphs to explain our meaning— stopping to define *success,* for instance, in a paper on successful small businesses, or giving the sense of a technical term in an engineering study. But we may also define words at essay length, especially when they are abstract, complicated, or controversial. Drawing on other methods of development, such as example or comparison and contrast, you might devote an entire essay to the debated phrase *family values,* the current uses of the word *monopoly* in business, or the meanings of the term *personality* in a particular psychological theory.

Cause-and-Effect Analysis (Chapter 12)

Why did the subject happen? What were or may be its consequences?

By analyzing causes and effects, we determine the events that brought about an outcome (the causes) or the events that resulted or may result from an occurrence (the effects). Like everyone else, you probably consider causes and effects many times a day: Why is the traffic so heavy? What will happen if I major in communications rather than business? In writing you'll also draw often on cause-and-effect analysis, perhaps explaining why the school's basketball team has been so successful this year, what made a bridge collapse, or how a new stoplight has worsened rush-hour traffic. You'll use the method for persuasion, too, as in arguing that the family, not the mass media, bears responsibility for children's violence (focusing on causes) or that adult illiteracy threatens American democracy (focusing on possible effects).

Argument and Persuasion (Chapter 13)

Why do I believe as I do about the subject? Why do others have different opinions? How can I convince others to accept my opinion or believe as I do?

With argument and persuasion, purpose and method coincide: the aim is to find agreement with readers, change their minds, or move them to action. You'll construct arguments in your classes, as when you dispute someone else's interpretation of data, and also in work and in life, as when you identify and propose a solution for a problem or protest a tax bill. In writing argument and persuasion, you may draw on several or all of the other methods of development.

ORGANIZING

Writers vary in the extent to which they arrange their material before they begin drafting, but most do establish some plan. A good time to do so is after you've explored your subject and developed a good stock of ideas about it. Before you begin drafting, you can look over what you've got and consider the best ways to organize it.

Creating a Plan

A writing plan may consist of a list of key points, a fuller list including specifics as well, or even a detailed formal outline—whatever gives order to your ideas and provides some direction for your writing.

As you'll see in later chapters, many of the methods of development suggest specific structures, most notably description, narration, classification, process analysis, and comparison and contrast. But even when the organization is almost built into the method, you'll find that some subjects demand more thoughtful plans than others. You may be able to draft a straightforward narrative of a personal experience with very little advance planning. But a nonpersonal narrative, or even a personal one involving complex events and time shifts, may require more thought about arrangement.

Though some sort of plan is almost always useful when drafting, resist any temptation at this stage to pin down every detail in its proper place. A huge investment in planning can hamper you during drafting, making it difficult to respond to new ideas and even new directions that may prove fruitful.

Thinking in Paragraphs

Most essays consist of three parts, an introduction and a conclusion (discussed in the next section) and the **body**, the most substantial and longest part that develops the main idea or thesis.

As you explore your subject, you will discover both ideas that directly support your thesis and more specific examples, details, and other evidence that support these ideas. In the following outline of Grace Patterson's "A Rock and a Hard Place" (pp. 56–58), you can see how each supporting idea, or subpoint, helps to build the thesis sentence:

THESIS SENTENCE   For the homeless people in America today, there are no good choices.

SUBPOINT   A "good choice" is one made from a variety of options determined and narrowed down by the chooser.

SUBPOINT   Homeless people do not necessarily choose to live on the streets.

SUBPOINT   The streets are the only alternative to shelters, which are dangerous and dehumanizing.

Patterson uses specific evidence to develop each subpoint in a paragraph. In essence, the paragraphs are like mini-essays with their own main ideas and support. (See pp. 35–36 for more on paragraph structure.)

When you seek a plan in your ideas, look first for your subpoints, the main supports for your thesis. Use these as your starting points to work out your essay one chunk (or paragraph) at a time. You can fill in the supporting evidence, the details and examples, in your organizational plan, or you can wait until you begin drafting to get into the specifics.

Considering the Introduction and Conclusion

You'll probably have to be drafting or revising before you'll know for sure how you want to begin and end your essay. Still, it can be helpful to consider the introduction and conclusion earlier, so you have a sense of how you might approach readers and what you might leave them with.

The basic opening and closing serve readers by demonstrating your interest in their needs and expectations:

- The **introduction** draws readers into the essay and focuses their attention on the main idea and purpose—often stated in a thesis sentence.
- The **conclusion** ties together the elements of the essay and provides a final impression for readers to take away with them.

These basic forms allow considerable room for variation. Especially as you are developing your writing skills, you will find it helpful to state your thesis sentence near the beginning of the essay; but sometimes you can place it effectively at the end, or you can let it direct what you say in the essay but never state it at all. One essay may need two paragraphs of introduction but only a one-sentence conclusion, whereas another essay may require no formal introduction but a lengthy conclusion. How you begin and end depends on your subject and purpose, the kind of essay you are writing, and the likely responses of your readers. Specific ideas for opening and closing essays are included in each chapter introduction and in the Glossary under *introductions* and *conclusions*.

DRAFTING

Drafting is the chance for you to give expression to your ideas, filling them out, finding relationships, drawing conclusions. If you are like most writers, you will discover much of what you have to say while drafting. In fact, if your subject is complex or difficult for you to write about, you may need several drafts just to work out your ideas and their relationships.

Writing, Not Revising

Some writers draft rapidly, rarely looking up from the paper or keyboard. Others draft more in fits and starts, gazing out the window or doodling as much as writing. Any method that works is fine, but one method rarely works: collapsing drafting and revising into one stage, trying to do everything at once.

Write first; then revise. Concentrate on *what* you are saying, not on *how* you are saying it. You pressure yourself needlessly if you try to produce a well-developed, coherent, interesting, and grammatically correct paper all at once. You may have trouble getting words on paper because you're afraid to make mistakes, or you may be distracted by mistakes from exploring your ideas fully. Awkwardness, repetition, wrong words, grammatical errors, spelling mistakes — these and other more superficial concerns can be attended to in a later draft. The same goes for considering your readers' needs: like many writers, you may find that attention to readers during the first draft inhibits the flow of ideas.

If you experience writer's block or just don't know how to begin your draft, start writing the part you're most comfortable with. Writing in paragraph chunks, as described on pages 27–28, will also make drafting more manageable. You can start with your thesis sentence— or at least keep it in view while you draft—as a reminder of your purpose and main idea. But if you find yourself pulled away from the thesis by a new idea, you may want to let go and follow, at least for a while. If your purpose and main idea change as a result of such exploration, you can always revise your thesis accordingly.

Grace Patterson's First Draft

Some exploratory work by the student Grace Patterson appears on pages 21 and 22. What follows is the first draft she subsequently wrote on homelessness. The draft is very rough, with frequent repetitions, wandering paragraphs, and many other flaws. But such weaknesses are not important at this early stage. The draft gave Patterson the opportunity to discover what she had to say, explore her ideas, and link them in rough sequence.

```
                    Title?
    In the essay, "The Box Man," Barbara Ascher says that
a homeless man who has chosen solitude can show the rest
of us how to "find [. . .] a friend in our own voice."
Maybe. But her case depends on the Box Man's choice, her
assumption that he had one.
    Discussions of the homeless often use the word
choice. Many people with enough money can accept the
condition of the homeless in America when they tell
themselves that many of the homeless chose their lives.
That the streets are in fact what they want. But it's not
fair to use the word choice here: the homeless don't get
to choose their lives the way most of the rest of us do.
For the homeless people in America today, there are no
good choices.
    What do I mean by a "good choice"? One made from a
variety of options determined and narrowed down by the
chooser. There is plenty of room for the chooser to make a
decision that he will be satisfied with. When I choose a
```

career, I expect to make a good choice. There is plenty of
interesting fields worth investigating, and there is lots
of rewarding work to be done. It's a choice that opens the
world up and showcases its possibilities. If it came time
for me to choose a career, and the mayor of my town came
around and told me that I had to choose between a life of
cleaning public toilets and operating a jackhammer on a
busy street corner, I would object. That's a lousy choice,
and I wouldn't let anyone force me to make it.

When the mayor of New York tried to take the homeless
off the streets, some of them didn't want to go. People
assumed that the homeless people who did not want to get
in the mayor's car for a ride to a city shelter chose to
live on the street. But just because some homeless people
chose the street over the generosity of the mayor does not
necessarily mean that life on the streets is their ideal.
We allow ourselves as many options as we can imagine, but
we allow the homeless only two: go to a shelter, or stay
where you are. Who narrowed down the options for the
homeless? Who benefits if they go to a shelter? Who
suffers if they don't?

Homeless people are not always better off in
shelters. I had a conversation with a man who had lived
on the streets for a long time. The man said that he had
spent some time in those shelters for the homeless, and
he told me what they were like. The shelters are crowded
and dirty and people have to wait in long lines for
everything. People are constantly being herded around and
bossed around. It's dangerous -- drug dealers, beatings,
theft. Dehumanizing. It matches my picture of hell. From
the sound of it, I couldn't spend two hours in a shelter,
never mind a whole night. I value my peace of mind and my
sleep too much, not to mention my freedom and autonomy.

When homeless people sleep in the street, though,
that makes the public uncomfortable. People with enough
money wish the homeless would just disappear. They don't

care where they go. Just out of sight. I've felt this way
too but I'm as uneasy with that reaction as I am at the
sight of a person sleeping on the sidewalk. And I tell
myself that this is more than a question of my comfort.
By and large I'm comfortable enough.

The homeless are in a difficult enough situation
without having to take the blame for making the rest of us
feel uncomfortable with our wealth. If we cannot offer the
homeless a good set of choices, the opportunity to choose
lives that they will be truly satisfied with then the
least we can do is stop dumping on them (?). They're
caught between a rock and a hard place: there are not
many places for them to go, and the places where they
can go afford nothing but suffering.

Chapter 3

WRITING

REVISING AND EDITING

The previous chapter took you through the first-draft stage of the writing process, when you have a chance to work out your meaning without regard for what others may think. This chapter describes the crucial next stages, when you actively consider your readers: revising to focus and shape the work and editing to clarify and polish.

REVISING

Revision means "re-seeing," looking at your draft as a reader sees it: mere words on a page that are only as clear, interesting, and significant as you have made them.

Looking at the Whole Draft

Revision involves seeing your draft as a whole, focusing mainly on your purpose and thesis, the support for your thesis, and the movement among ideas. You want to determine what will work and what won't for readers—where the draft strays from your purpose, leaves a hole in the development of your thesis, does not flow logically or smoothly, digresses, or needs more details. (See the revision checklist on p. 42.) Besides rewriting, you may need to cut whole paragraphs, condense paragraphs into sentences, add passages of explanation, or rearrange sections.

Revision is different from **editing**. In revising, you make fundamental changes in content and structure: you work below the surface of the draft. Then in editing, you make changes in the revised draft's sentences and words: you work on the surface, attending to style, grammar, punctuation, and the like. The separation of these two stages is important because attention to little changes distracts from a view of the whole. If you try to edit while you revise, you'll be more likely to miss the big picture. You may also waste effort perfecting sentences you'll later decide to cut.

Reading Your Own Work Critically

Perhaps the most difficult challenge in revising is reading your own work objectively, as a reader would. To gain something like a reader's critical distance from your draft, try one or more of the following techniques:

- Put your first draft aside for at least a few hours before attempting to revise it. You may have further thoughts in the interval, and you will be able to see your work more objectively when you return to it.
- Ask another person to read and comment on your draft. Your writing teacher may ask you and your classmates to exchange your drafts so that you can help each other revise. But even without such a procedure, you can benefit from others' responses. Keep an open mind to your readers' comments, and ask questions when you need more information.
- Make an outline of your draft by listing what you cover in each paragraph. Such an outline can show gaps, overlaps, and problems in organization. (See also pp. 27–28.)
- Read the draft aloud or into a tape recorder. Speaking the words and hearing them can help to create distance from them.
- Imagine you are someone else—a friend, perhaps, or a particular person in your intended audience—and read the draft through that person's eyes, as if for the first time.

- If you write on a word processor, print out a copy of your draft with double spacing. It's much easier to read text on paper than on a computer screen, and you can spread out the pages of a printout to see the whole paper at once. Once you've finished revising, making the changes on the computer requires little effort.

Revising for Purpose and Thesis

In the press of drafting, you may lose sight of why you are writing or what your main idea is. Both your purpose and your thesis may change as you work out your meaning, so that you start in one place and end somewhere else or even lose track of where you are.

Your first goal in revising, then, is to see that your essay is well focused. Readers should grasp a clear purpose right away, and they should find that you have achieved it at the end. They should see your main idea, your thesis, very early, usually by the end of the introduction, and they should think that you have proved or demonstrated the thesis when they reach the last paragraph.

Like many writers, you may sometimes start with one thesis and finish with another, in effect writing into your idea as you draft. To revise, you'll need to upend your essay, plucking your thesis out of the conclusion and starting over with it, providing the subpoints and details to develop it. You'll probably find the second draft much easier to write because you know better what you want to say, and the next round of revision will probably be much cleaner.

Revising for Unity

When a piece of writing has unity, all its parts are related: the sentences build the central idea of their paragraph, and the paragraphs build the central idea of the whole essay. Readers do not have to wonder what the essay is about or what a particular paragraph has to do with the rest of the piece.

Unity in Paragraphs

Earlier we saw how the body paragraphs of an essay are almost like mini-essays themselves, each developing an idea, or subpoint, that supports the thesis. (See pp. 27–28.) In fact, a body paragraph should have its own thesis, called its **topic**, usually expressed in a **topic**

sentence or sentences. The rest of the paragraph develops the topic with specifics.

In the following paragraph from the final draft of Grace Patterson's "A Rock and a Hard Place" (pp. 56–58), the topic sentence is italicized:

> *The fact is that homeless people are not always better off in shelters.*
> I recently had a conversation with a man named Alan who had lived on
> the streets for a long time. He said that he had spent some time in shel-
> ters for the homeless, and he told me what they are like. They're
> dangerous and dehumanizing. Drug dealing, beatings, and theft are com-
> mon. The shelters are dirty and crowded, so that residents have to wait
> in long lines for everything and are constantly being bossed around. No
> wonder some homeless people, including Alan, prefer the street: it af-
> fords some space to breathe, some autonomy, some peace for sleeping.

Notice that every sentence of this paragraph relates to the topic sentence. Patterson achieved this unity in revision (see p. 45). In her draft her last sentences focused on herself rather than the conditions of homeless shelters:

> It matches my picture of hell. From the sound of it, I couldn't spend two
> hours in a shelter, never mind a whole night. I value my peace of mind
> and my sleep too much, not to mention my freedom and autonomy.

If you look back at the full paragraph above, you'll see that Patterson deleted these sentences and substituted a final one that focused on the paragraph's topic, the conditions of the shelters for the homeless themselves.

Your topic sentences will not always fall at the very beginning of your paragraphs. Sometimes you'll need to create a transition from the preceding paragraph before stating the new paragraph's topic, or you'll build the paragraph to a topic sentence at the end, or you'll divide the statement between the beginning and the end. (Patterson's second paragraph, on p. 57, works this way, defining a good choice at the beginning and a bad choice at the end.) Sometimes, too, you'll write a paragraph with a topic but without a topic sentence. In all these cases, you'll need to have an idea for the paragraph and to unify the paragraph around that idea, so that all the specifics support and develop it.

Unity in Essays

Just as sentences must center on a paragraph's main idea, so paragraphs must center on the essay's main idea, or thesis. Readers who have to ask "What is the point?" or "Why am I reading this?" generally won't appreciate or accept the point.

Look back at the outline of Grace Patterson's essay on page 28. Her thesis sentences states, "For the homeless people in America today, there are no good choices," and each paragraph clearly develops this idea: what is a good choice, whether the homeless choose to live on the streets, and why shelters are not good alternatives to the streets.

This unity is true of Patterson's final draft but not of her first draft, where she drifted into considering how the homeless make other people uncomfortable. The topic could be interesting, but it blurred Patterson's focus on the homeless and their choices. Recognizing as much, Patterson deleted her entire second-to-last paragraph when she revised (see p. 45). Deleting this distracting passage also helped Patterson clarify her conclusion.

Like Patterson, you may be pulled in more than one direction by drafting, so that you digress from your thesis or pursue more than one thesis. Drafting and then revising are your chances to find and then sharpen your focus. Revising for unity strengthens your thesis.

Revising for Coherence

Writing is **coherent** when readers can follow it easily and can see how the parts relate to each other. The ideas develop in a clear sequence, the sentences and paragraphs connect logically, and the connections are clear and smooth. The writing flows.

Coherence in Paragraphs

Coherence starts as sentences build paragraphs. The example on the next page (also reprinted in Chapter 4 on description) shows several devices for achieving coherence in paragraphs:

- Repetition or restatement of key words (underlined twice in the example).
- Pronouns such as *it* and *they* that substitute for nouns such as *ice* and *birds* (circled in the example).
- Parallelism, the use of similar grammatical structures for related ideas of the same importance (underlined once in the example). See also page 50.

- Transitions that clearly link the parts of sentences and whole sentences (boxed in the example). See the Glossary, page 381, for a list of transitions.

Pastel icebergs roamed around us, some tens of thousands of years old. Great pressure can push the air bubbles out of the ice and compact it. Free of air bubbles, it reflects light differently, as blue. The waters shivered with the gooseflesh of small ice shards. Some icebergs glowed like dull peppermint in the sun — impurities trapped in the ice (phytoplankton and algae) tinted them green. Ethereal snow petrels flew around the peaks of the icebergs, while the sun shone through their translucent wings. White, silent, the birds seemed to be pieces of ice flying with purpose and grace. As they passed in front of an ice floe, they became invisible. Glare transformed the landscape with such force that it seemed like a pure color. When we went out in the inflatable motorized rafts called Zodiacs to tour the iceberg orchards, I grabbed a piece of glacial ice and held it to my ear, listening to the bubbles cracking and popping as the air trapped inside escaped. And that night, though exhausted from the day's spectacles and doings, I lay in my narrow bunk, awake with my eyes closed, while sunstruck icebergs drifted across the insides of my lids, and the Antarctic peninsula revealed itself slowly, mile by mile, in the small theater of my closed eyes.

—Diane Ackerman, from
A Natural History of the Senses

Check all your paragraphs to be sure that each sentence connects with the one preceding and that readers will see the connection without having to stop and reread. You may not need all the coherence devices Ackerman uses, or as many as she uses, but every paragraph you write will require some devices to stitch the sentences into a seamless cloth.

Coherence in Essays

Reading a coherent essay, the audience does not have to ask "What does this have to do with the preceding paragraph?" or "Where is the writer going here?" The connections are apparent, and the organization is clear and logical.

Transitions work between paragraphs as well as within them to link ideas. When the ideas in two paragraphs are closely related, a simple word or phrase at the start of the second one may be all that's needed to show the relation. In each example below, the italicized transition opens the topic sentence of the paragraph:

> *Moreover,* the rising costs of health care have long outstripped inflation.

> *However,* some kinds of health-care plans have proved much more expensive than others.

When a paragraph is beginning a new part of the essay or otherwise changing direction, a sentence or more at the beginning will help explain the shift. In the next example, the first sentence summarizes the preceding paragraph, the second introduces the topic of the new paragraph, and the third gives the paragraph's topic sentence:

> Traditional health-care plans have *thus* become an unaffordable luxury for most individuals and businesses. The majority of those with health insurance *now* find themselves in so-called managed plans. Though they do vary, managed plans share at least two features: they pay full benefits only when the insured person consults an approved doctor, and they require prior approval for certain procedures.

Notice that italicized transitions provide further cues about the relationship of ideas.

Though transitions can provide signposts to alert readers to movement from one idea to another, they can't achieve coherence by themselves. Just as important is an overall organization that directs readers in a familiar pattern:

- A **spatial organization** arranges information to parallel the way we scan people, objects, or places: top to bottom, left to right, front to back, near to far, or vice versa. This scheme is especially useful for description (Chapter 4).
- A **chronological organization** arranges events or steps as they occurred in time, first to last. Such an arrangement usually organizes a narrative (Chapter 5) or a process analysis (Chapter 9) and may also help with cause-and-effect analysis (Chapter 12).

- A **climactic organization** proceeds in order of climax, usually from least to most important, building to the most interesting example, the most telling point of comparison, the most significant argument. A climactic organization is most useful for example (Chapter 6), division or analysis (Chapter 7), classification (Chapter 8), comparison and contrast (Chapter 10), definition (Chapter 11), and argument and persuasion (Chapter 13), and it may also work for cause-and-effect analysis (Chapter 12).

The introduction to each method of development in Chapters 4–13 gives detailed advice on organizing with these arrangements and variations on them.

When revising your draft for coherence, try outlining it by jotting down the topic sentence of each paragraph and the key support for each topic. The exercise will give you some distance from your ideas and words, allowing you to see the structure like a skeleton. Will your readers grasp the logic of your arrangement? Will they see why you move from each idea to the next one? After checking the overall structure, be sure you've built in enough transitions between sentences and paragraphs to guide readers through your ideas.

Revising for Development

When you **develop** an idea, you provide concrete and specific details, examples, facts, opinions, and other evidence to make the idea vivid and true in readers' minds. Readers will know only as much as you tell them about your thesis and its support. Gaps, vague statements, and unsupported conclusions will undermine your efforts to win their interest and agreement.

Development begins in sentences, when you use the most concrete and specific words you can muster to explain your meaning. (See pp. 52–53.) At the level of the paragraph, these sentences develop the paragraph's topic. Then, at the level of the whole essay, these paragraphs develop the governing thesis.

The key to adequate development is a good sense of your readers' needs for information and reasons. The list of questions on page 20 can help you estimate these needs as you start to write; reconsidering the questions when you revise can help you see where your draft may fail to address, say, readers' unfamiliarity with your subject or possible resistance to your thesis.

The introduction to each method of development in Chapters 4–13 includes specific advice for meeting readers' needs when using the method to develop paragraphs and essays. When you sense that a paragraph or section of your essay is thin but you don't know how to improve it, you can also try the discovery techniques given on pages 20–23 or ask the questions for all the methods of development on pages 23–27.

Revising for Tone

The **tone** of writing is like the tone of voice in speech: it expresses the writer's attitude toward his or her subject and audience. In writing we express tone with word choice and sentence structure. Notice the marked differences in these two passages discussing the same information on the same subject:

> Voice mail can be convenient, sure, but for callers it's usually more trouble than it's worth. We waste time "listening to the following menu choices," when we just want the live person at the end. All too often, there isn't even such a person!

> For callers the occasional convenience of voice mail generally does not compensate for its inconveniences. Most callers would prefer to speak to a live operator but must wait through a series of choices to reach that person. Increasingly, companies with voice-mail systems do not offer live operators at all.

The first passage is informal, expresses clear annoyance, and with *we* includes the reader in that attitude. The second passage is more formal and more objective, reporting the situation without involving readers directly.

Tone can range from casual to urgent, humorous to serious, sad to elated, pleased to angry, personal to distant. The particular tone you choose for a piece of writing depends on your purpose and your audience. For most academic and business writing, you will be trying to explain or argue a point to your equals or superiors. Your readers will be interested more in the substance of your writing than in a startling tone, and indeed an approach that is too familiar or unserious or hostile could put them off. In other kinds of writing, you have more latitude. A warm and lighthearted tone may be just right for a personal narrative, and a touch of anger may help to grab the reader's attention in a letter to a magazine editor.

Tone is something you want to evaluate in revision, along with whether you've achieved your purpose and whether you've developed your thesis adequately for your audience. But adjusting tone is largely a matter of replacing words and restructuring sentences, work that could distract you from an overall view of your essay. If you think your tone is off-base, you may want to devote a separate phase of revision to it, after addressing unity, coherence, and the other matters discussed in this section on revision.

For advice on sentence structures and word choices, see the section on editing, beginning on page 46.

Using a Revision Checklist

The checklist below summarizes the advice on revision given here. Use the checklist to remind yourself what to look for in your first draft. But don't try to answer all the questions in a single reading of

---

CHECKLIST FOR REVISION

- What is your purpose in writing? Will it be clear to readers? Do you achieve it?
- What is your thesis? Where is it made clear to readers?
- How unified is your essay? How does each subpoint in your body paragraphs support your thesis? (Look especially at your topic sentences.) How does each sentence in the body paragraphs support the topic sentence of the paragraph?
- How coherent is your essay? Do repetition and restatement, pronouns, parallelism, and transitions link the sentences in paragraphs? Do transitions and overall organization smooth and clarify the flow of ideas?
- How well developed is your essay? Where might readers need more evidence to understand your ideas and find them convincing?
- What is the tone of your essay? How is it appropriate for your purpose and your audience?
- How does your introduction work to draw readers in and orient them to your purpose and thesis? How does your conclusion work to pull the essay together and give readers a sense of completion?

the draft. Instead, take the questions one by one, rereading the whole draft for each. That way you'll be able to concentrate on each element with minimal distraction from the others.

Note that the introductions to the methods of development in Chapters 4–13 also have their own revision checklists. Combining this list with the one for the method you're using will produce a more targeted set of questions. (The guide inside the back cover will direct you to the discussion you want.)

Grace Patterson's Revised Draft

Considering questions like those in the revision checklist led the student Grace Patterson to revise the rough draft we saw on pages 30–32. Patterson's revision follows. Notice that she made substantial cuts, especially of digressions near the end of the draft. She also revamped the introduction, tightened many passages, improved the coherence of paragraphs, and wrote a wholly new conclusion to sharpen her point. She did not try to improve her style or fix errors at this stage, leaving these activities for later editing.

᠁

Title?   A Rock and a Hard Place

In the essay/ "The Box Man/" Barbara Ascher says that

a homeless man who has chosen solitude can show the rest

of us how to "find [. . .] a friend in our own voice."
                     Ascher's
Maybe. But ~~her~~ case depends on the Box Man's choice, her

assumption that he had one.

Discussions of the homeless often use the word
                 of us with homes would like to think
choice. Many ~~people with enough money can accept the~~

~~condition of the homeless in America when they tell~~

~~themselves~~ that many of the homeless chose their lives.

~~That the streets are in fact what they want. But it's not~~

~~fair to use the word choice here: the homeless don't get~~

~~to choose their lives the way most of the rest of us~~

But

~~do.~~ ^F~~or~~ the homeless people in America today, there are no

good choices.

A good choice is

What do I mean by a "good choice"? ~~One~~ made from a

variety of options determined and narrowed down by the

chooser. There is plenty of room for the chooser to make a

decision that he will be satisfied with. When I choose a

career, I expect to make a good choice. There is plenty of

interesting fields worth investigating, and there is lots

of rewarding work to be done. ~~It's a choice that opens the~~

However,

~~world up and showcases its possibilities.~~ ^~~I~~f ~~it came time~~

~~for me to choose a career, and~~ the mayor of my town came

around and told me that I had to choose between a life of

cleaning public toilets and operating a jackhammer on a

busy street corner, I would object. That's a lousy choice,

and I wouldn't let anyone force me to make it.

people

When the mayor of New York tried to take ~~the~~ homeless^

he likewise offered them a bad choice.

off the streets, ^~~some of them didn't want to go. People~~

They could

~~assumed that the homeless people who did not want to~~^ get

or they could stay

in the mayor's car for a ride to a city shelter^~~chose to~~

People assumed that the homeless people who

~~live~~ on the street. ~~But just because some homeless people~~

refused a ride to the shelter wanted to live on the street. But that

~~chose the street over the generosity of the mayor does not~~

assumption is not necessarily true.

~~necessarily mean that life on the streets is their ideal.~~

We allow ourselves as many options as we can imagine, but

we allow the homeless only two~~, go to a shelter, or stay~~ both unpleasant.

~~where you are. Who narrowed down the options for the~~

~~homeless? Who benefits if they go to a shelter? Who~~

~~suffers if they don't?~~

Homeless people are not always better off in

shelters. Last Sunday, I had a conversation with a man who had lived

on the streets for a long time. ~~The man~~ He said that he had

spent some time in those shelters for the homeless, and

he told me what they were like. ~~The shelters are crowded~~ They're dangerous and

dehumanizing. Drug dealing, beatings, and theft are common.

~~and dirty and people have to wait in long lines for~~

The shelters are dirty and crowded, so that residents have to wait in

~~everything. People are constantly being herded around~~ and

long lines for everything and are constantly

bossed around. ~~It's dangerous--drug dealers, beatings,~~

~~theft. Dehumanizing. It matches my picture of hell. From~~

No wonder some homeless people prefer the street: some space to

~~the sound of it, I couldn't spend two hours in a shelter,~~

breathe, some autonomy, some peace for sleeping.

~~never mind a whole night. I value my peace of mind and my~~

~~sleep too much, not to mention my freedom and autonomy.~~

~~When homeless people sleep in the street, though,~~

that makes the public uncomfortable. People with enough

money wish the homeless would just disappear. They don't

care where they go. Just out of sight. I've felt this way

too but I'm as uneasy with that reaction as I am at the

sight of a person sleeping on the sidewalk. ~~And I tell~~

~~myself that this is more than a question of my comfort.~~

~~By and large I'm comfortable enough.~~

The homeless are in a difficult enough situation without having to take the blame for making the rest of us feel uncomfortable with our wealth. If we cannot offer the homeless a good set of choices, the opportunity to choose lives that they will be truly satisfied with then the least we can do is stop dumping on them (?). They're caught between a rock and a hard place: there are not many places for them to go, and the places where they can go afford nothing but suffering.

Focusing on the supposed choices the homeless have may make us feel better, but it distracts attention from the kinds of choices that are really being denied the homeless. The options we take for granted—a job with decent pay, an affordable home—do not belong to the homeless. They're caught between no shelter at all and shelter that dehumanizes, between a rock and a hard place.

EDITING

In editing you turn from global issues of purpose, thesis, unity, coherence, development, and tone to more particular issues of sentences and words. In a sense revision occurs beneath the lines, in the deeper meaning and structure of the essay. Editing occurs more between the lines, on the surface of the essay.

Like revision, editing requires that you gain some distance from your work so that you can see it objectively. Try these techniques:

- Work on a clean copy of your revised draft. If you write on a computer, edit on a printout rather than on the computer: it's more difficult to read text and spot errors on a screen.
- Read your revised draft aloud or into a tape recorder so you can hear the words. But be sure to read what you have actually written, not what you may have intended to write but didn't.
- To catch errors, try reading your draft backward sentence by sentence. You'll be less likely to get caught up in the flow of your ideas.

- Profit from your past writing experiences by keeping a personal checklist of problems that others have pointed out to you. Add this personal checklist to the one on page 42.

Making Sentences Clear and Effective

Clear and effective sentences convey your meaning concisely and precisely. In editing you want to ensure that readers will understand you easily, follow your ideas without difficulty, and stay interested in what you have to say.

Conciseness

In drafting, we often circle around our ideas, making various attempts to express them. As a result, sentences may use more words than necessary to make their points. To edit for conciseness, focus on the following changes:

- *Put the main meaning of the sentence in its subject, verb, and any object of the verb.* Generally, the subject should name the agent of your idea, the verb should describe what the agent did or was, and an object of the verb may name the receiver of the action. Notice the difference in these two sentences (the subjects and verbs are italicized):

    WORDY   According to some experts, the *use* of calculators by students *is* sometimes a reason why they fail to develop computational skills.

    CONCISE   According to some experts, *students* who use calculators sometimes *fail* to develop computational skills.

    By focusing on the key elements of the idea, the students and their occasional failure, the edited sentence saves seven words and is easier to follow.

- *Delete repetition and padding.* Words that don't contribute to your meaning will interfere with readers' understanding and interest. Watch out for unneeded repetition or restatement, such as that italicized in the following sentence:

    WORDY   Students *in the schools* should have ample practice in computational skills, *skills* such as long division and using fractions.

    CONCISE   Students should have ample practice in computational skills, such as long division and using fractions.

Padding occurs most often with empty phrases that add no meaning:

> WORDY   *In this particular regard, the nature of* calculators *is such that they* remove the drudgery from computation but can also *for all intents and purposes* interfere with the development of important cognitive skills.

> CONCISE   Calculators remove the drudgery from computation but can also interfere with the development of important cognitive skills.

- *Use the active voice.* In the active voice, a verb describes the action *by* the subject (*We grilled vegetables*), whereas in the passive voice a verb describes the action done *to* the subject (*Vegetables were grilled,* or, adding who did the action, *Vegetables were grilled by us*). The active voice usually conveys more information in fewer words than the passive. The active is also clearer, more direct, and more forceful because it always names the actor.

  > WORDY PASSIVE   Calculators *were withheld* from some classrooms by school administrators, and the math performance of students with and without the machines *was compared.*

  > CONCISE ACTIVE   School administrators *withheld* calculators from some classrooms and *compared* the math performance of students with and without the machines.

Emphasis

Once your sentences are as concise as you can make them, you'll want to see that they give the appropriate emphasis to your ideas. Readers will look for the idea of a sentence in its subject, verb, and any object of the verb (see also p. 47), and they will expect words and word groups to clarify or add texture to the idea by modifying it. You can emphasize the idea in various ways by altering the structure of the sentence:

- *Use subordination to stress the sentence's subject, verb, and object.* **Subordination** places less important information in words or word groups that modify the subject, verb, and object:

  > UNEMPHATIC   *Computers can manipulate film and photographs,* and *we can* no longer *trust these media* to represent reality. [The sentence has two subject-verb-object structures (both in italics), and they seem equally important.]

  > EMPHATIC   *Because* computers can manipulate film and photographs, we can no longer trust these media to represent reality.

[*Because* makes the first subject-verb-object group into a modifier, de-emphasizing the cause of the change and emphasizing the effect.]

The next example of subordination reduces word groups that are already subordinate to single words, thus emphasizing the main subject, verb, and object even more:

UNEMPHATIC   In a computer-manipulated photograph, a person *who is living now* can shake hands with a person *who is already dead.*

EMPHATIC   In a computer-manipulated photograph, a *living* person can shake hands with *a dead one.*

* *Use coordination to stress the equal importance of ideas.* Coordination uses *and, but, or,* or *nor* to join two or more ideas and emphasize their equality. It can link the ideas of separate sentences in one sentence:

  UNEMPHATIC   Two people may be complete strangers. A photograph can show them embracing.

  EMPHATIC   Two people may be complete strangers, *but* a photograph can show them embracing.

* *Place modifiers to give desired emphasis to ideas.* The end of a sentence is its most emphatic position, and the beginning is next most emphatic. Placing the sentence's subject, verb, and any object in one of these positions draws readers' attention to them. In these sentences the core idea is in italics:

  UNEMPHATIC   With computerized images, *filmmakers can entertain us,* placing historical figures alongside today's actors.

  EMPHATIC   With computerized images that place historical figures alongside today's actors, *filmmakers can entertain us.*

  EMPHATIC   *Filmmakers can entertain us* with computerized images that place historical figures alongside today's actors.

* *Use short sentences to underscore points.* A very short sentence amid longer sentences will focus readers' attention on a key point:

  UNEMPHATIC   Such images of historical figures and fictional characters have a disadvantage, however, in that they blur the boundaries of reality.

  EMPHATIC   Such images of historical figures and fictional characters have a disadvantage, however. They blur the boundaries of reality.

Parallelism

Parallelism is the use of similar grammatical structures for elements of similar importance, either within or among sentences.

> PARALLELISM WITHIN A SENTENCE   Smoking can *worsen heart disease* and *cause lung cancer.*

> PARALLELISM AMONG SENTENCES   Smoking has less well-known effects, too. *It can cause* gum disease. *It can impair* circulation of blood and other fluids. And *it can reduce* the body's supply of vitamins and minerals.

Parallelism can help relate sequential sentences, improving paragraph coherence (see p. 37). It also clarifies when sentences or elements within them are equivalent, so that readers see the relationship automatically. Without the signal of parallelism in the first sentence below, the reader must stop to work out that both italicized elements are nonmedical consequences:

> NONPARALLEL   Smoking has nonmedical consequences as well, including *loss of productivity* for smokers at work and *insurance expenses are high* for smokers.

> PARALLEL   Smoking has nonmedical consequences as well, including smokers' *loss of productivity* at work and *high expenses for insurance.*

Variety

Variety in the structure and length of sentences helps keep readers alert and interested, but it also does more. By emphasizing important points and de-emphasizing less important points, varied sentences make your writing clearer and easier to follow. The first passage below is adapted from "How Boys Become Men," an essay by Jon Katz. The second is the passage Katz actually wrote.

> UNVARIED   I was walking my dog last month past the playground near my house. I saw three boys encircling a fourth. They were laughing and pushing him. He was skinny and rumpled, and he looked frightened. One boy knelt behind him. Another pushed him from the front. The trick was familiar to any former boy. The victim fell backward.

> VARIED   Last month, walking my dog past the playground near my house, I saw three boys encircling a fourth, laughing and pushing him. He was skinny and rumpled, and he looked frightened. One boy knelt behind him while another pushed him from the front, a trick familiar to any former boy. He fell backward.

Katz's actual sentences work much better to hold and direct our attention because he uses several techniques to achieve variety:

- *Vary the lengths of sentences.* The eight sentences in the unvaried adaptation range from four to thirteen words. Katz's four sentences range from three to twenty-two words, with the long first sentence setting the scene and the short final sentence creating a climax.
- *Vary the beginnings of sentences.* Every sentence in the adaptation begins with its subject (*I, I, They, He, One boy, Another, The trick, The victim*). Katz, in contrast, begins one sentence with a transition and a modifier (*Last month, walking my dog past the playground near my house* [. . .]).
- *Vary the structure of sentences.* The sentences in the adaptation are all similar in structure, marching like soldiers down the page and making it difficult to pick out the important events of the story. Katz's version emphasizes the important events by making them the subjects and verbs of the sentences, turning the other information into modifiers that either precede or follow.

Choosing the Right Words

The words you use can have a dramatic effect on how readers understand your meaning, perceive your attitude, and respond to your thesis.

Denotation

The **denotation** of a word is its dictionary meaning, the literal sense without emotional overtones. Using a word with the wrong denotation muddies meaning. For instance, *reward* is different from *award,* and *sites* is different from *cites.* Substituting one for the other will confuse readers momentarily, and several such confusions can undermine readers' patience.

Consult a dictionary whenever you are unsure of a word's meaning. Be especially careful to distinguish between words with similar sounds but different meanings, such as *sites* and *cites* or *whether* and *weather,* and between words with related but distinct meanings, such as *reward* and *award* or *famous* and *infamous.* Keeping a list of the new words you acquire will help you build your vocabulary.

Connotation

A word's **connotations** are the emotional associations it produces in readers. *Bawling* denotes loud crying, but it connotes lack of control and dignity: we do not sympathize with bawlers. Writing that someone *bawled* will elicit a different reaction from readers than saying the person *wept* or *keened*—other kinds of crying with other connotations.

Using words with strong connotations can shape readers' responses to your ideas. For another example, consider the distinctions among *feeling, enthusiasm, passion,* and *mania.* Describing a group's *enthusiasm* for its cause is quite different from describing its *mania*: the latter connotes much more intensity, even irrationality. If your aim is to imply that the group's enthusiasm is excessive, and you think your readers will respond well to that characterization, then *mania* may be the appropriate word. But words can backfire if they set off inappropriate associations in readers.

A hardcover desk dictionary will usually distinguish among the connotations of words. You'll find a wider range of choices in a thesaurus, which lists words with similar meanings, but it won't provide definitions. Don't use a word from a thesaurus unless you are sure of its denotation and connotations, information you can find in a dictionary.

Choosing the Best Words

Attending to the established denotations and connotations of words will help you make correct and effective choices, but you can do more to convey your meaning clearly and interestingly if you opt for words that are specific, concrete, and fresh.

Concrete and Specific Words

Clear, exact writing balances abstract and general words, which provide outlines of ideas and things, with concrete and specific words, which limit and sharpen.

- **Abstract words** name ideas, qualities, attitudes, or states that we cannot perceive with our senses of sight, hearing, touch, smell, and taste: *liberty, hate, anxious, brave, idealistic.* **Concrete words,** in contrast, name objects, persons, places, or states that we can perceive with our senses: *newspaper, police officer, Mississippi River, red-faced, tangled, screeching.*

- **General words** name groups: *building, color, clothes.* **Specific words** name particular members of a group: *courthouse, red, trousers, black Levi's.*

You need abstract and general words for broad statements that set the course for your writing, conveying concepts or referring to entire groups. But you also need concrete and specific words to make meaning precise and vivid by appealing to readers' senses and experiences. The following examples show how much clearer and more interesting a sentence becomes when its abstractions and generalities are brought down to concrete and specific details:

> VAGUE   The pollution was apparent in the odor and color of the small stream.
>
> EXACT   The narrow stream, just four feet wide, smelled like rotten eggs and ran the greenish color of coffee with nonfat milk.

The first sentence leaves it to readers to imagine the size, odor, and color of the stream. A few readers may guess at details, but most won't bother: they'll just pass on without getting the picture. In contrast, the second sentence *shows* the stream just as the writer experienced it, in disturbing detail.

Concrete and specific language may seem essential only in description like that of the polluted stream, but it is equally crucial in any other kind of writing. Readers can't be expected to understand or agree with general statements unless they know what evidence the statements are based on. The evidence is in the details, and the details are in concrete and specific words.

Figures of Speech

You can make your writing concrete and specific, even lively and forceful, with **figures of speech,** expressions that imply meanings beyond or different from their literal meanings. Here are some of the most common figures:

- A **simile** compares two unlike things with the use of *like* or *as: The car spun around like a top. Coins as bright as sunshine lay glinting in the chest.*

- A **metaphor** also compares two unlike things, but more subtly, equating them without *like* or *as: The words shattered my fragile self-esteem. The laboratory was a prison, the beakers and test tubes her guards.*
- **Personification** is a simile or metaphor that attributes human qualities or powers to things or abstractions: *The breeze sighed and whispered in the grasses. The city squeezed me tightly at first but then relaxed its grip.*
- **Hyperbole** is a deliberate overstatement or exaggeration: *The dentist filled the tooth with a bracelet's worth of silver. The children's noise shook the walls and rafters.*

By briefly translating experiences and qualities into vividly concrete images, figures of speech can be economical and powerful. But be careful not to combine figures and thus create confusing or absurd images in readers' minds. This mixed metaphor conjures up conflicting images of bees and dogs: *The troops swarmed the field like pit bulls ready for a fight.*

Fresh Language

In trying for concrete and specific words, we sometimes resort to **clichés,** worn phrases that have lost their descriptive power: *tried and true, ripe old age, hour of need.* Many clichés are exhausted figures of speech, such as *heavy as lead, thin as a rail,* or *goes on forever.*

If you have trouble recognizing clichés in your writing, be suspicious of any expression you have heard or read before. When you do find a cliché, cure it by substituting plain language (for instance, *reliable* for *tried and true*) or by substituting a fresh figure of speech (*thin as a sapling* for *thin as a rail*).

Using an Editing Checklist

The checklist on the facing page summarizes the editing advice given in this section and adds a few other technical concerns as well. Some of the items will be more relevant for your writing than others: you may have little difficulty with variety in sentences but may worry that your language is too general. Concentrate your editing efforts where they're needed most, and then survey your draft to check for other problems.

CHECKLIST FOR EDITING

- How clear and concise is each sentence? Have you put the main meaning in the subject, verb, and any object of the verb? Is there repetition and padding to delete? Have you relied on the active voice of verbs?

- How well do sentences emphasize their main ideas with subordination, coordination, modifier placement, or length?

- Where is parallelism needed within or between sentences to increase clarity and coherence?

- Where should groups of sentences be more varied in length and structure to improve clarity and readability?

- Which words should be changed either because they have the wrong denotations or because their connotations are inappropriate for your meaning or your audience?

- Where should you make your meaning less abstract and general with concrete and specific words or with figures of speech? Where do clichés need editing?

- Where do sentences need editing for grammar or punctuation—so that, for instance, pronouns such as *he* and *him* are used correctly, subjects and verbs agree, sentences are complete, and apostrophes fall in the right places? Concentrate on finding errors that readers have pointed out in your work before.

- Where might spelling be a problem? Look up any word you're not absolutely sure of, or use your computer's spelling checker. (You'll still have to proofread a spell-checked paper, though, because the programs can't catch everything.)

Grace Patterson's Editing and Final Draft

The paragraph on the next page comes from the edited draft of Grace Patterson's "A Rock and a Hard Place." Then Patterson's full final draft appears with notes in the margins highlighting its thesis, structure, and uses of the methods of development. If you compare the final version with the first draft on pages 30–32, you'll see clearly how Patterson's revising and editing transformed the essay from a rough exploration of ideas to a refined, and convincing, essay.

EDITED PARAGRAPH

~~What do I mean by~~ A "good choice"? ~~A good choice~~ is one
made from a variety of options determined and narrowed
down by the chooser. ~~There is plenty of room for the
chooser to make a decision that he will be satisfied with.~~
When I choose a career, I expect to make a good choice.
There ~~is plenty of~~ are many interesting fields ~~worth~~ to investigate,
and there is ~~lots of~~ much rewarding work to ~~be done.~~ do. If the
mayor of my town ~~around and~~ suddenly told me that I ~~had~~ would have to choose
between a ~~life~~ career of cleaning public toilets and one of operating a
jackhammer on a busy street corner, I would object. That's
a ~~lousy~~ bad choice. ~~and I wouldn't let anyone force me to
make it.~~

FINAL DRAFT

A Rock and a Hard Place

In the essay "The Box Man" Barbara
Ascher says that a homeless man who has
chosen solitude can show the rest of us how
to "find [. . .] a friend in our own voice."
Maybe he can. But Ascher's case depends on
the Box Man's choice, her assumption that
he had one. Discussions of the homeless
often involve the word choice. Many of us
with homes would like to think that many of
the homeless chose their lives. But for the
homeless people in America today, there are
no good choices.

Introduction: establishes point of contention with Ascher's essay

Thesis sentence (see pp. 18–19)

A "good choice" is one made from a variety of options determined and narrowed down by the chooser. When I choose a career, I expect to make a good choice. There are many interesting fields to investigate, and there is much rewarding work to do. If the mayor of my town suddenly told me that I would have to choose between a career of cleaning public toilets and one of operating a jackhammer on a busy street corner, I would object. That's a <u>bad</u> choice.

Definition and comparison of good choices and bad choices

Examples

When the mayor of New York tried to remove the homeless people from the streets, he offered them a similarly bad choice. They could get in the mayor's car for a ride to a city shelter, or they could stay on the street. People assumed that the homeless people who refused a ride to the shelter <u>wanted</u> to live on the street. But the assumption is not necessarily true. We allow ourselves as many options as we can imagine, but we allow the homeless only two, both unpleasant.

Application of definition to homeless; analysis of choice offered

The fact is that homeless people are not always better off in shelters. I recently had a conversation with a man named Alan who had lived on the streets for a long time. He said that he had spent some time in shelters for the homeless, and he told me what they are like. They're dangerous and dehumanizing. Drug dealing, beatings, and theft are common. The shelters are dirty and crowded, so that residents have to wait in long lines for

Cause-and-effect analysis: why homeless avoid shelters

Description of shelter

everything and are constantly being bossed
around. No wonder some homeless people,   *Comparison of*
including Alan, prefer the street: it   *shelter and street*
affords some space to breathe, some
autonomy, some peace for sleeping.

    Focusing on the supposed choices the   *Conclusion: returns*
homeless have may make us feel better. But   *to good vs. bad*
                                                 choices; sums up
it distracts our attention from something   *with a familiar*
more important than our comfort: the   *image*
options we take for granted -- a job with
decent pay, an affordable home -- are denied
the homeless. These people are caught
between no shelter at all and shelter that
dehumanizes, between a rock and a hard
place.

Chapter 4

DESCRIPTION

Sensing the Natural World

USING THE METHOD

Whenever you use words to depict or re-create a scene, an object, a person, or a feeling, you use **description**. You draw on the perceptions of your five senses—sight, hearing, smell, taste, and touch—to understand and communicate your experience of the world. Description is a mainstay of conversation between people, and it is likely to figure in almost any writing situation: a letter home may describe a new roommate's spiky yellow hair; a laboratory report may describe the colors and odors of chemicals; a business memo may distinguish between the tastes of two competitors' chicken potpies.

Your purpose in writing and your involvement with the subject will largely determine how objective or subjective your description is.

- In **objective description** you strive for precision and objectivity, trying to convey the subject impersonally, without emotion. This is the kind of description required in scientific writing—for instance, a medical diagnosis or a report on an experiment in psychology—where cold facts and absence of feeling are essential for readers to judge the accuracy of procedures and results. It is also the method of news reports and of reference works such as encyclopedias.

- In **subject description,** in contrast, you draw explicitly on your emotions, giving an impression of the subject filtered through your experience of it. Instead of withdrawing to the background, you invest feelings in the subject and let those feelings determine which details to describe and how to describe them. Your state of mind—perhaps loneliness, anger, joy—can be re-created by reference to sensory details such as numbness, heat, or sweetness.

In general, you should favor objective description when your purpose is explanation and subjective description when your purpose is self-expression or entertainment. But the categories are not exclusive, and most descriptive writing mixes the two. A news report on a tropical storm, for instance, might objectively describe bent and broken trees, fallen wires, and lashing rains, but your selection of details would give a subjective impression of the storm's fearsomeness.

Whether objective or subjective or a mixture of the two, effective description requires a **dominant impression**—a central theme or idea about the subject to which readers can relate all the details. The dominant impression may be something you see in the subject, such as the apparent purposefulness of city pedestrians or the expressiveness of an actor. Or it may derive from your emotional response to the subject, perhaps pleasure (or depression) at all the purposefulness, perhaps admiration (or disdain) for the actor's technique. Whatever its source, the dominant impression serves as a unifying principle that guides your selection of details and the reader's understanding of the subject.

One aid to creating a dominant impression is a consistent **point of view,** a position from which you approach the subject. Point of view in description has two main elements:

- You take a real or imagined *physical* relation to the subject: you could view a mountain, for instance, from the bottom looking up, from fifteen miles away across a valley, or from an airplane passing overhead. The first two points of view are fixed because you remain in one position and scan the scene from there; the third is moving because you change position.

- You take a *psychological* relation to the subject, a relation partly conveyed by pronouns. In subjective description, where your feelings are part of the message, you might use *I* and *you* freely to narrow the distance between yourself and the subject and between yourself and the reader. But in the most objective, impersonal description, you will use *one* ("One can see the summit") or avoid self-reference altogether in order to appear distant from and unbiased toward the subject.

Once you establish a physical and psychological point of view, readers come to depend on it. Thus a sudden and inexplicable shift from one view to another—zooming in from fifteen miles away to the foot of a mountain, abandoning *I* for the more removed *one*—can disorient readers and distract them from the dominant impression you are trying to create.

ANALYZING DESCRIPTION IN PARAGRAPHS

David Mura (born 1952) is a poet, essayist, and critic. This paragraph comes from his book *Turning Japanese* (1991), a memoir of his time in Japan as a *sansei,* or a third-generation Japanese American. Mura describes Tokyo during the rainy season.

And then the rains of June came, the typhoon season. Every day endless streaks of gray drilled down from the sky. A note held, passing from monotone into a deeper, more permanent dirge. The air itself seemed to liquefy, like the insides of a giant invisible jellyfish. In the streets the patter grew into pools, then rushes and torrents. Umbrellas floated, black bobbing circles, close as the wings of bats in underground caves. In the empty lot across the street, the grass turned a deep, tropical green; then the earth itself seemed to bubble up in patches, foaming. In the country, square after square of rice field filled to the brim and overflowed. In the city, the city of labyrinths, the rain became another labyrinth, increased the density of inhabitants; everything seemed thicker, moving underwater.

Specific, concrete details (underlined once)

Figures of speech (underlined twice)

Point of view: moving; psychologically somewhat distant

Dominant impression: overwhelming, intense wetness

Diane Ackerman (born 1948) is a poet and essayist who writes extensively on the natural world. The following paragraph comes from *A*

Natural History of the Senses (1991), a prose exploration of sight, hearing, touch, taste, and smell.

Pastel icebergs roamed around us, some tens of thousand of years old. Great pressure can push the air bubbles out of the ice and compact it. Free of air bubbles, it reflects light differently, as blue. The waters shivered with the gooseflesh of small ice shards. Some icebergs glowed like dull peppermint in the sun — impurities trapped in the ice (phytoplankton and algae) tinted them green. Ethereal snow petrels flew around the peaks of the icebergs, while the sun shone through their translucent wings. White, silent, the birds seemed to be pieces of ice flying with purpose and grace. As they passed in front of an ice floe, they became invisible. Glare transformed the landscape with such force that it seemed like a pure color. When we went out in the inflatable motorized rafts called Zodiacs to tour the iceberg orchards, I grabbed a piece of glacial ice and held it to my ear, listening to the bubbles cracking and popping as the air trapped inside escaped. And that night, though exhausted from the day's spectacles and doings, I lay in my narrow bunk, awake with my eyes closed, while sunstruck icebergs drifted across the insides of my lids, and the Antarctic peninsula revealed itself slowly, mile by mile, in the small theater of my closed eyes.

Specific, concrete details (underlined once)

Figures of speech (underlined twice)

Point of view: fixed, then moving; psychologically close

Dominant impression: awesome, chilly brightness

DEVELOPING A DESCRIPTIVE ESSAY

Getting Started

The subject for a descriptive essay may be any object, place, person, or state of mind that you have observed closely enough or experienced sharply enough to invest with special significance. A chair, a tree, a room, a shopping mall, a movie actor, a passerby on the street, a feeling of fear, a sense of achievement — anything you have a strong impression of can prompt effective description.

When you have your subject, specify in a sentence the impression that you want to create for readers. The sentence will help keep you on track while you search for details, and later it may serve as the thesis of your essay. It should evoke a quality or an atmosphere or an effect, as these examples do:

His fierce anger at the world shows in every word and gesture.

The mall is a thoroughly unnatural place, like a space station in a science-fiction movie.

A sentence like one of these should give you a good start in choosing the sensory details that will make your description concrete and vivid. Observe your subject directly, if possible, or recall it as completely as you can. Jot down the details that seem to contribute most to the impression you're trying to convey. You needn't write the description of them yet—that can wait for drafting—but you do want to capture the possibilities in your subject. While exploring, try to remain alert to any variations in your dominant impression so that it can continue to guide your search.

At this stage you should start to consider the needs and expectations of your readers. If the subject is something readers have never seen or felt before, you will need enough objective details to create a complete picture in their minds. A description of a friend, for example, might focus on his distinctive voice and laugh, but readers will also want to know something about his appearance. If the subject is essentially abstract, like an emotion, you will need details to make it concrete for readers. And if the subject is familiar to readers, as a shopping mall or an old spruce tree on campus probably would be, you will want to skip obvious objective information in favor of fresh observations that will make readers see the subject anew.

Organizing

Though the details of a subject may not occur to you in any particular order, you should arrange them so that readers are not confused by your shifts among features. You can give readers a sense of the whole subject in the introduction to the essay: objective details of location or size or shape, the incident leading to a state of mind, or the reasons for describing a familiar object. In the introduction, also, you may want to state your thesis—the dominant impression you will create. An explicit thesis is not essential in description; sometimes you may prefer to let the details build to a conclusion. But the thesis should hover over the essay nonetheless, governing the selection of every detail and making itself as clear to readers as if it were stated outright.

The organization of the body of the essay depends partly on point of view and partly on dominant impression. If you take a moving point of view — say, strolling down a city street — the details will probably arrange themselves naturally. But a fixed point of view, scanning a subject from one position, requires your intervention. When the subject is a landscape, a person, or an object, you'll probably want to use a spatial organization: near to far, top to bottom, left to right, or vice versa. (See also p. 39.) Other subjects, such as a shopping mall, might be better treated in groups of features: shoppers, main concourses, insides of stores. Or a description of an emotional state might follow the chronological sequence of the event that aroused it (thus overlapping description and narration, the subject of the next chapter). The order itself is not important, as long as there is an order that channels readers' attention.

Drafting

The challenge of drafting your description will be bringing the subject to life. Whether it is in front of you or in your mind, you may find it helpful to consider the subject one sense at a time — what you can see, hear, smell, touch, taste. Of course, not all senses will be applicable to all subjects; a chair, for instance, may not have a noticeable odor, and you're unlikely to know its taste. But proceeding sense by sense can help you uncover details, such as the smell of a tree or the sound of a person's voice, that you may have overlooked.

Examining one sense at a time is also one of the best ways to conceive of concrete words and figures of speech to represent sensations and feelings. For instance, does *acid* describe the taste of fear? Does an actor's appearance suggest the smell of soap? Does a shopping mall smell like new dollar bills? In creating distinct physical sensations for readers, such representations make meaning inescapably clear. (See pp. 52–53 and the box opposite for more on specific, concrete language and figures of speech.)

Revising and Editing

When you are ready to revise and edit, use the following questions and box as a guide.

- *Have you in fact created the dominant impression you intended to create?* Check that you have plenty of specific details and that each one helps to pin down one crucial feature of your subject. Cut irrelevant details that may have crept in. What counts is not the number of details but their quality and the strength of the impression they make.
- *Are your point of view and organization clear and consistent?* Watch for confusing shifts from one vantage point or organizational scheme to another. Watch also for confusing and unnecessary shifts in pronouns, such as from *I* to *one* or vice versa. Any shifts in point of view or organization should be clearly essential for your purpose and for the impression you want to create.

FOCUS ON CONCRETE AND SPECIFIC LANGUAGE

For readers to imagine your subject, you'll need to use concrete, specific language that appeals to their experiences and senses. (See pp. 52–53 for the meanings of *concrete* and *specific*.) The first sentence below shows a writer's first-draft attempt to describe something she saw. After editing, the second sentence is much more vivid.

VAGUE   Beautiful, scented wildflowers were in the field.

CONCRETE AND SPECIFIC   Backlighted by the sun and smelling faintly sweet, an acre of tiny lavender flowers spread away from me.

The writer might also have used figures of speech (see pp. 53–54) to show what she saw: for instance, describing the field as "a giant's bed covered in a quilt of lavender dots" (a metaphor) or describing the backlighted flowers as "glowing like tiny lavender lamps" (a simile).

When editing your description, keep a sharp eye out for vague words such as *delicious, handsome, loud,* and *short* that force readers to create their own impressions or, worse, leave them with no impression at all. Using details that call on readers' sensory experiences, say why delicious or why handsome, how loud or how short. When stuck for a word, conjure up your subject and see it, hear it, touch it, smell it, taste it.

Note that *concrete* and *specific* do not mean "fancy": good description does not demand five-dollar words when nickel equivalents are just as informative. The writer who uses *rubiginous* instead of *rusty red* actually says less because fewer readers will understand the less common word and all readers will sense a writer showing off.

A NOTE ON THEMATIC CONNECTIONS

The writers represented in this chapter all set out to explore something in nature. They probably didn't decide consciously to write a description, but turned to the method intuitively as they chose to record the perceptions of their senses. In a paragraph, David Mura captures the dense unpleasantness of a seemingly endless downpour (p. 61). In another paragraph, Diane Ackerman describes the sharp, lasting images of a sea of icebergs (p. 62). Marta K. Taylor's essay on a nighttime car ride climaxes in a lightning storm (opposite). Larry Woiwode's essay on oranges depicts his childhood anticipation and enjoyment of sweet, ripe fruit (p. 72). And Joan Didion's essay on a wind coming from the mountains above Los Angeles shows how an air current can transform a city (p. 79).

Memory is the diary that we all carry about with us. —Oscar Wilde

A childhood is what anyone wants to remember of it. —Carol Shields

I might have seen more of America when I was a child if I hadn't had to spend so much of my time protecting my half of the back seat from incursions by my sister. —Calvin Trillin

Journal Response Recall a childhood event such as a family outing, a long car ride, a visit to an unfamiliar place, or an incident in your neighborhood. Imagine yourself back in that earlier time and write down details of what you experienced and how you felt.

Marta K. Taylor

Marta K. Taylor was born in 1970 and raised in Los Angeles. She attended a "huge" public high school there before being accepted into Harvard University. She graduated from Harvard in 1992 with a bachelor's degree in chemistry and from Harvard Medical School in 1998. She is now a resident physician in Chapel Hill, North Carolina, where she specializes in head and neck surgery.

Desert Dance

Taylor wrote this description of a nighttime ride when she was a freshman in college taking the required writing course. The essay was published in the 1988–89 edition of Exposé, *a collection of student writing published by Harvard.*

We didn't know there was a rodeo in Flagstaff. All the hotels were 1 filled, except the really expensive ones, so we decided to push on to Winslow that night. Dad must have thought we were all asleep, and so we should have been, too, as it was after one A.M. and we had been driving all day through the wicked California and Arizona desert on the first day of our August Family Trip. The back seat of our old station wagon was down, allowing two eleven-year-old kids to lie almost fully extended and still leaving room for the rusty green

Coleman ice-chest which held the packages of pressed turkey breast, the white bread, and the pudding snack-pacs that Mom had cleverly packed to save on lunch expenses and quiet the inevitable "Are we there yet?" and "How much farther?"

Jon was sprawled out on his back, one arm up and one arm down, 2 reminding me of Gumby or an outline chalked on the sidewalk in a murder mystery. His mouth was wide open and his regular breath rattled deeply in the back of his throat somewhere between his mouth and his nose. Beside the vibration of the wheels and the steady hum of the engine, no other sound disturbed the sacred silence of the desert night.

From where I lay, behind the driver's seat, next to my twin 3 brother on the old green patchwork quilt that smelled like beaches and picnics—salty and a little mildewed—I could see my mother's curly brown head slumped against the side window, her neck bent awkwardly against the seat belt, which seemed the only thing holding her in her seat. Dad, of course, drove—a motionless, soundless, protective paragon of security and strength, making me feel totally safe. The back of his head had never seemed more perfectly framed than by the reflection of the dashboard lights on the windshield; the short, raven-colored wiry hairs that I loved so much caught and played with, like tinsel would, the greenish glow with red and orange accents. The desert sky was starless, clouded.

Every couple of minutes, a big rig would pass us going west. The 4 lights would illuminate my mother's profile for a moment and then the roar of the truck would come and the sudden, the violent sucking rush of air and we would be plunged into darkness again. Time passed so slowly, unnoticeably, as if the whole concept of time were meaningless.

I was careful to make no sound, content to watch the rising and 5 falling of my twin's chest in the dim light and to feel on my cheek the gentle heat of the engine rising up through the floorboards. I lay motionless for a long time before the low rumbling, a larger sound than any eighteen-wheeler, rolled across the open plain. I lifted my head, excited to catch a glimpse of the rain that I, as a child from Los Angeles, seldom saw. A few seconds later, the lightning sliced the night sky all the way across the northern horizon. Like a rapidly growing twig, at least three or four branches, it illuminated the twisted forms of Joshua trees and low-growing cacti. All in silhouette—and only for a flash, though the image stayed many moments before my mind's eye in the following black.

The lightning came again, this time only a formless flash, as if God 6 were taking a photograph of the magnificent desert, and the long, straight road before us—empty and lonely—shone like a dagger. The trees looked like old men to me now, made motionless by the natural strobe, perhaps to resume their feeble hobble across the sands once the shield of night returned. The light show continued on the horizon though the expected rain never came. The fleeting, gnarled fingers grasped out and were gone; the fireworks flashed and frolicked and faded over and over—danced and jumped, acting out a drama in the quick, jerky movements of a marionette. Still in silence, still in darkness.

I watched the violent, gaudy display over the uninhabited, end- 7 less expanse, knowing I was in a state of grace and not knowing if I was dreaming but pretty sure I was awake because of the cramp in my neck and the pain in my elbow from placing too much weight on it for too long.

Meaning

1. What does Taylor mean by "state of grace" in paragraph 7? What associations does this phrase have? To what extent does it capture the dominant impression of this essay?
2. If you do not know the meaning of any of the words below, try to guess it from its context in Taylor's essay. Test your guesses in a dictionary, and then try to use each word in a sentence or two of your own.

paragon (3)	gnarled (6)	marionette (6)
silhouette (5)	frolicked (6)	gaudy (7)
strobe (6)		

Purpose and Audience

1. Why does Taylor open with the sentence "We didn't know there was a rodeo in Flagstaff"? What purposes does the sentence serve?
2. Even readers familiar with the desert may not have had Taylor's experience of it in a nighttime lightning storm. Where does she seem especially careful about describing what she saw? What details surprised you?

Method and Structure

1. What impression or mood is Taylor trying to capture in this essay? How does the precise detail of the description help to convey that mood?
2. Taylor begins her description inside the car (paragraphs 1–5) and then moves out into the landscape (5–7), bringing us back into the car in her

final thought. Why does she use such a sequence? Why do you think she devotes about equal space to each area?

3. Taylor's description is mainly subjective, invested with her emotions. Point to elements of the description that reveal emotion.

4. **Other Methods**   Taylor's description relies in part on narration (Chapter 5). How does narrative strengthen the essay's dominant impression?

Language

1. How does Taylor's tone help convey the "state of grace" she feels inside the car? Point out three or four examples of language that establish that mood.

2. Why do you think Taylor titles her essay "Desert Dance"?

3. Notice the words Taylor uses to describe Joshua trees (paragraphs 5–6). If you're already familiar with the tree, how accurate do you find Taylor's description? If you've never seen a Joshua tree, what do you think it looks like, based on Taylor's description? (Next time you're in the library, look the tree up in an encyclopedia to test your impression.)

4. Taylor uses similes to make her description vivid and immediate. Find several examples, and comment on their effectiveness. (See p. 53 for more on similes.)

5. Taylor's last paragraph is one long sentence. Does this long sentence work with or against the content and mood of the paragraph? Why and how?

Writing Topics

1. **Journal to Essay**   Using subjective description, expand your journal entry about a childhood event (p. 67) into an essay. Recalling details of sight, sound, touch, smell, even taste, build a dominant impression for readers of what the experience was like for you.

2. Taylor's essay illustrates her feelings not only about the desert but also about her father, mother, and twin brother. Think of a situation when you were intensely aware of your feelings about another person (friend or relative). Describe the situation and the person in a way that conveys those feelings.

3. **Cultural Considerations**   Though she had evidently seen the desert before, Taylor had not seen it the way she describes it in "Desert Dance." Write an essay in which you describe your first encounter with something new — for instance, a visit to the home of a friend from a different social or economic background, a visit to a big city or a farm, an unex-

pected view of your own backyard. Describe what you saw and your responses. How, if at all, did the experience change you?

4. **Connections**   Both Taylor and Diane Ackerman (in the paragraph on p. 62) experience awe at a natural wonder. In a brief essay, analyze how these writers convey their sense of awe so that it is concrete, not vague. Focus on their words and especially on their figures of speech. (See pp. 53–54 for more on figures of speech.)

Food is the most primitive form of comfort.   —Sheila Graham

There is nothing, absolutely nothing, that pleasures me more than a bowl of pasta and tomato sauce.   —Lynne Rossetto Kasper

There's something I've noticed about food: whenever there's a crisis, if you can get people to eating normally things get better.   —Madeleine L'Engle

Journal Response   Many children derive comfort from a particular food, such as a fruit, a flavor of ice cream, a grandparent's biscuits, or a home-cooked dish. What favored food do you associate with your childhood? Write a journal entry describing it and its associations.

Larry Woiwode

A fiction writer, poet, and essayist, Larry Woiwode was born in 1941 in Carrington, North Dakota, and grew up in rural North Dakota and Illinois. His perceptions of the harsh climates and stark landscapes of the West and Midwest have influenced his work, in which natural detail often reflects and represents characters' feelings. Woiwode attended the University of Illinois in the early 1960s and has earned his living as a writer and teacher ever since. He has published two collections of stories, Neumiller Stories *(1989) and* Silent Passages *(1993); a book of poems,* Even Tide *(1975); five novels,* What I'm Going to Do, I Think *(1969),* Beyond the Bedroom Wall *(1975),* Poppa John *(1981),* Born Brothers *(1988), and* Indian Affairs *(1992); and three books of nonfiction,* Acts: A Writer's Reflections on the Church, Writing, and His Own Acts *(1993),* So He Says *(1999), and* What I Think I Did: A Season of Survival in Two Acts *(2000). He has received many honors and prizes, including the fiction award from the American Academy and Institute of Arts and Letters. In 1995 he was made poet laureate of North Dakota, where he resides.*

Ode to an Orange

A critic has written that Woiwode's descriptions of nature can "hypnotize the senses" with their precision and vitality. In the following essay, first published in The Paris Review *in 1984, Woiwode turns his descriptive powers on a familiar fruit. While reading this description, recall your own experiences with oranges. When can you confirm Woiwode's impressions? When does he surprise you?*

Oh, those oranges arriving in the midst of the North Dakota winters   1
of the forties — the mere color of them, carried through the door in a
net bag or a crate from out of the white winter landscape. Their appearance was enough to set my brother and me to thinking that it
might be about time to develop an illness, which was the surest way
of receiving a steady supply of them.

"Mom, we think we're getting a cold."   2

"*We?* You mean, you two want an orange?"   3

This was difficult for us to answer or dispute; the matter seemed   4
moved beyond our mere wanting.

"If you want an orange," she would say, "why don't you ask for   5
one?"

"We want an orange."   6

"'We' again, '*We want an orange.*'"   7

"May we have an orange, please."   8

"That's the way you know I like you to ask for one. Now, why   9
don't each of you ask for one in that same way, but separately?"

"Mom . . ." And so on. There was no depth of degradation that   10
we wouldn't descend to in order to get one. If the oranges hadn't
wended their way northward by Thanksgiving, they were sure to arrive before the Christmas season, stacked first in crates at the depot,
filling that musty place, where pews sat back to back, with a spring-
time acidity, as if the building had been rinsed with a renewing elixir
that set it right for yet another year. Then the crates would appear at
the local grocery store, often with the top slats pried back on a few of
them, so that we were aware of a resinous smell of fresh wood in addition to the already orangy atmosphere that foretold the season
more explicitly than any calendar.

And in the broken-open crates (as if burst by the power of the or-   11
anges themselves), one or two of the lovely spheres would lie free of
the tissue they came wrapped in — always purple tissue, as if that
were the only color that could contain the populations of them in
their nestled positions. The crates bore paper labels at one end — of
an orange against a blue background, or of a blue goose against
an orange background — signifying the colorful otherworld (unlike our wintry one) that these phenomena had arisen from. Each
orange, stripped of its protective wrapping, as vivid in your vision as

a pebbled sun, encouraged you to picture a whole pyramid of them in a bowl on your dining room table, glowing in the light, as if giving off the warmth that came through the windows from the real winter sun. And all of them came stamped with a blue-purple name as foreign as the otherworld that you might imagine as their place of origin, so that on Christmas day you would find yourself digging past everything else in your Christmas stocking, as if tunneling down to the country of China, in order to reach the rounded bulge at the tip of the toe which meant that you had received a personal reminder of another state of existence, wholly separate from your own.

The packed heft and texture, finally, of an orange in your   12
hand—this is it!—and the eruption of smell and the watery fireworks as a knife, in the hand of someone skilled, like our mother, goes slicing through the skin so perfect for slicing. This gaseous spray can form a mist like smoke, which can then be lit with a match to create actual fireworks if there is a chance to hide alone with a match (matches being forbidden) and the peel from one. Sputtery ignitions can also be produced by squeezing a peel near a candle (at least one candle is generally always going at Christmastime), and the leftover peels are set on the stove top to scent the house.

And the ingenious way in which oranges come packed into their   13
globes! The green nib at the top, like a detonator, can be bitten off, as if disarming the orange, in order to clear a place for you to sink a tooth under the peel. This is the best way to start. If you bite at the peel too much, your front teeth will feel scraped, like dry bone, and your lips will begin to burn from the bitter oil. Better to sink a tooth into this greenish or creamy depression, and then pick at that point with the nail of your thumb, removing a little piece of the peel at a time. Later, you might want to practice to see how large a piece you can remove intact. The peel can also be undone in one continuous ribbon, a feat which maybe your father is able to perform, so that after the orange is freed, looking yellowish, the peel, rewound, will stand in its original shape, although empty.

The yellowish whole of the orange can now be divided into sec-   14
tions, usually about a dozen, by beginning with a division down the middle; after this, each section, enclosed in its papery skin, will be able to be lifted and torn loose more easily. There is a stem up the center of the section like a mushroom stalk, but tougher; this can be eaten. A special variety of orange, without any pits, has an extra

growth, or nubbin, like half of a tiny orange, tucked into its bottom. This nubbin is nearly as bitter as the peel, but it can be eaten, too; don't worry. Some of the sections will have miniature sections embedded in them and clinging as if for life, giving the impression that babies are being hatched, and should you happen to find some of these you've found the sweetest morsels of any.

If you prefer to have your orange sliced in half, as some people 15
do, the edges of the peel will abrade the corners of your mouth, making them feel raw, as you eat down into the white of the rind (which is the only way to do it) until you can see daylight through the orangy bubbles composing its outside. Your eyes might burn; there is no proper way to eat an orange. If there are pits, they can get in the way, and the slower you eat an orange, the more you'll find your fingers sticking together. And no matter how carefully you eat one, or bite into a quarter, juice can always fly or slip from a corner of your mouth; this happens to everyone. Close your eyes to be on the safe side, and for the eruption in your mouth of the slivers of watery meat, which should be broken and rolled fine over your tongue for the essence of orange. And if indeed you have sensed yourself coming down with a cold, there is a chance that you will feel it driven from your head—your nose and sinuses suddenly opening—in the midst of the scent of a peel and eating an orange.

And oranges can also be eaten whole—rolled into a spongy mass 16
and punctured with a pencil (if you don't find this offensive) or a knife, and then sucked upon. Then, once the juice is gone, you can disembowel the orange as you wish and eat away its pulpy remains, and eat once more into the whitish interior of the peel, which scours the coating from your teeth and makes your numbing lips and tip of your tongue start to tingle and swell up from behind, until, in the light from the windows (shining through an empty glass bowl), you see orange again from the inside. Oh, oranges, solid o's, light from afar in the midst of the freeze, and not unlike that unspherical fruit which first went from Eve to Adam and from there (to abbreviate matters) to my brother and me.

"Mom, we think we're getting a cold."   17

"You mean, you want an orange?"   18

This is difficult to answer or dispute or even to acknowledge, fi- 19
nally, with the fullness that the subject deserves, and that each orange bears, within its own makeup, into this hard-edged yet insubstantial, incomplete, cold, wintry world.

Meaning

1. Woiwode opens and closes his essay with the same thought: his mother's question, "You mean, you want an orange?" was "difficult for us to answer or dispute" (paragraphs 4, 19). Why was it difficult? What did the orange signify to Woiwode that made "the matter" greater than "mere wanting"?
2. What dominant impression of the orange does Woiwode create?
3. If you're unsure of any of the following words, try to guess what they mean from the context of Woiwode's essay. Then look them up to see if you were right. Use each word in a sentence or two of your own.

ode (title)	resinous (10)	feat (13)
degradation (10)	heft (12)	abrade (15)
wended (10)	detonator (13)	disembowel (16)
elixir (10)		

Purpose and Audience

1. In repeating his reflection on his mother's question in paragraphs 4 and 19, Woiwode changes verb tense from past (for example, "This *was* difficult," 4) to present ("This *is* difficult," 19). What does this shift reveal about the grown Woiwode's reason for writing about his experiences and feelings as a child? To what extent are "North Dakota winters of the forties" (1) and "this [. . .] wintry world" (19) the same or different?
2. An ode usually praises some person or object. Is Woiwode's praise for the orange weakened by the unpleasant sensations he sometimes describes, such as bitterness (paragraph 14) or burning eyes (15)? Why, or why not?
3. Woiwode could expect his readers to be familiar with his subject: most of us have eaten an orange. To what extent does he succeed in making this familiar object and experience fresher and more significant? What details surprised you? What details evoked your own experiences?

Method and Structure

1. Woiwode mingles straightforward objective description and emotion-laden subjective description. Locate two or three examples of each kind in paragraphs 13–16. What does each kind contribute to the essay? How does combining the two types help Woiwode achieve his purpose?
2. In the body of the essay (paragraphs 10–16), Woiwode describes the orange from a number of perspectives. What topic does each of these paragraphs cover? Is the sequence of topics logical? Why, or why not?

3. **Other Methods**   Woiwode uses several methods of development in addition to description—for instance, paragraphs 1–10 are narrative (Chapter 5), and paragraphs 13–14 divide the orange into its parts (Chapter 7). Most notably, paragraphs 13–16 analyze three processes (Chapter 9), three ways of eating an orange. Why does Woiwode explain these processes so painstakingly?

Language

1. An ode is usually a poem written in exalted language. Find language in Woiwode's essay that seems literary or poetic. What does Woiwode convey by such language? Is it excessive, do you think, or appropriate? Why?
2. In paragraph 11, Woiwode gradually shifts pronouns, from *we* and *our* to *you* and *your*. Do you find this shift disconcerting or effective? Why?
3. How many of the five senses does Woiwode appeal to in this extended description? Find words or phrases that seem especially precise in conveying sensory impressions.
4. To describe a bowl of oranges, Woiwode uses images of heat and light: it was "glowing in the light, as if giving off the warmth that came through the windows from the real winter sun" (paragraph 11). Locate other words or phrases in the essay that evoke heat and light. How does this imagery contribute to the essay?

Writing Topics

1. **Journal to Essay**   Write an essay about a food you ate as a child that summons especially vibrant images. Your subject could be the comfort food you wrote of in your journal entry (p. 72), or it could be one that you detested and avoided. Describe the object of your attachment or revulsion in order to reveal both its physical attributes and its significance to you.
2. Although Woiwode's essay is written with greater skill and range of vocabulary than a small boy would be capable of, the essay reveals the many facets of a small boy's emotional life. Write an essay in which you analyze the boyish concerns and observations evident in "Ode to an Orange," demonstrating how Woiwode captures the workings of a boy's mind. Consider, for example, the way he compares the orange to a hand grenade (paragraph 13).
3. **Cultural Considerations**   Our attitudes toward foods are often influenced by the family, community, or larger culture in which we grew up. Think of feelings that you have about a particular food that seem due at

least partly to other people. In an essay describe the food and your feelings about it and explain the origins of your feelings as best you can.

4. **Connections**   Woiwode's tone when he describes oranges is almost rev-
erential. Compare and contrast his attitude toward his subject with Joan
Didion's attitude toward the Santa Ana wind (next page). Does Didion's
tone indicate that she admires the destructive force she writes about? Be
sure to include examples from both essays to support your comparison.

It's an ill wind that blows nobody any good. —Proverb

Meanings, moods, the whole scale of our inner experience, find in nature the "correspondences" through which we may know our boundless selves.
—Kathleen Raine

How we are all more or less creatures of Sun, Shadow, and Imagination, impressed or depressed by weather! —The Gardener

Journal Response Write a journal entry about a natural phenomenon that affected you, such as a lightning storm, a hurricane, or a blizzard. How did the event make you act and feel?

Joan Didion

One of America's leading nonfiction writers, Joan Didion consistently applies a journalist's eye for detail and a terse, understated style to the cultural dislocation pervading modern American society. She was born in 1934 in Sacramento, a fifth-generation Californian, and she has attended closely to the distinctive people and places of the American West. After graduating from the University of California at Berkeley in 1956, Didion lived for nearly a decade in New York City before returning permanently to California. She has contributed to many periodicals, and her essays have been published in Slouching Towards Bethlehem *(1968),* The White Album *(1979), Salvador (1983),* Essays and Conversations *(1984),* Miami *(1987),* After Henry *(1992), and* Political Fictions *(2001). Didion has also published five novels:* Run River *(1963),* Play It as It Lays *(1970),* A Book of Common Prayer *(1977),* Democracy *(1984), and* The Last Thing He Wanted *(1996). With her husband, the writer John Gregory Dunne, she has written screenplays for movies, among them* Panic in Needle Park *(1971),* A Star Is Born *(1976),* True Confessions *(1981), and* Up Close and Personal *(1996).*

The Santa Ana

In describing the violent effects of a hot, dry wind on Los Angeles, Didion ranges typically outward from herself to the people figuring in local news reports. "The Santa Ana" first appeared in The Saturday Evening Post *in 1967 and later appeared as part of "Los Angeles Notebook," an essay collected in* Slouching Towards Bethlehem.

There is something uneasy in the Los Angeles air this afternoon, some   1
unnatural stillness, some tension. What it means is that tonight a
Santa Ana will begin to blow, a hot wind from the northeast whining
down through the Cajon and San Gorgonio Passes, blowing up
sandstorms out along Route 66, drying the hills and the nerves to
the flash point. For a few days now we will see smoke back in
the canyons, and hear sirens in the night. I have neither heard nor
read that a Santa Ana is due, but I know it, and almost everyone I
have seen today knows it too. We know it because we feel it. The
baby frets. The maid sulks. I rekindle a waning argument with the
telephone company, then cut my losses and lie down, given over to
whatever it is in the air. To live with the Santa Ana is to accept,
consciously or unconsciously, a deeply mechanistic view of human
behavior.

I recall being told, when I first moved to Los Angeles and was liv-   2
ing on an isolated beach, that the Indians would throw themselves
into the sea when the bad wind blew. I could see why. The Pacific
turned ominously glossy during a Santa Ana period, and one woke in
the night troubled not only by the peacocks screaming in the olive
trees but by the eerie absence of surf. The heat was surreal. The sky
had a yellow cast, the kind of light sometimes called "earthquake
weather." My only neighbor would not come out of her house for
days, and there were no lights at night, and her husband roamed the
place with a machete. One day he would tell me that he had heard a
trespasser, the next a rattlesnake.

"On nights like that," Raymond Chandler[1] once wrote about the   3
Santa Ana, "every booze party ends in a fight. Meek little wives feel
the edge of the carving knife and study their husbands' necks. Anything can happen." That was the kind of wind it was. I did not know
then that there was any basis for the effect it had on all of us, but it
turns out to be another of those cases in which science bears out folk
wisdom. The Santa Ana, which is named for one of the canyons it
rushes through, is a *foehn* wind, like the *foehn* of Austria and
Switzerland and the *hamsin* of Israel. There are a number of
persistent malevolent winds, perhaps the best known of which are the
mistral of France and the Mediterranean sirocco, but a *foehn* wind
has distinct characteristics: it occurs on the leeward slope of a moun-

---

[1] Chandler (1888–1959) is best known for his detective novels featuring Philip
Marlowe. [Editor's note.]

tain range and, although the air begins as a cold mass, it is warmed as it comes down the mountain and appears finally as a hot dry wind. Whenever and wherever a *foehn* blows, doctors hear about headaches and nausea and allergies, about "nervousness," about "depression." In Los Angeles some teachers do not attempt to conduct formal classes during a Santa Ana, because the children become unmanageable. In Switzerland the suicide rate goes up during the *foehn*, and in the courts of some Swiss cantons the wind is considered a mitigating circumstance for crime. Surgeons are said to watch the wind, because blood does not clot normally during a *foehn*. A few years ago an Israeli physicist discovered that not only during such winds, but for the ten or twelve hours which precede them, the air carries an unusually high ratio of positive to negative ions. No one seems to know exactly why that should be; some talk about friction and others suggest solar disturbances. In any case the positive ions are there, and what an excess of positive ions does, in the simplest terms, is make people unhappy. One cannot get much more mechanistic than that.

Easterners commonly complain that there is no "weather" at all in   4
Southern California, that the days and the seasons slip by relentlessly, numbingly bland. That is quite misleading. In fact the climate is characterized by infrequent but violent extremes: two periods of torrential subtropical rains which continue for weeks and wash out the hills and send subdivisions sliding toward the sea; about twenty scattered days a year of the Santa Ana, which, with its incendiary dryness, invariably means fire. At the first prediction of a Santa Ana, the Forest Service flies men and equipment from northern California into the southern forests, and the Los Angeles Fire Department cancels its ordinary non-firefighting routines. The Santa Ana caused Malibu to burn the way it did in 1956, and Bel Air in 1961, and Santa Barbara in 1964. In the winter of 1966–67 eleven men were killed fighting a Santa Ana fire that spread through the San Gabriel Mountains.

Just to watch the front-page news out of Los Angeles during a   5
Santa Ana is to get very close to what it is about the place. The longest single Santa Ana period in recent years was in 1957, and it lasted not the usual three or four days but fourteen days, from November 21 until December 4. On the first day 25,000 acres of the San Gabriel Mountains were burning, with gusts reaching 100 miles an hour. In town, the wind reached Force 12, or hurricane force, on the Beaufort Scale; oil derricks were toppled and people ordered off the downtown streets to avoid injury from flying objects. On November 22 the fire in the San Gabriels was out of control. On November 24

six people were killed in automobile accidents, and by the end of the week the Los Angeles *Times* was keeping a box score of traffic deaths. On November 26 a prominent Pasadena attorney, depressed about money, shot and killed his wife, their two sons, and himself. On November 27 a South Gate divorcée, twenty-two, was murdered and thrown from a moving car. On November 30 the San Gabriel fire was still out of control, and the wind in town was blowing eighty miles an hour. On the first day of December four people died violently, and on the third the wind began to break.

It is hard for people who have not lived in Los Angeles to realize   6 how radically the Santa Ana figures in the local imagination. The city burning is Los Angeles's deepest image of itself: Nathanael West perceived that, in *The Day of the Locust;* and at the time of the 1965 Watts riots what struck the imagination most indelibly were the fires.[2] For days one could drive the Harbor Freeway and see the city on fire, just as we had always known it would be in the end. Los Angeles weather is the weather of catastrophe, of apocalypse, and, just as the reliably long and bitter winters of New England determine the way life is lived there, so the violence and the unpredictability of the Santa Ana affect the entire quality of life in Los Angeles, accentuate its impermanence, its unreliability. The wind shows us how close to the edge we are.

Meaning

1. Does Didion describe purely for the sake of describing, or does she have a thesis she wants to convey? If so, where does she most explicitly state this thesis?
2. What is the dominant impression Didion creates of the Santa Ana wind? What effect does it have on residents of Los Angeles?
3. Explain what Didion means by a "mechanistic view of human behavior" (paragraph 1). What would the opposite of such a view of human behavior be?
4. How might Didion's last sentence have two meanings?
5. Based on their context in the essay, try to guess the meanings of any of the following words that you don't know. Test your guesses in a dictio-

---

[2] *The Day of the Locust* (1939), a novel about Hollywood, ends in riot and fire. The August 1965 disturbances in the Watts neighborhood of Los Angeles resulted in millions of dollars in damage from fires. [Editor's note.]

nary, and then try out your knowledge of each word by using it in sentences of your own.

flash point (1)	malevolent (3)	derricks (5)
mechanistic (1)	leeward (3)	indelibly (6)
ominously (2)	cantons (3)	apocalypse (6)
surreal (2)	mitigating (3)	accentuate (6)
machete (2)	incendiary (4)	

Purpose and Audience

1. Why do you think Didion felt compelled to write about the Santa Ana? Consider whether she might have had a dual purpose.
2. What kind of audience is Didion writing for? Primarily people from Los Angeles? How do you know? Does Didion identify herself as an Angelina?

Method and Structure

1. Didion doesn't describe the Santa Ana wind itself as much as its effects. Why does she approach her subject this way? What effects does she focus on?
2. Didion alternates between passages of mostly objective and mostly subjective description. Trace this movement throughout the essay.
3. What is the function of the quotation from Raymond Chandler at the beginning of paragraph 3? How does it serve as a transition?
4. **Other Methods** The essay is full of examples (Chapter 6) of the wind's effects on human beings. How do these examples help Didion achieve her purpose?

Language

1. Note Didion's frequent use of the first person (*I* and *we*) and of the present tense. What does she achieve with this point of view?
2. What is the effect of the vivid imagery in paragraph 2? In what way is this imagery "surreal" (fantastic or dreamlike)?

Writing Topics

1. **Journal to Essay** Using Didion's essay as a model, write a descriptive essay about something that annoys, frightens, or even crazes you and others. Your subject could be a natural phenomenon, such as the one

you described in your journal entry (p. 79), or something else: bumper-to-bumper traffic at rush hour, long lines at the department of motor vehicles or another government agency, lengthy and complicated voice-mail menus that end up in busy signals. You may use examples from your own experience and observation, from experiences you have read or heard about, or, like Didion, from both sources.

2. Didion tries to explain the Santa Ana phenomenon scientifically in paragraph 3 as having something to do with an excess of positive ions in the air. But she admits that nobody knows why there are more positive than negative ions or why that fact should translate into human unhappiness. To what extent do you think our moods can be explained by science? Are our emotions simply the by-products of brain chemistry, as some scientists would suggest? Write an essay, using description and narration (Chapter 5), about someone you know (or know of) whose moods are affected by forces beyond his or her control. Be sure to include enough detail to create a vivid portrait for your readers.

3. **Cultural Considerations**   Didion perceives the Santa Ana as a cultural phenomenon in Los Angeles that affects the attitudes, relationships, and activities of residents "just as the reliably long and bitter winters of New England determine the way life is lived there" (paragraph 6). Consider a place you know well and describe how some aspect of the climate or weather affects the culture, "the way life is lived," not only during a particular event or season but throughout the year.

4. **Connections**   Both Didion and Marta K. Taylor, in "Desert Dance" (p. 67), describe dramatic natural phenomena that occur in the American West. Compare the way Taylor describes a desert lightning storm in paragraphs 5 and 6 of her essay to Didion's description, in paragraph 2, of the surreal landscape of the Santa Ana. How does each writer combine striking images and original figures of speech to convey a strong sense of mood and a feeling in the reader that he or she is there? Do you think one author's description is more successful than the other's? Why?

Writing with the Method
Description

Choose one of the following topics, or any topic they suggest, for an essay developed by description. The topic you decide on should be something you care about so that description is a means of communicating an idea, not an end in itself.

PEOPLE

1. An exceptionally neat or messy person
2. A person whose appearance and mannerisms are at odds with his or her real self
3. A person you admire or respect
4. An irritating child
5. A person who intimidates you (teacher, salesperson, doctor, police officer, fellow student)

PLACES

6. A shopping mall
7. A frightening place
8. A place near water (ocean, lake, pond, river, swimming pool)
9. A place you daydream about
10. A prison cell, police station, or courtroom
11. A cellar, attic, or garage
12. Your room

ANIMALS AND THINGS

13. Birds at a bird feeder
14. A work of art
15. A pet or an animal in a zoo
16. A favorite childhood toy
17. A prized possession
18. The look and taste of a favorite or detested food

SCENES

19. The devastation caused by a natural disaster
20. A scene of environmental destruction
21. A yard sale or flea market
22. Late night or early morning
23. The scene at a concert (rock, country, folk, classical, jazz)

85

SENSATIONS

24. Waiting for important news
25. Being freed of some restraint
26. Sunday afternoon
27. Writing
28. Skating, running, body surfing, skydiving, or some other activity
29. Extreme hunger, thirst, cold, heat, or fatigue

Writing About the Theme
Sensing the Natural World

1. Some of the writers in this chapter recognize that nature can be difficult to cope with. Joan Didion's description of the Santa Ana wind (p. 79) and David Mura's description of rain (p. 61) are most notable in this respect, but even Larry Woiwode's celebration of the orange (p. 72) mentions that parts of it are bitter and that the peel can abrade the corners of one's mouth. Write a descriptive essay about a place or thing that is special to you, paying close attention to its blemishes as well as its beauty.

2. All of the writers in this chapter demonstrate strong feelings for the place, thing, or phenomenon they describe, but the writers vary considerably in the way they express their feelings. For example, Joan Didion's own discomfort in the Santa Ana wind colors all of her perceptions, whereas Larry Woiwode's description of oranges is celebratory. Write an essay analyzing the tone of these and the three other selections in this chapter: David Mura's paragraph on typhoons, Diane Ackerman's paragraph on icebergs (p. 62), and Marta K. Taylor's "Desert Dance" (p. 67). Discuss which pieces you find most effective and why.

3. Each writer in this chapter vividly describes a specific place or thing that represents some larger, abstract concept: for example, Larry Woiwode's oranges represent childhood, and Marta Taylor's desert lightning represents the awesomeness of nature. Think of a specific, tangible place or thing in your life that represents some larger, abstract idea and write a descriptive essay exploring this relationship.

Chapter 5

NARRATION

Recalling Childhood

USING THE METHOD

To **narrate** is to tell a story, to relate a sequence of events that are linked in time. We narrate when we tell of a funny experience, report a baseball game, or trace a historical event. By arranging events in an orderly progression, we illuminate the stages leading to a result.

Sometimes the emphasis in narration is on the story itself, as in fiction, biography, autobiography, some history, and much journalism. But often a narrative serves some larger point, as when a paragraph or a brief story about an innocent person's death helps to strengthen an argument for stricter handling of drunk drivers. When used as a primary means of developing an essay, such pointed narration usually relates a sequence of events that led to new knowledge or had a notable outcome. The point of the narrative—the idea the reader is to take away—then determines the selection of events, the amount of detail devoted to them, and their arrangement.

Though narration arranges events in time, narrative time is not real time. An important event may fill whole pages, even though it took only minutes to unfold; and a less important event may be dispensed with in a sentence, even though it lasted hours. Suppose, for instance, that a writer wants to narrate the experience of being mugged in order to show how courage came unexpectedly to his aid. He might provide a slow-motion account of the few minutes' encounter with the muggers, including vivid details of the setting and of the attackers' appearance, a moment-by-moment replay of his emotions, and exact dialogue. At the same time, he will compress events that merely fill in background or link main events, such as how he got to the scene of the mugging or the follow-up questioning by a police detective. And he will entirely omit many events, such as a conversation overheard at the police station, that have no significance for his point.

The point of a narrative influences not only which events are covered and how fully but also how the events are arranged. There are several possibilities:

- A straight chronological sequence is usually the easiest to manage because it relates events in the order of their actual occurrence. It is particularly useful for short narratives, for those in which the last event is the most dramatic, or for those in which the events preceding and following the climax contribute to the point being made.
- The final event, such as a self-revelation, may come first, followed by an explanation of the events leading up to it.
- The entire story may be summarized first and then examined in detail.
- **Flashbacks** — shifts backward rather than forward in time — may recall events whose significance would not have been apparent earlier. Flashbacks are common in movies and fiction: a character in the midst of one scene mentally replays another.

In addition to providing a clear organization, you can also help readers by adopting a consistent **point of view**, a position relative to the events, conveyed in two main ways:

- Pronouns indicate your place in the story: the first-person *I* if you are a direct participant; the third-person *he, she, it,* and *they* if you are an observer or reporter.

- Verb tense indicates your relation in time to the sequence of events: present (*is, run*) or past (*was, ran*).

Combining the first-person pronoun with the present tense can create great immediacy ("I feel the point of the knife in my back"). At the other extreme, combining third-person pronouns with the past tense creates more distance and objectivity ("He felt the point of the knife in his back"). In between extremes, you can combine first person with past tense ("I felt . . .") or third person with present tense ("He feels . . ."). The choice depends on your actual involvement in the narrative and on your purpose.

ANALYZING NARRATION IN PARAGRAPHS

Michael Ondaatje (born 1943) is a poet, fiction writer, essayist, and filmmaker. The following paragraph is from *Running in the Family* (1982), Ondaatje's memoir of his childhood in Ceylon, now called Sri Lanka, off the southern tip of India.

After my father died, a grey cobra came into the house. My stepmother loaded the gun and fired at point blank range. The gun jammed. She stepped back and reloaded but by then the snake had slid out into the garden. For the next month this snake would often come into the house and each time the gun would misfire or jam, or my stepmother would miss at absurdly short range. The snake attacked no one and had a tendency to follow my younger sister Susan around. Other snakes entering the house were killed by the shotgun, lifted with a long stick and flicked into the bushes, but the old grey cobra led a charmed life. Finally one of the old workers at Rock Hill told my stepmother what had become obvious, that it was my father who had come to protect his family. And in fact, whether it was because the chicken farm closed down or because of my father's presence in the form of a snake, very few other snakes came into the house again.

Chronological order

Past tense

Transitions (underlined)

Point of view: participant

Purpose: to relate a colorful, mysterious story

Andre Dubus (1936–99) wrote essays and fiction. This paragraph comes from his essay "Under the Lights," which was published first in the *Village Voice* and then in Dubus's collection *Broken Vessels* (1991).

In the spring of 1948, in the first softball game during the afternoon hour of physical education in the dusty schoolyard, the two captains chose teams and, as always, they chose other boys until only two of us remained. I batted last, and first came to the plate with two or three runners on base, and while my teammates urged me to try for a walk, and the players on the field called Easy out, Easy out, I watched the softball coming in waist high, and stepped and swung, and hit it over the right fielder's head for a double. My next time at bat I tripled to center. From then on I brought my glove to school, hanging from a handlebar.

Chronological order

Past tense

Transitions (under-lined)

Point of view: direct participant

Purpose: to relate the author's trans-formation into a baseball player

DEVELOPING A NARRATIVE ESSAY
Getting Started

You'll find narration useful whenever relating a sequence of events can help you make a point, sometimes to support the thesis of a larger paper, sometimes *as* the thesis of a paper. If you're assigned a narrative essay, probe your own experiences for a situation such as an argument involving strong emotion, a humorous or embarrassing incident, a dramatic scene you witnessed, or a learning experience like a job. If you have the opportunity to do research, you might choose a topic dealing with the natural world (such as the Big Bang scenario for the origin of the universe) or an event in history or politics (such as how a local activist worked to close down an animal-research lab).

Whatever your subject, you should have some point to make about it: Why was the incident or experience significant? What does it teach or illustrate? Phrase this point in a sentence if you can at this stage (later it can serve as your thesis sentence). For instance:

I used to think small-town life was boring, but one taste of the city made me appreciate the leisurely pace of home.

A recent small earthquake demonstrated the hazards of inadequate civil-defense measures.

Sometimes you may need to draft your story before the point of it becomes clear to you, especially if the experience was personal and too recent to have sunk in.

Explore your subject by listing all the events in sequence as they happened. At this stage you may find the traditional journalist's questions helpful:

- Who was involved?
- What happened?
- When did it happen?
- Where did it happen?
- Why did it happen?
- How did it happen?

These questions will lead you to examine your subject from all angles. Then you need to decide which events should be developed in great detail because they are central to your point; which merit compression because they merely contribute background or tie the main events together; and which should be omitted altogether because they add nothing to your point and might clutter your narrative.

While you are weighing the relative importance of events, consider also what your readers need to know in order to understand and appreciate your narrative.

- What information will help locate readers in the narrative's time and place?
- How will you expand and compress events to keep readers' attention?
- What details about people, places, and feelings will make the events vivid for readers?
- What is your attitude toward the subject—lighthearted, sarcastic, bitter, serious?—and how will you convey it to readers in your choice of events and details?
- What should your point of view be? Do you want to involve readers intimately by using the first person and the present tense? Or does that seem overdramatic, less appropriate than the more detached, objective view that would be conveyed by the past tense or the third person or both?

Organizing

Narrative essays often begin without formal introductions, instead drawing the reader in with one of the more dramatic events in the sequence. But you may find an introduction useful to set the scene for your narrative, summarize the events leading up to it, or otherwise establish the context for it. Such an opening may lead to a statement of your thesis so that readers know why you are bothering to tell them your story. Then again, to intensify the drama of your story you may decide to withhold your thesis sentence for the conclusion or omit it altogether. (Remember, though, that the thesis must be evident to readers even if it isn't stated: the narrative needs a point.)

The arrangement of events in the body of your essay depends on the actual order in which they occurred and the point you want to make. To narrate a trip during which one thing after another went wrong, you might find a strict chronological order most effective. To narrate an earthquake that began and ended in an instant, you might sort simultaneous events into groups—say, what happened to buildings and what happened to people—or you might arrange a few people's experiences in order of increasing drama. To narrate your experience of city life, you might interweave events in the city with contrasting flashbacks to your life in a small town, or you might start by relating one especially bad experience in the city, drop back to explain how you ended up in that situation, and then go on to tell what happened afterward. Narrative time can be manipulated in any number of ways, but your scheme should have a purpose that your readers can see, and you should stick to it.

Let the ending of your essay be determined by the effect you want to leave with readers. You can end with the last event in your sequence, or the one you have saved for last, if it conveys your point and provides a strong finish. Or you can summarize the aftermath of the story if it contributes to the point. You can also end with a formal conclusion that states your point—your thesis—explicitly. Such a conclusion is especially useful if your point unfolds gradually throughout the narrative and you want to emphasize it at the finish.

Drafting

Drafting a narrative can be less of a struggle than drafting other kinds of papers, especially if you're close to the events and you use a straight chronological order. But the relative ease of storytelling can be misleading if it causes you to describe events too quickly or write without making a point. While drafting, be as specific as possible. Tell what the people in your narrative were wearing, what expressions their faces held, how they gestured, what they said. Specify the time of day, and describe the weather and the surroundings (buildings, vegetation, and the like). All these details may be familiar to you, but they won't be to your readers.

At the same time, try to remain open to what the story means to you, so that you can convey that meaning in your selection and description of events. If you know before you begin what your thesis is, let it guide you. But the first draft may turn out to be a search for your thesis, so that you'll need another draft to make it evident in the way you relate events.

In your draft you may want to experiment with dialogue — quotations of what participants said, in their words. Dialogue can add immediacy and realism as long as it advances the narrative and doesn't ramble beyond its usefulness. In reconstructing dialogue from memory, try to recall not only the actual words but also the sounds of speakers' voices and the expressions on their faces — information that will help you represent each speaker distinctly. And keep the dialogue natural sounding by using constructions typical of speech. For instance, most speakers prefer contractions like *don't* and *shouldn't* to the longer forms *do not* and *should not;* and few speakers begin sentences with *although,* as in the formal-sounding "Although we could hear our mother's voice, we refused to answer her."

Whether you are relating events in strict chronological order or manipulating them for some effect, try to make their sequence in real time and the distance between them clear to readers. Instead of signaling sequence with the monotonous *and then . . . and then . . . and then* or *next . . . next . . . next,* use informative transitions that signal the order of events (*afterward, earlier*), the duration of events (*for an hour, in that time*), or the amount of time between events (*the next morning, a week later*). (See the Glossary under *transitions* for a list of such expressions.)

Revising and Editing

When your draft is complete, revise and edit it by answering the following questions and considering the information in the box.

- *Is the point of your narrative clear, and does every event you relate contribute to it?* Whether or not you state your thesis, it should be obvious to readers. They should be able to see why you have lingered over some events and compressed others, and they should not be distracted by insignificant events and details.

- *Is your organization clear?* Be sure that your readers will understand any shifts backward or forward in time.
- *Have you used transitions to help readers follow the sequence of events?* Transitions such as *meanwhile* or *soon afterward* serve a dual purpose: they keep the reader on track, and they link sentences and paragraphs so that they flow smoothly. (For more information, see pp. 38 and 39 and the Glossary under *transitions*.)
- *If you have used dialogue, is it purposeful and natural?* Be sure all quoted speeches move the action ahead. And read all dialogue aloud to check that it sounds like something someone would actually say.

FOCUS ON VERBS

Narration depends heavily on verbs to clarify and enliven events. Strong verbs sharpen meaning and encourage you to add other informative details:

WEAK The wind *made* an awful noise.

STRONG The wind *roared* around the house and *rattled* the trees.

Forms of *make* (as in the example above) and forms of *be* (as in the next example) can sap the life from narration:

WEAK The noises *were* alarming to us.

STRONG The noises *alarmed* us.

Verbs in the active voice (the subject does the action) usually pack more power into fewer words than verbs in the passive voice (the subject is acted upon):

WEAK PASSIVE We *were besieged* in the basement by the wind, as the water at our feet *was swelled* by the rain.

STRONG ACTIVE The wind *besieged* us in the basement, as the rain *swelled* the water at our feet.

(See also p. 48 on active versus passive voice.)

While strengthening verbs, also ensure that they're consistent in tense. The tense you choose for relating events, present or past, should not shift unnecessarily.

INCONSISTENT TENSES We *held* a frantic conference to consider our options. It *takes* only a minute to decide to stay put.

CONSISTENT TENSE We *held* a frantic conference to consider our options. It *took* only a minute to decide to stay put.

A NOTE ON THEMATIC CONNECTIONS

All the authors in this chapter saw reasons to articulate key events in their childhoods, and for that purpose narration is the obvious choice. Michael Ondaatje, in a paragraph, recalls his stepmother's inability to kill a cobra, perhaps because it embodied his dead father (p. 90). Andre Dubus, in another paragraph, records his transformation from a bench warmer to a baseball player (p. 91). Langston Hughes's essay pinpoints the moment during a church revival when he lost his faith (opposite). Gavin Rember's essay recalls a disturbing boyhood experience at the welfare department (p. 102). And Annie Dillard's essay recounts the ecstasy of being chased by an adult for pelting his car with a snowball (p. 108).

Nothing is more restful than conformity. — Elizabeth Bowen

We all try to be alike in our youth. — Alec Tweedie

This above all: to thine own self be true, / And it must follow, as the night the day, / Thou canst not then be false to any man. — William Shakespeare

Journal Response When have you experienced a powerful desire to think, look, or act like others, especially your peers? Write a journal entry about your experience.

Langston Hughes

A poet, fiction writer, playwright, critic, and humorist, Langston Hughes described his writing as "largely concerned with depicting Negro life in America." He was born in 1902 in Joplin, Missouri, and grew up in Illinois, Kansas, and Ohio. After dropping out of Columbia University in the early 1920s, Hughes worked at odd jobs while struggling to gain recognition as a writer. His first book of poems, The Weary Blues *(1925), helped seed the Harlem Renaissance, a flowering of African American music and literature centered in the Harlem district of New York City during the 1920s. The book also generated a scholarship that enabled Hughes to finish college at Lincoln University. In all of his work — including* The Negro Mother *(1931),* The Ways of White Folks *(1934),* Shakespeare in Harlem *(1942),* Montage of a Dream Deferred *(1951),* Ask Your Mama *(1961), and* The Best of Simple *(1961) — Hughes captured and projected the rhythms of jazz and the distinctive speech, subtle humor, and deep traditions of African American people. He died in New York City in 1967.*

Salvation

A chapter in Hughes's autobiography, The Big Sea *(1940), "Salvation" is a simple yet compelling narrative about a moment of deceit and disillusionment for a boy of twelve. As you read Hughes's account, notice how the opening two sentences set up every twist of the story.*

I was saved from sin when I was going on thirteen. But not really *1*
saved. It happened like this. There was a big revival at my Auntie
Reed's church. Every night for weeks there had been much preaching,

singing, praying, and shouting, and some very hardened sinners had been brought to Christ, and the membership of the church had grown by leaps and bounds. Then just before the revival ended, they held a special meeting for children, "to bring the young lambs to the fold." My aunt spoke of it for days ahead. That night, I was escorted to the front row and placed on the mourner's bench with all the other young sinners, who had not yet been brought to Jesus.

My aunt told me that when you were saved you saw a light, and 2 something happened to you inside! And Jesus came into your life! And God was with you from then on! She said you could see and hear and feel Jesus in your soul. I believed her. I have heard a great many old people say the same thing and it seemed to me they ought to know. So I sat there calmly in the hot, crowded church, waiting for Jesus to come to me.

The preacher preached a wonderful rhythmical sermon, all 3 moans and shouts and lonely cries and dire pictures of hell, and then he sang a song about the ninety and nine safe in the fold, but one little lamb was left out in the cold. Then he said: "Won't you come? Won't you come to Jesus? Young lambs, won't you come?" And he held out his arms to all us young sinners there on the mourner's bench. And the little girls cried. And some of them jumped up and went to Jesus right away. But most of us just sat there.

A great many old people came and knelt around us and prayed, 4 old women with jet-black faces and braided hair, old men with work-gnarled hands. And the church sang a song about the lower lights are burning, some poor sinners to be saved. And the whole building rocked with prayer and song.

Still I kept waiting to *see* Jesus. 5

Finally all the young people had gone to the altar and were 6 saved, but one boy and me. He was a rounder's son named Westley. Westley and I were surrounded by sisters and deacons praying. It was very hot in the church, and getting late now. Finally Westley said to me in a whisper: "God damn! I'm tired o' sitting here. Let's get up and be saved." So he got up and was saved.

Then I was left all alone on the mourner's bench. My aunt came 7 and knelt at my knees and cried, while prayers and songs swirled all around me in the little church. The whole congregation prayed for me alone, in a mighty wail of moans and voices. And I kept waiting serenely for Jesus, waiting, waiting — but he didn't come. I wanted to see him, but nothing happened to me. Nothing! I wanted something to happen to me, but nothing happened.

I heard the songs and the minister saying: "Why don't you come?   8
My dear child, why don't you come to Jesus? Jesus is waiting for you.
He wants you. Why don't you come? Sister Reed, what is this child's
name?"

"Langston," my aunt sobbed.   9

"Langston, why don't you come? Why don't you come and be   10
saved? Oh, Lamb of God! Why don't you come?"

Now it was really getting late. I began to be ashamed of myself,   11
holding everything up so long. I began to wonder what God thought
about Westley, who certainly hadn't seen Jesus either, but who was
now sitting proudly on the platform, swinging his knickerbockered
legs and grinning down at me, surrounded by deacons and old
women on their knees praying. God had not struck Westley dead for
taking his name in vain or for lying in the temple. So I decided that
maybe to save further trouble, I'd better lie, too, and say that Jesus
had come, and get up and be saved.

So I got up.   12

Suddenly the whole room broke into a sea of shouting, as they   13
saw me rise. Waves of rejoicing swept the place. Women leaped in the
air. My aunt threw her arms around me. The minister took me by the
hand and led me to the platform.

When things quieted down, in a hushed silence, punctuated by a   14
few ecstatic "Amens," all the new young lambs were blessed in the
name of God. Then joyous singing filled the room.

That night, for the last time in my life but one—for I was a big   15
boy twelve years old—I cried. I cried, in bed alone, and couldn't
stop. I buried my head under the quilts, but my aunt heard me. She
woke up and told my uncle I was crying because the Holy Ghost had
come into my life, and because I had seen Jesus. But I was really crying because I couldn't bear to tell her that I had lied, that I had de-
ceived everybody in the church, that I hadn't seen Jesus, and that now
I didn't believe there was a Jesus anymore, since he didn't come to
help me.

Meaning

1. What is the main point of Hughes's narrative? What change occurs in
   him as a result of his experience?
2. What finally makes Hughes decide to get up and be saved? How does
   this decision affect him afterward?

3. What do you make of the title and the first two sentences? What is Hughes saying here about "salvation"?

4. If you are unfamiliar with any of the following words, try to guess what they mean from the context of Hughes's essay. Test your guesses in a dictionary, and then try to use each word in a sentence or two of your own.

dire (3)
rounder (6)
deacons (6)

Purpose and Audience

1. Why do you think Hughes wrote "Salvation" as part of his autobiography more than two decades after the experience? Was his purpose simply to express feelings prompted by a significant event in his life? Did he want to criticize his aunt and the other adults in the congregation? Did he want to explain something about childhood or about the distance between generations? What passages support your answer?

2. What does Hughes seem to assume about his readers' familiarity with the kind of service he describes? What details help make the procedure clear?

3. How do dialogue, lines from hymns, and details of other sounds (paragraphs 3–10) help re-create the increasing pressure Hughes feels? What other details contribute to this sense of pressure?

Method and Structure

1. Why do you think Hughes chose narration to explore the themes of this essay? Can you imagine an argumentative essay (Chapter 13) that would deal with the same themes? What might its title be?

2. Where in his narrative does Hughes insert explanations, compress time by summarizing events, or jump ahead in time by omitting events? Where does he expand time by drawing moments out? How does each of these insertions and manipulations of time relate to Hughes's main point?

3. In paragraph 1 Hughes uses several transitions to signal the sequence of events and the passage of time: "for weeks," "Then just before," "for days ahead," "That night." Where does he use similar signals in the rest of the essay?

4. **Other Methods**   Hughes's narrative also explains a process (Chapter 9): we learn how a revival meeting works. Why is this process analysis essential to the essay?

Language

1. What does Hughes's language reveal about his adult attitudes toward his experience? Does he feel anger? bitterness? sorrow? guilt? shame? amusement? What words and passages support your answer?
2. Hughes relates his experience in an almost childlike style, using many short sentences and beginning many sentences with *And*. What effect do you think he is trying to achieve with this style?
3. Hughes expects to "see" Jesus when he is saved (paragraphs 2, 5, 7), and afterward his aunt thinks that he has "seen" Jesus (15). What does each of them mean by *see*? What is the significance of the difference in Hughes's story?

Writing Topics

1. **Journal to Essay**   Continuing from your journal entry (p. 97), write a narrative essay about a time when others significantly influenced the way you thought, looked, or acted—perhaps against your own true beliefs or values. What was the appeal of the others' attitudes, appearance, or behavior? What did you gain by conforming? What did you lose? Use specific details to explain how and why the experience affected you.
2. Hughes says, "I have heard a great many old people say the same thing and it seemed to me they ought to know" (paragraph 2). Think of a piece of information or advice that you heard over and over again from adults when you were a child. Write a narrative essay about an experience in which you were helped or misled by that information or advice.
3. **Cultural Considerations**   It seems that Hughes wants to be saved largely because of the influence of his family and his community. Westley (paragraphs 6 and 11) represents another kind of influence, peer pressure, that often works against family and community. Think of an incident in your own life when you felt pressured by peers to go against your parents, religion, school, or another authority. Write a narrative essay telling what happened and making it clear why the situation was important to you. What were the results?
4. **Connections**   When Hughes doesn't see Jesus and then lies to satisfy everyone around him, he feels betrayed and pained. How does Hughes's experience differ from the one cheerfully reported by Michael Ondaatje (paragraph, p. 90), in which a potentially deadly snake is said to be Ondaatje's deceased father, "come to protect his family"? Write an essay analyzing what elements these narratives have in common and any significant differences between them.

Bad memories are best forgotten. —Popular saying

Perhaps one day this too will be pleasant to remember. —Virgil

That which is bitter to endure may be sweet to remember. —Thomas Fuller

Journal Response In a journal entry, look back on a time in your past when you had a troubling or challenging experience. Try to convey why the experience was difficult. Has your perspective on the experience changed over time?

Gavin Rember

Gavin Rember was born in 1981 in Denver, Colorado. He spent the first part of his life living with his mother in a handful of towns throughout the Colorado Rocky Mountains. He returned to Denver in 1989, attending East High School and the University of Denver. He reports that his true passion is photography and his favorite subjects are people and urban life.

Closing Doors

"Closing Doors" first appeared in the University of Denver's Breaking Ground: Guide to First Year English. *In this essay Rember re-creates through sounds and sights his experience as a young child visiting the Denver welfare office.*

A lonely child screams for her mother. A couple bickers, the woman begins to sob. I sit in silence, trying to drown out the noise. These sights and sounds represent the instability of my childhood. Years later, in the sanctuary of my bedroom, I recall the discomfort of the welfare office. 1

The Denver Department of Social Services office was located in a strip mall, behind a Vietnamese Market and a restaurant called The Organ Grinder. Skydeck Liquors, Kim Hong Jewelry, and Plaza Mexico Salon Eldorado, and other small businesses scattered the mall. A vast asphalt parking lot sat ominously before the strip mall, which sprawled nearly half the length of a city block. Hideous shrubs grew near the entrance—an attempt at landscaping gone horribly 2 awry. The exterior façade was all glass. It had a reflective coating, which gave an effect similar to that of a two-way mirror. White metal railings rose from the steps and ancient rust stained the sidewalk at their base.

Inside the building, everything seemed inconsistent. The waiting 3 area was filthy, unorganized, and overcrowded. Plastic chairs awaited the welfare-hopefuls, after they took a number. A large indicator above the counter would tell which number the overworked staff was serving, a dismal reminder of the crying, throbbing, aching mass of humanity yet to be served. The carpet, a dingy blue, clashed with its surroundings. The blandness of the building and its furnishings radiated with the blandness of government. The one exception could be found in the walls, which were painted a bright white and a gaudy purple. These flashy colors gave the impression that the social services facility was child friendly.

However, the Department of Social Services was not child friendly. 4 Perhaps that's one of the reasons I hated it so much. A sign in the waiting room read: "PARENTS PLEASE SILENCE YOUR CHILDREN." Another demanded, "PLEASE KEEP CHILDREN OFF COUNTER TOPS." The government offered no day-care services of any kind. Parents brought their children to the office, making them sit for hours waiting to see a caseworker. Fortunately I had to visit only a few times.

The visions of people I encountered there remain clear in my 5 mind. The office was always full of people, many of whom were immigrants who spoke little if no English. The screams of infants and cries of toddlers echoed throughout the building. Out of view of the social workers, abusive parents with few parenting skills would rebuke, spank, or hit their children.

The caseworker assigned to my mother and me was a middle- 6 aged white woman. She wore a red nylon jacket with red-and-white striped cuffs, brown pants, and a white shirt. Perhaps she held a second job driving a bus, I guessed from her clothing. Her lifeless gaze told a sad story. She hated her job, but years of it had desensitized her to its depressing reality.

I hated this place. To me, it symbolized the height of my family's 7 instabilities. It shrouded me in embarrassment: not only having to visit the office, but the humiliation of having to use food stamps at the grocery store. By using them, I felt we were telling everyone that we were a family of limited means, that we were poor.

I know my mother didn't want to take me along. She resented 8 what I had to go through by being there. She had little choice. I'm an

only child of a single mom. My mother is an artist; her work often reflects crucial parts of her life, and in turn, a great deal of it reflects
me. She's painted all of her life, and she is extremely talented. However, like many artists, her income fluctuates dramatically. One year
we relied on food stamps, and the next we traveled to Europe.

Because my mother's income was so inconsistent, we moved   9
around quite a bit. In all, I've gone to over ten different schools and
lived in just as many houses. Despite the moving, I had a good childhood. After I was born (at St. Luke's Hospital in Denver), we moved
in with my great aunt in Greeley. Shortly after, we went west to Rifle,
a small ranching town an hour east of the Utah-Colorado border. My
mom painted, and I attended school. We lived in several houses in
Rifle and then moved to Glenwood Springs in 1985. We lived there
for several years, moving from place to place many times.

In 1988, rent rose so high that we were forced to move again. We   10
lived in a tent for two months that summer until we found a house in
New Castle, a small town on the Colorado River, located about 150
miles west of Denver. My mother had no success with her art there
and felt that moving to the city was the best choice. We had only
lived in New Castle for a year and had no real reason to stay. We
packed up our two dogs, three cats, and the rest of our belongings
and left for Denver.

We found a house for rent in north Denver and moved in. I   11
started school that September, and we started our life over once
again. Because of financial instability, we were forced to go on food
stamps. Every month, my mom and I would go to the Denver Department of Social Services to pick them up. The social services office was
the most depressing place I have ever been in my life.

Through all of this, my bedroom was a place of refuge. The   12
safety of my room always welcomed me. There I could be alone, far
from the screaming children and chaos of the social services office.
But it wasn't until we bought our first house in 1991 that I had a true
sanctuary. Previous houses weren't homes; they were temporary
places to stay for a year or less. The house we bought on Adams
Street was permanent. I could live there without the threat of leaving
looming above me.

Recently, I went back to the social services office on Alameda and   13
Federal. I parked and walked to the building. Above the entrance, the
sign still reads: "Denver Department of Social Services." Posted on the
inside of a door, a piece of paper reads: "DENVER HUMAN SERVICES DE-
PARTMENT WILL BE CLOSED AT THIS LOCATION PERMANENTLY."

The railing leading to the stairs rattled with icy gusts of wind. *14* The once prominent bushes dwindled in the chilly September sun. Old dry hoses snaked their way between the dying plants. I moved toward the window. The reflective covering peeled inward from the edges, allowing me to see into sections of the glass. Inside, the blue carpet remained. Dark spots on the floor revealed where desks and other large furnishings had once been. In one of the rooms, a solitary wooden chair faced outward toward the window. The chair, like many other artifacts inside, seemed out of place. A dusty yellow computer monitor sat sideways beside the chair, its power cord intertwined with unused phone cords.

Back in my car, I sat in silence — with no noise to drown out my *15* thoughts. In the distance, a young boy ran across the parking lot. I watched as he disappeared behind a building. I looked back at the social services office. The doors weren't simply closed on the outside. For me they had closed a chapter that signified the instability of my life. My hatred for this place had diminished. The uneasiness I had once felt was replaced with a sense of tranquility. It was the tranquility I needed to find peace in my life.

Meaning

1. In paragraph 1 Rember begins to "recall the discomfort of the welfare office." Do you think the main point of this essay is this experience or something else? How does Rember feel about this experience?

2. Why do you think Rember felt that the "social services office was the most depressing place I have ever been in my life" (paragraph 11)? What are the main reasons why he hated it so much? In your answer, consider not only Rember's description of the office, but also what the place represented to him.

3. The title of the essay is "Closing Doors." Rember returns to this image at the end of his essay (paragraph 15). What doors are closed? What does the image of closed doors represent for Rember? (See *image* in the Glossary.)

4. If you are unsure of the meanings of any of the following words, try to guess them from the context of Rember's essay. Look the words up in a dictionary to test your guesses, and then use each word in a sentence or two of your own.

sanctuary (1)	dingy (3)	fluctuates (8)
ominously (2)	gaudy (3)	dwindled (14)
awry (2)	desensitized (6)	
façade (2)	shrouded (7)	

Purpose and Audience

1. It can be very difficult to recall a painful experience in your life, yet Rember chooses to do so. What do you believe is his purpose in recording these visits to the social services office: to understand that experience? to tell his peers about his childhood? something else?
2. Do you think that Rember wrote this essay with a particular audience in mind? Does he assume that his readers are familiar with being on welfare, with welfare offices, or with the Colorado towns he describes? What evidence in the text supports your answers?

Method and Structure

1. What features of narration make it ideal for describing a childhood experience like the one documented by Rember?
2. Rember does not organize his experiences in chronological order but instead uses flashbacks to tell his reader about his past. (For example, paragraph 1 begins with a dramatic flashback.) Why do you believe he jumps between time periods? How does this manipulation of narrative time serve the overall purpose of the essay?
3. **Other Methods**   In addition to narration, Rember includes some cause-and-effect arguments (Chapter 12) to explain his visits to the welfare office. Why does he feel the need to offer reasons for his family's economic plight?

Language

1. Rember uses many adjectives to enrich his prose, particularly when he is describing the interior and exterior of the social services office: the waiting area is "filthy, unorganized, and overcrowded" but painted in "bright," "gaudy," and "flashy" colors (paragraph 3), and the sun is "chilly" (14). How effective is Rember's use of descriptive adjectives in setting the scene for the reader? How do these adjectives reflect how he feels about the social services office?
2. Why does Rember begin the essay in the present tense (paragraph 1)? What is the effect of this passage?

Writing Topics

1. **Journal to Essay**   In "Closing Doors" Rember revisits a place that was important to him as a child and reopens a door that had been closed for some time. In your journal entry (p. 102) you opened a memory from

your own past. Now elaborate on that memory in a brief narrative essay. Include details of the episode that will make this memory more vivid and real for your readers. What perspective can you bring to your experience now that you didn't have then?

2. "Closing Doors" relies on narrative in order to recount a sad and difficult experience. Using the same method, write an essay in which you recapture one of the happiest or most exciting times in your childhood: for example, playing childhood games with your neighbors, being read to by a parent or grandparent, going on vacation, or receiving something you deeply desired. Use straightforward chronological time if that works best, or, like Rember, experiment with verb tenses, flashbacks, and time shifts.

3. **Cultural Considerations**   Rember is particularly conscious of his own reaction to the social services office, but it is likely that the other people there had their own strong reactions. Write an essay in which you imagine the point of view of either Rember's mother or the social worker. How would this person describe the office and her feelings about being there?

4. **Connections**   Both Rember and Marta K. Taylor, in "Desert Dance" (p. 67), write about experiences they had as children. Rember recalls times of unhappiness and instability; Taylor, in contrast, recaptures a "state of grace." Write an essay comparing the two writers' uses of narrative time, dramatic incidents, and language as means of showing readers their experiences.

We wove a web in childhood, a web of funny air.   —Charlotte Brontë

When she was good, she was very, very good, / But when she was bad she was horrid.   —Henry Wadsworth Longfellow

Go directly—see what she's doing, and tell her she mustn't.   —*Punch*

Journal Response   In a short journal entry, reflect on a time you misbehaved as a child. Was it exciting? scary? How did the adults in your life react?

Annie Dillard

A poet and essayist, Annie Dillard is part naturalist, part mystic. She was born in 1945 in Pittsburgh. Growing up in that city, she was an independent child given to exploration and reading. (As an adult, she reads nearly a hundred books a year.) After graduating from Hollins College in the Blue Ridge Mountains of Virginia, Dillard settled in the area to investigate her natural surroundings and to write. Her early books were Tickets for a Prayer Wheel *(1974), a collection of poems, and* Pilgrim at Tinker Creek *(1974), a series of related essays that demonstrate Dillard's intense, passionate involvement with the world of nature and the world of the mind.* Pilgrim *earned her national recognition and a Pulitzer Prize. It was followed by* Holy the Firm *(1977), a prose poem;* Teaching a Stone to Talk *(1982), a collection of essays;* Living by Fiction *(1982), a collection of critical essays;* Encounters with Chinese Writers *(1984); the autobiography* An American Childhood *(1987);* The Writing Life *(1989); and* The Living *(1992). More recently, Dillard published* Mornings Like This: Found Poems *(1995) and a collection of essays,* For the Time Being *(1999). In 1999 she was inducted into the American Academy of Arts and Letters. Dillard currently lives in North Carolina and is Writer in Residence at Wesleyan University.*

The Chase

In her autobiography, An American Childhood, *Dillard's enthusiasm for life in its many forms colors her recollections of her own youth. "The Chase" (editor's title) is a self-contained chapter from the book that narrates a few minutes of glorious excitement.*

Some boys taught me to play football. This was fine sport. You   1
thought up a new strategy for every play and whispered it to the oth-

ers. You went out for a pass, fooling everyone. Best, you got to throw yourself mightily at someone's running legs. Either you brought him down or you hit the ground flat out on your chin, with your arms empty before you. It was all or nothing. If you hesitated in fear, you would miss and get hurt: you would take a hard fall while the kid got away, or you would get kicked in the face while the kid got away. But if you flung yourself wholeheartedly at the back of his knees—if you gathered and joined body and soul and pointed them diving fearlessly—then you likely wouldn't get hurt, and you'd stop the ball. Your fate, and your team's score, depended on your concentration and courage. Nothing girls did could compare with it.

Boys welcomed me at baseball, too, for I had, through enthusiastic practice, what was weirdly known as a boy's arm. In winter, in the snow, there was neither baseball nor football, so the boys and I threw snowballs at passing cars. I got in trouble throwing snowballs, and have seldom been happier since. 2

On one weekday morning after Christmas, six inches of new snow 3 had just fallen. We were standing up to our boot tops in snow on a front yard on trafficked Reynolds Street, waiting for cars. The cars traveled Reynolds Street slowly and evenly; they were targets all but wrapped in red ribbons, cream puffs. We couldn't miss.

I was seven; the boys were eight, nine, and ten. The oldest two 4 Fahey boys were there—Mikey and Peter—polite blond boys who lived near me on Lloyd Street, and who already had four brothers and sisters. My parents approved of Mikey and Peter Fahey. Chickie McBride was there, a tough kid, and Billy Paul and Mackie Kean too, from across Reynolds, where the boys grew up dark and furious, grew up skinny, knowing, and skilled. We had all drifted from our houses that morning looking for action, and had found it here on Reynolds Street.

It was cloudy but cold. The cars' tires laid behind them on the 5 snowy street a complex trail of beige chunks like crenellated castle walls. I had stepped on some earlier; they squeaked. We could have wished for more traffic. When a car came, we all popped it one. In the intervals between cars we reverted to the natural solitude of children.

I started making an iceball—a perfect iceball, from perfectly 6 white snow, perfectly spherical, and squeezed perfectly translucent so no snow remained all the way through. (The Fahey boys and I considered it unfair actually to throw an iceball at somebody, but it had been known to happen.)

I had just embarked on the iceball project when we heard tire 7
chains come clanking from afar. A black Buick was moving toward
us down the street. We all spread out, banged together some regular
snowballs, took aim, and, when the Buick drew nigh, fired.

A soft snowball hit the driver's windshield right before the 8
driver's face. It made a smashed star with a hump in the middle.

Often, of course, we hit our target, but this time, the only time 9
in all of life, the car pulled over and stopped. Its wide black door
opened; a man got out of it, running. He didn't even close the car
door.

He ran after us, and we ran away from him, up the snowy 10
Reynolds sidewalk. At the corner, I looked back; incredibly, he was
still after us. He was in city clothes: a suit and tie, street shoes. Any
normal adult would have quit, having sprung us into flight and made
his point. This man was gaining on us. He was a thin man, all action.
All of a sudden, we were running for our lives.

Wordless, we split up. We were on our turf; we could lose our- 11
selves in the neighborhood backyards, everyone for himself. I paused
and considered. Everyone had vanished except Mike Fahey, who
was just rounding the corner of a yellow brick house. Poor Mikey, I
trailed him. The driver of the Buick sensibly picked the two of us to
follow. The man apparently had all day.

He chased Mikey and me around the yellow house and up a 12
backyard path we knew by heart: under a low tree, up a bank,
through a hedge, down some snowy steps, and across the grocery
store's delivery driveway. We smashed through a gap in another
hedge, entered a scruffy backyard and ran around its back porch and
tight between houses to Edgerton Avenue; we ran across Edgerton to
an alley and up our own sliding woodpile to the Halls' front yard; he
kept coming. We ran up Lloyd Street and wound through mazy backyards toward the steep hilltop at Willard and Lang.

He chased us silently, block after block. He chased us silently 13
over picket fences, through thorny hedges, between houses, around
garbage cans, and across streets. Every time I glanced back, choking
for breath, I expected he would have quit. He must have been as
breathless as we were. His jacket strained over his body. It was an
immense discovery, pounding into my hot head with every sliding,
joyous step, that this ordinary adult evidently knew what I thought
only children who trained at football knew: that you have to fling
yourself at what you're doing, you have to point yourself, forget
yourself, aim, dive.

Mikey and I had nowhere to go, in our own neighborhood or out 14 of it, but away from this man who was chasing us. He impelled us forward; we compelled him to follow our route. The air was cold; every breath tore my throat. We kept running, block after block; we kept improvising, backyard after backyard, running a frantic course and choosing it simultaneously, failing always to find small places or hard places to slow him down, and discovering always, exhilarated, dismayed, that only bare speed could save us—for he would never give up, this man—and we were losing speed.

He chased us through the backyard labyrinths of ten blocks be- 15 fore he caught us by our jackets. He caught us and we all stopped.

We three stood staggering, half blinded, coughing, in an obscure 16 hilltop backyard: a man in his twenties, a boy, a girl. He had released our jackets, our pursuer, our captor, our hero: he knew we weren't going anywhere. We all played by the rules. Mikey and I unzipped our jackets. I pulled off my sopping mittens. Our tracks multiplied in the backyard's new snow. We had been breaking new snow all morning. We didn't look at each other. I was cherishing my excitement. The man's lower pants legs were wet; his cuffs were full of snow, and there was a prow of snow beneath them on his shoes and socks. Some trees bordered the little flat backyard, some messy winter trees. There was no one around: a clearing in a grove, and we the only players.

It was a long time before he could speak. I had some difficulty at 17 first recalling why we were there. My lips felt swollen; I couldn't see out of the sides of my eyes; I kept coughing.

"You stupid kids," he began perfunctorily. 18

We listened perfunctorily indeed, if we listened at all, for the 19 chewing out was redundant, a mere formality, and beside the point. The point was that he had chased us passionately without giving up, and so he had caught us. Now he came down to earth. I wanted the glory to last forever.

But how could the glory have lasted forever? We could have run 20 through every backyard in North America until we got to Panama. But when he trapped us at the lip of the Panama Canal, what precisely could he have done to prolong the drama of the chase and cap its glory? I brooded about this for the next few years. He could only have fried Mikey Fahey and me in boiling oil, say, or dismembered us piecemeal, or staked us to anthills. None of which I really wanted, and none of which any adult was likely to do, even in the spirit of fun. He could only chew us out there in the Panamanian jungle, after months or years of exalting pursuit. He could only begin, "You stupid kids," and continue in his ordinary Pittsburgh accent with his normal righteous anger and the usual common sense.

If in that snowy backyard the driver of the black Buick had cut off our heads, Mikey's and mine, I would have died happy, for nothing has required so much of me since as being chased all over Pittsburgh in the middle of winter—running terrified, exhausted—by this sainted, skinny, furious red-headed man who wished to have a word with us. I don't know how he found his way back to his car.   21

Meaning

1. What lesson did Dillard learn from the experience of the chase? Where is her point explicitly revealed?

2. In paragraph 2 Dillard writes, "I got in trouble throwing snowballs, and have seldom been happier since." What exactly is Dillard saying about the relationship between trouble and happiness? Do you think she is recommending "getting in trouble" as a means to happiness? Why, or why not?

3. If you do not know the meanings of the following words, try to guess them from the context of Dillard's essay. Test your guesses in a dictionary, and then try to use each word in a sentence or two of your own.

crenellated (5)	compelled (14)	perfunctorily (18, 19)
translucent (6)	improvising (14)	redundant (19)
embarked (7)	labyrinths (15)	exalting (20)
impelled (14)	obscure (16)	

Purpose and Audience

1. What seems to be Dillard's purpose in "The Chase": to encourage children to get into trouble? to encourage adults to be more tolerant of children who get into trouble? something else?

2. In her first paragraph, Dillard deliberately shifts from the first-person point of view (using *me*) to the second (using *you*). What is the effect of this shift, and how does it contribute to Dillard's purpose?

Method and Structure

1. Why do you think Dillard chose narration to illustrate her point about the difference between children and adults? What does she gain from this method? What other methods might she have used?

2. In this straightforward narrative, Dillard expands some events and summarizes others: for instance, she provides much more detail about the

chase in paragraph 12 than in paragraphs 13 and 14. Why might she first provide and then pull back from the detail in paragraph 12?

3. How does the last sentence of paragraph 2—"I got in trouble throwing snowballs, and have seldom been happier since"—serve to set up the story Dillard is about to tell?

4. **Other Methods** Dillard makes extensive use of description (Chapter 4). Locate examples of this method and analyze what they contribute to the essay as a whole.

Language

1. How would you characterize Dillard's style? How does the style reflect the fact that the adult Dillard is writing from a child's point of view?

2. What does Dillard mean by calling the man who chases her "sainted" (paragraph 21)? What is her attitude toward this man? What words and passages support your answer?

3. Consider Dillard's description of cars: traveling down the street, they looked like "targets all but wrapped in red ribbons, cream puffs" (paragraph 3), and their tires in the snow left "a complex trail of beige chunks like crenellated castle walls" (5). What is the dominant impression created here?

Writing Topics

1. **Journal to Essay** Write a narrative essay about the incident of misbehavior you explored in your journal entry (p. 108). Use the first-person, *I*, strong verbs, and plenty of descriptive details to render vividly the event and its effects on you and others.

2. Write a narrative essay about a time you discovered that "an ordinary adult" knew some truth you thought only children knew. What was that truth, and why did you believe until that moment that only children knew it? What did this adult do to change your mind?

3. Though Dillard focuses on a time when no harm was done, the consequences of throwing snowballs at moving cars could be quite serious. Rewrite the essay from the point of view of someone who would *not* glorify the children's behavior—the man driving the Buick, for instance, or one of the children's parents. How might one of these people narrate these events? On what might he or she focus?

4. **Cultural Considerations** Childhood pranks like throwing snowballs at cars are tolerated more in some cultural groups than in others. In a narrative essay, retell an event in your childhood when you felt you were testing the rules of behavior in your culture. Make your motivations as clear as possible, and reflect on the results of your action.

5. **Connections**   Annie Dillard and Larry Woiwode ("Ode to an Orange,"
p. 72) share an exuberant attitude toward their childhoods, at least toward the small portions they describe in their essays. But Woiwode focuses on a concrete, specific object, while Dillard focuses on an event.
Write an essay examining the effects each essay has on you, and why.
What techniques does each writer use to create these effects?

Writing with the Method
Narration

Choose one of the following topics, or any other topic they suggest, for an essay developed by narration. The topic you decide on should be something you care about so that narration is a means of communicating an idea, not an end in itself.

FRIENDS AND RELATIONS

1. Gaining independence
2. A friend's generosity or sacrifice
3. A significant trip with your family
4. A wedding or funeral
5. An incident from family legend

THE WORLD AROUND YOU

6. An interaction you witnessed while taking public transportation
7. A storm, a flood, an earthquake, or another natural event
8. The history of your neighborhood
9. The most important minutes of a particular game in baseball, football, basketball, or some other sport
10. A school event, such as a meeting, demonstration, or celebration
11. A time when a poem, story, film, song, or other work left you feeling changed

LESSONS OF DAILY LIFE

12. Acquiring and repaying a debt, either psychological or financial
13. An especially satisfying run, tennis match, bicycle tour, one-on-one basketball game, or other sports experience
14. A time when you confronted authority
15. A time when you had to deliver bad news
16. A time when a new, eagerly anticipated possession proved disappointing
17. Your biggest social blunder

FIRSTS

18. Your first day of school, as a child or more recently
19. The first time you met someone who became important to you
20. The first performance you gave
21. A first date

ADVENTURES

22. An episode of extrasensory perception
23. An intellectual journey: discovering a new field, pursuing a subject, solving a mystery
24. A trip to an unfamiliar place

Writing About the Theme
Recalling Childhood

1. While growing up inevitably involves fear, disappointment, and pain, there is usually security and joy as well. Michael Ondaatje clearly finds comfort in his dead father's reappearance as a cobra (p. 90), Andre Dubus finally earns the respect of his classmates on the softball field (p. 91), and Annie Dillard relishes the thrill of being chased (p. 108). Write a narrative essay about a similarly mixed experience from your childhood, making sure to describe your feelings vividly so that your readers share them with you.

2. The vulnerability of children is a recurring theme in the essays and paragraphs in this chapter. Andre Dubus, Langston Hughes (p. 97), and Gavin Rember (p. 102) all write in some way about psychological pain. After considering each writer's situation individually, write an essay analyzing the differences among these situations. Based on these narratives, which writers seem to have the most in common? Which of their responses seem unique to children? Which are most likely to be outgrown?

3. Childhood is full of epiphanies, or sudden moments of realization, insight, or understanding. Langston Hughes and Annie Dillard both report such moments at the ends of their essays: Hughes loses faith in a Jesus who would not help him in church, and Dillard recognizes that any experience of glorious happiness must end. Write a narrative essay in which you tell of events leading to an epiphany when you were growing up. Make sure both the events themselves and the nature of the epiphany are vividly clear.

Chapter 6

EXAMPLE

Using Language

USING THE METHOD

An **example** represents a general group or an abstract concept or quality. Steven Spielberg is an example of the group of movie directors. A friend's calling at 2:00 A.M. is an example of her inconsiderateness—or desperation. We habitually use examples to bring general and abstract statements down to earth so that listeners or readers will take an interest in them and understand them.

As this definition indicates, the chief purpose of examples is to make the general specific and the abstract concrete. Since these operations are among the most basic in writing, it is easy to see why illustration or exemplification (the use of example) is among the most common methods of writing. Examples appear frequently in essays developed by other methods. In fact, as diverse as they are, all the essays in this book employ examples for clarity, support, and liveliness. If the writers had not used examples, we might have only a vague sense of their meaning or, worse, might supply mistaken meanings from our own experiences.

118

While nearly indispensable in any kind of writing, examples may also serve as the dominant method of developing a thesis. For instance:

- Generalizations about trends: "The cable box could become the most useful machine in the house."
- Generalizations about events: "Some members of the audience at *The Rocky Horror Picture Show* were stranger than anything in the movie."
- Generalizations about institutions: "A mental hospital is no place for the mentally ill."
- Generalizations about behaviors: "The personalities of parents are sometimes visited on their children."
- Generalizations about rituals: "A funeral benefits the dead person's family and friends."

Each of the quoted ideas could form the central assertion (the thesis) of an essay, and as many examples as necessary would then support it.

How many examples are necessary? That depends on your subject, your purpose, and your intended audience. Two basic patterns are possible:

- A single **extended example** of several paragraphs or several pages fills in needed background and gives the reader a complete view of the subject from one angle. For instance, the purpose of a funeral might be made clear with a narrative and descriptive account of a particular funeral, the family and friends who attended it, and the benefits they derived from it.
- **Multiple examples,** from a few to dozens, illustrate the range covered by the generalization. The strangeness of a movie's viewers might be captured with three or four very strange examples. But supporting the generalization about mental hospitals might demand many examples of patients whose illnesses worsened in the hospital or (from a different angle) many examples of hospital practices that actually harm patients.

Sometimes a generalization merits support from both an extended example and several briefer examples, a combination that provides depth along with range. For instance, half the essay on mental hospitals might be devoted to one patient's experiences and the other half to brief summaries of others' experiences.

ANALYZING EXAMPLES IN PARAGRAPHS

Lewis Thomas (1913–93) was a medical doctor, researcher, and administrator widely known for his engaging, perceptive essays on science, health, and society. The following paragraph is from "Communication," an essay in Thomas's last collection, *The Fragile Species* (1992).

No amount of probing with electrodes inserted into the substance of the brain, no array of electro-encephalographic tracings, can come close to telling you what the brain is up to, while a simple declarative sentence can sometimes tell you everything. <u>Sometimes a phrase will do to describe what human beings in general are like, and even how they look at themselves.</u> There is an ancient Chinese phrase, dating back millennia, which is still used to say that someone is in a great hurry, in too much of a hurry. It is *zou-ma guan-hua; zou* means "traveling," *ma* means "horse," *guan* is "looking at," *hua* is "flowers." The whole phrase means riding on horseback while looking, or trying to look, at the flowers. Precipitously, as we might say, meaning to look about while going over a cliff.

Generalization and topic sentence (underlined)

Single detailed example

William Lutz (born 1940) is an expert on doublespeak, which he defines as "language that conceals or manipulates thought. It makes the bad seem good, the negative appear positive, the unpleasant appear attractive or at least tolerable." In this paragraph from his book *Doublespeak* (1989), Lutz illustrates one use of this deceptive language.

<u>Because it avoids or shifts responsibility, double-speak is particularly effective in explaining or at least glossing over accidents.</u> An air force colonel in charge of safety wrote in a letter that rocket boosters weighing more than 300,000 pounds "have an explosive force upon surface impact that is sufficient to exceed the accepted overpressure threshold of physiological damage for exposed personnel." In English: if a 300,000-pound booster rocket falls on you, you

Generalization and topic sentence (underlined)

Two examples

probably won't survive. In 1985 three American soldiers were killed and sixteen were injured when the
first stage of a Pershing II missile they were unloading
suddenly ignited. There was no explosion, said Major
Michael Griffen, but rather "an unplanned rapid igni-
tion of solid fuel."

DEVELOPING AN ESSAY BY EXAMPLE

Getting Started

You will need examples whenever your experiences, observations, or
reading lead you to make a general statement: the examples give readers evidence for the statement, so that they see its truth. An appropriate
subject for an example paper is likely to be a general idea you have
formed about people, things, the media, or any other feature of your
life. Say, for instance, that over the past several years you have seen
many made-for-television movies dealing effectively with a sensitive
issue such as incest, domestic violence, or AIDS. There is your subject:
some TV movies do a good job of dramatizing and explaining difficult
social issues. It is a generalization about TV movies based on what you
know of individual movies. This statement could serve as the thesis of
an essay, the point you want readers to take away. A clear thesis is crucial for an example paper because without it readers can only guess
what your illustrations are intended to show.

After arriving at your thesis, you should make a list of all the perti-
nent examples. This stage may take some thought and even some further reading or observation. While making the list, keep your intended
readers at the front of your mind: what do they already know about
your subject, and what do they need to know in order to accept your
thesis? In illustrating the social value of TV movies for readers who believe television is worthless or even harmful, you might concentrate on
the movies that are most relevant to readers' lives, providing enough
detail about each to make readers see the relevance.

Organizing

Most example essays open with an introduction that engages readers'
attention and gives them some context to relate to. You might begin
the paper on TV movies, for instance, by briefly narrating the plot of

one movie. The opening should lead into your thesis sentence so that readers know what to expect from the rest of the essay.

Organizing the body of the essay may not be difficult if you use a single example, for the example itself may suggest a distinct method of development (such as narration) and thus an arrangement. But an essay using multiple examples usually requires close attention to arrangement so that readers experience not a list but a pattern. Some guidelines:

- With a limited number of examples—say, four or five—use a climactic organization (p. 40), arranging examples in order of increasing importance, interest, or complexity. Then the strongest and most detailed example provides a dramatic finish.
- With very many examples—ten or more—find some likenesses among examples that will allow you to treat them in groups. For instance, instead of covering fourteen TV movies in a shapeless list, you might group them by subject into movies dealing with family relations, those dealing with illness, and the like. (This is the method of classification discussed in Chapter 8.) Covering each group in a separate paragraph or two would avoid the awkward string of choppy paragraphs that might result from covering each example independently. And arranging the groups themselves in order of increasing interest or importance would further structure your presentation.

To conclude your essay, you may want to summarize by elaborating on the generalization of your thesis now that you have supported it. But the essay may not require a conclusion at all if you believe your final example emphasizes your point and provides a strong finish.

Drafting

While you draft your essay, remember that your examples must be plentiful and specific enough to support your generalization. If you use fifteen different examples, their range should allow you to treat each one briefly, in one or two sentences. But if you use only three examples, say, you will have to describe each one in sufficient detail to make up for their small number. And, obviously, if you use only a single example, you must be as specific as possible so that readers see clearly how it illustrates your generalization.

Revising and Editing

To be sure you've met the expectations that most readers hold for examples, revise and edit your draft by considering the following questions and the information in the box.

- *Are all examples, or parts of a single example, obviously relevant to your generalization?* Be careful not to get sidetracked by interesting but unrelated information.
- *Are the examples specific?* Examples bring a generalization down to earth only if they are well detailed. Simply naming representative TV movies and their subjects would not demonstrate their social value. Each movie would need a plot summary that shows how the movie fits and illustrates the generalization.

FOCUS ON SENTENCE VARIETY

While accumulating and detailing examples during drafting, you may find yourself writing strings of similar sentences:

> UNVARIED   One example of a movie about a disease is *In the Forest.* Another example is *The Beating Heart.* Another is *Tree of Life.* These three movies treat misunderstood or little known diseases in a way that increases the viewer's sympathy and understanding. *In the Forest* deals with a little boy who suffers from cystic fibrosis. *The Beating Heart* deals with a middle-aged woman who is weakening from multiple sclerosis. *Tree of Life* deals with a father of four who is dying from AIDS. All three movies show complex, struggling human beings caught blamelessly in desperate circumstances.

The writer of this paragraph was clearly pushing to add examples and to expand them — both essential for a successful essay — but the resulting passage needs editing so that the writer's labor isn't so obvious and the sentences are more varied and interesting:

> VARIED   Three movies dealing with disease are *In the Forest, The Beating Heart,* and *Tree of Life.* In these movies people with little-known or misunderstood diseases become subjects for the viewer's sympathy and understanding. A little boy suffering from cystic fibrosis, a middle-aged woman weakening from multiple sclerosis, a father of four dying from AIDS — these complex, struggling human beings are caught blamelessly in desperate circumstances.

For more on sentence variety, see page 50.

- *Do the examples, or the parts of a single example, cover all the territory mapped out by your generalization?* To support your generalization, you need to present a range of instances that fairly represents the whole. An essay on the social value of TV movies would be misleading if it failed to acknowledge that not *all* TV movies have social value. It would also be misleading if it presented several TV movies as representative examples of socially valuable TV when in fact they were the *only* instances of such TV.

- *Do your examples support your generalization?* You should not start with a broad statement and then try to drum up a few examples to prove it. A thesis such as "Children do poorly in school because they watch too much television" would require factual support gained from research, not the lone example of your little brother. If your little brother performs poorly in school and you attribute his performance to his television habits, then narrow your thesis so that it accurately reflects your evidence — perhaps "In the case of my little brother, at least, the more time spent watching television the poorer the grades."

A NOTE ON THEMATIC CONNECTIONS

The authors represented in this chapter all had something to say about language — how we use it, abuse it, or change from it. Their ideas probably came to them through examples as they read, talked, and listened, so naturally they use examples to demonstrate those ideas. In one paragraph, Lewis Thomas draws on a single example to show how much meaning a phrase can pack (p. 120). In another, William Lutz uses two examples to illustrate how evasive doublespeak can be (p. 120). Kim Kessler's essay explores the emergence of the expression *blah blah blah* to end sentences (opposite). Kirk Johnson questions the common assumption that today's slang is contributing to a decline in the English language (p. 130). And Perri Klass's essay grapples with why doctors use peculiar and often cruel jargon and how it affects them (p. 136).

Sometimes speech is no more than a device for saying nothing.
—Simone de Beauvoir

Continual eloquence is tedious.
—Blaise Pascal

One way of looking at speech is to say it is a constant stratagem to cover nakedness.
—Harold Pinter

Journal Response Pick a conversation filler that you have noticed, such as *you know*, or *I mean*. Why do people use these fillers? Do you use them yourself? Write a journal entry reacting to these words and phrases.

Kim Kessler

Kim Kessler was born in 1975 in New York City and grew up mostly in Greenwich, Connecticut, graduating from high school there. In 1997 she graduated from Brown University and took a job at Vanity Fair *magazine. She lives in New York City.*

Blah Blah Blah

Kessler published this essay in the Brown Daily Herald *in 1996, after noticing, she says, that she and her friends "had basically stopped talking to each other in complete sentences." With ample examples and analysis, Kessler questions the uses of the title expression in place of words that the speaker, for some reason, doesn't want to utter.*

"So he says to me, 'Well it just happened. I was this and that and 1
blah blah blah.'"

That's an actual quote. That was the statement one of my oh-so- 2
articulate friends made as an explanation of a certain situation. The
thing about it is that I figured I knew exactly what he meant. The
more important thing about it, the thing that makes this quote
notable, is that I feel as though I've been hearing it all over the place
these days. It has come to my attention in the last few weeks, maybe
even in the last couple of months, that it is common for peers of mine
to finish their sentences with "blah blah blah." Some people have
their own less common versions of the phrase—e.g., "yadda yadda"

or "etc., etc." — but it all amounts to the same thing. Rather than completing a thought or detailing an explanation, sentences simply fade away into a symbol of generic rhetoric.

I'm not quite sure what I think about this recently noticed phe-   3
nomenon quite yet. What does it mean that I can say "blah blah blah" to you and you consider it to be an acceptable statement?

I guess that there are a couple of good reasons for why this is   4
going on. First, it's a commentary on just how trite so many of those conversations we spend our time having really are. Using the phrase is a simple acknowledgment of the fact that what is about to be said has been said so many times before that it is pretty much an exercise in redundancy to say it again. Some folks "blah blah blah" me (yeah, it's a verb) when they're using the phrase as a shortcut; they are eager to get to the part of their story that *does* distinguish it from all the other stories out there. Other times people "blah blah blah" me when they think that it is not worth their time or their energy to actually re-count a story for my sake. In this case I feel dismissed, rejected. You can get "blah blahed" (past tense) in an inclusive way, too. In this scenario the "blah blah" construction is used to refer to something that both you and the speaker understand. This reflects a certain inti-macy between the speaker and the listener, an intimacy that tran-scends the need for the English language that strangers would need in order to communicate.

I have discovered quite a different use for the phrase. I have   5
found that because "blah blah" is an accepted part of our everyday discourse, and because people assume that with this phrase what you are referring to is indeed the same thing that they are thinking of, it is very easy to use this construction to lie. Well, maybe "lie" isn't the best word. It's usually more of a cover-up than a lie. I'll give an ex-ample to demonstrate my meaning here.

I'm walking across campus at some time on some Monday. I get   6
accosted by some acquaintance and have the gratuitous "How was your weekend?" conversation. He's asking me about my Saturday night. I reply: "It was good, you know . . . went out to dinner then to a party, blah blah blah." The acquaintance smiles and nods and then goes merrily on his way, his head filled with thoughts of me and my normal Saturday night. What he will never know (as long as he's not reading this) is that I ended that night walking many, many blocks home alone in the rain without a coat, carrying on my back, of all things, a trombone. He also does not know about the mini-

breakdown and moment of personal evaluation that my lonely, wet, trombone-carrying state caused me to have under a streetlight in the middle of one of those many blocks. He does not know these things because he has constructed his own end to my night to fill in for my "blah blah blah." (I hope you can all handle that open display of vulnerability. It's not very often that I share like that.)

"Blah blah blah" implies the typical. I tend to use it in place of the atypical, usually the atypical of the most embarrassing sort. For me, it's a cop-out. The accepted use of the phrase has allowed me a refuge, a wall of meaningless words with which to protect myself. I'm definitely abusing the term.   7

Maybe there are a couple of you readers who would want to interject here and remind me that not everybody tells the *whole* truth *all* of the time. (I'd guess that there would even be a hint of sarcasm in your voice as you said this to me.) Well, I realize that. I just feel the slightest twinge of guilt because my withholding of the truth has a deceptive element to it.   8

But, hey, maybe I'm not the only one. Maybe everyone is manipulating the phrase "blah blah blah." What if none of us really knows what anyone else is talking about anymore? What are the repercussions of this fill-in-the-blank type of conversation? I feel myself slipping into that very annoying and much too often frequented realm of the overly analytical, so I'm going to stop myself. To those of you who are concerned about this "blah blah" thing I am going to offer the most reasonable solution that I know of—put on your Walkman and avoid it all. The logic here is that the more time you spend with your Walkman on, the less time you spend having those aforementioned gratuitous conversations, and therefore the fewer "blah blahs" you'll have to deal with.   9

Meaning

1. How does Kessler's use of the phrase "blah blah blah" differ from the normal use, and why does her use bother her?
2. What is the "symbol of generic rhetoric" referred to in paragraph 2? What does Kessler mean by these words? (Consult a dictionary if you're not sure.) Does this sentence state Kessler's main idea? Why, or why not?
3. Try to guess the meanings of any of the following words you are unsure of, based on their context in Kessler's essay. Look the words up in a dictionary to test your guesses, and then use each word in a sentence of your own.

articulate (2)	transcends (4)	atypical (7)
phenomenon (3)	discourse (5)	interject (8)
trite (4)	accosted (6)	repercussions (9)
redundancy (4)	gratuitous (6)	

Purpose and Audience

1. What seems to be Kessler's purpose in this essay: to explain the various ways the phrase "blah blah blah" can be used? to argue against the overuse of the phrase? something else?
2. Whom did Kessler assume as her audience? (Look back at the note on the essay, p. 125, if you're not sure.) How do her subject, evidence, and tone reflect such an assumption?

Method and Structure

1. Why do you think Kessler chose to examine this linguistic phenomenon through examples? How do examples help her achieve her purpose in a way that another method might not? (Hint: What is lost when you skip from paragraph 5 to 7?)
2. What generalizations do the examples in paragraphs 4 and 6 support?
3. Which paragraphs fall into the introduction, body, and conclusion of Kessler's essay? What function does each part serve?
4. **Other Methods** Kessler's essay attempts to define the indefinable, an expression that would seem to have no meaning. What meanings does she find for "blah blah blah"? How does this use of definition (Chapter 11) help Kessler achieve her purpose?

Language

1. How would you characterize Kessler's tone: serious? light? a mix of both? How does this tone reflect her intended audience and her attitude toward her subject?
2. Point out instances of irony in the essay. (See *irony* in the Glossary.)
3. What does Kessler achieve by addressing the reader directly throughout the essay?

Writing Topics

1. **Journal to Essay** Reread your journal entry (p. 125), and then listen carefully for the conversation filler you've selected in the speech of your

friends, the talk you observe on campus or in online chat rooms, and the dialogue in television shows and movies. Form a generalization about the way the filler functions and the purpose or purposes it serves, and then, in an essay, support that generalization with plenty of examples.

2. Write an essay expressing your opinion of Kessler's essay. For instance, how did you react to her complaint that most of her conversations with her peers were "trite"or "gratuitous"? Do you think she is too critical of her peers? Agree or disagree with Kessler, supporting your opinion with your own examples.

3. **Cultural Considerations**   Although Kessler never explicitly says so, the phenomenon she writes about seems to apply mainly to people of her own generation. Think of an expression that you use when among a group to which you belong (family, ethnic group, others of your own gender, and so on) but feel constrained from using outside the group. Write an essay explaining and illustrating the uses of the expression in the group and the problems you experience using it elsewhere.

4. **Connections**   To what extent, if at all, does "blah blah blah" resemble the jargon of the medical profession as discussed by Perri Klass in "She's Your Basic L.O.L. in N.A.D." (p. 136)? After reading Klass's essay, list the purposes she believes medical jargon serves. Does "blah blah blah" serve similar or different purposes for Kessler and her peers? Spell your answer out in an essay, drawing on Klass's and Kessler's essays as well as your own experience for evidence.

Slang is a language that rolls up its sleeves, spits on its hands, and goes to work.
— Carl Sandburg

Every age has a language of its own; and the difference in the words is often far greater than in the thoughts.
— Augustus Hare

Correct English is the slang of prigs.
— George Eliot

Journal Response Think of one or more expressions that you use when speaking with friends or family but that you might not use in writing an essay — private code words that you use only with your family or slang expressions such as *duh, like,* and *yeah, right,* the subjects of the following essay. Write briefly about what these expressions mean to you and others who use them.

Kirk Johnson

Kirk Johnson was born in Salt Lake City, Utah. A Pulitzer-nominated writer for the New York Times *and an endurance runner, Johnson has written a book entitled* To the Edge: A Man, Death Valley, and the Mystery of Endurance *(2001). He lives in northern New Jersey with his wife and two sons.*

Today's Kids Are, Like, Killing the English Language

In "Today's Kids Are, Like, Killing the English Language," which first appeared in the New York Times, *Johnson takes a long look at the changes occurring in, like, the vocabulary of younger generations. Contrary to common opinion, Johnson holds, these changes are neither superficial nor dangerous.*

As a father of two preteen boys, I have in the last year or so become 1
a huge fan of the word *duh.* This is a word much maligned by educators, linguistic Brahmins and purists, but they are all quite wrong.

Duh has elegance. *Duh* has shades of meaning, even sophistica- 2
tion. *Duh* and its perfectly paired linguistic partner, *yeah, right,* are
the ideal terms to usher in the millennium and the information age,
and to highlight the differences from the stolid old twentieth century.

Even my sons might stop me at this point and quash my hyper- 3
bole with a quickly dispensed, "Yeah, right, Dad." But hear me out: I
have become convinced that *duh* and *yeah, right* have arisen to fill a
void in the language because the world has changed. Fewer questions
these days can effectively be answered with *yes* or *no,* while at the
same time, a tidal surge of hype and mindless blather threatens to
overwhelm old-fashioned conversation. *Duh* and *yeah, right* are the
cure.

Good old *yes* and *no* were fine for their time—the archaic, 4
black-and-white era of late industrialism that I was born into in the
1950s. The *yes*-or-*no* combo was hard and fast and most of all
simple: it belonged to the Manichean[1] red-or-dead mentality of the
cold war, to manufacturing, to *Father Knows Best* and *It's a Wonderful Life.*

The information-age future that my eleven-year-old twins own is 5
more complicated than *yes* or *no.* It's more subtle and supple, more
loaded with content and hype and media manipulation than my
childhood—or any adult's, living or dead—ever was.

And *duh,* whatever else it may be, is drenched with content. Be- 6
tween them, *duh* and *yeah, right* are capable of dividing all language
and thought into an exquisitely differentiated universe. Every statement and every question can be positioned on a gray scale of understatement or overstatement, stupidity or insightfulness, information
saturation or yawning emptiness.

And in an era when plain speech has become endangered by the 7
pressures of political correctness, *duh* and *yeah, right* are matchless
tools of savvy, winking sarcasm and skepticism: caustic without
being confrontational, incisive without being quite specific.

With *duh,* you can convey a response, throw in a whole basket 8
full of auxiliary commentary about the question or the statement
you're responding to, and insult the speaker all at once! As in this hypothetical exchange:

Parent: Good morning, son, it's a beautiful day.
Eleven-year-old boy: Duh.

---

[1] *Manichean* means dualistic. Manicheism is the belief that the world consists of dual
oppositions, such as good and evil. [Editor's note.]

And there is a kind of esthetic balance as well. *Yeah, right* is 9
the yin to *duh*'s yang, the antithesis to *duh*'s empathetic thesis.
Where *duh* is assertive and edgy, a perfect tool for undercutting
mindless understatement or insulting repetition, *yeah, right* is laid
back, a surfer's cool kind of response to anything overwrought or
oversold.

New York, for example, is *duh* territory, while Los Angeles is 10
yeah, right. Television commercials can be rendered harmless and
inert by simply saying, "yeah, right," upon their conclusion. Local
television news reports are helped out with a sprinkling of well-
placed *duh*s, at moments of stunning obviousness. And almost any
politician's speech cries out for heaping helpings of both at various
moments.

Adolescent terms like *like,* by contrast, scare me to death. While I 11
have become convinced through observation and personal experi-
mentation that just about any adult of even modest intelligence can
figure out how to use *duh* and *yeah, right* properly, *like* is different.
Like is hard. *Like* is, like, dangerous.

Marcel Danesi, a professor of linguistics and semiotics at the Uni- 12
versity of Toronto who has studied the language of youth and who
coined the term "pubilect" to describe the dialect of pubescence, said
he believes *like* is in fact altering the structure of the English language, making it more fluid in construction, more like Italian or some
other Romance language than good old hard-and-fast Anglo-Saxon.
Insert *like* in the middle of a sentence, he said, and a statement can be
turned into a question, a question into an exclamation, an exclamation into a quiet meditation.

Consider these hypothetical expressions: "If you're having broc- 13
coli for dinner, Mr. Johnson, I'm, like, out of here!" and "I was, like,
no way!" and perhaps most startlingly, "He was, like, duh!"

In the broccoli case, *like* softens the sentence. It's less harsh and 14
confrontational than saying flatly that the serving of an unpalatable
vegetable would require a fleeing of the premises.

In the second instance, *like* functions as a kind of a verbal quota- 15
tion mark, an announcement that what follows, "no way," is to be
heard differently. The quote itself can then be loaded up with any variety of intonation—irony, sarcasm, even self-deprecation—all depending on the delivery.

In the third example—"He was, like, duh!"—*like* becomes a 16
crucial helping verb for *duh,* a verbal springboard. (Try saying the
sentence without like and it becomes almost incomprehensible.)

But *like* and *duh* and *yeah, right,* aside from their purely linguis- 17
tic virtues, are also in many ways the perfect words to convey the
sense of reflected reality that is part of the age we live in. Image manipulation, superficiality, and shallow media culture are, for better or
worse, the backdrop of adolescent life.

Adults of the *yes*-or-*no* era could perhaps grow up firm in their 18
knowledge of what things "are," but in the Age of *Duh,* with images
reflected back from every angle at every waking moment, kids swim
in a sea of what things are "like." Distinguishing what is from what
merely seems to be is a required skill of an eleven-year-old today; *like*
reflects modern life, and *duh* and *yeah, right* are the tools with which
such a life can be negotiated and mastered.

But there is a concealed paradox in the Age of *Duh.* The informa- 19
tion overload on which it is based is built around the computer, and the
computer is, of course, built around — that's right — the good old *yes*-
or-*no* binary code: billions of microcircuits all blinking on or off, black
or white, current in or current out. Those computers were designed by
minds schooled and steeped in the world of *yes* or *no,* and perhaps it is
not too much of a stretch to imagine my sons' generation, shaped by the
broader view of *duh,* finding another path: binary code with attitude.
Besides, most computers I know already seem to have an attitude. Incorporating a little *duh* would at least give them a sense of humor.

Meaning

1. What is Johnson's main point? Underline the sentence that you believe
   best demonstrates his main idea.
2. Which slang terms does Johnson single out, and what do they contribute
   to the main point of his essay?
3. What is a paradox? What is the "paradox" that Johnson refers to in his
   last paragraph?
4. If you are uncertain of the meanings of any of the words listed below,
   try to guess them from the context of Johnson's essay. Then look them
   up to see how close your definitions were to those in the dictionary. Test
   out the new words by using each of them in a sentence or two.

Brahmins (1)	esthetic (9)	confrontational (14)
hyperbole (3)	antithesis (9)	self-deprecation (15)
hype (3)	overwrought (9)	springboard (16)
blather (3)	semiotics (12)	backdrop (17)
caustic (7)	unpalatable (14)	steeped (19)
incisive (7)		

Purpose and Audience

1. Do you think Johnson wants to provoke, educate, or entertain us? Or does he want to do all of these things? What evidence can you provide for your answer?
2. What clues can you find that this essay was originally published in the *New York Times*? For instance, what does Johnson seem to assume about his readers—that they're teenagers? adults? linguists? parents? Does he assume that they speak the slang he analyzes or that they approve of it? Provide examples from the essay to support your answers.
3. Johnson establishes his viewpoint in the first few paragraphs. What objections does he anticipate? How does he respond to them? How convinced are you by his response?

Method and Structure

1. Examine the quotations that Johnson offers as examples of *duh* and *yeah, right* and *like*. How well do they, along with Johnson's explanations of them, convey the meanings of the expressions? Are there places where you would like to see more examples?
2. Why do you think that Johnson does not mention *like* until halfway through the essay? Does this delay make the essay weaker or more interesting for you?
3. Weigh the evidence that Johnson gives to support his opinions. Which evidence is personal, and which is not? Are both the personal and the nonpersonal equally effective? Why, or why not?
4. **Other Methods**   Johnson's example essay is also a model of definition (Chapter 11) because he establishes the meanings of three slang terms. What are the meanings of *duh* and *yeah, right* and *like*? How is each distinct from the others?

Language

1. How would you characterize Johnson's tone in this essay—for instance, wise, argumentative, reassuring, humorous, serious, flippant, worried, irritated, confused, enthusiastic? Give examples to support your analysis. How is the tone appropriate (or not) for the audience you identified in question 2 under "Purpose and Audience"?
2. Johnson uses several pairs of contrasting words, such as "*yes*-or-*no*" and "red-or-dead." What similar pairs do you find? What is their significance for Johnson's thesis?
3. How does the author attempt to make his ideas accessible while also maintaining his sophistication? In your opinion, is this essay difficult to read, easy to read, or something in between? Why?

Writing Topics

1. **Journal to Essay**   Reread your journal entry and the quotations at the beginning of Johnson's essay (p. 130). Using specific examples, write an essay about the expression or expressions you use with friends or family. What shades of meaning do the expressions have? What situations do you use them in? How do others react to them?

2. You may not agree with Johnson's opinion that certain slang expressions are ideal for our modern world and actually enrich our language. Write an essay in which you consider the opposite view: that English is actually being harmed by terms such as *duh* and *yeah, right* and *like*. You may use examples from Johnson's essay or others of your own, but be sure to support your case.

3. **Cultural Considerations**   Many English speakers use words from other languages, nonstandard forms such as *ain't* or *can't hardly*, or slang such as *duh* or *yeah, right* — and many listeners find the language richer for these additions. Yet not all ways of speaking gain equal acceptance. Write an essay in which you examine how negative stereotyping may use the language of a particular group — an accent, say, or certain slang expressions — against the members of that group. In stereotyping, what connections are drawn between the language and the perceived or imagined qualities of its speakers? What purpose might such stereotyping serve for those who do it? What effect might it have on them?

4. **Connections**   Both Johnson and William Lutz, in a paragraph from *Doublespeak* (p. 120), discuss language use among a particular group. Johnson explains how his preteen sons and their friends use certain slang expressions to reflect the reality of the world around them. Lutz, in contrast, shows how carefully chosen terminology used by the military can actually obscure meaning. Write an essay in which you examine a form of doublespeak, jargon, or slang, such as the language of teachers, journalists, or college students. Does the language used clarify or confuse reality?

A passage is not plain English — still less is it good English — if we are obliged to read it twice to find out what it means.   —Dorothy Sayers

I'm bilingual. I speak English and I speak educationese.

—Shirley Hufstedler

You and I come by road or rail, but economists travel on infrastructure.

—Margaret Thatcher

Journal Response What words or expressions have you encountered in your college courses or in your college's rules and regulations that have confused, delighted, or irritated you? Write a brief journal entry describing the language and its effects on you.

Perri Klass

Perri Klass is a pediatrician and a writer of both fiction and nonfiction. She was born in 1958 in Trinidad and grew up in New York City and New Jersey. After obtaining a B.A. from Harvard University in 1979, she began graduate work in biology but then switched to medicine. Klass finished Harvard Medical School in 1986 and practices pediatrics in Boston. Her publications are extensive: short stories in Mademoiselle, Antioch Review, *and other magazines; two collections of stories,* I Am Having an Adventure *(1986) and* Love and Modern Medicine: Stories *(2001); two novels,* Recombinations *(1985) and* Other Women's Children *(1990); essays for the* New York Times, Discover, *and other periodicals; and two collections of essays,* A Not Entirely Benign Procedure *(1987) and* Baby Doctor: A Pediatrician's Training *(1992). She is the mother of two sons and one daughter.*

She's Your Basic
L.O.L. in N.A.D.

Most of us have felt excluded, confused, or even frightened by the jargon of the medical profession — that is, by the special terminology and abbreviations for diseases and procedures. In this essay Klass uses examples of such language, some of it heartless, to illustrate the pluses and minuses of becoming a doctor. The essay first appeared in 1984 as a "Hers" column in the New York Times.

"Mrs. Tolstoy is your basic L.O.L. in N.A.D., admitted for a soft 1
rule-out M.I.," the intern announces. I scribble that on my patient
list. In other words Mrs. Tolstoy is a Little Old Lady in No Apparent
Distress who is in the hospital to make sure she hasn't had a heart attack (rule out a myocardial infarction). And we think it's unlikely
that she has had a heart attack (a *soft* rule-out).

If I learned nothing else during my first three months of working 2
in the hospital as a medical student, I learned endless jargon and abbreviations. I started out in a state of primeval innocence, in which I
didn't even know that "s̄ C.P., S.O.B., N/V" meant "without chest
pain, shortness of breath, or nausea and vomiting." By the end I took
the abbreviations so for granted that I would complain to my mother
the English professor, "And can you believe I had to put down *three*
NG tubes last night?"

"You'll have to tell me what an NG tube is if you want me to sym- 3
pathize properly," my mother said. NG, nasogastric—isn't it obvious?

I picked up not only the specific expressions but also the patterns 4
of speech and the grammatical conventions; for example, you never
say that a patient's blood pressure fell or that his cardiac enzymes
rose. Instead, the patient is always the subject of the verb: "He
dropped his pressure." "He bumped his enzymes." This sort of construction probably reflects that profound irritation of the intern when
the nurses come in the middle of the night to say that Mr. Dickinson
has disturbingly low blood pressure. "Oh, he's gonna hurt me bad
tonight," the intern may say, inevitably angry at Mr. Dickinson for
dropping his pressure and creating a problem.

When chemotherapy fails to cure Mrs. Bacon's cancer, what we 5
say is, "Mrs. Bacon failed chemotherapy."

"Well, we've already had one hit today, and we're up next, but at 6
least we've got mostly stable players on our team." This means that
our team (group of doctors and medical students) has already gotten
one new admission today, and it is our turn again, so we'll get who-
ever is next admitted in emergency, but at least most of the patients
we already have are fairly stable, that is, unlikely to drop their
pressures or in any other way get suddenly sicker and hurt us bad.
Baseball metaphor is pervasive: a no-hitter is a night without any new
admissions. A player is always a patient—a nitrate player is a patient
on nitrates, a unit player is a patient in the intensive-care unit, and so
on, until you reach the terminal player.

It is interesting to consider what it means to be winning, or doing 7
well, in this perennial baseball game. When the intern hangs up the

phone and announces, "I got a hit," that is not cause for congratulations. The team is not scoring points; rather, it is getting hit, being bombarded with new patients. The object of the game from the point of view of the doctors, considering the players for whom they are already responsible, is to get as few new hits as possible.

These special languages contribute to a sense of closeness and   8
professional spirit among people who are under a great deal of stress. As a medical student, it was exciting for me to discover that I'd finally cracked the code, that I could understand what doctors said and wrote and could use the same formulations myself. Some people seem to become enamored of the jargon for its own sake, perhaps because they are so deeply thrilled with the idea of medicine, with the idea of themselves as doctors.

I knew a medical student who was referred to by the interns on   9
the team as Mr. Eponym because he was so infatuated with eponymous terminology,[1] the more obscure the better. He never said "capillary pulsation" if he could say "Quincke's pulses." He would lovingly tell over the multinamed syndromes — Wolff-Parkinson-White, Lown-Ganong-Levine, Henoch-Schonlein — until the temptation to suggest Schleswig-Holstein or Stevenson-Kefauver or Baskin-Robbins became irresistible to his less reverent colleagues.

And there is the jargon that you don't ever want to hear yourself   10
using. You know that your training is changing you, but there are certain changes you think would be going a little too far.

The resident was describing a man with devastating terminal   11
pancreatic cancer. "Basically he's C.T.D.," the resident concluded. I reminded myself that I had resolved not to be shy about asking when I didn't understand things. "C.T.D.?" I asked timidly.

The resident smirked at me. "Circling The Drain."   12

The images are vivid and terrible. "What happened to Mrs.   13
Melville?"

"Oh, she boxed last night." To box is to die, of course.   14

Then there are the more pompous locutions that can make the   15
beginning medical student nervous about the effects of medical training. A friend of mine was told by his resident, "A pregnant woman with sickle-cell represents a failure of genetic counseling."

Mr. Eponym, who tried hard to talk like the doctors, once ex-   16
plained to me, "An infant is basically a brainstem preparation." A brainstem preparation, as used in neurological research, is an animal

---

[1] *Eponymous* means "named after" — in this case, medical terminology is named after researchers. [Editor's note.]

whose higher brain functions have been destroyed so that only the most primitive reflexes remain, like the sucking reflex, the startle reflex, and the rooting reflex.

The more extreme forms aside, one most important function of 17 medical jargon is to help doctors maintain some distance from their patients. By reformulating a patient's pain and problems into a language that the patient doesn't even speak, I suppose we are in some sense taking those pains and problems under our jurisdiction and also reducing their emotional impact. This linguistic separation between doctors and patients allows conversations to go on at the bedside that are unintelligible to the patient. "Naturally, we're worried about adreno-C.A.," the intern can say to the medical student, and lung cancer need never be mentioned.

I learned a new language this past summer. At times it thrills me 18 to hear myself using it. It enables me to understand my colleagues, to communicate effectively in the hospital. Yet I am uncomfortably aware that I will never again notice the peculiarities and even atrocities of medical language as keenly as I did this summer. There may be specific expressions I manage to avoid, but even as I remark them, promising myself I will never use them, I find that this language is becoming my professional speech. It no longer sounds strange in my ears — or coming from my mouth. And I am afraid that as with any new language, to use it properly you must absorb not only the vocabulary but also the structure, the logic, the attitudes. At first you may notice these new alien assumptions every time you put together a sentence, but with time and increased fluency you stop being aware of them at all. And as you lose that awareness, for better or for worse, you move closer and closer to being a doctor instead of just talking like one.

Meaning

1. What point does Klass make about medical jargon in this essay? Where does she reveal her main point explicitly?
2. What useful purposes does medical jargon serve, according to Klass? Do the examples in paragraphs 9–16 serve these purposes? Why, or why not?
3. Try to guess the meanings of any of the following words on the next page that are unfamiliar. Check your guesses in a dictionary, and then use each word in a sentence or two of your own.

primeval (2)   syndromes (9)   locutions (15)
terminal (6)   reverent (9)   jurisdiction (17)
perennial (7)   pompous (15)

Purpose and Audience

1. What does Klass imply when she states that she began her work in the hospital "in a state of primeval innocence" (paragraph 2)? What does this phrase suggest about her purpose in writing the essay?
2. From what perspective does Klass write this essay: that of a medical professional? someone outside the profession? a patient? someone else? To what extent does she expect her readers to share her perspective? What evidence in the essay supports your answer?
3. Given that she is writing for a general audience, does Klass take adequate care to define medical terms? Support your answer with examples from the essay.

Method and Structure

1. Why does Klass begin the essay with an example rather than a statement of her main idea? What effect does this example produce? How does this effect support her purpose in writing the essay?
2. Although Klass uses many examples of medical jargon, she avoids the dull effect of a list by periodically stepping back to make a general statement about her experience or the jargon—for instance, "I picked up not only the specific expressions but also the patterns of speech and the grammatical conventions" (paragraph 4). Locate other places—not necessarily at the beginnings of paragraphs—where Klass breaks up her examples with more general statements.
3. **Other Methods**   Klass uses several other methods besides example, among them classification (Chapter 8), definition (Chapter 11), and cause-and-effect analysis (Chapter 12). What effects—positive and negative—does medical jargon have on Klass, other students, and doctors who use it?

Language

1. What is the tone of this essay? Is Klass trying to be humorous or tongue-in-cheek about the jargon of the profession, or is she serious? Where in the essay is the author's attitude toward her subject the most obvious?
2. Klass refers to the users of medical jargon as both *we/us* (paragraphs 1, 5, 6, 17) and *they/them* (7), and sometimes she shifts from *I* to *you*

within a paragraph (4, 18). Do you think these shifts are effective or distracting? Why? Do the shifts serve any function?

3. Klass obviously experienced both positive and negative feelings about mastering medical jargon. Which words and phrases in the last paragraph reflect positive feelings, and which negative?

Writing Topics

1. **Journal to Essay**   When she attended medical school, Perri Klass discovered a novel language to learn and with it some new attitudes. Working from your journal entry (p. 136), write an essay about new languages and attitudes you have encountered in college. Have you been confronted with different kinds of people (professors, other students) from the ones you knew before? Have you had difficulties understanding some words people use? Have you found yourself embracing ideas you never thought you would or speaking differently? Have others noticed a change in you that you may not have been aware of? Have you noticed changes in your precollege friends? Focus on a particular kind of obstacle or change, using specific examples to convey this experience to readers.

2. Klass likens her experience learning medical jargon to that of learning a new language (paragraph 18). If you are studying or have learned a second language, write an essay in which you explain the "new alien assumptions" you must make "every time you put together a sentence." Draw your examples not just from the new language's grammar and vocabulary but from its underlying logic and attitudes. For instance, does one speak to older people differently in the new language? make requests differently? describe love or art differently?

3. Klass's essay explores the "separation between doctors and patients" (paragraph 17). Has this separation affected you as a patient or as the relative or friend of a patient? If so, write an essay about your experiences. Did the medical professionals rely heavily on jargon? Was their language comforting, frightening, irritating? Based on your experience and on Klass's essay, do you believe that the separation between doctors and patients is desirable? Why, or why not?

4. **Cultural Considerations**   Most groups focused on a common interest have their own jargon. If you belong to such a group—for example, runners, football fans, food servers, engineering students—spend a few days listening to yourself and others use this language and thinking about the purposes it serves. Which aspects of this language seem intended to make users feel like insiders? Which seem to serve some other purpose, and what is it? In an essay, explain what this jargon reveals about the group and its common interest, using as many specific examples as you can.

5. **Connections**   Both Klass and Kirk Johnson, in "Today's Kids Are, Like, Killing the English Language" (p. 130), believe that the way we speak can signal our membership in a particular group of people: in this case, doctors or teenagers. Write an essay in which you examine the way another group of people, say, faculty members, politicians, or people from a particular region, use language to mark their group identity.

Writing with the Method

Example

Choose one of the following statements, or any other statement they suggest, and agree *or* disagree with it in an essay developed by one or more examples. The statement you decide on should concern a topic you care about so that the example or examples are a means of communicating an idea, not an end in themselves.

FAMILY

1. In happy families, talk is the main activity.
2. Grandparents relate more closely to their grandchildren than to their children.
3. Sooner or later, children take on the personalities of their parents.

BEHAVIOR AND PERSONALITY

4. Rudeness is on the rise.
5. Gestures and facial expressions often communicate what words cannot say.
6. Our natural surroundings when we are growing up contribute to our happiness or unhappiness as adults.

EDUCATION

7. The best courses are the difficult ones.
8. Education is an easy way to get ahead in life.
9. Students at schools with enforced dress codes behave better than students at schools without such codes.

POLITICS AND SOCIAL ISSUES

10. Talk radio can influence public policy.
11. Drug or alcohol addiction does not happen just to "bad" people.
12. True-life crime mimics TV and movies.
13. Unemployment is hardest on those over fifty years old.

MEDIA AND CULTURE

14. Bumper stickers are a form of conversation among Americans.
15. The Internet divides people instead of connecting them.
16. Good art can be ugly.

17. A craze or fad reveals something about the culture it arises in.
18. The best rock musicians treat social and political issues in their songs.
19. Television news programs are beauty pageants for untalented journalists.
20. The most rewarding books are always easy to read.

RULES FOR LIVING

21. Murphy's Law: If anything can go wrong, it will go wrong, and at the worst possible moment.
22. With enough motivation, a person can accomplish anything.
23. Lying may be justified by the circumstances.
24. Friends are people you can't always trust.

Writing About the Theme
Using Language

1. Lewis Thomas (p. 120), William Lutz (p. 120), and Perri Klass (p. 136) discuss the power of language with a good deal of respect. Thomas refers to its descriptive powers, Lutz to its effectiveness "in explaining [. . .] accidents," and Klass to its support as she became a doctor. Think of a time when you were in some way profoundly affected by language, and write an essay about this experience. Provide as many examples as necessary to illustrate both the language that affected you and how it made you feel.

2. Kim Kessler (p. 125) and Kirk Johnson (p. 130) both write about forms of language that do not obey traditional grammar rules and are considered incorrect by some people. As you see it, what are the advantages and disadvantages of using nonstandard language when speaking? How effective are these forms of language as ways to communicate? Write an essay answering these questions, using examples from the essays and your own experience.

3. Perri Klass writes that medical jargon "contribute[s] to a sense of closeness and professional spirit among people who are under a great deal of stress" (paragraph 8) and that it helps "doctors maintain some distance from their patients" (17). Write an essay in which you analyze the function of "doublespeak," as presented by William Lutz. Who, if anyone, is such language designed to help? The accident victims? Survivors of these victims? Someone else? Can a positive case be made for this language?

Chapter 7

DIVISION
OR ANALYSIS

Looking at Popular Culture

USING THE METHOD

Division and **analysis** are interchangeable terms for the same method. *Division* comes from a Latin word meaning "to force asunder or separate." *Analysis* comes from a Greek word meaning "to undo." Using this method, we separate a whole into its elements, examine the relations of the elements to one another and to the whole, and reassemble the elements into a new whole informed by the examination. The method is essential to understanding and evaluating objects, works, and ideas.

Analysis (as we will call it) is a daily occurrence in our lives, whether we ponder our relationships with others, decide whether a certain movie was worthwhile, or try to understand a politician's campaign promises. We also use analysis throughout this book, when looking at paragraphs and essays. And it is the basic operation in at least four other methods discussed in this book: classification

146

(Chapter 8), process analysis (Chapter 9), comparison and contrast (Chapter 10), and cause-and-effect analysis (Chapter 12).

At its most helpful, analysis builds on the separation into elements, leading to a conclusion about the meaning, significance, or value of the whole. This approach is essential to college learning, whether in discussing literature, reviewing a psychology experiment, or interpreting a business case. It is fundamental to work, from choosing a career to making sense of market research. And it informs and enriches life outside school or work, in buying a car, looking at art, or deciding whom to vote for. The method is the foundation of **critical thinking,** the ability to see beneath the surface of things, images, events, and ideas; to uncover and test assumptions; to see the importance of context; and to draw and support independent conclusions.

The subject of any analysis is usually singular — a freestanding, coherent unit, such as a bicycle or a poem, with its own unique constitution of elements. (In contrast, classification, the subject of the next chapter, usually starts with a plural subject, such as bicycles or the poems of the Civil War, and groups them according to their shared features.) You choose the subject and with it a **principle of analysis,** a framework that determines how you divide the subject and thus what elements you identify.

Sometimes the principle of analysis will be self-evident, especially when the subject is an object, such as a bicycle or a camera, that can be "undone" in only a limited number of ways. Most of the time, however, the principle you choose will depend on your view of the whole. In academic disciplines, businesses, and the professions, distinctive principles are part of what the field is about and are often the subject of debate within the field. In art, for instance, some critics see a painting primarily as a visual object and concentrate on its composition, color, line, and other formal qualities; other critics see a painting primarily as a social object and concentrate on its content and context (cultural, economic, political, and so on). Both groups use a principle of analysis that is a well-established way of looking at painting; yet each group finds different elements and thus meaning in a work.

There is, then, a great deal of flexibility in choosing a principle of analysis. But it should be appropriate for the subject and the field or discipline; it should be significant; and it should be applied thoroughly and consistently. Analysis is not done for its own sake but for a larger goal of illuminating the subject, perhaps concluding something about it, perhaps evaluating it. But even when the method culminates in evaluation—in the writer's judgment of the subject's value—the analysis should represent the subject as it actually is, in all its fullness and complexity. In analyzing a movie, for instance, a writer may emphasize one element, such as setting, and even omit some elements, such as costumes; but the characterization of the whole must still apply to *all* the elements. If it does not, readers can be counted on to notice; so the writer must single out any wayward element(s) and explain why they do not substantially undermine the framework and thus weaken the opinion.

ANALYZING DIVISION OR ANALYSIS IN PARAGRAPHS

Jon Pareles (born 1953) is the chief critic of popular music for the *New York Times*. The following paragraph comes from "Gather No Moss, Take No Prisoners, but Be Cool," a review of a concert by the rock guitarist Keith Richards.

Mr. Richards shows off by not showing off. He uses rhythm chords as a goad, not a metronome, slipping them in just ahead of a beat or skipping them entirely. The distilled twang of his tone has been imitated all over rock, but far fewer guitarists have learned his guerrilla timing, his coiled silences. When he switches to lead guitar, Mr. Richards goes not for long lines, but for serrated riffing, zinging out three or four notes again and again in various permutations, wringing from them the essence of the blues. The phrasing is poised and suspenseful, but it also carries a salutary rock attitude: that less is more, especially when delivered with utter confidence.

Principle of analysis (topic sentence underlined): elements of Richards's "not showing off"

1. Rhythm chords as goad (or prod)

2. Timing

3. Silences

4. Riffing (or choppy playing)

5. Confident, less-is-more attitude

Luci Tapahonso (born 1953) is a poet and teacher. This paragraph is from her essay "The Way It Is," which appears in *Sign Language*, a book of photographs (by Skeet McAuley) of life on the reservation for some Navajo and Apache Indians.

It is rare and, indeed, very exciting to see an Indian person in a commercial advertisement. Word travels fast when that happens. Nunzio's Pizza in

Principle of analysis (topic sentence underlined at end): elements of the commercial that appealed to Indians

Albuquerque, New Mexico, ran commercials featuring Jose Rey Toledo of Jemez Pueblo talking about his "native land—Italy" while wearing typical Pueblo attire—jewelry, moccasins, and hair tied in a chongo. Because of the ironic humor, because Indian grandfathers specialize in playing tricks and jokes on their grandchildren, and because Jose Rey Toledo is a respected and well-known elder in the Indian communities, word of this commercial spread fast among Indians in New Mexico. It was the cause of recognition and celebration of sorts on the reservations and in the pueblos. His portrayal was not in the categories which the media usually associate with Indians but as a typical sight in the Southwest. It showed Indians as we live today—enjoying pizza as one of our favorite foods, including humor and fun as part of our daily lives, and recognizing the importance of preserving traditional knowledge.

1. *Rarity of an Indian in a commercial*

2. *Indian dress*

3. *Indian humor*
4. *Indian tradition*
5. *Respected Indian spokesperson*

6. *Realism*

DEVELOPING AN ESSAY
BY DIVISION OR ANALYSIS
Getting Started

Analysis is one of the readiest methods of development: almost anything whole can be separated into its elements, from a lemon to a play by Shakespeare to an economic theory. In college and at work, many writing assignments will demand analysis with a verb such as *analyze, criticize, discuss, evaluate, interpret,* or *review.* If you need to develop your own subject for analysis, think of something whose meaning or significance puzzles or intrigues you and whose parts you can distinguish and relate to the whole—an object such as a machine, an artwork such as a poem, a media product such as a news broadcast, an institution such as a hospital, a relationship such as stepparenting, a social issue such as sheltering the homeless.

If you begin by seeking meaning or significance, you will be more likely to find a workable principle of analysis and less likely to waste time on a hollow exercise. Each question on the next page suggests a distinct approach to the subject's elements—a distinct principle—that makes it easier to isolate the elements and show their connection to one another. Each question could lead to a thesis sentence that states an opinion and reveals the principle of analysis.

QUESTION   To what extent is an enormously complex hospital a community in itself?

THESIS SENTENCE   The hospital encompasses such a wide range of personnel and services that it resembles a good-sized town.

QUESTION   What is the appeal of the front-page headlines in the local tabloid newspaper?

THESIS SENTENCE   The newspaper's front page routinely appeals to readers' fear of crime, anger at criminals, and sympathy for victims.

QUESTION   Why did a certain movie have such a powerful effect on you and your friends?

THESIS SENTENCE   The film is a unique and important statement of the private terrors of adolescence.

Note that all three thesis sentences imply an explanatory purpose— an effort to understand something and share that understanding with the reader. The third thesis sentence, however, conveys a persuasive purpose as well: the writer hopes that readers will accept her evaluation of the film. (See p. 153 for more on thesis sentences in division or analysis.)

Of course, the thesis must develop from and be supported by the evidence of the analysis—the elements of the subject, their interconnections, and their relation to the whole. Dissect your subject, looking at the actual, physical thing if possible, imagining it in your mind if necessary. Make detailed notes of all the elements you see, their distinguishing features, and how they help answer your starting question about meaning or significance. In analyzing someone's creation, tease out the creator's influences, assumptions, intentions, conclusions, and evidence. You may have to go outside the work for some of this information—researching an author's background, for instance, to uncover the political biases that may underlie his or her opinions. Even if you do not use all this information in your final draft, it will help you see the elements and help keep your analysis true to the subject.

At this point you should consider your readers' needs as well as the needs of your subject and your own framework:

- If the subject is familiar to readers (as, say, the newspaper's headlines might be), then your principle of analysis may not require much justification (as long as it's clear), but your details and examples must be vivid and convincing.
- If the subject is unfamiliar, then you should carefully explain your principle of analysis, define all specialized terms, distinguish parts from one another, and provide ample illustrations.
- If readers know your subject but may dispute your way of looking at it, then you should justify as well as explain your principle of analysis. You should also account for any evidence that may seem not to support your opinion by showing either why, in fact, the evidence is supportive or why it is unimportant. (If contrary evidence refuses to be dispensed with, you may have to rethink your approach.)

Organizing

In the introduction to your essay, let readers know why you are bothering to analyze your subject: Why is the subject significant? How might the essay relate to the experiences of readers or be useful to them? A subject unfamiliar to readers might be summarized or described, or part of it (an anecdote or quotation, say) might be used to tantalize readers. A familiar subject might be introduced with a surprising fact or an unusual perspective. An evaluative analysis might open with an opposing viewpoint.

In the body of the essay you'll need to explain your principle of analysis according to the guidelines above. The arrangement of elements and analysis should suit your subject and purpose: you can describe the elements and then offer your analysis, or you can introduce and analyze elements one by one. You can arrange the elements themselves from least to most important, least to most complex, most to least familiar, spatially, or chronologically. Devote as much space to each element as it demands: there is no requirement that all elements be given equal space and emphasis if their complexity or your framework dictates otherwise.

Most analysis essays need a conclusion that assembles the elements, returning readers to a sense of the whole subject. The conclusion can restate the thesis, summarize what the essay has contributed, consider the influence of the subject or its place in a larger picture, or (especially in an evaluation) assess the effectiveness or worth of the subject.

Drafting

If your subject or your view of it is complex, you may need at least two rough drafts of an analysis essay—one to discover what you think and one to clarify your principle, cover each element, and support your points with concrete details and vivid examples (including quotations if the subject is a written work). Plan on two drafts if you're uncertain of your thesis when you begin: you'll probably save time in the long run by attending to one goal at a time. Especially because the analysis essay says something about the subject by explaining its structure, you need to have a clear picture of the whole and relate each part to it.

Revising and Editing

When you revise and edit your essay, use the following questions and the box on the next page to uncover any weaknesses remaining in your analysis.

- *Is your principle of analysis clear?* The significance of your analysis and your view of the subject should be apparent throughout your essay.
- *Is your analysis complete?* Have you identified all elements according to your principle of analysis and determined their relations to one another and to the whole? If you have omitted some elements from your discussion, will the reason for their omission be clear to readers?
- *Is your analysis consistent?* Is your principle of analysis applied consistently to the entire subject (including any elements you have omitted)? Do all elements reflect the same principle, and are they clearly separate rather than overlapping? You may find it helpful to check your draft against your list of elements or your outline or to outline the draft itself.
- *Is your analysis well supported?* Is the thesis supported by clear assertions about parts of the subject, and are the assertions supported by concrete, specific evidence (sensory details, facts, quotations, and so on)? Do not rely on your readers to prove your thesis.
- *Is your analysis true to the subject?* Is your thesis unforced, your analysis fair? Is your new whole (your reassembly of the elements) faithful to the original? Be wary of leaping to a conclusion that distorts the subject.

FOCUS ON THE THESIS SENTENCE

A clear, informative thesis sentence (or sentences) is crucial in division or analysis because readers need to know your purpose in analyzing the subject and your principle of analysis. The sample sentences on page 150 convey both kinds of information. The following sentence, however, does not—with "do anything," it overstates and yet fails to specify a framework for analysis:

VAGUE   Advertisers will do anything to sell their products.

Compare this thesis sentence with the one from Shafeeq Sadiq's essay later in this chapter (p. 160). Here it is apparent that the writer will focus on the racist and sexist elements in advertising:

CLEAR   In general, these gimmicks [in advertisements] seem to enforce racial stereotypes and to view women in a negative way.

A well-focused thesis sentence benefits not only your readers but also you as writer, because it gives you a yardstick to judge the completeness, consistency, and supportiveness of your analysis. Don't be discouraged, though, if your thesis sentence doesn't come to you until *after* you've written a first draft and had a chance to discover your interest. Writing about your subject may be the best way for you to find its meaning and significance.

For more on thesis sentences, see pages 18–19.

A NOTE ON THEMATIC CONNECTIONS

Because it is everywhere, and everywhere taken for granted, popular culture is a tempting and challenging target for writers. Having chosen to write critically about a disturbing, cheering, or intriguing aspect of popular culture, all the authors represented in this chapter naturally pursued the method of division or analysis. A paragraph by Jon Pareles dissects the unique playing style of the rock guitarist Keith Richards (p. 148). Another paragraph, by Luci Tapahonso, analyzes a pizza commercial that especially appealed to Native Americans (p. 148). Sarah Coleman's essay asks just what we are watching when we view a "reality" show on television (next page). Shafeeq Sadiq's essay finds plenty of political incorrectness in advertising (p. 160). And Margaret Visser's essay considers what besides food we buy when we visit McDonald's (p. 165).

All television is educational television. The question is: What is it teaching?
—Nicholas Johnson

When television is good, nothing is better. But when television is bad, nothing is worse.
—Newton Minow

Television is chewing gum for the eyes.
—Frank Lloyd Wright

Journal Response   Reflect for a few moments on what you consider to be the worst show on TV. Write a journal entry explaining what is so bad about the show, trying to get down as many details as you can.

Sarah Coleman

Born in London in 1965, Sarah Coleman studied English at Cambridge University and fine art at London University. She then moved to the United States to attend Columbia University, where she earned an M.F.A. in creative writing in 1993. Her essays and reviews have appeared in Art News, *the* Boston Phoenix, New York Newsday, Photo Metro, Salon, *the* San Francisco Chronicle, *and the* World Press Review. *She currently works as a freelance writer in New York, where, she says, she spends more time watching television than she should.*

The Distorting Mirror of Reality TV

In this essay written especially for The Compact Reader, *Coleman examines one of the hottest trends in the media—reality TV. Her careful analysis leads to a sharp critique of the shows' portrayal of "reality."*

Take ten people. Put them (a) on an island, (b) in a locked house, or (c) in a desert. Turn on some television cameras, give them strange tests to perform as a group, and ask them to vote one person out of the group each week. In between, watch them fight, lie, eat, wash, fall in love. The last player left will win a big pot of money. This is the basic premise of a popular form of entertainment called "reality television." 1

154

The idea of watching people behave spontaneously on television   2
isn't a new one. MTV's hugely successful show *The Real World* debuted in 1992, and way back in the television dark ages of the 1940s,
Allen Funt's *Candid Camera* began using hidden cameras to catch ordinary people reacting to strange events. No doubt there exists some
ancient civilization in which entrepreneurs knocked holes in their
neighbors' wall and called their friends together to peep. But the new
crop of reality shows seems different somehow: meaner, tougher, and
less connected with reality than ever before.

Let's start with the contestants. Most producers of reality TV   3
shows would like you to believe they've picked a group of people
who span a broad spectrum of human diversity. But if you took the
demographics of the average reality show and applied them to the
population at large, you'd end up with a society that was 90 percent
white, young, and beautiful. In fact, though reality TV pretends to
hold up a mirror to society, its producers screen players in much the
same way as the producers of television commercials and Hollywood
movies screen their actors. For ethnic minorities, old people, the un-
beautiful, and the disabled, the message is harsh: even in "reality"
you don't exist.

Nor do stereotypes disappear once a contestant makes it into the   4
cast of a reality show. Players who can't wait until they appear on
television as themselves are often surprised to find that viewers see
only one side of their personality. To make the shows more dramatic,
it helps if viewers can easily identify each player as a particular type
of person, so producers find cast members' most obvious traits and
accentuate them through careful editing. The hunk, the girl next
door, the know it all, and the flirt: these are all popular recurring
"characters" on reality shows. With this kind of simplification, the
complexity that makes real people so interesting is gone; instead,
these "real" people are no more profound than the average soap
opera character.

Reality shows' view of human potential is similarly diminished.   5
In movies and soaps, evil characters often capture our imagination,
but their badness is effective because it contrasts with other characters' goodness. In reality TV, every character is a villain. Since the
shows are set up as contests with a single winner, naked self-interest
is the force motivating each contestant. To walk away with the
jackpot, players must be wily and calculating. They must charm other
players into letting them stick around, but be ready to crush anyone
who stands in the way of their success. What we see here is really a

refined form of mud wrestling. Cynics might argue that it is nothing more than real life with the gloves off—but if humans are that ruthlessly self-interested, how do we account for inspirational figures from Mahatma Gandhi to Nelson Mandela?[1] Real people are capable of nobility to differing degrees, but reality TV gives us a world where nobody can be trusted and where manipulation and backstabbing are rewarded with big cash prizes.

This eat-or-be-eaten mentality is often underscored by the shows'   6
exotic locations. Crystal clear water cascades over craggy rocks, a red cardinal's feathers are lit by the setting sun, but we see that even amid all this natural beauty people are still petty and conniving. No wonder one show continually showed shots of crocodiles poking their snouts out of murky river water: the producers wanted us to remember that every paradise has its poison-filled serpent, every jungle its tiger.

In other ways, reality shows are less reminiscent of movies and   7
mud wrestling than of another form of popular entertainment: the ancient Roman fight to the death between gladiators and lions. By eliminating one contestant each week, the shows offer us a symbolic form of public execution (one show even used that term to describe the way it dispatches its losers). We enjoy the suspense of seeing who will be eliminated, and perhaps we enjoy the loser's humiliation (after all, it's not "us"). The "executions" also offer the fantasy that annoying people can be banished from our lives. This is a place where irritating, self-absorbed types usually get their comeuppance, unless they make themselves useful to the group by hunting or cooking. Of course, real life is never that convenient: annoying people have a habit of sticking around, and they usually don't bring you fish.

Flimsy people in search of money and glory: Is that what we hu-   8
mans are all about? Reality TV puts forward a dark view of humanity in the guise of light entertainment. While it's fun to see "real" people (however reduced) on television—and to gossip about them the next day—it's depressing to think that their decency and ours is being hijacked in the name of entertainment. Nor are the shows' producers the only cynics in this game. With winners appearing every-

[1]Mahatma Gandhi (1869–1948), the Indian political and spiritual leader, led a campaign of nonviolent civil opposition against British rule. His efforts led to India's independence from Great Britain in 1947. Nelson Mandela (born 1918), the first black president of South Africa (1994–99), helped to bring about democratic political change in his country. He fought against racial segregation and won the Nobel Peace Prize in 1993. [Editor's note.]

where from *Playboy* to lip-salve commercials, and sore losers suing producers for alleged results-fixing, it seems everyone is exploiting everyone here. Andy Warhol[2] once predicted, "In the future everyone will be world-famous for fifteen minutes." Could he have foreseen how ugly people would make themselves for their moment in the spotlight?

Meaning

1. What is Coleman's thesis? Where does she state it explicitly?
2. According to Coleman, how do producers of reality TV shows turn the contestants into stereotypes? In your answer consider her points about the physical characteristics of the people who are typically cast on the shows and how producers and editors manipulate shots and story lines.
3. What do you think Coleman means when she writes, "it's depressing to think that [the contestants'] decency and ours is being hijacked in the name of entertainment" (paragraph 8)? According to Coleman, what qualities does reality TV bring out in both the contestants and the audience?
4. Based on their context in Coleman's essay, try to guess the meanings of any of the following words that you are unsure of. Test your guesses in a dictionary, and then try to use each word in a sentence or two of your own.

premise (1)	demographics (3)	conniving (6)
debuted (2)	accentuate (4)	reminiscent (7)
entrepreneurs (2)	wily (5)	alleged (8)
spectrum (3)	petty (6)	

Purpose and Audience

1. What do you think was Coleman's purpose in writing this essay? Does she want to shock, inform, persuade, or entertain her readers? What evidence from the text supports your viewpoint?
2. What assumptions does Coleman make about her audience? Does she assume that her readers are familiar with reality TV shows? How familiar with such shows would readers have to be in order to understand Coleman's analysis?

---

[2] Andy Warhol (1928–87) was an American artist and filmmaker, a founder of the Pop Art movement. [Editor's note.]

Method and Structure

1. What is the subject of Coleman's analysis, and what elements of this subject does she analyze? How does she reassemble these elements into a new whole? Support your answer with evidence from the essay.
2. Coleman begins her essay by presenting a formula, which she calls "the basic premise of a popular form of entertainment" (paragraph 1). How does beginning with this formula foreshadow the conclusions she draws from her analysis of reality TV shows?
3. A division or analysis essay needs concrete, specific examples to support each element of the analysis. In paragraph 4 Coleman provides examples of the way characters are stereotyped once they get on the show. What examples does she give of the plot and setting of reality TV shows? How convincing are these examples for her overall analysis?
4. **Other Methods**   In addition to analysis, Coleman uses argument and persuasion (Chapter 13) to convince readers of her negative view of reality TV. How does she build her argument? Find specific examples of evidence she uses to support her argument.

Language

1. Describe the author's tone: Is it basically personal and informal? angry? serious? What examples can you provide to support your answer?
2. Coleman uses humor in her analysis of reality TV, as when she writes that reality TV is "really a refined form of mud wrestling" (paragraph 5) or "annoying people have a habit of sticking around, and they usually don't bring you fish" (7). How does Coleman's use of humor contribute to the overall tone of the essay?

Writing Topics

1. **Journal to Essay**   In your journal entry (p. 154) you reflected on a TV show that you dislike. Now analyze the show carefully to uncover the elements you dislike. For example, like Coleman, do you object to the depiction of characters? Does the show stereotype groups of people? Is the show just a waste of time, or does it have a deeper negative effect parallel to Coleman's perception of "a dark view of humanity"? Does the show you picked have any redeeming qualities that lead you to watch it despite its weaknesses?
2. Using the method of division or analysis, write an essay in which you describe a TV show or movie that you particularly enjoyed. Just as Coleman took reality shows apart to criticize them, explain what elements contributed to the appeal of the show or movie you selected. Did

its appeal rest mostly on the actors involved, the places depicted, the story line, or other features? Did it make you think about who you were as a person or change your view of the world? If it was merely good "entertainment," describe what made it so.

3. **Cultural Considerations** In the Western world, we watch a lot of television: most of us watch it every day. Some people feel that TV can expand our vision of the world by showing us different people and places and exposing us to new ideas and issues. Others argue that TV narrows our views, inundating us with shallow content designed to please the crowd. What is your opinion about the effects of TV? Do you think that your viewing habits have an essentially positive or negative effect on you? Write an essay in which you explain how you think TV affects you.

4. **Connections** Coleman and Judith Ortiz Cofer, in "Don't Misread My Signals" (p. 307), both refer to the creation of negative stereotypes about a particular group. In fact, both writers assign some blame to the media. Write an essay in which you analyze the effects of the media on perpetuating and/or creating stereotypes, drawing on both essays and your own understanding of this issue.

You can tell the ideals of a nation by its advertisements. —Norman Douglas

The art of publicity is a black art. —Learned Hand

Advertising may be described as the science of arresting the human intelligence long enough to get money from it. —Stephen Leacock

Journal Response Think of a TV commercial that you object to because it is offensive or annoying in some way. Write about why it bothers you so much.

Shafeeq Sadiq

Shafeeq Sadiq was born in 1977 in Stockton, California, the son of Pakistani immigrants. He grew up in Stockton, graduated from high school in nearby Manteca, and obtained an A.A. degree from San Joaquin Delta College in Stockton. Sadiq now majors in economics at the University of California at Davis and in his free time enjoys body building.

Racism and Sexism in Advertising

In this strong critique of advertising tactics, Sadiq offers detailed examples to support his assertions. The essay was published in the 1997 Delta Winds, *a collection of student writing from San Joaquin Delta College.*

It seems as if everywhere you turn, someone is trying to be politically correct. Whether it involves minorities or women, racist and sexist comments are no longer tolerated in places such as the school yard and the workplace. Why is it, then, that minorities and women are constantly being exploited in everyday advertisements? Television, magazines, and billboards no longer show products, but rather show gimmicks in order to sell their product. In general, these gimmicks seem to enforce racial stereotypes and to view women in a negative way.

It appears that on every channel, there is another television commercial trying to sell its product with beautiful women. These commercials can range from selling beer to selling cars. Who can forget the gorgeous blonde standing next to the green Geo Storm, proudly exclaiming, "A man likes a woman who knows how to drive a stick!"? Advertisements like these, though seemingly aimed toward women, are exploiting them en route to the actual target: men. This commercial would routinely air during sporting events, when the majority of the viewers are male. It fits in well with the other commercials which, more often than not, have to do with beer.

Beer companies have been notorious for exploiting women in 3 their everyday promotions. Watching a football game, you can usually find an attractive young lady being swept off her feet by a less than attractive man after he opens the beer of his choice. Or, if you are lucky, you can witness several young women materializing on a desert island with the male drinker after, of course, he opens his can of beer. These advertisements present women as a goal, a trophy if you will, that can only be attained with the proper beverage. These women seldom have anything to say besides "Yes," making them seem like unintelligent sex objects.

Unfortunately, the exploitation does not stop with women. Beer 4 commercials exploit minorities as well. Black Entertainment Television frequently airs malt liquor commercials directed at African-American buyers. These ads usually involve a hip-hop rap artist who visits an unusually quiet ghetto community. When he brings the malt liquor, the entire neighborhood breaks into song and dance, with the very attractive African-American woman saying, "Things are back to the way they used to be." How did things used to be? Were there no peaceful afternoons in the 'hood? African-Americans can't be happy in a calm, serene environment? Though there are no racial slurs uttered, the entire commercial perpetuates stereotypes of the African-American community. They must sing and dance in the streets, trying to live life the way it used to be, before they were confined to the monotony of a good job and a quiet neighborhood. Perhaps the commercial maker is trying to say that African-Americans, as a whole, have been subdued by society.

African-Americans are not the only minority group exploited in 5 advertising; Arab Americans are victims as well. On September 16, 1996, *Newsweek* magazine printed a two-page advertisement for a well-known computer company. This ad depicted an Arab man from an unknown Arab country, wearing his native garb and standing next to a camel. There are boxes of computer parts in the corner of the page. The ad reads, "Some computer companies don't make their own parts. Makes you wonder where they get them." This advertisement insinuates that if these parts were made in an Arab country, they would somehow be inferior. Though the country is not mentioned by name, the message is still very clear.

Perhaps the most stereotyped people, when it comes to advertis- 6
ing, are Indian-Americans, those whose families originated in India. To my recollection, there has never been a major commercial involving an Indian-American who didn't speak with a ridiculously exaggerated accent. The most recent perpetrator, MCI, promotes a dime-a-minute service featuring an Indian-American with a very thick and pronounced accent stereotypically driving a New York City taxicab. The actor will never be an American who happens to be of Indian descent. For the company, using Indian-Americans in this manner might add to the comic value of the commercial. But it is safe to say that to most Indian-Americans, it is no laughing matter.

Racism and sexism are problems that go unnoticed in advertising 7
today. Nevertheless, they must be dealt with. The only winners in these types of ads are the advertisers themselves, who make money when you buy the product. There needs to be a public awakening, for racism and sexism should not be used in any situation, especially not to sell products. Advertisers need to take responsibility for their own actions and to end this type of exploitation. If they do not, we the consumer can always force them. After all, we have the dollars and the sense.

Meaning

1. What is Sadiq's thesis? Where does he state it explicitly?
2. In your own words, explain the process, described in paragraphs 2 and 3, by which advertisers use women to sell products to men. What, besides the product, are they selling?
3. What is wrong, in Sadiq's opinion, with a beer company's depicting African Americans having a good time?
4. What does Sadiq mean in paragraph 6 when he says, "The actor will never be an American who happens to be of Indian descent"? As opposed to what?
5. If you are unfamiliar with any of the following words, try to guess their meanings from the context in which Sadiq uses them. Look the words up in a dictionary to check your guesses, and then use each one in a sentence or two of your own.

gimmicks (1)	materialize (3)	monotony (4)
notorious (3)	perpetuates (4)	perpetrator (6)

Purpose and Audience

1. What do you think Sadiq's purpose was in writing this essay: to ask readers who think that racism and sexism have disappeared from advertising to reconsider? to convince advertisers to change their ways? something else?
2. What assumptions does Sadiq seem to make about his readers—their gender or age, their attitudes toward stereotypes of gender or race, their attitudes toward advertising, and so on?

Method and Structure

1. Why do you think Sadiq chose the method of analysis to talk about sexism and racism in advertising? How does the method help Sadiq achieve his purpose?
2. Each example Sadiq cites is a mini-analysis of a television commercial or magazine ad. By breaking down the commercial into its elements, he creates a new whole, a new way of looking at the commercial, that might not have been apparent before. Show how this analysis works in paragraph 5 of the essay, using the annotated paragraphs on pages 148–49 as a guide.
3. What does Sadiq accomplish in his first and last paragraphs?
4. Why do you think Sadiq cites more examples of racism than of sexism in advertising? Does he seem to think racism is more important or more widespread?
5. **Other Methods** The advertisements Sadiq analyzes are all examples (Chapter 6) used to illustrate racism or sexism in advertising, and each of these examples includes description (Chapter 4). What does this description contribute to Sadiq's thesis?

Language

1. How would you describe Sadiq's tone? How seriously does he take his subject? Is the tone appropriate, given his purpose?
2. Sadiq occasionally uses irony in analyzing advertisements, as in "Or, if you are lucky, you can witness several young women materializing on a desert island with the male drinker after, of course, he opens his can of beer" (paragraph 3) or "Were there no peaceful afternoons in the 'hood? African-Americans can't be happy in a calm, serene environment?" (4). Is the irony effective? Why, or why not? (See *irony* in the Glossary.)

Writing Topics

1. **Journal to Essay**   Expand your journal entry about a TV commercial (p. 160) into a full essay analyzing the commercial. Describe the commercial, and pinpoint why you find it annoying or offensive. Make sure your essay has a controlling thesis that draws together all the points of your analysis and asserts why the commercial has the effect it does. Alternatively, you could choose a commercial you think is unusually entertaining, amusing, or moving and explain why it works.

2. How did you react to Sadiq's essay? Do you agree with him that too many commercials remain sexist or racist in an age of supposed tolerance? Or do you find his complaints to be exaggerated, the offenses he points out rare or minor? Write an essay of your own responding to Sadiq's essay. Be sure to include examples to support your view.

3. **Cultural Considerations**   Sadiq is critical of an advertisement on Black Entertainment Television that he sees as depicting African Americans in a negative light. However, what if the ad was created by African Americans for African Americans? Would it still seem to stereotype? And if so, do the members of a minority group have a license to employ stereotypes about themselves, either in jest or as a way of deflating the stereotypes? Write an essay in which you state your position on this issue and support it using examples.

4. **Connections**   Write a two-paragraph comparison of paragraph 4 of Sadiq's essay and the paragraph by Luci Tapahonso on page 148. Each paragraph analyzes a single advertisement, but their tones are quite different. How do the words used by each author convey his or her attitude toward the advertisement?

The ordinary human being would sooner starve than live on brown bread and raw carrots. —George Orwell

Bread that must be sliced with an axe is bread that is too nourishing. —Fran Lebowitz

I'm president of the United States, and I'm not going to eat any more broccoli! —George Bush (father of the current president, George W. Bush)

Journal Response What kinds of junk food do you regularly consume: mints or chewing gum? salty snacks like potato chips? sweet, fatty foods like ice cream, cookies, and candy? fast food like cheeseburgers and French fries? Write about the junk food you ingest, describing when and where you eat it and the reasons you do so. (If you've sworn off junk food, what kinds did you consume in the past? When, where, and why?)

Margaret Visser

Born in 1940 in South Africa, Margaret Visser was raised in Zambia and lived in England, France, Iraq, and the United States before settling in Toronto, Canada. (She is a naturalized citizen of Canada.) Visser was educated at the University of Toronto, where she earned a B.A. (1970), an M.A. (1973), and a Ph.D. in classics (1980). She taught classics at York University in Toronto and has published articles in scholarly and popular periodicals. Visser also appears on television and radio, discussing her discoveries about the history and social mythology of everyday life. "The extent to which we take everyday objects for granted," she says, "is the precise extent to which they govern and inform our lives." Four books illuminate this important territory: Much Depends on Dinner *(1986),* The Rituals of Dinner *(1991),* The Way We Are *(1994), and* The Geometry of Love *(2001).*

The Ritual of Fast Food

In this excerpt from The Rituals of Dinner, *an investigation of table manners, Visser analyzes the fast-food restaurant. What do we seek when we visit such a place? How does the management oblige us? Success hinges on predictability.*

An early precursor of the restaurant meal was dinner served to the public at fixed times and prices at an eating house or tavern. Such a

1

meal was called, because of its predetermined aspects, an "ordinary," and the place where it was eaten came to be called an "ordinary," too. When a huge modern business conglomerate offers fast food to travellers on the highway, it knows that its customers are likely to desire No Surprises. They are hungry, tired, and not in a celebratory mood; they are happy to pay—provided that the price looks easily manageable—for the safely predictable, the convenient, the fast and ordinary.

Ornamental formalities are pruned away (tables and chairs are   2 bolted to the floor, for instance, and "cutlery" is either nonexistent or not worth stealing); but rituals, in the sense of behaviour and expectations that conform to preordained rules, still inform the proceedings. People who stop for a hamburger—at a Wendy's, a Harvey's, a McDonald's, or a Burger King—know exactly what the building that houses the establishment should look like; architectural variations merely ring changes on rigidly imposed themes. People want, perhaps even need, to *recognize* their chain store, to feel that they know it and its food in advance. Such an outlet is designed to be a "home away from home," on the highway, or anywhere in the city, or for Americans abroad.

Words and actions are officially laid down, learned by the staff   3 from handbooks and teaching sessions, and then picked up by customers in the course of regular visits. Things have to be called by their correct names ("Big Mac," "large fries"); the McDonald's rubric in 1978 required servers to ask "Will that be with cheese, sir?" "Will there be any fries today, sir?" and to close the transaction with "Have a nice day." The staff wear distinctive garments; menus are always the same, and even placed in the same spot in every outlet in the chain; prices are low and predictable; and the theme of cleanliness is proclaimed and tirelessly reiterated. The company attempts also to play the role of a lovable host, kind and concerned, even parental: it knows that blunt and direct confrontation with a huge faceless corporation makes us suspicious, and even badly behaved. So it stresses its love of children, its nostalgia for cozy warmth and for the past (cottage roofs, warm earth tones), or its clean, brisk modernity (glass walls, smooth surfaces, red trim). It responds to social concerns— when they are insistent enough, sufficiently widely held, and therefore "correct." McDonald's for example, is at present busy showing how much it cares about the environment.

Fast-food chains know that they are ordinary. They *want* to be   4 ordinary, and for people to think of them as almost inseparable from the idea of everyday food consumed outside the home. They are happy to allow their customers time off for feasts—on Thanksgiving, Christmas, and so on—to which they do not cater. Even those comparatively rare holiday times, however, are turned to a profit, because the companies know that their favourite customers—law-abiding families—are at home together then, watching television, where carefully placed commercials will spread the word concerning new fast-food products, and re-imprint the image of the various chain stores for later, when the long stretches of ordinary times return.

Families are the customers the fast-food chains want: solid citizens in groups of several at a time, the adults hovering over their children, teaching them the goodness of hamburgers, anxious to bring them up to behave typically and correctly. Customers usually maintain a clean, restrained, considerate, and competent demeanour as they swiftly, gratefully, and informally eat. Fast-food operators have recently faced the alarming realization that crack addicts, craving salt and fat, have spread the word among their number that French fries deliver these substances easily, ubiquitously, cheaply, and at all hours. Dope addicts at family "ordinaries"! The unacceptability of such a thought was neatly captured by a news story in *The Economist* (1990) that spelled out the words a fast-food proprietor can least afford to hear from his faithful customers, the participants in his polite and practiced rituals: the title of the story was "Come on Mabel, let's leave." The plan to counter this threat included increasing the intensity of the lighting in fast-food establishments—drug addicts, apparently, prefer to eat in the dark.

The formality of eating at a restaurant belonging to a fast-food chain depends upon the fierce regularity of its product, its simple but carefully observed rituals, and its environment. Supplying a hamburger that adheres to perfect standards of shape, weight, temperature, and consistency, together with selections from a pre-set list of trimmings, to a customer with fiendishly precise expectations is an enormously complex feat. The technology involved in performing it has been learned through the expenditure of huge sums on research, and after decades of experience—not to mention the vast political and economic ramifications involved in maintaining the supplies of cheap beef and cheap buns. But these costs and complexities are, with tremendous care, hidden from view. We know of course that, say, a Big Mac is a cultural construct: the careful control expended upon it is one of the things we are buying. But McDonald's manages—it must do so if it is to succeed in being ordinary—to provide a "casual" eating experience. Convenient, innocent simplicity is what the technology, the ruthless politics, and the elaborate organization serve to the customer.

Meaning

1. In paragraph 6 Visser writes, "Supplying a hamburger that adheres to perfect standards of shape, weight, temperature, and consistency [. . .] to a customer with fiendishly precise expectations is an enormously complex feat." How does this statement illustrate Visser's main idea?
2. What do you think Visser means by the statement that "a Big Mac is a cultural construct" (paragraph 6)?
3. If any of the following words are new to you, try to guess their meanings from the context of Visser's essay. Test your guesses in a dictionary, and then use each new word in a sentence or two.

precursor (1)	cater (4)	ubiquitously (5)
conglomerate (1)	hovering (5)	proprietor (5)
pruned (2)	demeanour (5)	expenditure (6)
preordained (2)	(American spelling:	ramifications (6)
rubric (3)	demeanor)	
reiterated (3)		

Purpose and Audience

1. What is Visser's purpose in writing this essay: to propose more interesting surroundings and menus at fast-food restaurants? to argue that the patrons of these establishments are too demanding? to explain how these chains manage to satisfy so many customers? something else?
2. Whom does Visser seem to imagine as her audience? Is she writing for sociologists? for managers at corporations such as McDonald's and Burger King? for diners who patronize fast-food restaurants? What evidence in the essay supports your answer?

Method and Structure

1. How does Visser's analysis, breaking the fast-food experience down into its elements, help her achieve her purpose?
2. Into what elements does Visser divide the fast-food restaurant? Be specific, supporting your answer with examples from the text.
3. **Other Methods** In addition to analysis, Visser employs example (Chapter 6) and description (Chapter 4) to illustrate the predictable nature of fast-food restaurants, most extensively in paragraph 3. In para-

graph 5 she also uses cause-and-effect analysis (Chapter 12) to explain both why crack addicts began to frequent chain restaurants and why these restaurants couldn't risk including addicts among their clientele. What does this cause-and-effect analysis add to the analysis of fast-food restaurants? How would addicts, whose money is presumably as good as anyone else's, interfere with the operation of these restaurants?

Language

1. What is Visser's tone? How seriously does she take her subject?
2. Visser writes that McDonald's used to require its servers to ask patrons, depending on their order, "Will that be with cheese, sir?" or "Will there be any fries today, sir?" (paragraph 3). What would be the purpose of such questions? How would you characterize this use of language?
3. According to Visser, people who patronize fast-food restaurants "want, perhaps even need, to *recognize* their chain store" (paragraph 2); they are looking for "the safely predictable, the convenient, the fast and ordinary" (1). Find other instances in the essay where Visser describes the people who eat in these restaurants. What portrait emerges of these customers? How does this portrait contribute to Visser's overall message?

Writing Topics

1. **Journal to Essay** Building on your journal entry (p. 165), write an essay in which you analyze your behavior as a consumer of junk food. Make a list of all the elements that constitute this activity and the setting in which it occurs. In your essay examine each element to show what it contributes to the whole. Be sure your principle of analysis is clear to readers.
2. In her last paragraph, Visser writes that the "costs and complexities" of providing "a 'casual' eating experience" in a fast-food restaurant are "hidden from view." Does this seem appropriate to you, or would you rather know what the corporation feeding you puts into its operation, such as the "economic ramifications involved in maintaining the supplies of cheap beef and cheap buns"? Write an essay exploring the issues this question raises for you.
3. **Cultural Considerations**   All of us have probably experienced a particular moment (or perhaps many moments) when we were willing to dine out on anything *but* fast food. What, at these moments, do you think we are seeking? Following Visser's example, write an essay analyzing the "culture" of a particular *non*chain restaurant. How does the management deliver what the customer wants?

4. **Connections**   Like Visser, Sarah Coleman, in "The Distorting Mirror of
Reality TV" (p. 154), writes seriously about a subject that some people
would consider trivial and unworthy of serious attention. How informative and useful do you find such analyses of popular culture? Where does
each essay tell us something significant about ourselves, or, in contrast,
where does it fail in trying to make the trivial seem important? Is popular culture — magazines, television, Hollywood movies, self-help books,
toys, fast-food restaurants — best looked at critically, best ignored, or
best simply enjoyed? Explain your answers in an essay, using plenty of
examples to support your thesis.

Writing with the Method
Division or Analysis

Choose one of the following topics, or any other topic they suggest, for an essay developed by analysis. The topic you decide on should be something you care about so that analysis is a means of communicating an idea, not an end in itself.

PEOPLE, ANIMALS, OBJECTS

1. The personality of a friend or relative
2. The personality of a typical politician, teacher, or other professional
3. An animal such as a cat, dog, horse, cow, spider, or bat
4. A machine or appliance such as a car engine, harvesting combine, laptop computer, hair dryer, toaster, or sewing machine
5. A nonmotorized vehicle such as a skateboard, an in-line skate, a bicycle, or a snowboard
6. A building such as a hospital, theater, or sports arena

IDEAS

7. The perfect city
8. The perfect crime
9. A theory or concept in a field such as psychology, sociology, economics, biology, physics, engineering, or astronomy
10. The evidence in a political argument (written, spoken, or reported in the news)
11. A liberal arts education

ASPECTS OF CULTURE

12. A style of dress or "look" such as that associated with the typical businessperson, jock, rap musician, or outdoors enthusiast
13. A typical hero or villain in science fiction, romance novels, war movies, or movies or novels about adolescents
14. A television or film comedy
15. A literary work: short story, novel, poem, essay
16. A visual work: painting, sculpture, building
17. A musical work: song, concerto, symphony, opera
18. A performance: sports, acting, dance, music, speech
19. The slang of a particular group or occupation

Writing About the Theme
Looking at Popular Culture

1. The essays by Sarah Coleman (p. 154), Shafeeq Sadiq (p. 160), and Margaret Visser (p. 165) all include the theme that what you see — whether in entertainment, advertising, or fast-food restaurants — is not all you get. Think of something you have used, seen, or otherwise experienced that made you suspect a hidden message or agenda. Consider, for example, a childhood toy, a popular breakfast cereal, a political speech, a magazine, a textbook, a video game, a movie, or a visit to a theme park such as Disney World. Using the essays in this chapter as models, write an analysis of your subject, making sure to divide it into distinct elements, and conclude by reassembling these elements into a new whole.

2. Margaret Visser writes that "a Big Mac is a cultural construct: the careful control expended upon it is one of the things we are buying." In what way is Keith Richards's guitar playing, as described by Jon Pareles (p. 148), also part of a cultural construct? Consider the myths surrounding guitars and famous rock-and-roll guitar players, such as Elvis Presley, Chuck Berry, Jimi Hendrix, and Eric Clapton. Write an essay explaining the attitudes and expectations invested in rock guitar playing in our society. Examine the language, setting, and atmosphere surrounding guitars and guitarists, whether in clubs, at rock concerts, or on music videos.

3. Luci Tapahonso (p. 148) and Shafeeq Sadiq both analyze television advertising. Sadiq calls for a "public awakening" to racist and sexist advertising. Tapahonso, in contrast, thinks that Native Americans found cause for celebration in a positive commercial that showed "Indians as we live today." What do you think of television advertising? Is Sadiq's concern justified, or are the ads he singles out unusual? How common are ads like the one Tapahonso analyzes? Consider ads you've seen, or pay close attention to the ads as you're watching television over a week or so. Then write an essay addressing whether advertisers seem to treat the differences among people fairly or to exploit those differences. Are there notable exceptions in either case?

Chapter 8

CLASSIFICATION

Sorting Thoughts and Behaviors

USING THE METHOD

We **classify** when we sort things into groups: kinds of cars, styles of writing, types of psychotherapy. Because it creates order, classification helps us make sense of our physical and mental experience. With it, we see the correspondences among like things and distinguish them from unlike things. We can name things, remember them, discuss them.

Writers classify primarily to explain a pattern in a subject that might not have been noticed before: for instance, a sportswriter might observe that basketball players tend to fall into one of three groups based on the aggressiveness of their play. Sometimes, writers also classify to persuade readers that one group is superior: the sportswriter might argue that one style of basketball play is more effective than the other two.

Classification is a three-step process:

- Separate things into their elements, using the method of division or analysis (previous chapter).
- Isolate the similarities among the elements.
- Group or classify the things based on those similarities, matching like with like.

The diagram below illustrates a classification essay that appears later in this chapter, "The People Next Door" by Jonathan R. Gould Jr. (p. 181). Gould's subject is neighbors, and he sees four distinct kinds:

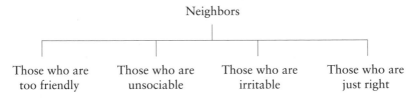

Neighbors

| Those who are too friendly | Those who are unsociable | Those who are irritable | Those who are just right |

All the members of Gould's overall group share at least one characteristic: they have been Gould's neighbors. The members of each subgroup also share at least one characteristic: they are too friendly, for instance, or unsociable. The people in each subgroup are independent of each other, and none of them is essential to the existence of the subgroup: the kind of neighbor would continue to exist even if at the moment Gould didn't live next door to such a person.

The number of groups in a classification scheme depends entirely on the basis for establishing the classes in the first place. There are two systems:

- In a complex classification like that used for neighbors, each individual fits firmly into one class because of at least one distinguishing feature shared with all members of that class but not with any members of any other classes. All the too-friendly neighbors are overly friendly, but none of the unsociable, irritable, or just-right neighbors is.
- In a binary or two-part classification, two classes are in opposition to each other, such as constructive and destructive neighbors. Often, one group has a certain characteristic that the other group lacks. For instance, neighbors could be classified into those who respect your privacy and those who don't. A binary scheme

is useful to emphasize the possession of a particular characteristic, but it is limited if it specifies nothing about the members of the "other" class except that they lack the trait. (An old joke claims that there are two kinds of people in the world—those who classify, and all others.)

Sorting items demands a **principle of classification** that determines the groups by distinguishing them. For instance, Gould's principle in identifying four groups of neighbors is their behavior toward him and his family. Principles for sorting a year's movies might be genre (action-adventures, comedies, dramas); place of origin (domestic, foreign); or cost of production (low-budget, medium-priced, high-budget). Your choice of a principle depends on your interest.

Although you may emphasize one class over the others, the classification itself must be complete and consistent. A classification of movies by genre would be incomplete if it omitted comedies. It would be inconsistent if it included action-adventures, comedies, dramas, low-budget films, and foreign films: such a system mixes *three* principles (genre, cost, origin); it omits whole classes (what of high-budget domestic dramas?); and it overlaps other classes (a low-budget foreign action-adventure would fit in three different groups).

ANALYZING CLASSIFICATION IN PARAGRAPHS

Max Eastman (1883–1969) was a political organizer and tract writer and also a poet and scholar of Russian. This paragraph comes from his book *Enjoyment of Poetry* (1913).

A simple experiment will distinguish two types of human nature. Gather a throng of people and pour them into a ferryboat. By the time the boat has swung into the river you will find that a certain proportion have taken the trouble to climb upstairs in order to be out on deck and see what is to be seen as they cross over. The rest have settled indoors to think what they will do upon reaching the other side, or perhaps lose themselves in apathy or tobacco smoke. But leaving out those apathetic, or addicted to a single enjoyment, we may divide all the alert passengers on the boat into two classes: those

Principle of classification (topic sentences underlined toward end): attitude toward experience and goals

1 | *1. Poetic people: focused on experience*

2 | *2. Practical people: focused on goals*

who are interested in crossing the river, and those   1
who are merely interested in getting across. And we   2
may divide all the people on the earth, or all the
moods of people, in the same way. Some of them are
chiefly occupied with attaining ends, and some with   2
receiving experiences. The distinction of the two will   1
be more marked when we name the first kind practical, and the second poetic, for common knowledge
recognizes that a person poetic or in a poetic mood   1
is impractical, and a practical person is intolerant of   2
poetry.

Daniel Goleman (born 1940) is a psychologist who consults and writes on "emotional intelligence." He previously wrote for the *New York Times,* and the following paragraph comes from a 1992 *Times* column headlined "As Addiction Medicine Gains, Experts Debate What It Should Cover."

Dr. [Harvey] Milkman, in a theory often cited by those who are stretching the boundaries of addiction, proposed in the mid-1980s that there are three kinds of addiction, each marked by the change they produce in emotional states. The first involves substances or activities that are calming, including alcohol, tranquilizers, overeating, and even watching television. The second involves becoming energized, whether by cocaine and amphetamines, gambling, sexual activity, or high-risk sports like parachute-jumping. The third kind of addiction is to fantasy, whether induced by psychedelic drugs or, for example, by sexual thoughts.

Principle of classification (topic sentence underlined): change produced in emotional states

1. Calming addiction

2. Energizing addiction

3. Fantasy-producing addiction

DEVELOPING AN ESSAY BY CLASSIFICATION
Getting Started

Classification essays are often assigned in college courses. When you need to develop your own subject for a classification essay, think of one large class of things whose members you've noticed fall into subclasses, such as study habits, midnight grocery shoppers, or political fund-raising appeals. Be sure that your general subject forms a class in its own right—that all its members share at least one important quality. Then look for your principle of classification, the quality or qualities that distinguish some members from others, providing poles for the members to group themselves around. One such principle for political fund-raising appeals might be the different methods of delivery, including letters, telephone calls, advertisements, telethons, social gatherings, and rallies.

Your principle of classification may suggest a thesis sentence, but be sure the sentence also conveys a *reason* for the classification so that the essay does not become a dull list of categories. The following tentative thesis sentence is mechanical; the revision is more interesting.

> TENTATIVE THESIS SENTENCE   Political fund-raising appeals are delivered in any of six ways.
>
> REVISED THESIS SENTENCE   Of the six ways to deliver political fund-raising appeals, the three that rely on personal contact are generally the most effective.

(Note that the revised thesis sentence implies a further classification based on whether the appeals involve personal contact or not.)

While generating ideas for your classification, keep track of them in a list, diagram, or outline to ensure that your principle is applied thoroughly (all classes) and consistently (each class relating to the principle). Fill in the list, diagram, or outline with the distinguishing features of each class and with examples that will clarify your scheme. Be sure to consider your readers' needs. The principle for classifying a familiar subject such as study habits might need little justification, although the classes themselves would need to be enlivened with vivid examples. An unfamiliar subject, in contrast, might require considerable care in explaining the principle of classification as well as attention to the details.

Organizing

The introduction to a classification essay should make clear why the classification is worthwhile: What situation prompted the essay? What do readers already know about the subject? What use might they make of the information you will provide? Unless your principle of classification is self-evident, you may want to explain it briefly—though save extensive explanation for the body of the essay. Do state your principle in a thesis sentence, so that readers know where you're taking them.

In the body of the essay the classes may be arranged in order of decreasing familiarity or increasing importance or size—whatever pattern provides the emphasis you want and clarifies your scheme for readers. You should at least mention each class, but some classes may demand considerable space and detail.

A classification essay often ends with a conclusion that restores the wholeness of the subject. Among other uses, the conclusion might summarize the classes, comment on the significance of one particular class in relation to the whole, or point out a new understanding of the whole subject gained from the classification.

Drafting

For the first draft of your classification, your main goal will be to establish your scheme: spelling out the purpose and principle of classification and defining the groups so that they are complete and consistent, covering the subject without mixing principles or overlapping. The more you've been able to plan your scheme, the less difficult the draft will be. If you can also fill in the examples and other details needed to develop the groups, do so. But you may want to save this important work for revision, as discussed in the box opposite.

Revising and Editing

The following questions and the information in the box opposite can help you revise and edit your classification.

- *Will readers see the purpose of your classification?* Let readers know early why you are troubling to classify your subject, and keep this purpose evident throughout the essay.
- *Is your classification complete?* Your principle of classification should create categories that encompass every representative of the general subject. If some representatives will not fit the scheme, you may have to create a new category or revise the existing categories to include them.
- *Is your classification consistent?* Consistency is essential to save readers from confusion or irritation. Make sure all the classes reflect the same principle and that they do not overlap. Remedy flaws by adjusting the classes or creating new ones.

FOCUS ON PARAGRAPH DEVELOPMENT

A crucial aim of revising a classification is to make sure each group is clear: what's counted in, what's counted out, and why. You'll provide the examples and other details that make the groups clear as you develop the paragraph(s) devoted to each group.

The following paragraph gives just the outline of one group in a four-part classification of ex-smokers into zealots, evangelists, the elect, and the serene:

> The second group, evangelists, does not condemn smokers but encourages them to quit. Evangelists think quitting is easy, and they preach this message, often earning the resentment of potential converts.

Contrast this bare-bones adaptation with the actual paragraphs written by Franklin E. Zimring in his essay "Confessions of a Former Smoker" (p. 192):

> By contrast, the antismoking evangelist does not condemn smokers. Unlike the zealot, he regards smoking as an easily curable condition, as a social disease, and not a sin. The evangelist spends an enormous amount of time seeking and preaching to the unconverted. He argues that kicking the habit is not *that* difficult. After all, *he* did it; moreover, as he describes it, the benefits of quitting are beyond measure and the disadvantages are nil.
>
> The hallmark of the evangelist is his insistence that he never misses tobacco. Though he is less hostile to smokers than the zealot, he is resented more. Friends and loved ones who have been the targets of his preachments frequently greet the resumption of smoking by the evangelist as an occasion for unmitigated glee.

In the second sentence of both paragraphs, Zimring explicitly contrasts evangelists with zealots, the group he previously defined. And he does more as well: he provides specific examples of the evangelist's message (first paragraph) and of others' reactions to him (second paragraph). These details pin down the group, making it distinct from other groups and clear in itself.

For more on paragraph development through specifics, see pages 40–41.

A NOTE ON THEMATIC CONNECTIONS

Writers classify the thoughts and behaviors of human beings more than any other subject, perhaps because the method gives order and even humor to our many psychological quirks and curious actions. The authors in this chapter mine thoughts and behaviors for information and for humor. In a paragraph Max Eastman identifies two classes of people, the practical and the poets (p. 175). Also in a paragraph Daniel Goleman sorts addictions by the emotional changes they produce (p. 176). Jonathan Gould's essay finds four kinds of next-door neighbors (opposite). Marion Winik's essay categorizes her friends into nine groups (p. 186). And Franklin Zimring's essay explores the four varieties of ex-smokers (p. 192).

We make our friends; we make our enemies; but God makes our next-door neighbor.
— G. K. Chesterton

Good fences make good neighbors.
— Proverb

For what do we live, but to make sport for our neighbours, and laugh at them in our turn?
— Jane Austen

Journal Response   Jot down a list of neighbors you have now and have had in the past. Then write a short journal entry about the different kinds of neighbors you have encountered.

—————— *Jonathan R. Gould Jr.* ——————

Jonathan R. Gould Jr. was born in 1968 in Little Falls, New York, and grew up on a dairy farm in nearby Ft. Plain. Graduating from Little Falls Baptist Academy, he was valedictorian of his class. He served three years in the U.S. Army, specializing in administration and computer programming. At the State University of New York at Oneonta, he was an honors student, received the Provost Award for academic distinction, and obtained a B.S. in mathematics education. Gould currently works for an Internet service provider in Oneonta, where he lives with his wife and three children.

The People Next Door

From his experiences in many different settings, Gould identifies four types of neighbors, only one of which could be considered truly neighborly. Gould wrote this essay in 1994 for a writing course at SUNY.

I have moved more often than I care to remember. However, one 1 thing always stays the same no matter where I have been. There is always a house next door, and that house contains neighbors. Over time, I have begun putting my neighbors into one of four categories: too friendly, unsociable, irritable, and just right.

Neighbors who are too friendly can be seen just about anywhere. 2 I mean that both ways. They exist in every neighborhood I have ever lived in and seem to appear everywhere I go. For some strange reason these people become extremely attached to my family and stop in as many as eight to ten times a day. No matter how tired I appear to be, nothing short of opening the door and suggesting they leave will make them go home at night. (I once told an unusually friendly neighbor that his house was on fire, in an attempt to make him leave, and he still took ten minutes to say goodbye.) What is truly interesting about these people is their strong desire to cook for us even though they have developed no culinary skill whatsoever. (This has always proved particularly disconcerting since they stay to watch us eat every bite as they continually ask if the food "tastes good.")

The unsociable neighbor is a different story altogether. For reasons of his own, he has decided to pretend that we do not exist. I have always found that one or two neighbors of this type are in my neighborhood. It is not easy to identify these people, because they seldom leave the shelter of their own house. To be honest, the only way I know that someone lives in their building is the presence of a name on the mailbox and the lights shining through the windows at night. My wife often tries to befriend these unique people, and I have to admire her courage. However, even her serenity is shaken when she offers our neighbors a fresh-baked apple pie only to have them look at her as if she intended to poison them.

Probably the most difficult neighbor to deal with is the irritable neighbor. This individual probably has several problems, but he has reduced all those problems down to one cause—the proximity of my family to his residence. Fortunately, I have only encountered this type of neighbor in a handful of settings. (He is usually too busy with one group of "troublemakers" to pick up a new set.) The times that I have encountered this rascal, however, have proved more than enough for my tastes. He is more than willing to talk to me. Unfortunately, all he wants to tell me is how miserable my family is making him. Ignoring this individual has not worked for me yet. (He just adds my "snobbishness" to his list of faults that my family displays.) Interestingly, this fellow will eat anything my wife (bless her soul) might make in an attempt to be sociable. Even though he never has anything good to say about the food, not a crumb will be left on the plate when he is finished (which leads me to wonder just how starved and impoverished he must be).

At the risk of sounding like Goldilocks, there is also a neighbor who is "just right." One of the most wonderful things about this neighbor is that there has always been at least one everywhere I have gone. We meet often (though not too often), and our greetings are always sincere. Occasionally, our families will go out to eat or to shop, or just sit and talk. We tend to spend as much time at their house as they do at ours (two to three times a month), and everyone knows just when it is time to say goodnight. For some reason, this neighbor knows how to cook, and we frequently exchange baked goods as well as pleasantries. For obvious reasons, this type of neighbor is my favorite.

As I mentioned before, each type of neighbor I have encountered is   6
a common sight in any neighborhood. I have always felt it was important to identify the type of neighbors that were around me. Then I am better able to maintain a clear perspective on our relationship and understand their needs. After all, people do not really change; we just learn how to live with both the good and the bad aspects of their behavior.

Meaning

1. Where does Gould state his thesis?
2. What is the difference between unsociable and irritable neighbors in Gould's classification?
3. From their context in Gould's essay, try to guess the meanings of any of the following words that are unfamiliar to you. Check your definitions against a dictionary's, and then write a sentence or two using each new word.

culinary (2)   proximity (4)   pleasantries (5)
disconcerting (2)   impoverished (4)

Purpose and Audience

1. Why do you suppose Gould wrote this essay? Where does he give the clearest indication?
2. Does Gould make any assumptions about his audience? Does he seem to be writing for a certain type of reader?

Method and Structure

1. Why do you think Gould chose the method of classification to write about the subject of neighbors? How does the method help him achieve his purpose?
2. What is Gould's principle of classification? Do you think his classification is complete and consistent? How else might he have sorted neighbors?
3. Why do you think Gould stresses the fact that he has encountered most of these types of neighbors everywhere he has lived?

4. What does Gould accomplish in his conclusion?
5. **Other Methods**   Gould's categories lend themselves to comparison and contrast (Chapter 10). Based on his descriptions, what are the differences between the too-friendly neighbor and the just-right neighbor?

Language

1. What is Gould's tone? How seriously does he take the problem of difficult neighbors?
2. Point out several instances of hyperbole or overstatement in the essay. What effect do these have?

Writing Topics

1. **Journal to Essay**   In your journal entry (p. 181) you began a process of classification by focusing on neighbors you have had. Now think of a group to which you belong—a religious organization, your family, a club or committee, even a writing class. Write a classification essay in which you sort the group's members into categories according to a clear principle of classification. Be sure to label and define each type for your readers, to provide examples, and to position yourself in one of the categories. What does your classification reveal about the group as a whole?
2. Most of us have had at least one colorful or bothersome neighbor at some time or another—a busybody, a recluse, a peeping Tom. Write a descriptive essay (with some narration) about an interesting neighbor you have known or a narrative essay (with some description) about a memorable run-in with a neighbor.
3. Television has provided us with a large array of eccentric neighbors—from the Nortons in *The Honeymooners* to Rhoda Morgenstern in *The Mary Tyler Moore Show* to Cosmo Kramer in *Seinfeld*. Write an essay in which you classify the kinds of neighbors depicted on TV. You may borrow Gould's principle of classification if it fits, or come up with an alternative one of your own.
4. **Cultural Considerations**   "Good fences make good neighbors," says a character in Robert Frost's poem "Mending Wall," and many people in our live-and-let-live society would seem to agree. Is the best neighbor an invisible one? Or do we lose something when we ignore those who are literally closest to us? Write an essay giving a definition of what it means to be a good neighbor. Or, if you prefer, write an essay in which you compare and contrast neighboring habits in different types of communities you have lived in or know of.

5. **Connections**   Franklin Zimring's "Confession of a Former Smoker" (p. 192), like Gould's essay, takes a large group of people and sorts them into a small number of clearly defined categories. This goal is quite ambitious because the authors are trying to account for wide variations among a large number of individuals. In your opinion, which essay provides the most comprehensive categorization? Are there groups that either author has failed to mention?

I get by with a little help from my friends.
— John Lennon and Paul McCartney

If a man does not make new acquaintances as he advances through life, he will soon find himself alone. — Samuel Johnson

We need new friends. Some of us are cannibals who have eaten their old friends up; others must have ever-renewed audiences before whom to reenact an ideal version of their lives. — Logan Pearsall Smith

Journal Response Draw up a list of your friends. Include people you see on a regular basis and others you haven't seen for a while. Can you sort them into categories — for instance, by the places you see them, the things you discuss with them, the ways they make you feel, or their importance to you?

Marion Winik

Marion Winik was born in New York City in 1958. She received her B.A. from Brown University and her M.F.A. from Brooklyn College. Perhaps best known as a commentator for National Public Radio's All Things Considered, *Winik has also published in well-known print periodicals, such as* Parenting, Cosmopolitan, *the* Philadelphia Inquirer, *and* Utne Reader. *Her books include* Telling: Confessions, Concessions, and Other Flashes of Light *(1995) and* First Comes Love *(1997), a memoir about life with her gay, AIDS-infected husband. She's also the author of* The Lunch Box Chronicles *(1999), which deals with single parenthood in the nineties.*

What Are Friends For?

In "What Are Friends For?" Winik locates various kinds of friends, from "Far-away" to "Hero" to "Friends You Love to Hate." The essay appears in Winik's collection Telling: Confessions, Concessions, and Other Flashes of Light.

I was thinking about how everybody can't be everything to each other, but some people can be something to each other, thank God, from the ones whose shoulder you cry on to the ones whose half-slips you borrow to the nameless ones you chat with in the grocery line. 1

Buddies, for example, are the workhorses of the friendship world, the people out there on the front lines, defending you from loneliness 2 and boredom. They call you up, they listen to your complaints, they celebrate your successes and curse your misfortunes, and you do the same for them in return. They hold out through innumerable crises before concluding that the person you're dating is no good, and even then understand if you ignore their good counsel. They accompany you to a movie with subtitles or to see the diving pig at Aquarena Springs. They feed your cat when you are out of town and pick you up from the airport when you get back. They come over to help you decide what to wear on a date. Even if it is with that creep.

What about family members? Most of them are people you just 3 got stuck with, and though you love them, you may not have very much in common. But there is that rare exception, the Relative Friend. It is your cousin, your brother, maybe even your aunt. The two of you share the same views of the other family members. Meg never should have divorced Martin. He was the best thing that ever happened to her. You can confirm each other's memories of things that happened a long time ago. Don't you remember when Uncle Hank and Daddy had that awful fight in the middle of Thanksgiving dinner? Grandma always hated Grandpa's stamp collection; she probably left the windows open during the hurricane on purpose.

While so many family relationships are tinged with guilt and 4 obligation, a relationship with a Relative Friend is relatively worry free. You don't even have to hide your vices from this delightful person. When you slip out Aunt Joan's back door for a cigarette, she is already there.

Then there is that special guy at work. Like all the other people 5 at the job site, at first he's just part of the scenery. But gradually he starts to stand out from the crowd. Your friendship is cemented by jokes about coworkers and thoughtful favors around the office. Did you see Ryan's hair? Want half my bagel? Soon you know the names of his turtles, what he did last Friday night, exactly which model CD player he wants for his birthday. His handwriting is as familiar to you as your own.

Though you invite each other to parties, you somehow don't 6 quite fit into each other's outside lives. For this reason, the friendship may not survive a job change. Company gossip, once an infallible source of entertainment, soon awkwardly accentuates the distance between you. But wait. Like School Friends, Work Friends share certain memories which acquire a nostalgic glow after about a decade.

A Faraway Friend is someone you grew up with or went to 7 school with or lived in the same town as until one of you moved away. Without a Faraway Friend, you would never get any mail addressed in handwriting. A Faraway Friend calls late at night, invites you to her wedding, always says she is coming to visit but rarely shows up. An actual visit from a Faraway Friend is a cause for celebration and binges of all kinds. Cigarettes, Chips Ahoy, bottles of tequila.

Faraway Friends go through phases of intense communication, 8 then may be out of touch for many months. Either way, the connection is always there. A conversation with your Faraway Friend always helps to put your life in perspective: when you feel you've hit a dead end, come to a confusing fork in the road, or gotten lost in some crackerbox subdivision of your life, the advice of the Faraway Friend—who has the big picture, who is so well acquainted with the route that brought you to this place—is indispensable.

Another useful function of the Faraway Friend is to help you re- 9 member things from a long time ago, like the name of your seventh-grade history teacher, what was in that really good stir-fry, or exactly what happened that night on the boat with the guys from Florida.

Ah, the Former Friend. A sad thing. At best a wistful memory, at 10 worst a dangerous enemy who is in possession of many of your deepest secrets. But what was it that drove you apart? A misunderstanding, a betrayed confidence, an unrepaid loan, an ill-conceived flirtation. A poor choice of spouse can do in a friendship just like that. Going into business together can be a serious mistake. Time, money, distance, cult religions: all noted friendship killers. You quit doing drugs, you're not such good friends with your dealer anymore.

And lest we forget, there are the Friends You Love to Hate. They 11 call at inopportune times. They say stupid things. They butt in, they boss you around, they embarrass you in public. They invite themselves over. They take advantage. You've done the best you can, but they need professional help. On top of all this, they love you to death and are convinced they're your best friend on the planet.

So why do you continue to be involved with these people? Why 12 do you tolerate them? On the contrary, the real question is, What would you do without them? Without Friends You Love to Hate, there would be nothing to talk about with your other friends. Their problems and their irritating stunts provide a reliable source of conversation for everyone they know. What's more, Friends You Love to Hate make you feel good about yourself, since you are obviously in so much better shape than they are. No matter what these people do, you will never get rid of them. As much as they need you, you need them too.

At the other end of the spectrum are Hero Friends. These people   13
are better than the rest of us, that's all there is to it. Their career is something you wanted to be when you grew up — painter, forest ranger, tire-
less doer of good. They have beautiful homes filled with special handmade things presented to them by villagers in the remote areas they
have visited in their extensive travels. Yet they are modest. They never
gossip. They are always helping others, especially those who have suffered a death in the family or an illness. You would think people like
this would just make you sick, but somehow they don't.

A New Friend is a tonic unlike any other. Say you meet her at a   14
party. In your bowling league. At a Japanese conversation class, perhaps. Wherever, whenever, there's that spark of recognition. The first
time you talk, you can't believe how much you have in common. Suddenly, your life story is interesting again, your insights fresh, your
opinion valued. Your various shortcomings are as yet completely invisible.

It's almost like falling in love.   15

Meaning

1. What is Winik's thesis? How does it relate to the question she poses in
   the title?
2. What label does Winik assign to each category of friend that she establishes? What functions does each group fulfill?
3. Winik concludes her essay by describing the experience of meeting a
   New Friend (paragraph 14). How is a New Friend different from other
   types of friends, and why does Winik compare this experience with falling in love?
4. Try to guess the meanings of the following words from their context in
   Winik's essay. Look up the words in a dictionary to check your guesses.
   Then use each word in a sentence or two of your own.

counsel (2)	binges (7)	inopportune (11)
tinged (4)	crackerbox (8)	butt in (11)
cemented (5)	wistful (10)	tonic (14)
infallible (6)	ill-conceived (10)	
nostalgic (6)	lest (11)	

Purpose and Audience

1. Winik begins her essay by saying, "I was thinking about [. . .]" (paragraph 1). What does this introductory sentence reveal about her purpose?

2. Is the essay addressed to both male and female readers? In your opinion, is it accessible to both sexes? Why, or why not? According to the information presented in this essay, does Winik believe that friends can be of either sex?

Method and Structure

1. Some people would not think of classifying relationships as intimate as friendships into such clear-cut categories. Does Winik's choice of method surprise you? Do you find it effective? What does this method enable her to do?

2. What is Winik's principle of classification? Does she group her friends based on differences among them independent of her or on differences in their relationships with her? Why do you think she just mentions but doesn't explain School Friends (paragraph 6)? Do you understand what she means by this category? Is it a flaw in the essay that Winik does not explain the category?

3. In paragraph 3 Winik asks "What about family members?" as a transition to the category of Relative Friends. Study how she moves from one category to another in the rest of the essay. Are her transitions appropriate and effective? Why, or why not?

4. **Other Methods**   How does Winik use definition (Chapter 11) to differentiate her categories of friends? Where in the essay does she seem to take the most care with definition? Why do you think she gives more attention to some categories than to others?

Language

1. Winik sometimes uses actual lines from conversation but without quotation marks. For example, in paragraph 3 she writes, "The two of you share the same views of the other family members. Meg should never have divorced Martin. He was the best thing that ever happened to her." Locate two other passages where dialogue blends into the text. What is the effect of this use of dialogue?

2. Winik sometimes omits words (such as *If* at the beginning of "You quit doing drugs, you're not such good friends with your dealer anymore," paragraph 10) or uses sentence fragments (such as "Even if it is with that creep," 2). Why do you think she chooses to break some rules of writing?

3. Winik uses several metaphors in the essay—for example, "Buddies [. . .] are the workhorses of the friendship world" (paragraph 2). Find other examples of metaphor. What do they contribute to the essay? (If necessary, review *metaphor* in the Glossary.)

Writing Topics

1. **Journal to Essay** Write an essay about one of the categories of friends that you described in your journal entry (p. 186) — for example, friends you study with childhood friends, or friends you confide in. Using the method of classification, examine the *functions* this category of friend performs. What activities do you do with them that you don't do with others? What do you talk about? How relaxed or tense, happy or irritated, do they make you feel? Why are they significant to you? For each function, provide plenty of examples for readers.

2. Winik uses classification to explore friendship. Use the same method to develop your own essay about people with whom you do *not* get along. What categories do they fall into — for example, are some gossipy, others arrogant, still others unreliable? (Detail the categories with plenty of examples.) What does your dislike of these types of people ultimately reveal about yourself and your values?

3. **Cultural Considerations** Americans have a reputation for being very friendly, so that a stranger might smile, wish you a nice day, or even suggest having coffee together. What, in your view, is the appropriate way to interact (or not interact) with a stranger? In answering, ignore situations that might be risky, such as deserted nighttime streets or strangers who look clearly threatening. Think instead of a safe situation, such as a long line at the grocery store or coffee shop or the waiting room of a doctor's office. What are your "rules" for initiating conversation and for responding to a stranger's overtures? What informs your rules: experience? personality? upbringing? To what extent do you think your rules are invented by you or bred into you?

4. **Connections** Both Winik and Jonathan R. Gould Jr., in "The People Next Door" (p. 181), classify common relationships: Winik distinguishes nine categories of friends, while Gould pinpoints four types of neighbors. Write an essay in which you compare the two essays. How persuasive do you find each writer's groups? Which comes closest to your own experiences with friends or neighbors? Why?

It has been said that cigarettes are the only products that, if used according to the manufacturer's instructions, have a very high chance of killing you.

—Michael Buerk

This very night I am going to leave off tobacco! Surely there must be some other world in which this unconquerable purpose shall be realized.

—Charles Lamb

I gave up smoking four years, two weeks, and five days ago. But who misses it?

—Sandra Scoppettone

Journal Response   Write a short journal entry about smoking or smokers. Have you ever smoked? Have you given up smoking? Do you know anyone who has quit or who struggles to quit? How do you view smokers?

Franklin E. Zimring

A teacher and scholar of the law, Franklin E. Zimring writes soberly about pornography, capital punishment, drug control, and other fiery subjects. He was born in 1942 in Los Angeles, received a B.A. in 1963 from Wayne State University, and earned a doctorate in law in 1967 from the University of Chicago. He taught law at Chicago until 1985 and also directed the Center for Studies in Criminal Justice. Then he moved to the University of California at Berkeley, where he now teaches and also directs the Earl Warren Legal Institute. In addition to numerous articles for scholarly and popular periodicals, Zimring has written a number of distinguished books, among them Confronting Youth Crime *(1978),* Capital Punishment and the American Agenda *(with Gordon Hawkins, 1986),* American Youth Violence *(1998), and* Punishment and Democracy: Three Strikes and You're Out in California *(2000). Calling himself "an involuntary writer," Zimring believes that "to undertake research is to commit oneself to report it."*

Confessions of a Former Smoker

In this essay Zimring reports research somewhat off his usual legal path: an ex-smoker himself, he carefully classifies four kinds of quitters. The essay first appeared in Newsweek *on April 20, 1987.*

Americans can be divided into three groups—smokers, nonsmokers, *1*
and that expanding pack of us who have quit. Those who have never
smoked don't know what they're missing, but former smokers, ex-
smokers, reformed smokers can never forget. We are veterans of a
personal war, linked by that watershed experience of ceasing to
smoke and by the temptation to have just one more cigarette. For almost all of us ex-smokers, smoking continues to play an important
part in our lives. And now that it is being restricted in restaurants
around the country and will be banned in almost all indoor public
places in New York state starting next month, it is vital that
everyone understand the different emotional states cessation of
smoking can cause. I have observed four of them; and in the interest of science I have classified them as those of the zealot, the evangelist, the elect, and the serene. Each day, each category gains new
recruits.

Not all antitobacco zealots are former smokers, but a substantial *2*
number of fire-and-brimstone opponents do come from the ranks of
the reformed. Zealots believe that those who continue to smoke are
degenerates who deserve scorn, not pity, and the penalties that will
deter offensive behavior in public as well. Relations between these
people and those who continue to smoke are strained.

One explanation for the zealot's fervor in seeking to outlaw to- *3*
bacco consumption is his own tenuous hold on abstaining from
smoking. But I think part of the emotional force arises from sheer
envy as he watches and identifies with each lung-filling puff. By making smoking in public a crime, the zealot seeks reassurance that he
will not revert to bad habits; give him strong social penalties and he
won't become a recidivist.

No systematic survey has been done yet, but anecdotal evidence *4*
suggests that a disproportionate number of doctors who have quit
smoking can be found among the fanatics. Just as the most enthusiastic revolutionary tends to make the most enthusiastic counterrevolu-
tionary, many of today's vitriolic zealots include those who had been
deeply committed to tobacco habits.

By contrast, the antismoking evangelist does not condemn smok- *5*
ers. Unlike the zealot, he regards smoking as an easily curable condition, as a social disease, and not a sin. The evangelist spends an
enormous amount of time seeking and preaching to the unconverted.
He argues that kicking the habit is not *that* difficult. After all, *he* did
it; moreover, as he describes it, the benefits of quitting are beyond
measure and the disadvantages are nil.

The hallmark of the evangelist is his insistence that he never 6
misses tobacco. Though he is less hostile to smokers than the zealot,
he is resented more. Friends and loved ones who have been the targets of his preachments frequently greet the resumption of smoking
by the evangelist as an occasion for unmitigated glee.

Among former smokers, the distinctions between the evangelist 7
and the elect are much the same as the differences between proselytiz-
ing and nonproselytizing religious sects. While the evangelists preach
the ease and desirability of abstinence, the elect do not attempt to
convert their friends. They think that virtue is its own reward and
subscribe to the Puritan theory of predestination. Since they have
proved themselves capable of abstaining from tobacco, they are
therefore different from friends and relatives who continue to smoke.
They feel superior, secure that their salvation was foreordained.
These ex-smokers rarely give personal testimony on their conversion.
They rarely speak about their tobacco habits, while evangelists talk
about little else. Of course, active smokers find such bluenosed[1] behavior far less offensive than that of the evangelist or the zealot, yet
they resent the elect simply because they are smug. Their air of self-
satisfaction rarely escapes the notice of those lighting up. For active
smokers, life with a member of the ex-smoking elect is less stormy
than with a zealot or evangelist, but it is subtly oppressive nonetheless.

I have labeled my final category of former smokers the serene. 8
This classification is meant to encourage those who find the other
psychic styles of ex-smokers disagreeable. Serenity is quieter than
zealotry and evangelism, and those who qualify are not as self-
righteous as the elect. The serene ex-smoker accepts himself and also
accepts those around him who continue to smoke. This kind of serenity does not come easily, nor does it seem to be an immediate option
for those who have stopped. Rather it is a goal, an end stage in a
process of development during which some former smokers progress
through one or more of the less-than-positive psychological points en
route. For former smokers, serenity is thus a positive possibility that
exists at the end of the rainbow. But all former smokers cannot reach
that promised land.

What is it that permits some former smokers to become serene? I 9
think the key is self-acceptance and gratitude. The fully mature former

---

[1] *Bluenosed* means straitlaced and moralistic, deriving perhaps from the perceived
character of people from cold northern climates. [Editor's note.]

smoker knows he has the soul of an addict and is grateful for the knowledge. He may sit up front in an airplane, but he knows he belongs in the smoking section in back. He doesn't regret that he quit smoking, nor any of his previous adventures with tobacco. As a former smoker, he is grateful for the experience and memory of craving a cigarette.

Serenity comes from accepting the lessons of one's life. And ex-   10
smokers who have reached this point in their worldview have much to be grateful for. They have learned about the potential and limits of change. In becoming the right kind of former smoker, they developed a healthy sense of self. This former smoker, for one, believes that it is better to crave (one hopes only occasionally) and not to smoke than never to have craved at all. And by accepting that fact, the reformed smoker does not need to excoriate, envy, or disassociate himself from those who continue to smoke.

Meaning

1. What is the author's thesis? What reasons does he give for classifying?
2. In which category does Zimring place himself, and what does he say about this group in relation to the others?
3. Try to guess the meanings of any of the following words that are unfamiliar. Test your guesses in a dictionary, and then come up with a sentence or two using each new word.

watershed (1)	deter (2)	nil (5)
cessation (1)	tenuous (3)	unmitigated (6)
zealot (1)	abstaining (3)	proselytizing (7)
evangelist (1)	recidivist (3)	predestination (7)
elect (1)	anecdotal (4)	foreordained (7)
serene (1)	vitriolic (4)	excoriate (10)
degenerates (2)		

Purpose and Audience

1. What do you suppose Zimring's purpose is? Do you think his classification is really motivated by "the interest of science" (paragraph 1)?
2. Who is Zimring's intended audience? What in the text supports your answer?
3. What do you think of Zimring's categories? Are they complete? convincing? If you know people in these categories, do they match Zimring's description?

Method and Structure

1. How does or doesn't the method of classification lend itself to Zimring's purpose?
2. Summarize each of the groups Zimring identifies (even those he does not discuss in detail). What is their relation to one another?
3. What do you notice about Zimring's organization and the space he devotes to each category? Why would he present his categories at different lengths? Do some of the categories get shortchanged?
4. **Other Methods**   In addition to classification, Zimring uses a number of other methods to convey his ideas effectively: description (Chapter 4), example (Chapter 6), division or analysis (Chapter 7), comparison and contrast (Chapter 10), definition (Chapter 11), and cause-and-effect analysis (Chapter 12). Locate at least one instance of each, and consider how these methods contribute to the discussion as a whole.

Language

1. Consider the labels Zimring devises for each category. What connotations do these words have? How do these words and their connotations contribute to Zimring's overall tone? (If necessary, see p. 52 on connotation and pp. 41–42 on tone.)
2. Zimring uses a lot of "five-dollar words," many of which appear in the vocabulary list. He also avoids use of the first-person *I*. How do his diction and point of view relate to his purpose and to his audience?

Writing Topics

1. **Journal to Essay**   Building on your journal entry about your own experience with smoking or with smokers (p. 192), write a response to Zimring's essay. Does it amuse you? irritate you? something else? Do you find the categories and the descriptions of people fair, given that Zimring is not entirely serious? Does Zimring's essay lead you to sympathize with ex-smokers? Do you object to Zimring's view that smoking (or quitting smoking) is a subject to be written about lightly?
2. Using Zimring's essay as a model, write an essay classifying some group of people with whom you are quite familiar (teachers, bosses, or sales clerks, for example). Sort your subject into classes according to a consistent principle, and make sure to provide plenty of details to clarify the classes you decide on. Write an essay in which you explain your classification.
3. **Cultural Considerations**   Smoking is a battlefield in our culture, with feelings running high on all sides. In a thoughtful, well-reasoned essay, establish your position on smoking in outdoor places, such as outdoor restaurants, sports stadiums, or the street. In expressing your opinion,

consider and acknowledge opposing views—for instance, the smoker's right to enjoy smoke or the nonsmoker's right to enjoy smoke-free air.

4. **Connections**   In his paragraph on page 176, Daniel Goleman writes about addictions as calming, energizing, or fantasy-producing. Based on what you know about smoking, either from experience or from reading about or observing smokers, does it fall into one or more of these categories? Write a brief essay in which you explain what you understand smokers gain from their addiction. In other words, why do people smoke?

Writing with the Method
Classification

Choose one of the following topics, or any other topic they suggest, for an essay developed by classification. The topic you decide on should be something you care about so that classification is a means of communicating an idea, not an end in itself.

PEOPLE

1. People you like (or dislike)
2. Boring people
3. Laundromat users
4. Teachers or students
5. Friends or coworkers
6. Computer users
7. Mothers or fathers

PSYCHOLOGY AND BEHAVIOR

8. Friendships
9. Ways of disciplining children
10. Ways of practicing religion
11. Obsessions
12. Diets
13. Dreams

THINGS

14. Buildings on campus
15. Junk foods
16. Computer games
17. Trucks

SPORTS AND PERFORMANCE

18. Styles of baseball pitching, tennis serving, football tackling, or another sports skill
19. Runners
20. Styles of dance, guitar playing, acting, or another performance art

COMMUNICATIONS MEDIA

21. Young male or female movie stars
22. Talk-show hosts

23. Electronic discussion groups
24. Sports announcers
25. Television programs
26. Radio stations
27. Magazines or newspapers

Writing About the Theme

Sorting Thoughts and Behaviors

1. Max Eastman (p. 175) claims that there are two types of human beings: those who are poetic and those who are practical. Write an essay in which you apply Eastman's classification to Franklin Zimring's categories of reformed smokers (p. 192). Be sure to define each type for your readers and explain why you assign Zimring's groups the way you do. Remember to use evidence from Zimring's essay to support your idea.

2. Jonathan Gould (p. 181), Marion Winik (p. 186), and Franklin Zimring classify and label people with some intention to amuse readers. However, not all labels used to classify people are harmless. Consider, for example, labels based on gender or race or sexual orientation. Write an essay in which you discuss both the benefits and the costs of assigning labels to people — for those using the labels, for those being labeled, and for society as a whole. Give plenty of specific examples.

3. Try adapting the categories of Max Eastman or Daniel Goleman (p. 176), to create your own classification of relationships among people. Using Eastman's scheme, are some relationships poetic and some practical? Using Goleman's scheme, do relationships provide calm or energy or fantasy?

Chapter 9

PROCESS ANALYSIS

Examining Writing Practices

USING THE METHOD

Game rules, car-repair manuals, cookbooks, science textbooks—these and many other familiar works are essentially process analyses. They explain how to do something (play Monopoly, tune a car), how to make something (a carrot cake), or how something happens (how our hormones affect our behavior, how a computer stores and retrieves data). That is, they explain a sequence of actions with a specified result (the **process**) by dividing it into its component steps (the **analysis**). Almost always, the purpose of process analysis is to explain, but sometimes a parallel purpose is to prove something about the process or to evaluate it: to show how easy it is to change a tire, for instance, or to urge dieters to follow a weight-loss plan on the grounds of its safety and effectiveness.

Process analysis overlaps several other methods discussed in this book. The analysis is actually the method examined in Chapter 7—dividing a thing or concept into its elements. And we analyze a process much as we analyze causes and effects (Chapter 12), except that cause-and-effect analysis asks mainly *why* something happens or *why* it has certain results, whereas process analysis asks mainly *how* something happens. Process analysis also overlaps narration (Chapter 5), for the steps of the process are almost always presented in chronological sequence. But narration recounts a unique sequence of events with a unique result, whereas process analysis explains a series of steps with the same predictable result. You might narrate a particularly exciting baseball game, but you would analyze the process— the rules—of any baseball game.

Processes occur in several varieties, including mechanical (a car engine), natural (cell division), psychological (acquisition of sex roles), and political (the electoral process). Process analyses generally fall into one of two types:

- In a **directive** process analysis, you tell how to do or make something: bake a cake, repair a bicycle, negotiate a deal, write a process analysis. You outline the steps in the process completely so that the reader who follows them can achieve the specified result. Generally, you address the reader directly, using the second-person *you* ("You should concentrate on the words that tell you what to do") or the imperative (commanding) mood of verbs ("Add one egg yolk and stir vigorously"). (See also p. 207.)
- In an **explanatory** process analysis, you provide the information necessary for readers to understand the process, but more to satisfy their curiosity than to teach them how to perform it. You may address the reader directly, but the third-person *he, she, it,* and *they* are more common.

Whether directive or explanatory, process analyses usually follow a chronological sequence. Most processes can be divided into phases or stages, and these in turn can be divided into steps. The stages of changing a tire, for instance, may be jacking up the car, removing the flat, putting on the spare, and lowering the car. The steps within, say, jacking up the car may be setting the emergency brake, blocking the other wheels, loosening the bolts, positioning the jack, and raising the car. Following a chronological order, you cover the stages in sequence and, within each stage, cover the steps in sequence.

To ensure that the reader can duplicate the process or understand how it unfolds, you must fully detail each step and specify the reasons for it. In addition, you must be sure that the reader grasps the sequence of steps, their duration, and where they occur. To this end, transitional expressions that signal time and place—such as *after five minutes, meanwhile, to the left,* and *below*—can be invaluable in process analysis.

Though a chronological sequence is usual for process analysis, you may have to interrupt or modify it to suit your material. You may need to pause in the sequence to provide definitions of specialized terms or to explain why a step is necessary or how it relates to the preceding and following steps. In an essay on how to change a tire, for instance, you might stop briefly to explain that the bolts should be slightly loosened *before* the car is jacked up in order to prevent the wheel from spinning afterward.

ANALYZING PROCESSES IN PARAGRAPHS

William Strunk Jr. (1869–1946) and **E. B. White** (1899–1985) met as teacher and student, respectively, at Cornell University. The following paragraph comes from White's 1959 version of Strunk's 1918 *Elements of Style.* The book is now a classic work on the use of the English language. White was also well known for his essays, verse, and children's fiction.

Write in a way that draws the reader's attention to the sense and substance of the writing, rather than to the mood and temper of the author. If the writing is solid and good, the mood and temper of the writer will eventually be revealed and not at the expense of the work. Therefore, the <u>first</u> piece of advice is this: to achieve style, begin by affecting none—that is, place yourself in the background. A careful and honest writer does not need to worry about style. <u>As you become proficient</u> in the use of language, your style will emerge, because you yourself will emerge, and <u>when this happens</u> you will find it increasingly easy to break through the barriers that separate you from other minds, other hearts—which is, of course, the purpose of writing, as well as its principal reward. Fortunately, the act of composition, or creation, disciplines the mind; writing is one way to go about thinking, and the practice and habit of writing not only drain the mind but supply it, too.

Directive process analysis: tells how to achieve style in writing

Process divided into three steps, each signaled with a transition (underlined)

Goals and result of the process

Nora Ephron (born 1941) is a screenwriter, director, essayist, and novelist known for her sharp wit and strong female characters. This paragraph comes from "Revision and Life," an essay first published in 1986 in the *New York Times Book Review*. (When she wrote this paragraph, Ephron composed on a typewriter. Even if she now uses a computer for writing, as seems likely, her process may well remain much the same.)

I learned as a journalist to revise on deadline. I learned to write an article a paragraph at a time— and to turn it in a paragraph at a time—and I arrived at the kind of writing and revising I do, which is basically a kind of typing and retyping. I am a great believer in this technique for the simple reason that I type faster than the wind. What I generally do is to start an article and get as far as I can—sometimes no farther in than a sentence or two—before running out of steam, ripping the piece of paper from the typewriter and starting all over again. I type over and over until I have got the beginning of the piece to the point where I am happy with it. I then am ready to plunge into the body of the article itself. This plunge usually requires something known as a transition. I approach a transition by completely retyping the opening of the article leading up to it in the hope that the ferocious speed of my typing will somehow catapult me into the next section of the piece. This does not work—what in fact catapults me into the next section is a concrete thought about what the next section ought to be about—but until I have the thought the typing keeps me busy, and keeps me from feeling something known as blocked.

Explanatory process analysis: tells how the author drafts and revises

Transitions (underlined) signal sequence

Process divided into steps

Details of the last step

Goal of process

DEVELOPING AN ESSAY BY PROCESS ANALYSIS

Getting Started

You'll find yourself writing process analyses for your courses in school (for instance, explaining how a drug affects brain chemistry), in memos at work (recommending a new procedure for approving cost estimates), or in life outside work (giving written directions to your home). To find a subject when an assignment doesn't make one obvious, examine your interests or hobbies or think of something whose workings you'd like to research in order to understand them better. Explore the subject by listing chronologically all the necessary stages and steps.

While you are exploring your subject, decide on the point of your analysis and express it in a thesis sentence that will guide your writing and tell your readers what to expect. The simplest thesis states what the process is and its basic stages. For instance:

> Building a table is a three-stage process of cutting, assembling, and finishing.

But you can increase your readers' interest in the process by also conveying your reason for writing about it. You might assert that a seemingly difficult process is actually quite simple, or vice versa:

> Changing a tire does not require a mechanic's skill or strength; on the contrary, a ten-year-old child can do it.

> Windsurfing may look easy, but it demands the knowledge of an experienced sailor and the balance of an acrobat.

You might show how the process demonstrates a more general principle:

> The process of getting a bill through Congress illustrates majority rule at work.

Or you might assert that a process is inefficient or unfair:

> The overly complicated registration procedure forces students to waste two days each semester standing in line.

Remember your readers while you are generating ideas and formulating your thesis. Consider how much background information they need, where specialized terms must be defined, and where examples must be given. Especially if you are providing directions, consider what special equipment readers will need, what hitches they may encounter, and what the interim results should be. To build a table, for instance, what tools would readers need? What should they do if the table wobbles even after the corners are braced? What should the table feel like after the first sanding or the first varnishing?

Organizing

Many successful process analyses begin with an overview of the process to which readers can relate each step. In such an introduction you can lead up to your thesis sentence by specifying when or where the process occurs, why it is useful or interesting or controversial, what its result is, and the like. Especially if you are providing directions, you can also use the introduction (perhaps a separate paragraph) to provide essential background information, such as the materials readers will need.

After the introduction, you should present the stages distinctly, perhaps one or two paragraphs for each, and usually in chronological order. Within each stage, also chronologically, you then cover the necessary steps. This chronological sequence helps readers see how a process unfolds or how to perform it themselves. Try not to deviate from it unless you have good reason to—perhaps because your process requires you to group simultaneous steps or your readers need definitions of terms, reasons for steps, connections between separated steps, and other explanations.

A process essay may end simply with the result. But you might conclude with a summary of the major stages, with a comment on the significance or usefulness of the process, or with a recommendation for changing a process you have criticized. For an essay providing directions, you might state the standards by which readers can measure their success or give an idea of how much practice may be necessary to master the process.

Drafting

While drafting your process analysis, concentrate on getting in as many details as you can: every step, how each relates to the one before and after, how each contributes to the result. In revising you can always delete unnecessary details and connective tissue if they seem cumbersome, but in the first draft it's better to overexplain than underexplain.

Drafting a process analysis is a good occasion to practice a straightforward, concise writing style, for clarity is more important than originality of expression. Stick to plain language and uncomplicated sentences. If you want to dress up your style a bit, you can always do so after you have made yourself clear.

Revising and Editing

When you've finished your draft, ask a friend to read it. If you have explained a process, he or she should be able to understand it. If you have given directions, he or she should be able to follow them, or imagine following them. Then examine the draft yourself against the questions on the next page and the information in the box below.

FOCUS ON CONSISTENCY

While drafting a directive process analysis, telling readers how to do something, you may start off with subjects or verbs in one form and then shift to another form because the original choice felt awkward. These shifts occur most often with the subjects *a person* or *one:*

> INCONSISTENT   To keep the car from rolling while changing the tire, *one* should first set the car's emergency brake. Then *one* should block the three other tires with objects like rocks or chunks of wood. Before raising the car, *you* should loosen the bolts of the wheel.

To repair the inconsistency here, you could stick with *one* for the subject (*one should loosen*), but that usually sounds stiff. It's better to revise the earlier subjects to be *you:*

> CONSISTENT   To keep the car from rolling while changing the tire, *you* should set the car's emergency brake. Then *you* should block the three other tires with objects like rocks or chunks of wood. Before raising the car, *you* should loosen the bolts of the wheel.

Sometimes, writers try to avoid *one* or *a person* or even *you* with passive verbs that don't require actors:

> INCONSISTENT   To keep the car from rolling while changing the tire, you should first set the car's emergency brake. Then the other three tires *should be blocked* with objects like rocks or chunks of wood.

But the passive is wordy and potentially confusing, especially when directions should be making it clear who does what. (See p. 48 for more on passive verbs.)

One solution to the problem of inconsistent subjects and passive verbs is to use the imperative, or commanding, form of verbs, in which *you* is understood as the subject:

> CONSISTENT   To keep the car from rolling while changing the tire, first *set* the car's emergency brake. Then *block* the three other tires with objects like rocks or chunks of wood.

- *Have you adhered to a chronological sequence?* Unless there is a compelling and clear reason to use some other arrangement, the stages and steps of your analysis should proceed in chronological order. If you had to depart from that order — to define or explain or to sort out simultaneous steps — the reasons should be clear to your readers.
- *Have you included all necessary steps and omitted any unnecessary digressions?* The explanation should be as complete as possible but not cluttered with information, however interesting, that contributes nothing to the readers' understanding of the process.
- *Have you accurately gauged your readers' need for information?* You don't want to bore readers with explanations and details they don't need. But erring in the other direction is even worse, for your essay will achieve little if readers cannot understand it.
- *Have you shown readers how each step fits into the whole process and relates to the other steps?* If your analysis seems to break down into a multitude of isolated steps, you may need to organize them more clearly into stages.
- *Have you used plenty of informative transitions?* Transitions such as *at the same time* and *on the other side of the machine* indicate when steps start and stop, how long they last, and where they occur. (A list of such expressions appears in the Glossary under *transitions*.) The expressions should be as informative as possible; signals such as *first . . . second . . . third . . . fourteenth* and *next . . . next* do not help indicate movement in space or lapses in time, and they quickly grow tiresome.

A NOTE ON THEMATIC CONNECTIONS

The authors represented in this chapter set out to examine the steps involved in writing, and for that purpose process analysis is the natural choice of method. In a paragraph, William Strunk Jr. and E. B. White direct writers on how to "achieve style" (p. 203). Nora Ephron, in another paragraph, explains how she drafts and revises her work (p. 204). Jeffrey Voccola's essay recommends a procrastination technique for avoiding writing altogether (opposite). Anne Lamott's essay offers tips for getting that crucial first draft down on paper (p. 215). And Garrison Keillor's essay explains how to write a letter, a task that may seem harder than it actually is (p. 221).

Never put off until tomorrow what you can do today. —Proverb

Never do today what you can put off until tomorrow.

—Variation on the proverb

Never put off until tomorrow what you can put off until the day after tomorrow. —Variation on the variation

Journal Response   At one time or another, everyone has put off an important task, finding other things to do instead of focusing on the job. In a paragraph, describe one such event in your life—a time when you missed a crucial deadline because you deliberately avoided preparing for it.

Jeffrey Voccola

Born in 1971, Jeffrey Voccola grew up in Stratford, Connecticut. After graduating from Sacred Heart University, where he majored in business management, Voccola went on to earn an M.S. in English from Southern Connecticut State University in 1998 and an M.F.A. in creative writing from Emerson College in 2001. Voccola teaches fiction workshops in Boston, and his short stories have been published in Whirligig, Beacon Street Review, *and* Folio.

The Art of Procrastination

In the following essay, Voccola explains his special twist on a process that many students know well—procrastinating when faced with an essay assignment. Voccola wrote this piece especially for The Compact Reader.

The assignment is no different from any he has done throughout the semester—another essay, one more link in a chain of grades. What makes this occasion unusual is that days have passed, yet he is still without a topic. He has never experienced writer's block before. He wonders how a person can be expected to write on command, to turn on inspiration like flicking a light switch. He consults his professor, who handles the situation without alarm. She tells him not to force it, that she is certain an idea will come. After all, he's done quite well on his essays in the past. Don't worry, she says. She knows that he is bright enough to get through this. We'll just see about that, he thinks. His professor obviously does not understand the severity of his problem.

Another day closer to his deadline and still nothing, but he is not 2 without options. The plan is simple: avoid the essay at all costs. If by the evening before it's due nothing has come to him, he can simply prattle off the first feeble idea that pops into his head. Then, when his professor sees his inadequate essay, it will be her fault for having had faith in him in the first place.

He need only keep clear of the essay for two more days and the 3 burden will no longer be his. There is an art to true and effective procrastination. The idea is to occupy the mind and body with anything but the impending task. There are many weapons he can choose, but for writer's block of this magnitude he must bring out the heaviest artillery. He must choose a preoccupation so mundane that the task itself is avoided on a daily basis: he must clean.

His dorm room is average sized with a small bathroom leading 4 off to one side. As he surveys the mess in his room, he admits to himself that maybe, just maybe, he should have tried this particular form of procrastination sooner. No matter, the more time consuming the better. He rolls up his sleeves and gets to work. He starts off slowly, gathering dirty laundry off the floor, straightening his bed, stacking books and papers into a neat pile, but eventually things get serious. He begins organizing his CDs, putting each into its respective case, sliding each case into the rack alphabetically. Occasionally, the essay slips into his mind, but only briefly. Though it's winter, he pictures his professor sitting on the beach and sipping a daiquiri while she laughs about the assignment. The image makes him clean harder.

With the first layer of clutter removed from each surface, he sees 5 the room as when he first moved in. He can now walk on the floor without having to step over or around or on objects. His desk is clear enough to write on. He can even use his bed without having to push items onto the floor. With all these surfaces exposed, he sees where the real cleaning needs to take place. The floor could use a good sweeping, the desk, computer, and bookshelves a dusting. There is no turning back.

Unfortunately, the only tools he owns for the job are a dustpan 6 and brush, but he is undaunted. On his hands and knees he sweeps the floor clean, even worming himself under the bed to get the most elusive clumps of dust, carefully flicking the trash into the pan. He grabs a dirty T-shirt to wipe each surface, stirring a cloud of tiny specks into the sunlight that angles through the window. With such mindless work, it is only natural to think about the very thing he is trying to avoid. The essay still looms in the distance. He decides to take things up a notch, out of desperation. He moves to the bathroom.

Making circles of scouring powder in the tub, he imagines the   7
bird's-eye view of a hurricane, the swirl of a galaxy, and wonders if inspiration has arrived without his knowing. With so many possible topics before him, how can he be certain he will pick the right one? He tries not to think of the essay as a whole, but rather just one small portion of it, just the first page. It's easier that way.

And while he rinses the tub something miraculous happens,   8
something unforeseen. He gets an idea. It's a small idea, not strong enough to carry an entire essay, but perhaps one that may lead to others. Nevertheless, it's there, taking up space in his mind. This in no way proves his professor's theory, he tells himself. It is simply a random occurrence, nothing more. Regardless, he writes it down.

Hours have passed since his cleaning began, and he feels the guilt   9
of avoiding his schoolwork return. He knows what he has to do, what step he has to take next. This is a step taken only in the direst of circumstances. And so in a desperate attempt to keep his epic bout with procrastination going, he considers the unthinkable: the toilet.

As far as he knows, there is no right or wrong way to go about   10
cleaning this object. He dumps disinfectant into the bowl until the water turns a rich turquoise blue. He picks up the toilet brush and swirls it in the basin as if it were a witch's caldron. He scrubs, paying careful attention to every tucked-under portion of the bowl. He even cleans down around the base of the toilet, that hard-to-reach area where it touches the floor. He is looking for a shine worthy of a television commercial.

When he flushes the last of the suds away, a chill comes over   11
him. He is done. He knows he must now move onto another form of procrastination since this one has been exhausted. There are many other possibilities: Frisbee, eating, sleeping, hanging out with friends, exercise, watching television, listening to the CDs that are now organized—to name a few—and, if all else fails, reading. Yet he finds himself, for some strange reason, sitting at his computer, the screen clear from Windex, elaborating on his previous idea. He did not plan on doing this, it just happened. He finds himself typing, knowing that if the work becomes at all frustrating he can always exchange it for any number of available distractions. But for now he is focused, attacking his topic, formulating a strong, yet elegant thesis.

He does not dwell on the process that has occurred. He does not 12
analyze the situation. He is so engrossed in his writing, so rapt in his
own words, that he hardly even notices when his buddy steps into the
room and says, "What happened in here?"

Meaning

1. What exactly is *procrastination?* How does the essay explain it? Do you
   think Voccola really believes, as he says in the title, that procrastination
   is an art?
2. In paragraph 11 we learn that "for some strange reason" the student
   finds himself working on the very task he had been avoiding for days.
   What is ironic about this outcome? (If you need a definition of *irony,*
   consult the Glossary.)
3. Given the irony noted above, how would you express Voccola's thesis?
   Is it stated in paragraph 3 ("There is an art to true and effective procrastination. The idea is to occupy the mind and body with anything but the
   impending task.")? Or is it broader?
4. If you are not familiar with any of the following words, try to guess their
   meanings based on their context in Voccola's essay. Check your guesses
   in a dictionary, and then use each new word in a sentence or two.

prattle (2)	undaunted (6)	caldron (10)
impending (3)	direst (9)	engrossed (12)
mundane (3)	bout (9)	rapt (12)

Purpose and Audience

1. Is Voccola actually trying to teach readers how to procrastinate, or do
   you think he has a different purpose in mind?
2. While a student, Voccola composed this essay especially for the student
   readers of *The Compact Reader.* What images and references show that
   he is deliberately trying to appeal to other students?

Method and Structure

1. Why is process analysis a particularly useful method for developing
   Voccola's ideas?
2. Voccola's process analysis details not only the student's actions but also
   his thoughts. Are both necessary? Why, or why not?
3. Point out transitional words and phrases that Voccola uses as guideposts
   in his process analysis.

4. **Other Methods**   Voccola uses specific details to describe the student's thoughts and actions so they are concrete and vivid (Chapter 4). In paragraph 4, for instance, he doesn't just assert that the student cleaned and straightened the room but says specifically what he did with particular objects (laundry, bed, CDs, and so on); and he has the student not just resent his teacher but imagine her at the beach, laughing. Find similarly specific details in the first three sentences of paragraph 6. What do they do that a general statement of the student's actions would not?

Language

1. How seriously does Voccola take his subject? How can you tell?
2. Throughout the essay, Voccola uses the third person ("The student . . . he"), seeming to describe the thoughts and actions of someone besides himself. How would the essay have been different if Voccola had written in the first person ("I")? To see the difference, try rewriting paragraph 1 in the first person.
3. Voccola uses several figures of speech to describe the student's thoughts and actions. For instance, turning on inspiration is "like flicking a light switch" (paragraph 1)—a simile. And to procrastinate the student "bring[s] out the heaviest artillery" (3)—a metaphor. What other figures of speech do you notice in the essay? Which do you find most effective? (See pp. 53–54 if you need help identifying figures of speech.)

Writing Topics

1. **Journal to Essay**   In your journal entry (p. 209) you wrote about a time when you procrastinated instead of tackling an important job. Now write an essay about that event, telling the story in concrete, specific detail, providing insights into your thoughts as well as your actions, making the incident come alive. (Use humor, too, if it comes naturally.) What conclusions can you draw about your experience?
2. Write a process analysis explaining how to do a task that you have struggled with in the past but have now mastered, such as organizing your computer files, painting or wallpapering a room, or cooking a meal. Explain the process step by step so that a reader could follow it, and be sure to cover solutions to problems that may be encountered along the way. For instance, in organizing computer files, how should one label folders and documents? What should one do when a downloaded document gets lost on the computer? How should one manage multiple drafts of a writing assignment?
3. **Cultural Considerations**   In some cultures young adults may not leave their parents' home until they marry and set up their own households. In the United States, in contrast, young adults often expect (and are ex-

pected) to live independently of their parents whether married or not. How would you define *independence* for American young adults? (See Chapter 11 if you need help with definition.) What freedoms does independence entail? What responsibilities? What problems can occur for the newly independent person?

4. **Connections**   Like Voccola, Anne Lamott, in "The Crummy First Draft" (next page), discusses the act of writing. However, unlike Voccola, whose student does not begin the task until he becomes inspired, Lamott advocates starting to write whether you feel like it or not. In an essay, compare and contrast these two authors' methods. Then explain which method is more effective for you, giving examples from various experiences with writing. If neither method works for you, what does?

Getting past "Once upon a time" requires concentration.   —Susan Isaacs

Giving birth to a book is always an abominable torture for me.

—Emile Zola

A man may write at any time, if he will set himself doggedly to it.

—Samuel Johnson

Journal Response   Describe what usually happens when you begin a writing project. Is the blank paper or screen an invitation or an obstacle? Do the words flow freely or haltingly or not at all? Do you feel creative? competent? helpless? tortured?

Anne Lamott

Anne Lamott is a well-known writing teacher and author of novels and best-selling nonfiction, including Bird by Bird *(1994),* Traveling Mercies *(1999), and* All New People *(1999). She has taught at the University of California, Davis, and at writing workshops across the country. Lamott's biweekly diary in the online magazine* Salon, *"Word by Word," which ran from 1996 to 1999, was voted "The Best of the Web" by* Time *magazine.* Bird by Bird with Annie *(1999) documents a year of Lamott's life, which Amazon.com characterizes as that of "your run-of-the-mill recovering alcoholic and drug addict, born-again Christian, left-wing liberal, and single mother who just so happens to have written* New York Times–*best-selling books." Lamott lives in northern California with her son.*

The Crummy First Draft

Lamott's Bird by Bird *is an inspiring and often very funny guide to writing. In this excerpt from the book, Lamott advises others how to begin writing by silencing their noisy inner critics.*

For me and most of the other writers I know, writing is not rapturous. In fact, the only way I can get anything written at all is to write really, really crummy first drafts.   1

The first draft is the child's draft, where you let it all pour out and then let it romp all over the place, knowing that no one is going   2 to see it and that you can shape it later. You just let this childlike part of you channel whatever voices and visions come through and onto the page. If one of the characters wants to say "Well, so what, Mr. Poopy Pants?" you let her. No one is going to see it. If the kid wants to get into really sentimental, weepy, emotional territory, you let him. Just get it all down on paper, because there may be something great in those six crazy pages that you would never have gotten to by more rational, grown-up means. There may be something in the very last line of the very last paragraph on page six that you just love, that is so beautiful or wild that you now know what you're supposed to be writing about, more or less, or in what direction you might go — but there was no way to get to this without first getting through the first five and a half pages.

I used to write food reviews for *California* magazine before it   3 folded. (My writing food reviews had nothing to do with the magazine folding, although every single review did cause a couple of canceled subscriptions. Some readers took umbrage at my comparing mounds of vegetable puree with various ex-presidents' brains.) These reviews always took two days to write. First I'd go to a restaurant several times with a few opinionated, articulate friends in tow. I'd sit there writing down everything anyone said that was at all interesting or funny. Then on the following Monday I'd sit down at my desk with my notes, and try to write the review. Even after I'd been doing this for years, panic would set in. I'd try to write a lead, but instead I'd write a couple of dreadful sentences, XX them out, try again, XX everything out, and then feel despair and worry settle on my chest like an x-ray apron. It's over, I'd think, calmly. I'm not going to be able to get the magic to work this time. I'm ruined. I'm through. I'm toast. Maybe, I'd think, I can get my old job back as a clerk-typist. But probably not. I'd get up and study my teeth in the mirror for a while. Then I'd stop, remember to breathe, make a few phone calls, hit the kitchen and chow down. Eventually I'd go back and sit down at my desk, and sigh for the next ten minutes. Finally I would pick up my one-inch picture frame, stare into it as if for the answer, and every time the answer would come: all I had to do was to write a really crummy first draft of, say, the opening paragraph. And no one was going to see it.

So I'd start writing without reining myself in. It was almost just   4 typing, just making my fingers move. And the writing would be *terrible*. I'd write a lead paragraph that was a whole page, even though the entire review could only be three pages long, and then I'd start writing up descriptions of the food, one dish at a time, bird by bird, and the critics would be sitting on my shoulders, commenting like cartoon characters. They'd be pretending to snore, or rolling their eyes at my overwrought descriptions, no matter how hard I tried to tone those descriptions down, no matter how conscious I was of what a friend said to me gently in my early days of restaurant reviewing. "Annie," she said, "it is just a piece of *chick*en. It is just a bit of *cake*."

But because by then I had been writing for so long, I would eventually let myself trust the process — sort of, more or less. I'd write a first draft that was maybe twice as long as it should be, with a self-indulgent and boring beginning, stupefying descriptions of the meal, lots of quotes from my black-humored friends that made them sound more like the Manson girls[1] than food lovers, and no ending to speak of. The whole thing would be so long and incoherent and hideous that for the rest of the day I'd obsess about getting creamed by a car before I could write a decent second draft. I'd worry that people would read what I'd written and believe that the accident had really been a suicide, that I had panicked because my talent was waning and my mind was shot.

The next day, though, I'd sit down, go through it all with a colored pen, take out everything I possibly could, find a new lead somewhere on the second page, figure out a kicky place to end it, and then write a second draft. It always turned out fine, sometimes even funny and weird and helpful. I'd go over it one more time and mail it in.

Then, a month later, when it was time for another review, the whole process would start again, complete with the fears that people would find my first draft before I could rewrite it.

Almost all good writing begins with terrible first efforts. You need to start somewhere. Start by getting something — anything — down on paper. A friend of mine says that the first draft is the down draft — you just get it down. The second draft is the up draft — you fix it up. You try to say what you have to say more accurately. And the third draft is the dental draft, where you check every tooth, to see if it's loose or cramped or decayed, or even, God help us, healthy.

What I've learned to do when I sit down to work on a crummy first draft is to quiet the voices in my head. First there's the vinegar-

---

[1] The Manson girls were young, troubled members of the cult led by Charles Manson (born 1934). In 1969 Manson and some of his followers were convicted of murder in California. [Editor's note.]

lipped Reader Lady, who says primly, "Well, *that's* not very interesting, is it?" And there's the emaciated German male who writes these Orwellian[2] memos detailing your thought crimes. And there are your parents, agonizing over your lack of loyalty and discretion; and there's William Burroughs,[3] dozing off or shooting up because he finds you as bold and articulate as a houseplant; and so on. And there are also the dogs: let's not forget the dogs, the dogs in their pen who will surely hurtle and snarl their way out if you ever *stop* writing, because writing is, for some of us, the latch that keeps the door of the pen closed, keeps those crazy, ravenous dogs contained. [. . .]

Close your eyes and get quiet for a minute, until the chatter starts   10
up. Then isolate one of the voices and imagine the person speaking as a mouse. Pick it up by the tail and drop it into a mason jar. Then isolate another voice, pick it up by the tail, drop it in the jar. And so on. Drop in any high-maintenance parental units, drop in any contractors, lawyers, colleagues, children, anyone who is whining in your head. Then put the lid on, and watch all these mouse people clawing at the glass, jabbering away, trying to make you feel crummy because you won't do what they want—won't give them more money, won't be more successful, won't see them more often. Then imagine that there is a volume-control button on the bottle. Turn it all the way up for a minute, and listen to the stream of angry, neglected, guilt-mongering voices. Then turn it all the way down and watch the frantic mice lunge at the glass, trying to get to you. Leave it down, and get back to your crummy first draft.

A writer friend of mine suggests opening the jar and shooting   11
them all in the head. But I think he's a little angry, and I'm sure nothing like this would ever occur to you.

Meaning

1. What is Lamott's thesis? Which sentences best convey her main idea?
2. According to Lamott, what role can other people, real or imaginary, play in the writing process? Are they helpful?
3. Review the comment by Lamott's friend (paragraph 8) that "the first draft is the down draft [. . .]. The second draft is the up draft [. . .]. And

[2] In his novel *1984*, the British writer George Orwell (1903–50) depicts a futuristic world in which a totalitarian government controls citizens' behavior and thoughts. [Editor's note.]

[3] The American novelist William Burroughs (1914–97) wrote experimental and often surreal works on drug addiction and other aspects of contemporary life. [Editor's note.]

the third draft is the dental draft [. . .]." What do you think is the difference in the writer's approach and focus at each stage? In what ways, if any, do these stages relate to your own approach to writing?

4. What do you think Lamott means when she says that "writing is, for some of us, the latch that keeps the door of the pen closed, keeps those crazy, ravenous dogs contained" (paragraph 9). What might the dogs and control of them stand for in this image?

5. Some of the following words may be new to you. Before looking them up in a dictionary, try to guess their meanings from their context in Lamott's piece. Then use each new word in a sentence or two.

overwrought (4)	waning (5)	ravenous (9)
self-indulgent (5)	emaciated (9)	guilt-mongering (10)
stupefying (5)	hurtle (9)	

Purpose and Audience

1. What is the purpose of Lamott's piece? To advise inexperienced writers? To relate her own difficulties with writing? Both, or something else? How do you know?

2. Lamott's book *Bird by Bird,* the source of this piece, is subtitled *Some Instructions on Writing and Life.* Who do you believe would find Lamott's advice most useful? Will it be useful to you? Why, or why not?

Method and Structure

1. In paragraph 4 Lamott says that she wrote food reviews "one dish at a time" and "bird by bird" (a metaphor from earlier in her book, meaning one step at a time). What steps does her process analysis outline for overcoming obstacles?

2. Process analysis can be explanatory or directive (see p. 202), and Lamott's piece has good examples of both types. In which paragraphs does Lamott use each type or combine them? What does each type contribute? Is the mixture effective? Why, or why not?

3. What transitions does Lamott use to guide the reader through the steps of her process analysis? Is her use of transitions effective?

4. **Other Methods**   Paragraphs 3–7 narrate Lamott's experience writing food reviews for a magazine. What is the effect of this story?

Language

1. Although trying to be encouraging, Lamott uses many negative adjectives to describe her own first efforts: for example, "terrible" (paragraph 4)

and "incoherent" (5). Find some other examples of negative adjectives. Why do you think Lamott uses so many of them?

2. What is Lamott's tone? How seriously does she take the difficulties facing the writer?

3. Lamott uses several original images, such as the "vinegar-lipped Reader Lady" (paragraph 9). List some images that made a particular impression on you, and explain their effect.

Writing Topics

1. **Journal to Essay**   Review the quotations at the beginning of Lamott's essay and the journal entry you wrote in response to the suggestion there (p. 215). Then write an essay that explains your own writing process (in general or on a specific project) as you progress from idea to final draft. Enliven the process with specific methods and incidents—techniques of procrastination, ripping up draft after draft, listening to and silencing (or not) your own imagined voices, and so on. Try to draw some conclusions about what the writing process means to you.

2. Writing is, of course, only one way to communicate ideas. Other forms of communication can also be difficult: speaking up in class, making a presentation to a group of people, meeting with a teacher, interviewing for a job, making an important telephone call. Write a process analysis in which you first examine an oral encounter that was particularly difficult for you and then offer advice about how best to tackle such a situation.

3. **Cultural Considerations**   We are usually taught to respect our parents and other authority figures, but Lamott advises writers to ignore them while composing. Is her advice justified in your view? Are there times when we can, even should, disregard authority? Write an essay about a time when you felt you could accomplish something only by disregarding the advice of someone you would normally listen to—or, in contrast, when you heeded advice even though it held you back or ignored advice and eventually regretted doing so. How difficult was your action? How did the situation turn out? Looking back, do you believe you did the right thing?

4. **Connections**   Lamott stresses the importance of ignoring the perspectives of others in order to hear your own voice, and in "Salvation" (p. 97), Langston Hughes writes of a powerful experience in which his own experience caused him to break with his peers and his elders. Citing examples from your own experience and, if you like, from Lamott's and Hughes's essays, write an essay that examines our obligations to others versus our obligations to ourselves. When are we justified in following our own paths regardless of what others think, and when are we not?

I am sorry for people who can't write letters. —Elizabeth Bishop

You say you have nothing to write about. Well, you can at least write about that—*or else simply the phrase our elders used to start a letter with: "If you are well, well and good; I am well." That will do for me*—*it is all that matters.* —Pliny the Younger

I would any day as soon kill a pig as write a letter. —Alfred, Lord Tennyson

Journal Response   Letter writing has had a rebirth since the advent of e-mail. How is written correspondence different from telephone conversation? What can make a letter or an e-mail message hard to write? What was the most difficult letter or e-mail you ever had to compose? Write a paragraph or two in which you consider the virtues and difficulties of corresponding.

Garrison Keillor

Garrison Keillor was born in Anoka, Minnesota, in 1942, the third of six children. He went to Anoka High School and then to the University of Minnesota, where he majored in English and worked at the university's newspaper and its radio station. After graduation Keillor went to work for Minnesota Public Radio, quitting every so often to write. In 1974 his live variety show A Prairie Home Companion *debuted on Saturday afternoons, and it continues running today, broadcast on public radio. Keillor has written several story collections, novels, and children's books, including* Happy to Be Here *(1981),* Lake Wobegon Days *(1985),* Leaving Home *(1987), and* Lake Wobegon: Summer 1956 *(2001). "Writing," Keillor says, "is pure entrepreneurship and a great way of life. And then, if you do a radio show every Saturday, you have a built-in social life. So it's a pretty good deal."*

How to Write
a Personal Letter

In the essay reprinted here, which first appeared in the books section of the London Times, *Keillor gives advice and support to letter writers. The impulse that moves us to write letters, he believes, is the same that moves a rock star to sing his heart out in front of 123,000 people: "We want to be known."*

We shy persons need to write a letter now and then, or else we'll dry   1
up and blow away. It's true. And I speak as one who loves to reach
for the phone, dial the number, and talk. The telephone is to shyness
what Hawaii is to February; it's a way out of the woods. *And yet:* a
letter is better.

Such a sweet gift—a piece of handmade writing, in an envelope   2
that is not a bill, sitting in our friend's path when she trudges
home from a long day spent among wahoos and savages, a day our
words will help repair. They don't need to be immortal, just sincere.
She can read them twice and again tomorrow: *You're someone I care
about, Corinne, and think of often, and every time I do, you make
me smile.*

We need to write; otherwise nobody will know who we are. They   3
will have only a vague impression of us as A Nice Person, because,
frankly, we don't shine at conversation, we lack the confidence to thrust
our faces forward and say, "Hi, I'm Heather Hooten; let me tell you
about my week." Mostly we say "Uh-huh" and "Oh really." People
smile and look over our shoulder, looking for someone else to meet.

So a shy person sits down and writes a letter. To be known by   4
another person—to meet and talk freely on the page—to be close
despite distance. To escape from anonymity and be our own sweet
selves and express the music of our souls.

Same thing that moves a giant rock star to sing his heart out in   5
front of 123,000 people moves us to take ballpoint in hand and write
a few lines to our dear Aunt Eleanor. *We want to be known.* We
want her to know that we have fallen in love, that we quit our job,
that we're moving to New York, and we want to say a few things
that might not get said in casual conversation: *Thank you for what
you've meant to me. I am very happy right now.*

The first step in writing letters is to get over the guilt of *not* writ-   6
ing. You don't "owe" anybody a letter. Letters are a gift. The burning shame you feel when you see unanswered mail makes it harder to
pick up a pen and makes for a cheerless letter when you finally do.
I feel bad about not writing, but I've been so busy, etc. Skip this. Few
letters are obligatory, and they are *Thanks for the wonderful gift* and
I am terribly sorry to hear about George's death and *Yes, you're wel-
come to stay with us next month.* Write these promptly if you want
to keep your friends. Don't worry about the others, except love letters, of course. When your true love writes *Dear Light of My Life,
Joy of My Heart, O Lovely Pulsating Core of My Sensate Life,* some
response is called for.

Some of the best letters are tossed off in a burst of inspiration, so   7
keep your writing stuff in one place where you can sit down for a few
minutes and—*Dear Roy, I am in the middle of an essay but thought
I'd drop you a line. Hi to your sweetie too*—dash off a note to a pal.
Envelopes, stamps, address book, everything in a drawer so you can
write fast when the pen is hot.

A blank white 8″ × 11″ sheet can look as big as Montana if the   8
pen's not so hot—try a smaller page and write boldly. Get a pen that
makes a sensuous line, get a comfortable typewriter, a friendly word
processor—whichever feels easy to the hand.

Sit for a few minutes with the blank sheet of paper in front of   9
you, and meditate on the person you will write to, let your friend
come to mind until you can almost see her or him in the room with
you. Remember the last you saw each other and how your friend
looked and what you said and what perhaps was unsaid between
you, and when your friend becomes real to you, start to write.

Write the salutation—*Dear* You—and take a deep breath and   10
plunge in. A simple declarative sentence will do, followed by another
and another. Tell us what you're doing and tell it like you were talking to us. Don't think about grammar, don't think about style, don't
try to write dramatically, just give us your news. Where did you go,
who did you see, what did they say, what do you think?

If you don't know where to begin, start with the present: *I'm sit-*   11
*ting at the kitchen table on a rainy Saturday morning. Everyone is
gone and the house is quiet.* Let your simple description of the present moment lead to something else; let the letter drift gently along.

The toughest letter to crank out is one that is meant to impress,   12
as we all know from writing job applications; if it's hard work to slip
off a letter to a friend, maybe you're trying too hard to be terrific. A
letter is only a report to someone who already likes you for reasons
other than your brilliance. Take it easy.

Don't worry about form. It's not a term paper. When you come   13
to the end of one episode, just start a new paragraph. You can go
from a few lines about the sad state of pro football to the fight with
your mother to your fond memories of Mexico to your cat's urinary-
tract infection to a few thoughts on personal indebtedness and on to
the kitchen sink and what's in it. The more you write, the easier it
gets, and when you have a True True Friend to write to, a *compadre*,
a soul sibling, then it's like driving a car; you just press on the gas.

Don't tear up the page and start over when you write a bad   14
line—try to write your way out of it. Make mistakes and plunge on.

Let the letter cook along and let yourself be bold. Outrage, confusion, love—whatever is in your mind, let it find a way to the page. Writing is a means of discovery, always, and when you come to the end and write *Yours ever* or *Hugs and Kisses,* you'll know something you didn't when you wrote *Dear Pal.*

Probably your friend will put your letter away, and it'll be read   15
again a few years from now—and it will improve with age. And forty years from now, your friend's grandkids will dig it out of the attic and read it, a sweet and precious relic of the ancient eighties that gives them a sudden clear glimpse of you and her and the world we old-timers knew. You will have then created an object of art. Your simple lines about where you went, who you saw, what they said, will speak to those children, and they will feel in their hearts the humanity of our times.

You can't pick up a phone and call the future and tell them about   16
our times. You have to pick up a piece of paper.

Meaning

1. What do you believe is the main idea of this essay? Underline the sentence or phrase that you think best states Keillor's thesis.
2. According to the author, what are some of the main reasons we write letters?
3. Keillor inserts several personal opinions into his essay. Respond to the following comments, explaining why you agree or disagree. "You don't owe anybody a letter. Letters are a gift" (paragraph 6). When writing a letter, "don't think about grammar, don't think about style" (10). "Writing is a means of discovery" (14).
4. If any of the following words are unfamiliar to you, try to determine their meanings from their context in Keillor's essay. Test your guesses using a dictionary, and then make up sentences of your own using the words.

wahoos (2)	obligatory (6)	declarative (10)	relic (15)
anonymity (4)	sensuous (8)	drift (11)	
cheerless (6)	salutation (10)	outrage (14)	

Purpose and Audience

1. What, in your opinion, is the author's principal purpose? Does he most want to inform, instruct, or entertain us? How do you know?
2. Keillor states in his first sentence that he is shy ("we shy persons"). Is he writing only for other shy people, or can anyone benefit from his advice?

3. Did you get any good advice from this essay about how to write a letter or about how to write in general? What lessons will you take away from the essay?

Method and Structure

1. Why do you think the method of process analysis suits Keillor's essay? In addition to telling us how to write a letter, what does Keillor tell us *not* to do?
2. Where does the process analysis part of the essay—the part where Keillor begins to outline the steps involved in letter writing—actually begin, and how are these steps linked together? What does Keillor do before he starts describing this process? Is it useful or distracting to have such a long introduction?
3. Examine the quotations from letters that Keillor includes in italic type. Why do you think he chose these examples? How do they enrich the essay?
4. **Other Methods**   The author draws parallels between letter writing to friends and other kinds of communication, such as telephone calls (paragraphs 1 and 16), job-application letters (12), and term papers (13). What are the chief differences he cites?

Language

1. Keillor's language has enormous variety. For example, he informally refers to his pens and papers as his "writing stuff" (paragraph 7) but then gives instructions on how to write the "salutation" (10), or greeting. List words from the essay that seem to be either quite formal or rather informal. Why do you think Keillor uses such varied vocabulary?
2. Generally, writers are advised to avoid clichés—phrases that have become tired from overuse—but Keillor uses several, such as "music of our souls" (paragraph 4), "Yours ever" (14), and "Light of My Life" (6). Why do you think Keillor uses these familiar phrases?
3. What does the author's language imply about his background, his family and friends, and his sense of humor? Give specific examples.

Writing Topics

1. **Journal to Essay**   Reread your journal entry and the quotations at the beginning of the essay (p. 221). Write an essay about your experiences as a letter writer, including both traditional and e-mail correspondence. Focus on any problems you have had either getting around to writing or

actually drafting a letter. If you find differences between traditional letters and e-mail, try to account for them. How can your writing course and Keillor's essay help you overcome the problems you've had?

2. Using Keillor's essay as a model, write a process analysis in which you explain how to handle some challenge of communicating with others — for example, apologizing, introducing yourself, complaining, or disagreeing. Like Keillor, provide plenty of examples so your readers will have a clear idea of the challenge and its solution.

3. **Cultural Considerations**   Before the invention of the phone, the fax machine, and e-mail, people used to communicate almost exclusively by writing and mailing letters to one another. It seems as if hardly anyone writes letters for the mail anymore; what fills our mailboxes instead is flyers, junk mail, and bills. Write an essay in which you consider what has been gained or lost by modern forms of communication. Use examples from your own life to illustrate the benefits of communicating with others in these different ways.

4. **Connections**   Both Keillor and Anne Lamott, in "The Crummy First Draft" (p. 215), recognize the obstacles that can arise when we put pen to paper. Keillor focuses on letter writing, Lamott on writing in general. What similar advice does each author offer? Are there any points where they seem to disagree? Which essay is more helpful to you in overcoming writers' block? Why?

Writing with the Method

Process Analysis

Choose one of the following topics, or any other topic they suggest, for an essay developed by process analysis. The topic you decide on should be something you care about so that process analysis is a means of communicating an idea, not an end in itself.

TECHNOLOGY AND THE ENVIRONMENT

1. How an engine or other machine works
2. How the Internet works
3. Winterizing a car
4. Setting up a recycling program in a home or an office
5. How solar energy can be converted into electricity

EDUCATION AND CAREER

6. How children learn to dress themselves, play with others, read, or write
7. Reading a newspaper
8. Interviewing for a job
9. Succeeding in biology, history, computer science, or another course
10. Learning a foreign language
11. Coping with a bad boss

ENTERTAINMENT AND HOBBIES

12. Keeping a car in good shape
13. Making a model car, airplane, or ship
14. Performing a magic trick
15. Playing a board or card game, or performing one maneuver in that game
16. Throwing a really *bad* party
17. Playing a sport or a musical instrument
18. Making great chili or some other dish

HEALTH AND APPEARANCE

19. Getting physically fit
20. Climbing a mountain
21. Dieting
22. Cutting or dyeing one's own hair

FAMILY AND FRIENDS

23. Offering constructive criticism to a friend
24. Driving your parents, brother, sister, friend, or roommate crazy
25. Minimizing sibling rivalry
26. Making new friends in a new place

Writing About the Theme

Examining Writing Practices

1. What do the selections by Garrison Keillor (p. 221), Anne Lamott (p. 215), and Jeffrey Voccola (p. 209) tell you about the difficulties involved in producing a piece of written work? According to these authors, why do we resist committing ourselves on paper? Why do we feel insecure about writing? How can we overcome these obstacles? Write an essay exploring the answers to these questions, referring to the authors' ideas and to your own experiences with the writing process.

2. The authors in this chapter explore the writing process, each focusing on a certain kind or element of writing—from William Strunk Jr. and E. B. White on achieving style (p. 203) to Garrison Keillor on letter writing to Anne Lamott on getting a first draft down to Jeffrey Voccola on avoiding writing. Think of kinds of writing that you do in your day-to-day life (such as composing e-mail or notes to your housemates), or that you do less often (such as drafting a letter to the editor or a memo summing up a club meeting). Write an essay describing the difficulties and pitfalls in that particular kind of writing, paying particular attention to how it is different from other forms of writing that you do.

3. Being creative can involve different approaches from different people. Nora Ephron (p. 204) seems to need the structure of a regular routine. Anne Lamott just starts, no matter where she's going. Jeffrey Voccola cannot start until he has exhausted all forms of procrastination. Write an essay exploring your creative process, such as when you make a new dish from a cookbook or craft something in a carpentry workshop or write an essay. What are the steps you usually take when you set out to produce something?

Chapter 10

COMPARISON AND CONTRAST

Distinguishing Ourselves from Others

USING THE METHOD

An insomniac watching late-night television faces a choice between two World War II movies broadcasting at the same time. To make up his mind, he uses the dual method of comparison and contrast.

- **Comparison** shows the similarities between two or more subjects: the similar broadcast times and topics of the two movies force the insomniac to choose between them.
- **Contrast** shows the differences between subjects: the different actors, locations, and reputations of the two movies make it possible for the insomniac to choose one.

As in the example, comparison and contrast usually work together because any subjects that warrant side-by-side examination usually resemble each other in some respects and differ in others. (Since comparison and contrast are so closely related, the terms *comparison* and *compare* will be used from now on to designate both.)

230

You'll generally write a comparison for one of two purposes:

- To explain the similarities and differences between subjects so as to make either or both of them clear.
- To evaluate subjects so as to establish their advantages and disadvantages, strengths and weaknesses.

The explanatory comparison does not take a position on the relative merits of the subjects; the evaluative comparison does, and it usually concludes with a preference or a suggested course of action. In an explanatory comparison you might show how new income-tax laws differ from old laws. In an evaluative comparison on the same subject, you might argue that the old laws were more equitable than the new ones are.

Whether explanatory or evaluative, comparisons treat two or more subjects in the same general class or group: tax laws, religions, attitudes toward marriage, diseases, advertising strategies, diets, contact sports, friends. You may define the class to suit your interest— for instance, you might focus on Tuesday night's television shows, on network news programs, or on old situation comedies. The class likeness ensures that the subjects share enough features to make comparison worthwhile. With subjects from different classes, such as an insect and a tree, the similarities are so few and differences so numerous—and both are so obvious—that explaining them would be pointless.

In writing a comparison, you not only select subjects from the same class but also, using division or analysis, identify the features shared by the subjects. These **points of comparison** are the attributes of the class and thus of the subjects within the class. For instance, the points of comparison for diets may be forbidden foods, allowed foods, speed of weight loss, and nutritional quality; for air pollutants they may be sources and dangers to plants, animals, and humans. These points help you arrange similarities and differences between subjects, and, more important, they ensure direct comparison rather than a random listing of unrelated characteristics.

In an effective comparison a thesis or controlling idea governs the choice of class, points of comparison, and specific similarities and differences, while also making the comparison worthwhile for the reader. The thesis of an evaluative comparison generally emerges naturally because it coincides with the writer's purpose of supporting a preference for one subject over another:

THESIS SENTENCE (EVALUATION)   The two diets result in similarly rapid weight loss, but Harris's requires much more self-discipline and is nutritionally much riskier than Marconi's.

In an explanatory comparison, however, the thesis does more than merely reflect the general purpose of explaining. It should go beyond the obvious and begin to identify the points of comparison. For example:

TENTATIVE THESIS SENTENCE (EXPLANATION)   Rugby and American football are the same in some respects and different in others.

REVISED THESIS SENTENCE (EXPLANATION)   Though rugby requires less strength and more stamina than American football, the two games are very much alike in their rules and strategies.

The examples above suggest other decisions you must make when writing a comparison:

- Should the subjects be treated in equal detail, or should one be emphasized over the others? Generally, give the subjects equal emphasis when they are equally familiar or are being evaluated (as the diets are in the example above). Stress one subject over the others when it is less familiar (as rugby is in this country).
- Should the essay focus on similarities or differences, or both? Generally, stress them equally when all the points of comparison are equally familiar or important. Stress the differences between subjects usually considered similar (such as diets) or the similarities between subjects usually considered different (such as rugby and American football).

With two or more subjects, several points of comparison, many similarities and differences, and a particular emphasis, comparison clearly requires a firm organizational hand. You have two options for arranging a comparison:

- **Subject-by-subject,** in which you group the points of comparison under each subject so that the *subjects* are covered one at a time.
- **Point-by-point,** in which you group the subjects under each point of comparison so that the *points* are covered one at a time.

The following brief outlines illustrate the different arrangements as they might be applied to diets:

Subject-by-subject	*Point-by-point*
Harris's diet	Speed of weight loss
Speed of weight loss	Harris's diet
Required self-discipline	Marconi's diet
Nutritional risk	Required self-discipline
Marconi's diet	Harris's diet
Speed of weight loss	Marconi's diet
Required self-discipline	Nutritional risk
Nutritional risk	Harris's diet
	Marconi's diet

Since the subject-by-subject arrangement presents each subject as a coherent unit, it is particularly useful for comparing impressions of subjects: the dissimilar characters of two friends, for instance. However, covering the subjects one at a time can break an essay into discrete pieces and strain readers' memories, so this arrangement is usually confined to essays that are short or that compare several subjects briefly. For longer papers requiring precise treatment of the individual points of comparison — say, an evaluation of two proposals for a new student-aid policy — the point-by-point arrangement is more useful. Its chief disadvantage is that the reader can get lost in details and fail to see any subject as a whole. Because each arrangement has its strengths and weaknesses, you may sometimes combine the two in a single work, using the divided arrangement to introduce or summarize overall impressions of the subjects and using the alternating arrangement to deal specifically with the points of comparison

ANALYZING COMPARISON AND CONTRAST IN PARAGRAPHS

Michael Dorris (1945–97) was a fiction and nonfiction writer who, as a member of the Modoc tribe, explored Native American issues and experiences. The following paragraph comes from "Noble Savages? We'll Drink to That," first published in the *New York Times* in April 1992.

For centuries, flesh and blood Indians have been as-signed the role of a popular-culture metaphor. Today, their evocation instantly connotes fuzzy images of Nature, the Past, Plight, or Summer Camp. War-

Subject-by-subject organization

bonneted <u>apparitions</u> pasted to football helmets or baseball caps act as opaque, impermeable <u>curtains</u>, solid walls of <u>white noise</u> that for many citizens block or distort all vision of the nearly two million <u>Native Americans today</u>. And why not? <u>Such honoring</u> relegates <u>Indians</u> to the long ago and <u>thus</u> makes them magically disappear from public consciousness and conscience. What do the 300 federally recognized <u>tribes</u>, and <u>their</u> various complicated treaties governing land rights and protections, <u>their</u> crippling teenage suicide rates, <u>their</u> manifold health problems <u>have in common with</u> jolly (or menacing) cartoon caricatures, wistful braves, or raven-tressed Mazola girls?

1. The image in popular culture

Comparison clarified by transitions (underlined once) and repetition and restatement (underlined twice) (see p. 238–39)

2. The reality of Native American life

Suzanne Britt (born 1946) has written for many newspapers and magazines, and she has also published several collections of essays. The following paragraph comes from "That Lean and Hungry Look," first published in 1978 in the "My Turn" column of *Newsweek on Campus*.

Some people say the business about the jolly <u>fat person</u> is a myth, that all of us <u>chubbies</u> are neurotic, sick, sad people. I <u>disagree</u>. <u>Fat people</u> may not be chortling all day long, <u>but</u> they're a hell of a lot *nicer* than the wizened and shriveled. <u>Thin people</u> turn surly, mean, and hard at a young age because <u>they</u> never learn the value of a hot-fudge sundae for easing tension. <u>Thin people</u> don't like gooey soft things because <u>they</u> themselves are neither gooey nor soft. <u>They</u> are crunchy and dull, like carrots. <u>They</u> go straight to the heart of the matter <u>while</u> <u>fat people</u> let things stay all blurry and hazy and vague, the way things actually are. <u>Thin people</u> want to face the truth. <u>Fat people</u> know there is no truth. One of my <u>thin</u> friends is always staring at complex, unsolvable problems and saying, "The key thing is . . ." <u>Fat people</u> never say <u>that</u>. <u>They</u> know there isn't any such thing as the key thing about anything.

Point-by-point comparison

1. Personality

2. Food preferences (related to personality)

3. Outlook

Comparison clarified by transitions (underlined once) and repetition and restatement (underlined twice) (see p. 238–39)

DEVELOPING AN ESSAY
BY COMPARISON AND CONTRAST

Getting Started

Whenever you observe similarities or differences between two or more members of the same general class—activities, people, ideas, things, places—you have a possible subject for comparison and contrast. Just be sure that the subjects are worth comparing and that you can do the job in the space and time allowed. For instance, if you have a week to complete a three-page paper, don't try to show all the similarities and differences between country-and-western music and rhythm-and-blues. The effort can only frustrate you and irritate your readers. Instead, limit the subjects to a manageable size—for instance, the lyrics of a representative song in each type of music—so that you can develop the comparisons completely and specifically.

To generate ideas for a comparison, explore each subject separately to pick out its characteristics, and then explore the subjects together to see what characteristics one suggests for the other. Look for points of comparison. Early on, you can use division or analysis (Chapter 7) to identify points of comparison by breaking the subjects' general class into its elements. A song lyric, for instance, could be divided into story line or plot, basic emotion, and special language such as dialect or slang. After you have explored your subjects fully, you can use classification (Chapter 8) to group your characteristics under the points of comparison. For instance, you might classify characteristics of two proposals for a new student-aid policy into qualifications for aid, minimum and maximum amounts to be made available, and repayment terms.

While you are shaping your ideas, you should begin formulating your controlling idea, your thesis. As discussed on pages 231–32, the thesis should reflect your answers to these questions:

- Do the ideas suggest an explanatory or evaluative comparison?
- If explanatory, what point will the comparison make so that it does not merely recite the obvious?
- If evaluative, what preference or recommendation will you express?
- Will you emphasize both subjects equally or stress one over the other?
- Will you emphasize differences or similarities, or both?

As you gain increasing control over your material, consider also the needs of your readers:

- Do they know your subjects well, or should you take special care to explain one or both of them?
- Will your readers be equally interested in similarities and differences, or will they find one more enlightening than the other?
- If your essay is evaluative, are your readers likely to be biased against your preference? If so, you will need to support your case with plenty of specific reasons.

Most readers know intuitively how a comparison works, so they will expect you to balance your comparison feature for feature. In other words, all the features you mention for the first subject should be mentioned as well for the second, and any features not mentioned for the first subject should not suddenly materialize for the second.

Organizing

Your readers' needs and expectations can also help you plan your essay's organization. An effective introduction to a comparison essay often provides some context for readers — the situation that prompts the comparison, for instance, or the need for the comparison. Placing your thesis sentence in the introduction also informs readers of your purpose and point, and it may help keep you focused while you write.

For the body of the essay, choose the arrangement that will present your material most clearly and effectively. Remember that the subject-by-subject arrangement suits brief essays comparing dominant impressions of the subjects, whereas the point-by-point arrangement suits longer essays requiring emphasis on the individual points of comparison. If you are torn between the two — wanting both to sum up each subject and to show the two side by side — then a combined arrangement may be your wisest choice.

A rough outline like the models on page 233 can help you plan the basic arrangement of your essay and also the order of the subjects and points of comparison. If your subjects are equally familiar to your readers and equally important to you, then it may not matter which subject you treat first, even in a subject-by-subject arrangement. But if one subject is less familiar or if you favor one, then that one should probably come second. You can also arrange the points themselves to reflect their importance and your readers' knowledge: from least to most significant or complex, from most to least familiar. Be sure to use the same order for both subjects.

The conclusion to a comparison essay can help readers see the whole picture: the chief similarities and differences between two subjects compared in a divided arrangement, or the chief characteristics of subjects compared in an alternating arrangement. In addition, you may want to comment on the significance of your comparison, advise readers on how they can use the information you have provided, or recommend a specific course of action for them to follow. As with all other methods of development, the choice of conclusion should reflect the impression you want to leave with readers.

Drafting

Drafting your essay gives you the chance to spell out your comparison so that it supports your thesis or, if your thesis is still tentative, to find your idea by writing into it. You can use paragraphs to help manage the comparison as it unfolds:

- In a subject-by-subject arrangement, if you devote two paragraphs to the first subject, try to do the same for the second subject. For both subjects, try to cover the points of comparison in the same order and group the same ones in paragraphs.
- In a point-by-point arrangement, balance the paragraphs as you move back and forth between subjects. If you treat several points of comparison for the first subject in one paragraph, do the same for the second subject. If you apply a single point of comparison to both subjects in one paragraph, do the same for the next point of comparison.

This way of drafting will help you achieve balance in your comparison and see where you may need more information to flesh out your subjects and your points. If the finished draft seems to march too rigidly in its pattern, you can always loosen things up when revising (see below).

Revising and Editing

When you are revising and editing your draft, use the following questions and the information in the box to be certain that your essay meets the principal requirements of the comparative method.

- *Are your subjects drawn from the same class?* The subjects must have notable differences *and* notable similarities to make comparison worthwhile—though, of course, you may stress one group over the other.
- *Does your essay have a clear purpose and say something significant about the subject?* Your purpose of explaining or evaluating and the point you are making should be evident in your thesis *and* throughout the essay. A vague, pointless comparison will quickly bore readers.
- *Do you apply all points of comparison to both subjects?* Even if you emphasize one subject, the two subjects must match feature for feature. An unmatched comparison may leave readers with unanswered questions or weaken their confidence in your authority.
- *Does the pattern of comparison suit readers' needs and the complexity of the material?* Although readers will appreciate a clear organization and roughly equal treatment of your subjects and points of comparison, they will also appreciate some variety in the way you move back and forth. You needn't devote a sentence to each point, first for one subject and then for the other, or alternate subjects sentence by sentence through several paragraphs. Instead, you might write a single sentence on one point or subject but four sentences on the other—if that's what your information requires.

FOCUS ON PARAGRAPH COHERENCE

With several points of comparison and alternating subjects, a comparison will be easy for your readers to follow only if you frequently clarify what subject and what point you are discussing. To help readers keep your comparison straight, you can rely on the techniques of paragraph coherence discussed on page 389, especially on transitions and on repetition or restatement:

- Transitions like those listed on page 389 act as signposts to tell readers where you, and they, are headed. Some transitions indicate that you are shifting between subjects, either finding resemblances between them (*also, like, likewise, similarly*) or finding differences (*but, however, in contrast, instead, unlike, whereas, yet*). Other transitions indicate that you are moving on to a new point (*in addition, also, furthermore, moreover*).

> Traditional public schools depend for financing, of course, on tax receipts and on other public money like bonds, and as a result they generally open enrollment to all students without regard to background, skills, or special needs. Magnet schools are *similarly* funded by public money. *But* they often require prospective students to pass a test or other hurdle for admission. *In addition, whereas* traditional public schools usually offer a general curriculum, magnet schools often focus on a specialized program emphasizing an area of knowledge or competence, such as science and technology or performing arts.

- Repetition or restatement of labels for your subjects or for your points of comparison makes clear the topic of each sentence. In the passage above, the repetitions of *traditional public schools* and *magnet schools* and the substitution of *they* for each clarify the subjects of the comparison. The restatements of *financing/public money/funded, enrollment/admission,* and *curriculum/program* clarify the points of comparison.

See the sample paragraphs on pages 233–34 for additional examples of these two techniques.

A NOTE ON THEMATIC CONNECTIONS

Each writer represented in this chapter uses comparison and contrast to show the similarities or the differences between individuals or groups. The paragraph by Michael Dorris contrasts media images of Native Americans with the group's reality (p. 233). Another paragraph, by Suzanne Britt (p. 234), takes a humorous look at the different personalities connected to different body types. Russell Baker describes a young boy searching for his own destiny while grappling with the expectations of a strict mother (next page), while Reena Nadler writes about carving out an identity different from that of her twin sister (p. 251). And the essay by Leanita McClain distinguishes the reality of being a middle-class African American from the misperceptions of both blacks and whites (p. 258).

*In youth our most bitter disappointments, our brightest hopes and
ambitions, are known only to ourselves.*   —Elizabeth Cady Stanton

*Ambition may be all right, but it sure can get a fellow into a lot of hard
work.*   —Popular saying

*Everybody must learn this lesson somewhere—that it costs something to be
what you are.*   —Shirley Abbott

Journal Response   When you were a child, adults probably asked you,
"What do you want to be when you grow up?" What did you reply? Write a
journal entry in which you describe your childhood ambitions.

Russell Baker

*Russell Baker was born in 1925 in Loudoun County, Virginia. He moved
quickly into journalism after attending Johns Hopkins University. In 1947 he
began working for the* Baltimore Sun; *later he moved to the* New York
Times, *where he began writing his column, "Observer," in 1962. Baker is a
two-time Pulitzer Prize winner, once in 1989 for his newspaper commentary
and again in 1982 for his memoir* Growing Up. *He has published many other
books as well, including* An American in Washington (1961), Poor Russell's
Almanac (1971), *and* The Good Times (1989). *He currently hosts the public
television series* Masterpiece Theatre. *He is a fellow of the American Academy of Arts and Sciences and a member of the American Academy of Arts
and Letters. Baker retired from the* New York Times *in 1998 and lives in
Leesburg, Virginia.*

Gumption

In this essay from Growing Up, *Baker reminisces about his failure in childhood to "make something" of himself, at least by his mother's light. The vo-
cation of writer sounded more agreeable to the eight-year-old Baker than the
role of newspaper salesman, since "what writers did couldn't even be classified as work."*

I began working in journalism when I was eight years old. It was my   *1*
mother's idea. She wanted me to "make something" of myself and,

after a levelheaded appraisal of my strengths, decided I had better start young if I was to have any chance of keeping up with the competition.

The flaw in my character which she had already spotted was the 2 lack of "gumption." My idea of a perfect afternoon was lying in front of the radio rereading my favorite Big Little Book *Dick Tracy Meets Stooge Viller*. My mother despised inactivity. Seeing me having a good time in repose, she was powerless to hide her disgust. "You've got no more gumption than a bump on a log," she said. "Get out in the kitchen and help Doris do those dirty dishes."

My sister Doris, though two years younger than I, had enough 3 gumption for a dozen people. She positively enjoyed washing dishes, making beds, and cleaning the house. When she was only seven she could carry a piece of short-weighted cheese back to the A&P, threaten the manager with legal action, and come back triumphantly with the full quarter-pound we'd paid for and a few extra ounces thrown in for forgiveness. Doris could have made something of herself if she hadn't been a girl. Because of this defect, however, the best she could hope for was a career as a nurse or schoolteacher, the only work that capable females were considered up to in those days.

This must have saddened my mother, this twist of fate that had 4 allocated all the gumption to the daughter and left her with a son who was content with Dick Tracy and Stooge Viller. If disappointed, though, she wasted no energy on self-pity. She would make me make something of myself whether I wanted to or not. "The Lord helps those who help themselves," she said. That was the way her mind worked.

She was realistic about the difficulty. Having sized up the mate- 5 rial the Lord had given her to mold, she didn't overestimate what she could do with it. She didn't insist that I grow up to be president of the United States.

Fifty years ago parents still asked boys if they wanted to grow up 6 to be president, and asked it not jokingly but seriously. Many parents who were hardly more than paupers still believed their sons could do it. Abraham Lincoln had done it. We were only sixty-five years from Lincoln. Many a grandfather who walked among us could remember Lincoln's time. Men of grandfatherly age were the worst for asking if you wanted to grow up to be president. A surprising number of little boys said yes and meant it.

I was asked many times myself. No, I would say, I didn't want to 7 grow up to be president. My mother was present during one of these interrogations. An elderly uncle, having posed the usual question and exposed my lack of interest in the presidency, asked, "Well, what *do* you want to be when you grow up?"

I loved to pick through trash piles and collect empty bottles, tin 8 cans with pretty labels, and discarded magazines. The most desirable job on earth sprang instantly to mind. "I want to be a garbage man," I said.

My uncle smiled, but my mother had seen the first distressing evi- 9 dence of a bump budding on a log. "Have a little gumption, Russell," she said. Her calling me Russell was a signal of unhappiness. When she approved of me I was always "Buddy."

When I turned eight years old she decided that the job of starting 10 me on the road toward making something of myself could no longer be safely delayed. "Buddy," she said one day, "I want you to come home right after school this afternoon. Somebody's coming and I want you to meet him."

When I burst in that afternoon she was in conference in the par- 11 lor with an executive of the Curtis Publishing Company. She introduced me. He bent low from the waist and shook my hand. Was it true as my mother had told him, he asked, that I longed for the opportunity to conquer the world of business?

My mother replied that I was blessed with a rare determination 12 to make something of myself.

"That's right," I whispered. 13

"But have you got the grit, the character, the never-say-quit spirit 14 it takes to succeed in business?"

My mother said I certainly did. 15

"That's right," I said. 16

He eyed me silently for a long pause, as though weighing whether 17 I could be trusted to keep his confidence, then spoke man-to-man. Before taking a crucial step, he said, he wanted to advise me that working for the Curtis Publishing Company placed enormous responsibility on a young man. It was one of the great companies of America. Perhaps the greatest publishing house in the world. I had heard, no doubt, of the *Saturday Evening Post*?

Heard of it? My mother said that everyone in our house had 18 heard of the *Saturday Evening Post* and that I, in fact, read it with religious devotion.

Then doubtless, he said, we were also familiar with those two 19 monthly pillars of the magazine world, the *Ladies Home Journal* and the *Country Gentleman*.

Indeed we were familiar with them, said my mother.   20

Representing the *Saturday Evening Post* was one of the weighti- 21 est honors that could be bestowed in the world of business, he said. He was personally proud of being a part of that great corporation.

My mother said he had every right to be.   22

Again he studied me as though debating whether I was worthy of 23 a knighthood. Finally: "Are you trustworthy?"

My mother said I was the soul of honesty.   24

"That's right," I said.   25

The caller smiled for the first time. He told me I was a lucky 26 young man. He admired my spunk. Too many young men thought life was all play. Those young men would not go far in this world. Only a young man willing to work and save and keep his face washed and his hair neatly combed could hope to come out on top in a world such as ours. Did I truly and sincerely believe that I was such a young man?

"He certainly does," said my mother.   27

"That's right," I said.   28

He said he had been so impressed by what he had seen of me that 29 he was going to make me a representative of the Curtis Publishing Company. On the following Tuesday, he said, thirty freshly printed copies of the *Saturday Evening Post* would be delivered at our door. I would place these magazines, still damp with the ink of the presses, in a handsome canvas bag, sling it over my shoulder, and set forth through the streets to bring the best in journalism, fiction, and cartoons to the American public.

He had brought the canvas bag with him. He presented it with a 30 reverence fit for a chasuble. He showed me how to drape the sling over my left shoulder and across the chest so that the pouch lay easily accessible to my right hand, allowing the best in journalism, fiction, and cartoons to be swiftly extracted and sold to a citizenry whose happiness and security depended upon us soldiers of the free press.

The following Tuesday I raced home from school, put the canvas 31 bag over my shoulder, dumped the magazines in, and, tilting to the left to balance their weight on my right hip, embarked on the highway of journalism.

We lived in Belleville, New Jersey, a commuter town at the 32 northern fringe of Newark. It was 1932, the bleakest year of the Depression. My father had died two years before, leaving us with a few pieces of Sears, Roebuck furniture and not much else, and my mother had taken Doris and me to live with one of her younger brothers. This was my Uncle Allen. Uncle Allen had made something of himself by 1932. As salesman for a soft-drink bottler in Newark, he had an income of $30 a week; wore pearl-gray spats[1], detachable collars, and a three-piece suit; was happily married; and took in threadbare relatives.

With my load of magazines I headed toward Belleville Avenue. 33 That's where the people were. There were two filling stations at the intersection with Union Avenue, as well as an A&P, a fruit stand, a bakery, a barbershop, Zuccarelli's drugstore, and a diner shaped like a railroad car. For several hours I made myself highly visible, shifting positions now and then from corner to corner, from shop window to shop window, to make sure everyone could see the heavy black lettering on the canvas bag that said THE SATURDAY EVENING POST. When the angle of the light indicated that it was suppertime, I walked back to the house.

"How many did you sell, Buddy?" my mother asked. 34

"None." 35

"Where did you go?" 36

"The corner of Belleville and Union Avenues." 37

"What did you do?" 38

"Stood on the corner waiting for somebody to buy a *Saturday* 39 *Evening Post.*"

"You just stood there?" 40

"Didn't sell a single one." 41

"For God's sake, Russell!" 42

Uncle Allen intervened. "I've been thinking about it for some 43 time," he said, "and I've about decided to take the *Post* regularly. Put me down as a regular customer." And I handed him a magazine and he paid me a nickel. It was the first nickel I earned.

Afterwards my mother instructed me in salesmanship. I would 44 have to ring doorbells, address adults with charming self-confidence, and break down resistance with a sales talk pointing out that no one, no matter how poor, could afford to be without the *Saturday Evening Post* in the home.

I told my mother I'd changed my mind about wanting to succeed 45 in the magazine business.

---

[1] Once-fashionable cloth or leather coverings for the ankle and upper shoe, often worn in wet weather. [Editor's note.]

"If you think I'm going to raise a good-for-nothing," she replied, 46 "you've got another thing coming." She told me to hit the streets with the canvas bag and start ringing doorbells the instant school was out the next day. When I objected that I didn't feel any aptitude for salesmanship, she asked how I'd like to lend her my leather belt so she could whack some sense into me. I bowed to superior will and entered journalism with a heavy heart.

My mother and I had fought this battle almost as long as I could 47 remember. It probably started even before memory began, when I was a country child in northern Virginia and my mother, dissatisfied with my father's plain workman's life, determined that I would not grow up like him and his people, with calluses on their hands, overalls on their backs, and fourth-grade educations in their heads. She had fancier ideas of life's possibilities. Introducing me to the *Saturday Evening Post*, she was trying to wean me as early as possible from my father's world where men left with their lunch pails at sunup, worked with their hands until the grime ate into the pores, and died with a few sticks of mail-order furniture as their legacy. In my mother's vision of the better life there were desks and white collars, well-pressed suits, evenings of reading and lively talk, and perhaps — if a man were very, very lucky and hit the jackpot, really made something important of himself — perhaps there might be a fantastic salary of $5,000 a year to support a big house and a Buick with a rumble seat[2] and a vacation in Atlantic City.

And so I set forth with my sack of magazines. I was afraid of the 48 dogs that snarled behind the doors of potential buyers. I was timid about ringing the doorbells of strangers, relieved when no one came to the door, and scared when someone did. Despite my mother's instructions, I could not deliver an engaging sales pitch. When a door opened I simply asked, "Want to buy a *Saturday Evening Post*?" In Belleville few persons did. It was a town of thirty thousand people, and most weeks I rang a fair majority of its doorbells. But I rarely sold my thirty copies. Some weeks I canvassed the entire town for six days and still had four or five unsold magazines on Monday evening; then I dreaded the coming of Tuesday morning, when a batch of thirty fresh *Saturday Evening Post*s was due at the front door.

"Better get out there and sell the rest of those magazines 49 tonight," my mother would say.

[2] An open-air seat in the rear of early model cars. [Editor's note.]

I usually posted myself then at a busy intersection where a traffic 50
light controlled commuter flow from Newark. When the light turned
red I stood on the curb and shouted my sales pitch at the motorists.

"Want to buy a *Saturday Evening Post?*" 51

One rainy night when car windows were sealed against me I 52
came back soaked and with not a single sale to report. My mother
beckoned to Doris.

"Go back down there with Buddy and show him how to sell 53
these magazines," she said.

Brimming with zest, Doris, who was then seven years old, re- 54
turned with me to the corner. She took a magazine from the bag, and
when the light turned red she strode to the nearest car and banged
her small fist against the closed window. The driver, probably
startled at what he took to be a midget assaulting his car, lowered
the window to stare, and Doris thrust a *Saturday Evening Post*
at him.

"You need this magazine," she piped, "and it only costs a 55
nickel."

Her salesmanship was irresistible. Before the light changed half a 56
dozen times she disposed of the entire batch. I didn't feel humiliated.
To the contrary. I was so happy I decided to give her a treat. Leading
her to the vegetable store on Belleville Avenue, I bought three apples,
which cost a nickel, and gave her one.

"You shouldn't waste your money," she said. 57

"Eat your apple." I bit into mine. 58

"You shouldn't eat before supper," she said. "It'll spoil your ap- 59
petite."

Back at the house that evening, she dutifully reported me for 60
wasting a nickel. Instead of a scolding, I was rewarded with a pat on
the back for having the good sense to buy fruit instead of candy. My
mother reached into her bottomless supply of maxims and told Doris,
"An apple a day keeps the doctor away."

By the time I was ten I had learned all my mother's maxims by 61
heart. Asking to stay up past normal bedtime, I knew the refusal
would be explained with, "Early to bed and early to rise, makes a
man healthy, wealthy, and wise." If I whimpered about having to get
up early in the morning, I could depend on her to say, "The early
bird gets the worm."

The one I most despised was, "If at first you don't succeed, try, try 62
again." This was the battle cry with which she constantly sent me back

into the hopeless struggle whenever I moaned that I had rung every doorbell in town and knew there wasn't a single potential buyer left in Belleville that week. After listening to my explanation, she handed me the canvas bag and said, "If at first you don't succeed . . ."

Three years in that job, which I would gladly have quit after the 　63 first day except for her insistence, produced at least one valuable result. My mother finally concluded that I would never make something of myself by pursuing a life in business and started considering careers that demanded less competitive zeal.

One evening when I was eleven I brought home a short "compo- 　64 sition" on my summer vacation which the teacher had graded with an A. Reading it with her own schoolteacher's eye, my mother agreed that it was top-drawer seventh grade prose and complimented me. Nothing more was said about it immediately, but a new idea had taken life in her mind. Halfway through supper she suddenly interrupted the conversation.

"Buddy," she said, "maybe you could be a writer." 　65

I clasped the idea to my heart. I had never met a writer, had shown 　66 no previous urge to write, and hadn't a notion how to become a writer, but I loved stories and thought that making up stories must surely be almost as much fun as reading them. Best of all, though, and what really gladdened my heart, was the ease of a writer's life. Writers did not have to trudge through the town peddling from canvas bags, defending themselves against angry dogs, being rejected by surly strangers. Writers did not have to ring doorbells. So far as I could make out, what writers did couldn't even be classified as work.

I was enchanted. Writers didn't have to have any gumption at all. 　67 I did not dare tell anybody for fear of being laughed at in the schoolyard, but secretly I decided that what I'd like to be when I grew up was a writer.

Meaning

1. Throughout this essay, Baker refers to his lack of gumption as a child. What is *gumption*? In what ways does the young Baker exhibit a lack of gumption? How did this "flaw" contribute to Baker's becoming a writer?
2. Why does Baker's mother want him to be more ambitious? How does she try to encourage him to make something of himself? Is she ultimately successful?

3. What is Doris's "defect" (paragraph 3)? Does Baker really believe that this is a shortcoming in his sister? How can you tell?
4. Consider the economic climate of the times and the Baker family's financial circumstances. Why are these important factors in the story Baker tells?
5. If any of the words below are new to you, try to guess their meanings from their context in Baker's essay. Check your guesses against a dictionary's definitions, and then try to use each word in a sentence or two of your own.

appraisal (1)	chasuble (30)	legacy (47)
repose (2)	threadbare (32)	maxims (60)
mold (5)	aptitude (46)	whimpered (61)
paupers (6)	calluses (47)	trudge (66)
bestowed (21)	wean (47)	surly (66)
spunk (26)		

Purpose and Audience

1. What elements of Baker's story seem a bit exaggerated? How do these exaggerations serve Baker's apparent intentions in writing about his childhood?
2. What lesson might readers take from Baker's story?
3. Writing about life in the 1930s, Baker makes period references that might not be familiar to younger readers—the book *Dick Tracy Meets Stooge Viller*, for example, and the *Saturday Evening Post* magazine. Does he seem to assume that readers will understand such references? Can readers still enjoy the essay without being familiar with the period?

Method and Structure

1. Baker's essay is based primarily on contrasts between people who have gumption and those who don't. Point out the specific examples he uses to develop these contrasts. Does he seem to value one type more than the other?
2. Baker also suggests an implicit contrast between business-minded people and those who are more dreamy or artistic. How would you describe this contrast?
3. In what ways does Baker, an acclaimed journalist, create a sense of irony with the fact that he failed at selling magazines? (For a definition of *irony*, see the Glossary.)
4. **Other Methods** Baker relies heavily on narration (Chapter 5), focusing on remembered scenes in which dialogue plays a large part. Choose one or two such scenes, and consider what each contributes to Baker's point.

Language

1. Baker refers to the idea of gumption using a variety of different words, such as "grit" (paragraph 14) and "spunk" (26). Scan the text and find as many synonyms for this attitude as you can. What effect do you think Baker wanted to achieve with this statement?
2. In paragraph 61 Baker notes, "By the time I was ten I had learned all my mother's maxims by heart." What is a *maxim*? What do these maxims reveal about Baker's mother?
3. Baker establishes a pattern in reporting his interview with the representative of Curtis Publishing Company (paragraphs 11–29): the executive asks a question, the mother responds, and Baker agrees. What effect does this pattern achieve?
4. In addition to *gumption*, the essay includes a number of old-fashioned words and expressions: "short-weighted" (paragraph 3), "parlor" (11), "spats" (32), and "rumble seat" (47), for example. Why do you suppose Baker chose to use terms like these?

Writing Topics

1. **Journal to Essay**   In your journal entry (p. 240), you described your ambitions as a child. Have your goals changed since then? Write an essay in which you describe your current ambitions. If they have changed, pinpoint the people or experiences that have made you modify your expectations for your career. Do you believe that your plans will evolve in the future? Do you think that they could ever change completely?
2. Think of a relative or close friend who has personality traits different from yours. Write an essay in which you explore the differences, focusing on how the two of you behave in particular circumstances or respond to specific experiences. How do you account for these differences?
3. Write an essay about the effect that an older family member or friend had on you when you were growing up. Did the person try to mold you, as Baker's mother did? Did you enjoy the person's guidance, or did you rebel against it? What lessons did you learn from the person?
4. **Cultural Considerations**   In the United States young people often have jobs such as delivering newspapers, babysitting, or working as clerks. Write about a job you have had. Was it something you did just for money, because you wanted to, or because your parents forced you to? Did you enjoy the experience? What lessons did you learn from your employment? Do you think it is a good idea for young people to have jobs?
5. **Connections**   Like Baker, who writes about his mother's expectations for her son, Judy Brady writes about the expectations for wives in "I

Want a Wife" (p. 276). Baker achieves his effect through personal narrative, while Brady offers a more generalized, if sarcastic, definition. Think about how the essays would have been different if the authors had used each other's methods: that is, if Brady had told a story about her life and if Baker had described the perfect son. Then write an essay exploring the advantages and disadvantages of the techniques used by each author.

Resolve to be thyself. —Matthew Arnold

It is easier to live through someone else than to become complete yourself.
—Betty Friedan

Man's main task in life is to give birth to himself. —Eric Fromm

Journal Response Achieving our individuality—one of life's greatest challenges—often involves differentiating ourselves from others. In a short journal entry, compare yourself with a sibling or a peer. How are you similar to this person? How are you different?

Reena Nadler

Reena Nadler was born in 1984 and grew up in New York City, where she is currently attending school. Her interests are diverse: she is a member of the track and field team, a senior editor and columnist for her school's student-run magazine, and a peer leader committed to mentoring fellow classmates. Nadler also organizes school programs that encourage students to appreciate cultural diversity, and she has participated in a national student diversity leadership conference.

Chromosomes in Common

"Do you like being a twin?" is a question that Nadler frequently hears. In this essay, written for an English class on autobiography, she responds to this question by discussing how it feels always to be compared with her twin sister.

"Hey, Reena, do you like being a twin?" 1

"Is that your sister, Reena? You guys look exactly alike, that's so cute." 2

"Do you guys ever switch classes or take tests for the other one?" 3

"Hold on, stand together so I can compare you. Your nose is rounder, I think, Reena, and Susannah, your face is a little wider." 4

"Hey, stay next to each other, I want a picture of the two of you together." 5

"Yeah, let's get a picture of the twins." 6

251

Susannah and I sighed, moved next to each other and grinned for 7 the flash. We were in Disneyland, surrounded by a group of goggling friends, half of whom had been on Susannah's summer trip and had never met me and the other half of whom had been on my summer trip and had never met her. The flood of questions washed over my armor—armor built up after sixteen years of the same thing. I didn't say that the comments and comparisons always make me feel as if I have no identity. I didn't say that they always make me feel as if I'm on display, like all the cartoon characters that day at Disneyland. I didn't say that they always make me feel as if I am not myself, but simply a comparison to Susannah. I didn't say that they always put a layer of bitterness over one of the most precious things I have—my relationship with my sister. After all, I told myself, these were my friends. They meant well, and they couldn't help it if they couldn't understand. I have never met anyone who could know both me and my sister and not compare us, and that will last all my life.

The picture came out so well that one of my friends sent it to 8 me—the cute twins right next to each other in the foreground and some Disneyland trees in the background. It is a close-up down to our shoulders; Susannah and I are next to each other in similar shirts, hair pulled back, each with one arm raised, presenting our identities as twins to the flock of picture takers. We're both wearing that extra wide picture smile one gets when too many pictures in a row have been taken and the smile muscles are getting tired. Our faces reflect the wry sense of humor—the essence of armor—that we have developed because the alternative is animosity. The picture is in black and white; singularly appropriate because it presents only one dimension of its subjects. Our attention is not focused on each other but on the camera, both enjoying and despising the attention. Though we stand next to each other in space, the picture does not record our connection. Instead it is about the connection of each to the role she plays for the world.

So what is that other dimension, that intimate bond? There is an- 9 other picture of us, back from when we were two. We are sitting in a big plush golden brown armchair which served as the center and meeting place of the room we shared. The chair is wide enough to hold the two of us side by side, and long enough for our purple-pajamaed feet to barely reach the edge. We each have one of those large children's books in our laps, easily bigger than we are, and we look as though we are settling in for an evening of companionable reading. Two tufts of light brown hair wisp gently over two concentrated foreheads as each examines her book. Our shoulders lean up against each other and our books overlap; our hands are touching as we hold down the pages. Each is interested in her own endeavor, but a quick glance could reveal what interesting activity the other one is up to, and a word or two could enlist the other's help and attention in our own. Our comfortable companionship whispers that we are long accustomed to sharing space, sharing discoveries, living with the spheres of our lives intertwining, overlapping, fusing, and re-forming in response to each other.

Our favorite number is two. We can break a cookie perfectly down the middle. When it is time to go to bed, we will not cry to stay up with the grown-ups because anything interesting that will be going on is probably going to be right there between the two of us. When we are together there is a relaxation of boundaries that is almost like one self being alone. We do not understand the concept of being truly alone. 10

I have found, however, that often in life the more meaningful something is to a person, the more difficulties it raises. The difficulties of being a twin are not restricted to other people's reactions but are also often about this connection we have shared since we were little. When I had just turned thirteen, I had the best summer of my life. That year Susannah, disappointed with her experiences at our old camp, decided to build new experiences for herself in a new camp. For herself, and by herself. I was contented to stay at the old camp and try my first solo flight in familiar surroundings. That summer I laughed and cried and talked with my friends at camp. My friends, not ours. I had a place that was mine alone, a place to make memories that no one else would ever have but me. That idea may sound ordinary to other people, but to me it was the first time ever that my sense of my life and my identity expanded into its own perfect sphere. It was the first time I knew it could. But Susannah's new camp experiment was a failure—the atmosphere and the people there did not complement her, but crushed her. I came home two months later with my arms flung wide to the world and to its possibilities. She came back curled up into a ball. The next summer everything I had created for myself was threatened: Susannah asked me if she could come back to the old camp and share it with me, and she wanted to be in my bunk. She needed somewhere safe where she could revive, and she needed me to be that safety. I needed desperately to keep my one separate plateau. 11

No one knows how to share the way a twin does. Twins share a   12
family, a face, a body, a life. They swim in the same sea before birth
and develop hands, feet, eyes, ears, brains in conjunction. For up to
ten days after conception, during the planning of nearly all patterns
of personhood, they are even a single entity. How could I invite my
sister to share the one space I had exuberantly and painstakingly
carved around myself? How could I deny it to her? What could I do
with our needs in such direct opposition?

It is a very powerful thing when you realize that you love some-   13
one as much as you love yourself. Not just the concept dwelt on in
various religious texts, which is treating other people as you wish to
be treated, but knowing that in some deep and shrouded part of
yourself another person's needs are as important to you as your own.
It is a feeling of absolute selfishness and absolute generosity. I got my
only glimpse of this part of myself when I was thirteen. I decided that
my sister's needs were stronger than my own; she came to camp with
me. It is a decision I still feel in conflict about today.

This was not an ultimate sacrifice, however. Searching for an   14
identity and defining the boundaries and differences between oneself
and other people is an exploration that everyone is faced with. Only
with me, the search is much more complex and urgent. Far from
being an isolated story, the camp incident merely illustrates one of
many conflicts that have always been and will always be a part of my
life; I deal with other people's comments and questions about being a
twin and my reactions to them every day. Sometimes I don't want
Susannah to read a book I have loved or to have a teacher I have had
simply because I want something so desperately to be mine. Competition between us is both repressed and secretly flourishing.

Sometimes I look at her, so similar to me, and see all my insecuri-   15
ties incarnated in a person who is with me all the time and whom
people cannot distinguish from me. When I am uncomfortable with
myself, therefore, it often translates into hating my sister. I remember
my frustration once when I was very angry at my sister, and I caught
a glimpse of my crying face in the mirror—looking exactly like hers
does when she is upset. Ironically, the only person who truly understands these and many other conflicts is Susannah herself, and as in
everything else, we help each other through the experience. On the
track team, for example, we are especially protective and supportive
of one another by an unspoken instinctive agreement, because the
other option is to spoil the experience by hating the other one for

being on the team too. She is my partner in the conflicts caused by her as she is my partner in everything else.

So back to the question that began this essay: "Hey, Reena, do 16 you like being a twin?" The answer, I have found, is often so complex that it can be encompassed only in the experience of a lifetime. On another level, however, the answer is quite simple. I am Me, my sister is She, and together there is another entity, a We. I wouldn't trade it in for anything.

Meaning

1. In her opening paragraphs Nadler describes the way that friends treat her and her twin sister. How does she react to their "comments and comparisons"? Why?
2. Nadler refers to an "intimate bond" with Susannah (paragraph 9). How does this bond manifest itself during her life, and what benefits does it provide?
3. In paragraph 11, Nadler claims that "often in life the more meaningful something is to a person, the more difficulties it raises." In addition to dealing with the "group of goggling friends" (paragraph 7), what other conflicts is Nadler compelled to face as a result of being a twin? How does she attempt to resolve them? Is she successful?
4. Based on their context in Nadler's essay, try to guess the meanings of any of the following words that you don't already know. Test your guesses in a dictionary, and then use each new word in a sentence or two of your own.

goggling (7)	plateau (11)	shrouded (13)
wry (8)	exuberantly (12)	incarnated (15)
companionable (9)	painstakingly (12)	encompassed (16)
enlist (9)		

Purpose and Audience

1. What do you think might have prompted Nadler to write so personally about being a twin? What evidence from the text can you use to support your opinion?
2. Although this essay is certainly written from the particular perspective of an identical twin, to what extent can nontwins sympathize with Nadler's experience? How does she try to make sure that they can do so? Find

examples from the essay that show she is addressing people who might not share her experience.

Method and Structure

1. Why is comparison and contrast particularly well suited to Nadler's subject and purpose?
2. Where in the essay does Nadler focus on similarities between herself and her sister? Where does she focus on differences? Why do you think she might have chosen to organize her essay as she does?
3. **Other Methods** Narration (Chapter 5) features prominently in Nadler's essay, and in paragraphs 8 and 9 she uses description (Chapter 4) of photographic images to complement her comparison. What dimensions do these other methods add to the piece?

Language

1. What is the overall tone of the essay?
2. In her first paragraphs, Nadler quotes comments made by her friends at Disneyland. How do these quotations set up the main idea of the essay?
3. Nadler frequently uses words in pairs, such as "exuberantly and painstakingly" (paragraph 12), "deep and shrouded" (13), and "complex and urgent" (14). Find other paired words in the essay. How does this device help to mirror Nadler's experience?

Writing Topics

1. **Journal to Essay** As an identical twin, Nadler is in a special position to write an essay of comparison and contrast about herself and her sister. Most of us cannot entirely understand the experience of being so intimately involved with another person, yet certainly we have all struggled to differentiate ourselves from siblings or peers. Expanding on your journal entry (p. 251), write an essay in which you explore one of these relationships, focusing on moments that involved distancing yourself from others. For example, did you ever have a wonderful experience that a close brother or sister did not share, or did a rift ever form between you and a close friend?
2. Like Nadler, you may recall the first time you felt that your sense of your life and your identity "expanded into its own perfect sphere." Write an essay in which you describe an experience that made you feel you were on your own, independent and in charge of your own life. This could be, for example, the first time you drove a car alone, traveled

abroad, or left home for college. How did it feel to be so independent? Was it intimidating or liberating?

3. Deeply loving another person can often bring both joys and difficulties. In fact, most people would probably agree with Nadler when she states, "It is a very powerful thing when you realize that you love someone as much as you love yourself." Write an essay about a similarly meaningful relationship you have had in your life. Describe the ups and downs of this relationship, from feelings of support and tenderness to moments of conflict and anger.

4. **Cultural Considerations**   Contemporary U.S. society places great importance on the individual, encouraging people to "be themselves," to develop original insights and tastes, and to voice their own opinions. In contrast, many other cultures emphasize conformity for the greater good. Write an essay in which you explain how either the pressure to be yourself or the pressure to conform with others has affected you in a personal way. For example, how have these pressures affected your college experience in situations such as classroom participation or writing term papers? Do you often feel compelled to be different or to conform? How do you tend to react to these pressures?

5. **Connections**   Like Nadler, Russell Baker, in "Gumption" (p. 240), explores the relationship he had with his sister during childhood. Though the two authors undoubtedly faced parallel conflicts, the situations they describe could hardly be more dissimilar. Write a comparison of the two essays in which you explore the authors' tones and purposes.

What is repugnant to every human being is to be reckoned always as a member of a class and not as an individual person. —Dorothy L. Sayers

It is utterly exhausting being Black in America—physically, mentally, and emotionally. While many minority groups and women feel similar stress, there is no respite or escape from your badge of color.
—Marian Wright Edelman

Prejudices are the chains forged by ignorance to keep men apart.
—Countess of Blessington

Journal Response Stereotypes are so pervasive in our society that it is hard to avoid them. Write a journal entry about a stereotype that you have observed or experienced.

Leanita McClain

An African American journalist, Leanita McClain earned a reputation for honest, if sometimes bitter, reporting on racism in America. She was born in 1952 on Chicago's South Side and grew up in a housing project there. She attended Chicago State University and the Medill School of Journalism at Northwestern University. Immediately after graduate school she began working as a reporter at the Chicago Tribune, *and over the next decade she advanced to writing a twice-weekly column and serving as the first African American member of the paper's editorial board. In 1983 she published an essay in the* Washington Post, *"How Chicago Taught Me to Hate Whites," that expressed her anguish over a racially divisive election in Chicago. The essay caused a furious controversy that probably undermined McClain's already fragile psychological condition. Long suffering from severe depression, she committed suicide in 1984, at the age of thirty-two. In the words of her former husband, Clarence Page, she could no longer "distinguish between the world's problems and her own."*

The Middle-Class Black's Burden

McClain wrote this essay for the "My Turn" column in Newsweek *magazine in October 1980, and it was reprinted in a collection of her essays,* A Foot in Each World *(1986). As her comparison makes disturbingly clear, McClain's*

position as an economically successful African American subjected her to mistaken judgments by both blacks and whites.

I am a member of the black middle class who has had it with being 1 patted on the head by white hands and slapped in the face by black hands for my success.

Here's a discovery that too many people still find startling: when 2 given equal opportunities at white-collar pencil pushing, blacks want the same things from life that everyone else wants. These include the proverbial dream house, two cars, an above-average school, and a vacation for the kids at Disneyland. We may, in fact, want these things more than other Americans because most of us have been denied them so long.

Meanwhile, a considerable number of the folks we left behind in 3 the "old country," commonly called the ghetto, and the militants we left behind in their antiquated ideology can't berate middle-class blacks enough for "forgetting where we came from." We have forsaken the revolution, we are told, we have sold out. We are Oreos, they say, black on the outside, white within.

The truth is, we have not forgotten; we would not dare. We are 4 simply fighting on different fronts and are no less war weary, and possibly more heartbroken, for we know the black and white worlds can meld, that there can be a better world.

It is impossible for me to forget where I came from as long as I 5 am prey to the jive hustler who does not hesitate to exploit my childhood friendship. I am reminded, too, when I go back to the old neighborhood in fear—and have my purse snatched—and when I sit down to a business lunch and have an old classmate wait on my table. I recall the girl I played dolls with who now rears five children on welfare, the boy from church who is in prison for murder, the pal found dead of a drug overdose in the alley where we once played tag.

My life abounds in incongruities. Fresh from a vacation in Paris, 6 I may, a week later, be on the milk-run Trailways bus in Deep South backcountry attending the funeral of an ancient uncle whose world stretched only fifty miles and who never learned to read. Sometimes when I wait at the bus stop with my attaché case, I meet my aunt getting off the bus with other cleaning ladies on their way to do my neighbors' floors.

But I am not ashamed. Black progress has surpassed our greatest   7
expectations; we never even saw much hope for it, and the achievement has taken us by surprise.

In my heart, however, there is no safe distance from the wretched   8
past of my ancestors or the purposeless present of some of my contemporaries; I fear such a fate can reclaim me. I am not comfortably
middle class; I am uncomfortably middle class.

I have made it, but where? Racism still dogs my people. There   9
are still communities in which crosses are burned on the lawns of
black families who have the money and grit to move in.

What a hollow victory we have won when my sister, dressed in   10
her designer everything, is driven to the rear door of the luxury high
rise in which she lives because the cab driver, noting only her skin
color, assumes she is the maid, or the nanny, or the cook, but certainly not the lady of any house at this address.

I have heard the immigrants' bootstrap tales, the simplistic re-   11
proach of "why can't you people be like us." I have fulfilled the entry
requirements of the American middle class, yet I am left, at times,
feeling unwelcome and stereotyped. I have overcome the problems of
food, clothing and shelter, but I have not overcome my old nemesis,
prejudice. Life is easier, being black is not.

I am burdened daily with showing whites that blacks are people.   12
I am, in the old vernacular, a credit to my race. I am my brothers'
keeper, and my sisters', though many of them have abandoned me
because they think that I have abandoned them.

I run a gauntlet between two worlds, and I am cursed and blessed   13
by both. I travel, observe, and take part in both; I can also be used by
both. I am a rope in a tug of war. If I am a token in my downtown
office, so am I at my cousin's church tea. I assuage white guilt. I dis-
prove black inadequacy and prove to my parents' generation that
their patience was indeed a virtue.

I have a foot in each world, but I cannot fool myself about either. I   14
can see the transparent deceptions of some whites and the bitter hope-
lessness of some blacks. I know how tenuous my grip on one way of life
is, and how strangling the grip of the other way of life can be.

Many whites have lulled themselves into thinking that race rela-   15
tions are just grand because they were the first on their block to discuss crab grass with the new black family. Yet too few blacks and
whites in this country send their children to school together, entertain
each other, or call each other friend. Blacks and whites dining out together draw stares. Many of my coworkers see no black faces from

the time the train pulls out Friday evening until they meet me at the coffee machine Monday morning. I remain a novelty.

Some of my "liberal" white acquaintances pat me on the head, 16 hinting that I am a freak, that my success is less a matter of talent than of luck and affirmative action. I may live among them, but it is difficult to live with them. How can they be sincere about respecting me, yet hold my fellows in contempt? And if I am silent when they attempt to sever me from my own, how can I live with myself?

Whites won't believe I remain culturally different; blacks won't 17 believe I remain culturally the same.

I need only look in a mirror to know my true allegiance, and I am 18 painfully aware that, even with my off-white trappings, I am prejudged by my color.

As for the envy of my own people, am I to give up my career, my 19 standard of living, to pacify them and set my conscience at ease? No. I have worked for these amenities and deserve them, though I can never enjoy them without feeling guilty.

These comforts do not make me less black, nor oblivious to the 20 woe in which many of my people are drowning. As long as we are denigrated as a group, no one of us has made it. Inasmuch as we all suffer for every one left behind, we all gain for every one who conquers the hurdle.

Meaning

1. McClain states, "My life abounds in incongruities" (paragraph 6). What does the word *incongruities* mean? How does it apply to McClain's life?
2. What is the "middle-class black's burden" to which the title refers? What is McClain's main idea?
3. McClain writes that "there is no safe distance from the wretched past of my ancestors or the purposeless present of some of my contemporaries" (paragraph 8). What do you think she means by this statement?
4. If any of the words below are new to you, try to guess their meanings from their context in McClain's essay. Check your guesses against a dictionary's definitions, and then try to use each word in a sentence or two of your own.

proverbial (2)	nemesis (11)	tenuous (14)
antiquated (3)	vernacular (12)	amenities (19)
ideology (3)	gauntlet (13)	oblivious (20)
berate (3)	assuage (13)	denigrated (20)
reproach (11)		

Purpose and Audience

1. What seems to be McClain's primary purpose in this piece? Does she simply want to express her frustration at whites and blacks, or is she trying to do something else here?
2. Is McClain writing primarily to whites or to blacks or to both? What feelings do you think she might evoke in white readers? in black readers? What is *your* reaction to this essay?
3. McClain's essay poses several questions, including "I have made it, but where?" (paragraph 9) and "How can they be sincere about respecting me, yet hold my fellows in contempt?" (16). What is the purpose of such questions?

Method and Structure

1. What exactly is McClain comparing here? What are her main points of comparison?
2. Paragraph 6 on "incongruities" represents a turning point in McClain's essay. What does she discuss before this paragraph? What does she discuss after?
3. McClain uses many expressions to make her comparison clear, such as "Meanwhile" (paragraph 3) and "different fronts" (4). Locate three more such expressions, and explain what relationship each one establishes.
4. **Other Methods**   McClain relies on many other methods to develop her comparison. Locate one instance each of description (Chapter 4), narration (Chapter 5), example (Chapter 6), and cause-and-effect analysis (Chapter 12). What does each contribute to the essay?

Language

1. McClain sets the tone for this essay in the very first sentence. How would you describe this tone? Is it appropriate, do you think?
2. In her opening sentence, does McClain use the words *patted* and *slapped* literally? How would you explain her use of these words in the context of her essay?
3. Notice McClain's use of parallelism in paragraph 8: "I am not comfortably middle class; I am uncomfortably middle class." Locate two or three other uses of parallelism. How does this technique serve McClain's comparison? (For more on parallelism, see p. 50 and *parallelism* in the Glossary.)
4. In paragraph 16, McClain uses quotation marks around the term "liberal" in reference to her white acquaintances. Why do you think she uses the quotation marks here? What effect does this achieve?

Writing Topics

1. **Journal to Essay**   McClain writes about a stereotype that plagued her, and in your journal entry (p. 258) you explored a stereotype that you have noticed or experienced. Now think of a time when you were stereotyped because of your membership in a group (as an ethnic, religious, or sexual minority, as a woman or a man, as a jock, a "nerd," a "homeboy," and so on). How were you perceived and by whom? What about this perception was accurate? What was unfair? How did the experience affect you? Write a narrative in which you recount this experience. Write for a reader who is not a member of the stereotyped group, being sure to include enough detail to bring the experience to life.

2. McClain's essay reports in part her experience of conflict resulting from her growth beyond the boundaries of her childhood and community. Think of a time when you outgrew a particular group or community. What conflicts and satisfactions did you experience? Write an essay comparing your experience with McClain's.

3. **Cultural Considerations**   Are there any ways in which you feel, like McClain, that you have "a foot in each world"? These worlds might be related to race and affluence, as McClain's worlds are, or they might be aligned by gender, social class, religion, or some other characteristic. Write an essay describing your own experience in balancing these two worlds. Are there ways in which you appreciate having a dual membership, or is it only a burden? What have you learned from your experience?

4. **Connections**   Like McClain, Aliza Kimhachandra, in "Banana" (p. 313), writes poignantly about the burden of being classified as a member of a group. The two women face similar obstacles and issues, but their approaches to the issue and their attitudes toward the discrimination that they face are quite different. In an essay of your own, compare the tone and viewpoint of these two authors.

Writing with the Method
Comparison and Contrast

Choose one of the following topics, or any other topic they suggest, for an essay developed by comparison and contrast. The topic you decide on should be something you care about so that the comparison and contrast is a means of communicating an idea, not an end in itself.

EXPERIENCE

1. Two jobs you have held
2. Two experiences with discrimination
3. Your own version of an event you witnessed or participated in and someone else's view of the same event (perhaps a friend's or a newspaper reporter's)
4. A good and a bad job interview

PEOPLE

5. Your relationships with two friends
6. Someone before and after marriage or the birth of a child
7. Two or more candidates for public office
8. Two relatives

PLACES AND THINGS

9. A place as it is now and as it was years ago
10. Two cars
11. Contact lenses and glasses
12. Two towns or cities
13. Nature in the city and in the country

ART AND ENTERTAINMENT

14. The work of two artists or writers, or two works by the same artist or writer
15. Two or more forms of jazz, classical music, or rock music
16. Movies or television today and when you were a child
17. A novel and a movie or television show on which it's based
18. A high school or college football, baseball, or basketball game and a professional game in the same sport
19. The advertisements during two very different television programs, or in two very different magazines

EDUCATION AND IDEAS

20. Talent and skill
21. Learning and teaching
22. Two styles of teaching
23. Two religions
24. Humanities courses and science or mathematics courses
25. A passive student and an active student

Writing About the Theme
Distinguishing Ourselves from Others

1. The writers in this chapter wrestle with questions of identity, debating issues as diverse as the reality of life for members of a racial minority (Dorris, p. 233, and McClain, p. 258), the role of peers and family in the emergence of an individual (Nadler, p. 251, and Baker, p. 240), and the relationship between body shape and personality (Britt, p. 234). All five authors rely on comparison and contrast, but otherwise they go about their tasks very differently. Most notably, perhaps, their tones vary widely, from irony to honesty to anger. Choose the two works that seem most different in this respect, and analyze how the tone of each helps the author achieve his or her purpose. Give specific examples to support your ideas. Does your analysis lead you to conclude that one tone is likely to be more effective than another in comparing ourselves with others? (For more on tone, see pp. 41–42 and 343.)

2. Michael Dorris and Leanita McClain both refer to misperceptions of their minority group on the part of the dominant white society. Think of a minority group to which you belong: it could be based on race, ethnicity, language, sexual orientation, religion, physical disability, or any other characteristic. How is your minority perceived in the dominant culture, and how does this perception resemble or differ from the reality as you know it? Write an essay comparing the perception of and the reality of your group.

3. Some authors in this chapter suggest that stereotypes play a significant part in our perceptions of others. Michael Dorris refers to the "white noise" of Indian images in the media, McClain to a distorted image of African Americans, and Britt to perceptions about overweight and lean individuals. To what extent, if at all, are these misconceptions the result of media hype or distortion, whether in advertising, news stories, television programming, movies, or elsewhere? What else might contribute to the misconceptions in each case? Write an essay explaining how such notions arise in the first place. You could use the misconceptions identified by Dorris, Britt, and McClain for your examples, or you could supply examples of your own.

Chapter 11

DEFINITION

Clarifying Gender Roles

USING THE METHOD

Definition sets the boundaries of a thing, a concept, an emotion, or a value. In answering "What is it?" and also "What is it *not*?" definition specifies the main qualities of the subject and its essential nature. Since words are only symbols, pinning down their precise meanings is essential for us to understand ourselves and one another. Thus we use definition constantly, whether we are explaining a slang word like *dis* to someone who has never heard it or explaining what *culture* means on an essay examination.

There are several kinds of definition, each with different uses. One is the **formal definition,** usually a statement of the general class of things to which the word belongs, followed by the distinction(s) between it and other members of the class. For example:

	General class	*Distinction(s)*
A submarine is	a seagoing vessel	that operates underwater.
A parable is	a brief, simple story	that illustrates a moral or religious principle.
Pressure is	the force	applied to a given surface.
Insanity is	a mental condition	in which a defendant does not know right from wrong.

A formal definition usually gives a standard dictionary meaning of the word (as in the first two examples) or a specialized meaning agreed to by the members of a profession or discipline (as in the last two examples, from physics and criminal law, respectively). It is most useful to explain the basic meaning of a term that readers need to know in order to understand the rest of a discussion. Occasionally, you might also use a formal definition as a springboard to a more elaborate, detailed exploration of a word. For instance, you might define *pride* simply as "a sense of self-respect" before probing the varied meanings of the word as people actually understand it and then settling on a fuller and more precise meaning of your own devising.

This more detailed definition of *pride* could fall into one of two other types of definition: stipulative and extended. A **stipulative definition** clarifies the particular way you are using a word: you stipulate, or specify, a meaning to suit a larger purpose; the definition is part of a larger whole. For example, if you wanted to show how pride can destroy personal relationships, you might first stipulate a meaning of *pride* that ties in with that purpose. Though a stipulative definition may sometimes take the form of a brief formal definition, most require several sentences or even paragraphs. In a physics textbook, for instance, the physicist's definition of *pressure* quoted above probably would not suffice to give readers a good sense of the term and eliminate all the other possible meanings they may have in mind.

Whereas you use a formal or stipulative definition for some larger purpose, you write an **extended definition** for the sake of defining—that is, for the purpose of exploring a thing, quality, or idea in its full complexity and drawing boundaries around it until its meaning is complete and precise. Extended definitions usually treat subjects so complex, vague, or laden with emotions or values that people misunderstand or disagree over their meanings. The subject may be an abstract concept like *patriotism,* a controversial phrase like *beginnings of life,* a colloquial or slang expression like *hype,* a thing like *microcomputer,* a scientific idea like *natural selection,* even an everyday expression like *nagging.* Besides defining, your purpose may be to persuade readers to accept a definition (for instance, that life begins at conception, or at birth), to explain (what is natural selection?), or to amuse (nagging as exemplified by great nags).

As the variety of possible subjects and purposes may suggest, an extended definition may draw on whatever methods will best accomplish the goal of specifying what the subject encompasses and distinguishing it from similar things, qualities, or concepts. Several strategies are unique to definition:

- **Synonyms,** or words of similar meaning, can convey the range of the word's meanings. For example, you could equate *misery* with *wretchedness* and *distress.*
- **Negation,** or saying what a word does not mean, can limit the meaning, particularly when you want to focus on only one sense of an abstract term, such as *pride,* that is open to diverse interpretations.
- The **etymology** of a word—its history—may illuminate its meaning, perhaps by showing the direction and extent of its change (*pride,* for instance, comes from a Latin word meaning "to be beneficial or useful") or by uncovering buried origins that remain implicit in the modern meaning (*patriotism* comes from the Greek word for "father"; *happy* comes from the Old Norse word for "good luck").

You may use these strategies of definition alone or together, and they may occupy whole paragraphs in an essay-length definition; but they rarely provide enough range to surround the subject completely. To do that, you'll need to draw on the other methods discussed in this book. One or two methods may predominate: an essay on nagging, for instance, might be developed with brief narratives. Or several methods may be combined: a definition of *patriotism* could compare it with *nationalism,* analyze its effects (such as the actions people take on its behalf), and give examples of patriotic individuals. The goal is not to employ every method in a sort of catalog of methods but to use those which best illuminate the subject. By drawing on the appropriate methods, you define and clarify your perspective on the subject so that the reader understands the meaning exactly.

ANALYZING DEFINITION IN PARAGRAPHS

David Popenoe (born 1932), a professor of sociology at Rutgers University, has written numerous books and articles about family life and marriage in modern societies. This paragraph comes from his book *Life Without Father: Compelling New Evidence That Fatherhood and Marriage Are Indispensable for the Good of Children and Society* (1996).

What do fathers do? Partly, of course, it is simply being a second adult in the home. Bringing up children is demanding, stressful, and often exhausting. Two adults can support and spell each other; they can also offset each other's deficiencies and build on each other's strengths. Beyond that, fathers—men—bring an array of unique and irreplaceable qualities that women do not ordinarily bring. Some of these are familiar, if sometimes overlooked or taken for granted. The father as protector, for example, has by no means outlived his usefulness. And he is important as a role model. Teenage boys without fathers are notoriously prone to trouble. The pathway to adulthood for daughters is somewhat easier, but they still must learn from their fathers, as they cannot from their mothers, how to relate to men. They learn from their fathers about heterosexual trust, intimacy, and difference. They learn to appreciate their own femininity from the one male who is most special in their lives (assuming that they love and respect their fathers). Most important, through loving and being loved by their fathers, they learn that they are worthy of love.

Question—topic sentence—introduces role to be defined.

Roles and qualities of fathers:
  Second adult in home

Protector

Role model
  For sons

For daughters

Paula Gunn Allen (born 1939), one of the nation's foremost scholars of Native American literature, is also a poet, an essayist, and a novelist. The following paragraph is from "Where I Come from Is like This," an essay that appears in *The Sacred Hoop: Recovering the Feminine in American Indian Traditions* (1986).

An American Indian woman is primarily defined by her tribal identity. In her eyes, her destiny is necessarily that of her people, and her sense of herself

Topic sentence introduces and summarizes role to be defined.

as a woman is first and foremost prescribed by her tribe. The definitions of women's roles are as diverse as tribal cultures in the Americas. In some she is devalued, in others she wields considerable power. In some she is a familial/clan adjunct, in some she is as close to autonomous as her economic circumstances and psychological traits permit. But in no tribal definitions is she perceived in the same way as are women in Western industrial and postindustrial cultures.

Clarification of identity

Examples of role definitions

Contrast with Western definitions

DEVELOPING AN ESSAY BY DEFINITION
Getting Started

You'll sometimes be asked to write definition essays, as when a psychology exam asks for a discussion of *schizophrenia* or a political science assignment calls for an explanation of the term *totalitarianism*. To come up with a subject on your own, consider words that have complex meanings and are either unfamiliar to readers or open to varied interpretations. The subject should be something you know and care enough about to explore in great detail and surround completely. An idea for a subject may come from an overheard conversation (for instance, a reference to someone as "too patriotic"), a personal experience (a broken marriage you think attributable to one spouse's pride), or something you've seen or read (another writer's definition of *jazz*).

Begin exploring your subject by examining and listing its conventional meanings (consulting an unabridged dictionary may help here, and the dictionary will also give you synonyms and etymology). Also examine the differences of opinion about the word's meanings—the different ways, wrong or right, that you have heard or seen it used. Run through the other methods to see what fresh approaches to the subject they open up:

- How can the subject be described?
- What are some examples?
- Can the subject be divided into qualities or characteristics?
- Can its functions help define it?
- Will comparing and contrasting it with something else help sharpen its meaning?
- Do its causes or effects help clarify its sense?

Some of the questions may turn up nothing, but others may open your eyes to meanings you had not seen.

When you have generated a good list of ideas about your subject, settle on the purpose of your definition. Do you mostly want to explain a word that is unfamiliar to readers? Do you want to express your own view so that readers see a familiar subject from a new angle? Do you want to argue in favor of a particular definition or perhaps persuade readers to look more critically at themselves or their surroundings? Try to work your purpose into a tentative thesis sentence that asserts something about the subject. For example:

> Though generally considered entirely positive in meaning, *patriotism* in fact reflects selfish, childish emotions that have no place in a global society.

With a thesis sentence formulated, reevaluate your ideas in light of it and pause to consider the needs of your readers:

- What do readers already know about your subject, and what do they need to be told in order to understand it as you do?
- Are your readers likely to be biased for or against your subject? If you were defining *patriotism,* for example, you might assume that your readers see the word as representing a constructive, even essential value that contributes to the strength of the country. If your purpose were to contest this view, as implied by the thesis above, you would have to build your case carefully to win readers to your side.

Organizing

The introduction to a definition essay should provide a base from which to expand and at the same time explain to readers why the forthcoming definition is useful, significant, or necessary. You may want to report the incident that prompted you to define, say why the subject itself is important, or specify the common understandings, or misunderstandings, about its meaning. Several devices can serve as effective beginnings: the etymology of the word; a quotation from another writer supporting or contradicting your definition; or an explanation of what the word does *not* mean (negation). (Try to avoid the overused opening that cites a dictionary: "According to *The American Heritage Dictionary,* _____ means. . . ." Your readers have probably seen this opening many times before.) If it is not implied in the rest of your introduction, you may want to state your thesis so that readers know precisely what your purpose and point are.

The body of the essay should then proceed, paragraph by paragraph, to refine the characteristics or qualities of the subject, using the arrangement and methods that will distinguish it from anything similar and provide your perspective. For instance:

- You might draw increasingly tight boundaries around the subject, moving from broader, more familiar meanings to the one you have in mind.
- You might arrange your points in order of increasing drama.
- You might begin with your own experience of the subject and then show how you see it operating in your surroundings.

The conclusion to a definition essay is equally a matter of choice. You might summarize your definition, indicate its superiority to other definitions of the same subject, quote another writer whose view supports your own, or recommend that readers make some use of the information you have provided. The choice depends — as it does in any kind of essay — on your purpose and the impression you want to leave with readers.

Drafting

While drafting your extended definition, keep your subject vividly in mind. Say too much rather than too little about it to ensure that you capture its essence; you can always cut when you revise. And be sure to provide plenty of details and examples to support your view. Such evidence is particularly important when, as in the earlier example of patriotism, you seek to change readers' perceptions of your subject.

In definition the words you use are especially important. Abstractions and generalities cannot draw precise boundaries around a subject, so your words must be as concrete and specific as you can make them. You'll have chances during revising and editing to work on your words, but try during drafting to pin down your meanings. Use words and phrases that appeal directly to the senses and experiences of readers. When appropriate, use figures of speech to make meaning inescapably clear; instead of "Patriotism is childish," for example, write "The blindly patriotic person is like a small child who sees his or her parents as gods, all-knowing, always right." The connotations of words — the associations called up in readers' minds by words like *home, ambitious,* and *generous* — can contribute to your definition as well. But be sure that connotative words trigger associations suited to your purpose. And when you are trying to explain something precisely, rely most heavily on words with generally neutral meanings. (See pp. 52–54 for more on concrete and specific language and figures of speech. See p. 52 for more on connotation.)

Revising and Editing

When you are satisfied that your draft is complete, revise and edit it against the following questions and the information in the box.

- *Have you surrounded your subject completely and tightly?* Your definition should not leave gaps, nor should the boundaries be so broadly drawn that the subject overlaps something else. For instance, a definition of *hype* that focused on exaggerated and deliberately misleading claims should include all such claims (some political speeches, say, as well as some advertisements), and it should exclude appeals that do not fit the basic definition (some public-service advertising, for instance).
- *Does your definition reflect the conventional meanings of the word?* Even if you are providing a fresh slant on your subject, you can't change its meaning entirely or you will confuse your readers and perhaps undermine your own credibility. *Patriotism,* for example, could not be defined from the first as "hatred of foreigners," for that definition strays into an entirely different realm. The conventional meaning of "love of country" would have to serve as the starting point, though your essay might interpret the meaning in an original way.

FOCUS ON PARAGRAPH AND ESSAY UNITY

When drafting a definition, you may find yourself being pulled away from your subject by the descriptions, examples, comparisons, and other methods you use to specify meaning. Let yourself explore byways of your subject—doing so will help you discover what you think. But in revising you'll need to direct all paragraphs to your thesis and, within paragraphs, to direct all sentences to the paragraph topic. In other words, you'll need to ensure that your essay and its paragraphs are unified.

One way to achieve unity is to focus each paragraph on some part of your definition and then to focus each sentence within the paragraph on that part. Judy Brady's "I Want a Wife" (p. 276) proceeds in just such a pattern, as the following outline shows. The sentences from paragraphs 3–9 specify the paragraph topics. A look at Brady's essay will show you that each of the paragraphs elaborates on its topic.

THESIS (PARAGRAPH 2)   I [. . .] would like to have a wife.

PARAGRAPH 3   I want a wife who will work and send me to school. And [. . .] take care of my children.

PARAGRAPH 4   I want a wife who will take care of *my* physical needs.

PARAGRAPH 5   I want a wife who will not bother me with rambling complaints [. . .]. But I want a wife who will listen to me [. . .].

PARAGRAPH 6   I want a wife who will take care of the details of my social life.

PARAGRAPH 7   I want a wife who is sensitive to my sexual needs [. . .].

PARAGRAPH 8   I want the liberty to replace my present wife with another one.

PARAGRAPH 9   When I am through with school and have a job, I want my wife to quit working and remain at home [. . .].

If some part of your definition requires more than a single paragraph, by all means expand it. But keep the group of paragraphs focused on a single idea.

For more on unity in essays and paragraphs, see pages 35–37.

A NOTE ON THEMATIC CONNECTIONS

Gender is the core topic of this chapter. The authors represented here are all seeking to define, or redefine, gender roles that have undergone a profound revolution in the last century. David Popenoe, in a paragraph, considers the ever-important role a father plays in the lives of his children (p. 270), while Paula Gunn Allen, in another paragraph, explains the forces defining an American Indian woman (p. 270). Judy Brady's concern is more particular: in defining a wife, she characterizes the marital relationship (next page). Clay McCuistion ponders the dangers of thrusting gender roles on children (p. 282). And Noel Perrin (p. 287) takes a semihumorous look at just what it means now to be a man.

A woman's place is in the home.   —Mid-nineteenth-century proverb

Motherhood and homemaking are honorable choices for any woman,
provided it is the woman who makes those decisions.   —Molly Yard

We haven't come a long way, we've come a short way. If we hadn't come a
short way, no one would be calling us "baby."   —Elizabeth Janeway

Journal Response   Write a journal entry about gender roles today. How
have they changed in the past few decades? How might they continue to
evolve?

Judy Brady

Judy Brady was born in 1937 in San Francisco. She attended the University
of Iowa and graduated with a bachelor's degree in painting in 1962. Married
in 1960, by the mid-1960s she was raising two daughters. She began working
in the women's movement in 1969 and through it developed an ongoing
concern with political and social issues, especially women's rights. She be-
lieves that "as long as women continue to tolerate a society which places
profits above the needs of people, we will continue to be exploited as workers
and as wives." Besides the essay reprinted here, Brady has written articles for
various magazines and edited 1 in 3: Women with Cancer Confront an
Epidemic (1991), motivated by her own struggle with the disease. Divorced
from her husband, Judy Brady is cofounder of the Toxic Links Coalition
and a volunteer at the Women's Cancer Resource Center in Berkeley, Cali-
fornia.

I Want a Wife

Writing after eleven years of marriage, and before separating from her hus-
band, Brady here pins down the meaning of the word wife *from the perspec-*
tive of one person who lives the role. This essay was published in the first
issue of Ms. *magazine in December 1971, and it has since been reprinted*
widely. Is its harsh portrayal still relevant today?

I belong to that classification of people known as wives. I am A Wife.   1
And, not altogether incidentally, I am a mother.

Not too long ago a male friend of mine appeared on the scene 2
fresh from a recent divorce. He had one child, who is, of course, with
his ex-wife. He is looking for another wife. As I thought about him
while I was ironing one evening, it suddenly occurred to me that I,
too, would like to have a wife. Why do I want a wife?

I would like to go back to school so that I can become economically 3
independent, support myself, and, if need be, support those dependent
upon me. I want a wife who will work and send me to school. And
while I am going to school I want a wife to take care of my children. I
want a wife to keep track of the children's doctor and dentist appoint-
ments. And to keep track of mine, too. I want a wife to make sure my
children eat properly and are kept clean. I want a wife who will wash
the children's clothes and keep them mended. I want a wife who is a
good nurturant attendant to my children, who arranges for their
schooling, makes sure that they have an adequate social life with their
peers, takes them to the park, the zoo, etc. I want a wife who takes care
of the children when they are sick, a wife who arranges to be around
when the children need special care, because, of course, I cannot miss
classes at school. My wife must arrange to lose time at work and not
lose the job. It may mean a small cut in my wife's income from time to
time, but I guess I can tolerate that. Needless to say, my wife will
arrange and pay for the care of the children while my wife is working.

I want a wife who will take care of *my* physical needs. I want a wife 4
who will keep my house clean. A wife who will pick up after my children, a wife who will pick up after me. I want a wife who will keep my
clothes clean, ironed, mended, replaced when need be, and who will see
to it that my personal things are kept in their proper place so that I can
find what I need the minute I need it. I want a wife who cooks the meals,
a wife who is a *good* cook. I want a wife who will plan the menus, do
the necessary grocery shopping, prepare the meals, serve them pleas-
antly, and then do the cleaning up while I do my studying. I want a wife
who will care for me when I am sick and sympathize with my pain and
loss of time from school. I want a wife to go along when our family
takes a vacation so that someone can continue to care for me and my
children when I need a rest and change of scene.

I want a wife who will not bother me with rambling complaints 5
about a wife's duties. But I want a wife who will listen to me when I
feel the need to explain a rather difficult point I have come across in
my course of studies. And I want a wife who will type my papers for
me when I have written them.

I want a wife who will take care of the details of my social life.   6
When my wife and I are invited out by friends, I want a wife who will
take care of the babysitting arrangements. When I meet people at
school that I like and want to entertain, I want a wife who will have the
house clean, will prepare a special meal, serve it to me and my friends,
and not interrupt when I talk about things that interest me and my
friends. I want a wife who will have arranged that the children are fed
and ready for bed before my guests arrive so that the children do not
bother us. I want a wife who takes care of the needs of my guests so that
they feel comfortable, who makes sure that they have an ashtray, that
they are passed the hors d'oeuvres, that they are offered a second helping of the food, that their wine glasses are replenished when necessary,
that their coffee is served to them as they like it. And I want a wife who
knows that sometimes I need a night out by myself.

I want a wife who is sensitive to my sexual needs, a wife who   7
makes love passionately and eagerly when I feel like it, a wife who
makes sure that I am satisfied. And, of course, I want a wife who will
not demand sexual attention when I am not in the mood for it. I want
a wife who assumes the complete responsibility for birth control,
because I do not want more children. I want a wife who will remain
sexually faithful to me so that I do not have to clutter up my intellectual life with jealousies. And I want a wife who understands
that *my* sexual needs may entail more than strict adherence to
monogamy. I must, after all, be able to relate to people as fully as
possible.

If, by chance, I find another person more suitable as a wife than   8
the wife I already have, I want the liberty to replace my present wife
with another one. Naturally, I will expect a fresh, new life; my wife
will take the children and be solely responsible for them so that I am
left free.

When I am through with school and have a job, I want my wife   9
to quit working and remain at home so that my wife can more fully
and completely take care of a wife's duties.

My God, who *wouldn't* want a wife?   10

Meaning

1. In one or two sentences, summarize Brady's definition of a wife. Consider not only the functions she mentions but also the relationship she
portrays.

2. Brady provides many instances of a double standard of behavior and responsibility for the wife and the wife's spouse. What are the wife's chief responsibilities and expected behaviors? What are the spouse's?

3. If any of the words below are unfamiliar, try to guess what they mean from the context of Brady's essay. Look the words up in a dictionary to check your guesses, and then use each one in a sentence or two of your own.

nurturant (3)	replenished (6)	monogamy (7)
hors d'oeuvres (6)	adherence (7)	

Purpose and Audience

1. Why do you think Brady wrote this essay? Was her purpose to explain a wife's duties, to complain about her own situation, to poke fun at men, to attack men, to attack society's attitudes toward women, or something else? Was she trying to provide a realistic and fair definition of *wife*? What passages in the essay support your answers?

2. What does Brady seem to assume about her readers' gender (male or female) and their attitudes toward women's roles in society, relations between the sexes, and work inside and outside the home? Does she seem to write from the perspective of a particular age group or social and economic background? In answering these questions, cite specific passages from the essay.

3. Brady clearly intended to provoke a reaction from readers. What is *your* reaction to this essay: do you think it is realistic or exaggerated, fair or unfair to men, relevant or irrelevant to the present time? Why?

Method and Structure

1. Why would anybody need to write an essay defining a term like *wife*? Don't we know what a wife is already? How does Brady use definition in an original way to achieve her purpose?

2. Analyze Brady's essay as a piece of definition, considering its thoroughness, its specificity, and its effectiveness in distinguishing the subject from anything similar.

3. Analyze the introduction to Brady's essay. What function does paragraph 1 serve? In what way does paragraph 2 confirm Brady's definition? How does the question at the end of the introduction relate to the question at the end of the essay?

4. **Other Methods**   Brady develops her definition primarily by classification (Chapter 8). What does she classify, and what categories does she form? What determines her arrangement of these categories? What does the classification contribute to the essay?

Language

1. How would you characterize Brady's tone: whining, amused, angry, contemptuous, or what? What phrases in the essay support your answer? (If necessary, see pp. 41–42 and 343 on tone.)
2. Why does Brady repeat "I want a wife" in almost every sentence, often at the beginning of the sentence? What does this stylistic device convey about the person who wants a wife? How does it fit in with Brady's main idea and purpose?
3. Why does Brady never substitute the personal pronoun "she" for "my wife"? Does the effect gained by repeating "my wife" justify the occasionally awkward sentences, such as the last one in paragraph 3?
4. What effect does Brady achieve with the expressions "of course" (paragraphs 3, 7), "Needless to say" (3), "after all" (7), and "Naturally" (8)?

Writing Topics

1. **Journal to Essay**   Using your journal entry (p. 276) and ideas generated by Brady's essay, analyze a role that is defined by gender, such as that of a wife or husband, mother or father, sister or brother, daughter or son. First write down the responsibilities, activities, and relationships that define that role, and then elaborate your ideas into an essay defining this role as you see it. You could, if appropriate, follow Brady's model by showing how the role is influenced by the expectations of another person or people.
2. Combine the methods of definition and comparison (Chapter 10) in an essay that compares a wife or a husband you know with Brady's definition of either role. Be sure that the point of your comparison is clear and that you use specific examples to illustrate the similarities or differences you see.
3. **Cultural Considerations**   Brady's essay was written in the specific cultural context of 1971. Undoubtedly, many cultural changes have taken place since then, particularly changes in gender roles. However, one could also argue that much remains the same. Write an essay in which you compare the stereotypical role of a wife now with the role Brady defines. In addition to your own observations and experiences, consider contemporary images of wives that the media present—for instance, in television advertising or sitcoms.
4. **Connections**   Both Brady and David Popenoe (p. 270) make reference to the demands of children in a family, mentioning their needs to be fed, kept clean, clothed, entertained, and guided, among others. Brady complains that most of these tasks fall on women's shoulders and wishes that her spouse would help more, but Popenoe, while acknowledging the need to have two people involved, distinguishes the unique role that fa-

thers play in bringing up their children. Write an essay in which you examine and compare the roles that mothers and fathers play in their children's upbringing. Are there tasks for which one parent is particularly suited? Or is the gender of the parent less relevant than people sometimes think?

Macho—the genetic defect that makes men want to teach toddlers to box.

—Joyce Armor

Contrary to what clergymen and policemen believe, gentleness is biological and aggression is cultural.

—Stefen Themerson

I am asking you to say no to the values that have defined manhood through the ages—prowess, competition, victory—and to grow into a manhood that has not existed before.

—Nancy Mairs

Journal Response   Do you think boys and girls are brought up to adopt certain gender traits or roles, such as aggression or empathy, competition or cooperation, playing sports or playing with dolls, breadwinning or nurturing? Write a brief journal entry about your own experience.

Clay McCuistion

Clay McCuistion was born in 1978 in Hiawatha, Kansas. A senior at the University of Kansas, he majors in journalism and English. He has worked as an editor, a reporter, a columnist, and a cartoonist at the University Daily Kansan *and has held other reporting internships at smaller Kansas papers.*

Boyhood Games

In his essay "Boyhood Games," McCuistion discusses how typical gender roles bind individuals, labeling them from early childhood onward: "That's a central function of gender-based youth activities: putting in place societally imposed restrictions that make it easier to categorize people quickly."

As a child of three or four, I wore tangled yellow yarn on my head   1
and pretended to be Rapunzel. In a high, feminine voice, I spoke about letting down my beautiful hair to the prince below. I strutted around the house, acting royal and generally having a terrific time. I was not, like many other boys my age, playing baseball or football or soccer.

My parents decided that their children should be able to play   2
whatever games we wanted. So my brother played with toy trucks,

pieces of wood, and string. My sister watched carefully over her collection of Barbies. And I played Rapunzel.

The family didn't mind. We were all pursuing the amusements 3 that amused us individually. What other people thought—what society believed appropriate—didn't enter into the equation. My parents never forced any of us to play Little League or take ballet lessons or follow any gender-specific activity. I came to place a higher value on fulfilling my own goals and dreams than on caring what other people thought about me.

Through my parents' example, my life became more focused on 4 discovering and exploring my own talent and potential. The loosely supervised, gender blind games allowed me to transcend the culture that stifled many others my age. Other kids often had to fit themselves into categories imposed by society—even in the context of loving and nurturing families. Using these categories, the kids could be defined in simple, straightforward, and uncomplicated ways.

That's a central function of gender-based youth activities: putting 5 in place societally imposed restrictions that make it easier to categorize people quickly. If I were to don a catcher's mitt, cute numbered jersey, and cap, I would instantly become a model little boy. But I didn't want to appease the culture surrounding me. It was far more fun to make people think—to make them deal with me on my own terms.

The sports and games of youth, particularly those directed to- 6 ward little boys, don't just define boyness. They also instill a competitive sense that reverberates throughout adult life. Little boys are aggressive, the stereotype goes, and so let them play games that involve physical activity and controlled violence. Those who use violence in the most efficient way win. The stereotyping then continues in adulthood. Any competition, from a presidential campaign to an advertising campaign, can be represented as a high-stakes sporting event—an event played by males. Those who can run fast enough and eventually overpower the opposition are the ones who will win. And those who win are the best.

When I arrived in elementary school, fresh from my gender- 7 bending play times, I watched in astonishment as the other little boys clawed and punched each other playing kickball, dodgeball, or any of the multitude of rough playground sports. What were they doing, I wondered? Didn't they realize this hurt?

As I continued through school, I eventually understood. They did 8 realize it hurt. They did occasionally wonder at the futility of running a small ball up and down a field while others pummeled them. But they didn't think they could stop. Boys were expected to play games. Boys were expected to be competitive. The notion of gender roles was tightly wound up in the sporting event itself. Not to play would be to betray one's gender.

Many people don't feel comfortable rebelling against prescribed   9
gender roles until they reach college—or some kind of independence from their families and youthful friends. Once they define themselves on their own terms, the often-brutal childhood games become less necessary. But even if they give up playing, men are expected to watch sports. And if they don't watch them, they at least keep up on the scores so they can make small talk around the water cooler at work. The connection between competition and gender is still there.

Perhaps more men should have played at being Rapunzel as boys,   10
or whatever person or thing they wanted. Constraining ourselves to gender-stereotyped roles and constant competition can only slow us down. Anyone can experience the sense of free, uninhibited play I had as a boy. All it takes is a high voice and some yellow yarn.

Meaning

1. What is McCuistion's thesis in this essay? Where does he first express it directly? Where does he restate it?
2. In paragraphs 6–9 McCuistion offers his views about the negative consequences of gender stereotypes on boys and men. What are these stereotypes, and what are their consequences?
3. What advice does McCuistion offer to free men from the need to compete constantly?
4. Some of the words listed below may be new to you. If so, try to guess what they mean from their context in McCuistion's essay. See how close your definitions are to the dictionary's, and then use each new word in a sentence or two of your own.

strutted (1)	pummeled (8)
don (5)	constraining (10)
appease (5)	uninhibited (10)
reverberates (6)	

Purpose and Audience

1. Why do you think McCuistion wrote this essay? In what ways is he trying to influence the thinking of his readers?

2. Do you think McCuistion believes his readers will accept his ideas readily? Does he allow for disagreements they might have? Do you think his essay is likely to change the minds of readers who disagree with him?

Method and Structure

1. Why is definition a natural choice of method for an essay critiquing the way young people are encouraged to adopt prescribed gender roles? How does this method allow McCuistion to achieve his purpose?
2. **Other Methods**   McCuistion's essay also relies on example (Chapter 6) and cause-and-effect analysis (Chapter 12). Where do you see evidence of these methods? What do they contribute to the essay?

Language

1. What is McCuistion's tone? Defiant, flippant, reasoned, impassioned? How seriously does he take his subject?
2. Why does McCuistion call the games he played as a young child "gender-bending" (paragraph 7)? What meanings does the phrase imply?

Writing Topics

1. **Journal to Essay**   Expand your journal entry (p. 282) into an essay in which you consider the lessons in your own childhood about masculinity or femininity. For example, were you encouraged to or discouraged from wearing particular clothes, playing with certain toys, or engaging in any activities? How did such pressures—or their absence—affect you?
2. If you are a parent or expect to become one someday, how do or will you teach your children about gender roles and expectations? Should your son be allowed to play dress-up? Should your daughter be permitted to take boxing lessons? How would you define what behavior is and is not appropriate for each gender?
3. **Cultural Considerations**   At heart McCuistion argues that a culture should not stifle its members' differences but instead should encourage self-discovery and the diversity that would inevitably result. The extent to which diversity should be encouraged or even tolerated is, of course, a controversial topic in the United States, with opponents and proponents at both extremes and large numbers of middle-grounders. Write an essay in which you articulate your own stand on this issue. Assuming no one is hurt, what limits, if any, should there be on people's activities, styles of

dress, behaviors, or other attributes? How do you answer those who disagree with you?

4. **Connections**   Like McCuistion, Judy Brady, in "I Want a Wife" (p. 276),
is negative about traditional gender roles: McCuistion focuses on the
competitiveness and aggression expected of boys, while Brady considers
the submissiveness and career sacrifices expected of women. Despite the
similarities in topic, the authors' tones are quite different. Write an essay
exploring both the similarities and the differences in these two essays.

I'm not afraid to show my feminine side—it's part of what makes me a man.
—Gerard Depardieu

Macho does not prove mucho.   —Zsa Zsa Gabor

The feminine in the man is the sugar in the whisky. The masculine in the woman is the yeast in the bread. Without these ingredients the result is flat, without tang or flavor.
—Edna Ferber

Journal Response   Contemporary society defines masculinity and femininity in ways that were not thought possible a few decades ago. Reflect for a moment on how you define *manhood* or *womanhood*, and write a journal entry that includes your definition.

Noel Perrin

Noel Perrin was born in 1927 in New York City. He received degrees from Williams College, Duke University, and Cambridge University. The author of many books dealing with themes of nature, ecology, and New England, Perrin is well known for Giving Up the Gun: Japan's Reversion to the Sword, 1543–1879 *and four collections of essays in the "First Person Rural" series. Recent publications include an article in* Vermont Life *about electric cars, a guide in the* Chronicle of Higher Education *to colleges focused on environmental protection, and a monthly column in the* Dartmouth College *alumni magazine. Perrin is a former chair of the English department at Dartmouth and now teaches environmental literature.*

The Androgynous Man

"The Androgynous Man" first appeared in the New York Times *Sunday magazine as part of a series called "About Men." In the essay Perrin explores his idea of "spiritual androgyny": a crossing over in spirit between the masculine and feminine realms, freeing the self from limiting expectations and roles.*

The summer I was sixteen, I took a train from New York to Steam- 1
boat Springs, Colorado, where I was going to be assistant horse
wrangler at a camp. The trip took three days, and since I was much
too shy to talk to strangers, I had quite a lot of time for reading. I

287

read all of *Gone with the Wind.* I read all the interesting articles in a couple of magazines I had, and then I went back and read all the dull stuff. I also took all the quizzes, a thing of which magazines were even fuller then than now.

The one that held my undivided attention was called "How Masculine/Feminine Are You?" It consisted of a large number of inkblots. The reader was supposed to decide which of the four objects each blot most resembled. The choices might be a cloud, a steam engine, a caterpillar and a sofa.   2

When I finished the test, I was shocked to find that I was barely masculine at all. On a scale of 1 to 10, I was about a 1.2. Me, the horse wrangler? (And not just wrangler, either. That summer, I had to skin a couple of horses that died—the camp owner wanted the hides.)   3

The results of the test were so terrifying to me that for the first time in my life I did a piece of original analysis. Having unlimited time on the train, I looked at the "masculine" answers over and over, trying to find what it was that distinguished real men from people like me—and eventually I discovered two very simple patterns. It was "masculine" to think the blots looked like man-made objects and "feminine" to think they looked like natural objects. It was masculine to think they looked like things capable of causing harm, and feminine to think of innocent things.   4

Even at sixteen, I had the sense to see that the compilers of the test were using rather limited criteria—maleness and femaleness are both more complicated than *that*—and I breathed a huge sigh of relief. I wasn't necessarily a wimp, after all.   5

That the test did reveal something other than the superficiality of its makers I realized only many years later. What it revealed was that there is a large class of men and women both, to which I belong, who are essentially androgynous. That doesn't mean we're gay, or low in the appropriate hormones, or uncomfortable performing the jobs traditionally assigned our sexes. (A few years after that summer, I was leading troops in combat and, unfashionable as it now is to admit this, having a very good time. War is exciting. What a pity the twentieth century went and spoiled it with high-tech weapons.)   6

What it does mean to be spiritually androgynous is a kind of freedom. Men who are all-male, or he-man, or 100 percent red-blooded Americans, have a little biological set that causes them to be attracted to physical power, and probably also to dominance. Maybe even to watching football. I don't say this to criticize them. Completely mascu-   7 line men are quite often wonderful people: good husbands, good (although sometimes overwhelming) fathers, good members of society. Furthermore, they are often so unselfconsciously at ease in the world that other men seek to imitate them. They just aren't as free as us androgynes. They pretty nearly have to be what they are; we have a range of choices open.

The sad part is that many of us never discover that. Men who are   8
not 100 percent red-blooded Americans—say, those who are only 75 percent red-blooded—often fail to notice their freedom. They are too busy trying to copy the he-men ever to realize that men, like women, come in a wide variety of acceptable types. Why this frantic imitation? My answer is mere speculation, but not casual. I have speculated on this for a long time.

Partly they're just envious of the he-man's unconscious ease.   9
Mostly they're terrified of finding that there may be something wrong with them deep down, some weakness at the heart. To avoid discovering that, they spend their lives acting out the role that the he-man naturally lives. Sad.

One thing that men owe to the women's movement is that this   10
kind of failure is less common than it used to be. In releasing themselves from the single ideal of the dependent woman, women have more or less incidentally released a lot of men from the single ideal of the dominant male. The one mistake the feminists have made, I think, is in supposing that *all* men need this release, or that the world would be a better place if all men achieved it. It wouldn't. It would just be duller.

So far I have been pretty vague about just what the freedom of   11
an androgynous man is. Obviously it varies with the case. In the case I know best, my own, I can be quite specific. It has freed me most as a parent. I am, among other things, a fairly good natural mother. I like the nurturing role. It makes me feel good to see a child eat—and it turns me to mush to see a four-year-old holding a glass with both small hands, in order to drink. I even enjoyed sewing patches on the knees of my daughter Amy's Dr. Dentons when she was at the crawling stage. All that pleasure I would have lost if I had made myself stick to the notion of the paternal role that I started with.

Or take a smaller and rather ridiculous example. I feel free to kiss   12
cats. Until recently it never occurred to me that I would want to,

though my daughters have been doing it all their lives. But my elder daughter is now twenty-two, and in London. Of course, I get to look after her cat while she is gone. He's a big, handsome farm cat named Petrushka, very unsentimental, though used from kittenhood to being kissed on the top of the head by Elizabeth. I've gotten very fond of him (he's the adventurous kind of cat who likes to climb hills with you), and one night I simply felt like kissing him on the top of the head, and did. Why did no one tell me sooner how silky cat fur is?

Then there's my relation to cars. I am completely unembarrassed 13 by my inability to diagnose even minor problems in whatever object I happen to be driving, and don't have to make some insider's remark to mechanics to try to establish that I, too, am a "Man with His Machine."

The same ease extends to household maintenance. I do it, of 14 course. Service people are expensive. But for the last decade my house has functioned better than it used to because I've had the aid of a volume called *Home Repairs Any Woman Can Do*, which is pitched just right for people at my technical level. As a youth, I'd as soon have touched such a book as I would have become a transvestite. Even though common sense says there is really nothing sexual whatsoever about fixing sinks.

Or take public emotion. All my life I have easily been moved by 15 certain kinds of voices. The actress Siobhan McKenna's[1], to take a notable case. Give her an emotional scene in a play, and within ten words my eyes are full of tears. In boyhood, my great dread was that someone might notice. I struggled manfully, you might say, to suppress this weakness. Now, of course, I don't see it was a weakness at all, but as a kind of fulfillment. I even suspect that the true he-men feel the same way, or one kind of them does, at least, and it's only the poor imitators who have to struggle to repress themselves.

Let me come back to the inkblots, with their assumption that 16 masculine equates with machinery and science, and feminine with art and nature. I have no idea whether the right pronoun for God is He, She or It. But this I'm pretty sure of. If God could somehow be induced to take that test, God would not come out macho, and not feminismo, either, but right in the middle. Fellow androgynes, it's a nice thought.

---

[1]Siobhan McKenna (1923–86) was an Irish stage and movie actress. [Editor's note.]

Meaning

1. In paragraph 6 Perrin writes that "there is a large class of men and women both, to which I belong, who are essentially androgynous." What does *androgynous* mean? Is Perrin at ease with his androgynous identity?
2. In paragraphs 7–9 Perrin defines *manhood* across a kind of range or spectrum. What is this spectrum, and how does it relate to the inkblot test he describes in his opening paragraphs?
3. In paragraph 10 Perrin claims that men owe a debt to the women's movement. Explain what he believes feminists have contributed to society's understanding of manhood.
4. If any of the words below are unfamiliar, try to guess what they mean from the context of Perrin's essay. Look up the words in a dictionary to check your guesses, and then use each one in a sentence or two of your own.

compilers (5)	nurturing (11)	dread (15)
superficiality (6)	unsentimental (12)	suppress (15)

Purpose and Audience

1. Why do you think Perrin wrote this essay? Was he trying to justify or come to terms with his own masculinity? If not, what was he trying to do?
2. In his conclusion (paragraph 16), Perrin speaks directly to his "Fellow androgynes." What does this suggest about Perrin's vision of his readers?
3. How do you think Perrin expects his audience to react to this essay? Does he seem to assume his audience's agreement, does he write defensively to forestall criticism, or does he assume some other response? What in the essay makes you think as you do?

Method and Structure

1. Why is definition an appropriate method for Perrin to use in developing his ideas? What specific features of this method serve him?
2. In developing his definition, Perrin relies heavily on personal anecdotes. What do the anecdotes contribute to his essay? Do they weaken his case in any way?
3. **Other Methods** In what ways does Perrin use comparison and contrast (Chapter 10) as part of his definition? Why is this method important in developing his point?

Language

1. Perrin's vocabulary in this essay ranges from relatively formal to highly informal. For example, in paragraph 5 he uses the phrase "rather limited criteria" as well as the word "wimp." What does this range of vocabulary suggest about Perrin's role as a writer here?
2. In paragraph 8 Perrin writes that the point he is making is "mere speculation, but not casual." What does he mean?
3. Point out some examples that show Perrin appealing to his readers' sense of humor. What is the effect of these examples?

Writing Topics

1. **Journal to Essay**   In your journal entry (p. 287), you defined *manhood* or *womanhood* for yourself. Now write an essay in which you extend and support that definition (or definitions if you wish to explore both terms). Does your definition correspond to traditional assumptions about gender or is it more like Perrin's? What characteristics does your definition *not* include?
2. Based on your own experience, write an essay in which you define a stereotype you have encountered, not necessarily a gender stereotype. Examples include assumptions about jocks, techies, persons in wheelchairs, persons who are thin or heavy or have other physical characteristics, or racial differences.
3. **Cultural Considerations**   Despite the societal changes Perrin refers to, many gender-related issues continue to be a source of controversy and debate: coeducation vs. gender-specific classrooms, discrepancies between men's and women's earnings, what constitutes sexual harassment, parental roles within the family, gender stereotypes in the media, and so on. Choose one such controversy that interests you, and in an essay explore its various sides as well as your own position.
4. **Connections**   In this essay Perrin argues for a broader definition of manhood. Clay McCuistion, in "Boyhood Games" (p. 282), might agree with Perrin, but he is more critical of the negative effects of a narrow definition of masculinity. Write an essay in which you compare and contrast the opinions and tones of these two writers.

Writing with the Method
Definition

Choose one of the following topics, or any other topic they suggest, for an essay developed by definition. The topic you decide on should be something you care about so that definition is a means of communicating an idea, not an end in itself.

PERSONAL QUALITIES

1. Ignorance
2. Sophistication
3. Spirituality or worldliness
4. Selflessness or selfishness
5. Loyalty or disloyalty
6. Responsibility
7. A good sport
8. Hypocrisy

EXPERIENCES AND FEELINGS

9. A nightmare
10. A good teacher, coach, parent, or friend
11. A good joke or a tasteless joke
12. Religious faith

ASPIRATIONS

13. The Good Life
14. Success or failure
15. A good job

SOCIAL CONCERNS

16. Poverty
17. Education
18. Domestic violence
19. Substance abuse
20. Prejudice
21. An American ethnic group such as Italians, WASPs, Japanese, Norwegians, or Chinese

ART AND ENTERTAINMENT

22. Jazz or some other kind of music
23. A good novel, movie, or television program
24. Impressionist painting or some other school of art

IDEAS

25. Freedom
26. Nostalgia
27. Feminism
28. A key concept in a course you're taking

Writing About the Theme

Clarifying Gender Roles

1. Both Paula Gunn Allen (p. 270) and Judy Brady (p. 276) discuss womanhood not in isolation, but in conjunction with another role: Brady defines the tasks of a woman who is also a spouse, and Allen speaks of women who are also tribal members. Can we make accurate generalizations about gender roles without taking into account the other roles that men and women play? In other words, does it make any sense to talk about men's and women's roles in society without referring to other variables that might influence the way that men and women are defined? Answer in a brief essay, citing as examples the selections in this chapter and observations of your own.

2. The three male authors in this section deal with gender-related issues across a wide age spectrum. David Popenoe (p. 270) focuses on the role of the man as father, Clay McCuistion (p. 282) is concerned with the lessons imparted to young boys, and Noel Perrin (p. 287) looks at manhood well past youth. In your experience, which age group brings the difficult questions of gender and identity into the sharpest focus? During your life, has your definition of your gender changed at all? If so, how?

3. Judy Brady, Clay McCuistion, and Noel Perrin all speak of the changes that have beset our traditional notions of gender. How have gender roles changed since your parents or grandparents were your age? Do you think that these roles will continue to evolve? What predictions can you make about men's and women's roles in society in the future?

Chapter 12

CAUSE-AND-EFFECT ANALYSIS

Exploring the Influence of Cultural Identity

USING THE METHOD

Why did free agency become so important in professional baseball, and how has it affected the sport? What caused the recent warming of the Pacific Ocean, and how did the warming affect the earth's weather? We answer questions like these with **cause-and-effect analysis,** the method of dividing occurrences into their elements to find relationships among them. Cause-and-effect analysis is a specific kind of analysis, the method discussed in Chapter 7.

When we analyze **causes,** we discover which of the events preceding a specified outcome actually made it happen:

What caused Adolf Hitler's rise in Germany?
Why have herbal medicines become so popular?

When we analyze **effects,** we discover which of the events following a specified occurrence actually resulted from it:

What do we do for (or to) drug addicts when we imprison them?

What happens to our foreign policy when the president's advisers disagree over its conduct?

These are existing effects of past or current situations, but effects are often predicted for the future:

How would a cure for cancer affect the average life expectancy of men and women?

How might your decision to major in history affect your job prospects?

Causes and effects can also be analyzed together, as the questions opening this chapter illustrate.

Cause-and-effect analysis is found in just about every discipline and occupation, including history, social science, natural science, engineering, medicine, law, business, and sports. In any of these fields, as well as in writing done for college courses, your purpose in analyzing may be to explain or to persuade. In explaining why something happened or what its outcome was or will be, you try to order experience and pin down the connections in it. In arguing with cause-and-effect analysis, you try to demonstrate why one explanation of causes is more accurate than another or how a proposed action will produce desirable or undesirable consequences.

The possibility of arguing about causes and effects points to the main challenge of this method. Related events sometimes overlap, sometimes follow one another immediately, and sometimes connect over gaps in time. They vary in their duration and complexity. They vary in their importance. Analyzing causes and effects thus requires not only identifying them but also discerning their relationships accurately and weighing their significance fairly.

Causes and effects often do occur in a sequence, each contributing to the next in what is called a **causal chain**. For instance, an unlucky man named Jones ends up in prison, and the causal chain leading to his imprisonment can be outlined as follows: Jones's neighbor, Smith, dumped trash on Jones's lawn. In reprisal, Jones set a small brushfire in Smith's yard. A spark from the fire accidentally ignited Smith's house. Jones was prosecuted for the fire and sent to jail. In this chain each event is the cause of an effect, which in turn is the cause of another effect, and so on to the unhappy conclusion.

Identifying a causal chain partly involves sorting out events in time:

- **Immediate** causes or effects occur nearest an event. For instance, the immediate cause of a town's high unemployment rate may be the closing of a large manufacturing plant where many townspeople work.
- **Remote** causes or effects occur further away in time. The remote cause of the town's unemployment rate may be a drastic decline in the company's sales or (more remote) a weak regional or national economy.

Analyzing causes also requires distinguishing their relative importance in the sequence:

- **Major** causes are directly and primarily responsible for the outcome. For instance, if a weak economy is responsible for low sales, it is a major cause of the manufacturing plant's closing.
- **Minor** causes (also called **contributory** causes) merely contribute to the outcome. The manufacturing plant may have closed for the additional reason that the owners could not afford to make repairs to its machines.

As these examples illustrate, time and significance can overlap in cause-and-effect analysis: a weak economy, for instance, is both a remote and a major cause; the lack of funds for repairs is both an immediate and a minor cause.

Since most cause-and-effect relationships are complex, you should take care to avoid several pitfalls in analyzing and presenting them. One is a confusion of coincidence and cause — that is, an assumption that because one event preceded another, it must have caused the other. This error is nicknamed **post hoc,** from the Latin *post hoc, ergo propter hoc,* meaning "after this, therefore because of this." Superstitions often illustrate post hoc: a basketball player believes that a charm once ended her shooting slump, so she now wears the charm whenever she plays. But post hoc also occurs in more serious matters. For instance, the office of a school administrator is vandalized, and he blames the incident on a recent speech by the student-government president criticizing the administration. But the administrator has no grounds for his accusation unless he can prove that the speech incited the vandals. In the absence of proof, the administrator commits the error of post hoc by asserting that the speech caused the vandalism simply because the speech preceded the vandalism.

Another potential problem in cause-and-effect writing is **oversimplification.** You must consider not just the causes and effects that seem obvious or important but all the possibilities: remote as well as immediate, minor as well as major. One form of oversimplification confuses a necessary cause with a sufficient cause:

- A **necessary** cause, as the term implies, is one that must happen in order for an effect to come about; an effect can have more than one necessary cause. For example, if emissions from a factory cause a high rate of illness in a neighborhood, the emissions are a necessary cause.
- A **sufficient** cause, in contrast, is one that brings about the effect *by itself.* The emissions are not a sufficient cause of the illness rate unless all other possible causes—such as water pollution or infection—can be eliminated.

Oversimplification can also occur if you allow opinions or emotions to cloud the interpretation of evidence. Suppose that you are examining the reasons why a gun-control bill you opposed was passed by the state legislature. Some of your evidence strongly suggests that a member of the legislature, a vocal supporter of the bill, was unduly influenced by lobbyists. But if you attributed the passage of the bill solely to this legislator, you would be exaggerating the significance of a single legislator and you would be ignoring the opinions of the many others who also voted for the bill. To achieve a balanced analysis, you would have to put aside your own feelings and consider all possible causes for the bill's passage.

ANALYZING CAUSES AND EFFECTS IN PARAGRAPHS

Amy Tan (born 1952) is an essayist and a fiction writer. She won the National Book Award for *The Joy Luck Club* (1989), a novel about a relationship she knows firsthand: Chinese American daughters and their immigrant Chinese mothers. The following paragraph comes from Tan's essay "Mother Tongue," first published in *The Threepenny Review* in 1990.

I think my mother's English almost had an effect
on limiting my possibilities in life as well. Sociologists and linguists probably will tell you that a

person's developing language skills are more influenced by peers. But I do think that the language spoken in the family, especially in immigrant families which are more insular, plays a large role in shaping the language of the child. And I believe that it affected my results on achievement tests, IQ tests, and the SAT. While my English skills were never judged as poor, compared to math, English could not be considered my strong suit. In grade school I did moderately well, getting perhaps Bs, sometimes B-pluses, in English and scoring perhaps in the sixtieth or seventieth percentile on achievement tests. But those scores were not good enough to override the opinion that my true abilities lay in math and science, because in those areas I achieved As and scored in the ninetieth percentile or higher.

Cause (topic sentence underlined): the language spoken in an immigrant family

Effects:
Language proficiency of children

Test scores and grades

Perception of abilities

Sherman Alexie (born 1966) writes essays, fiction, poetry, and screenplays about the experiences of contemporary Native Americans. The following paragraph is from a 1998 *Cineaste* interview in which Alexie discusses his film *Smoke Signals*.

I always tell people that the five primary influences in my life are my father, for his nontraditional Indian stories, my grandmother for her traditional Indian stories, Stephen King, John Steinbeck, and *The Brady Bunch*. That's who I am. I think a lot of Indian artists like to pretend that they're not influenced by pop culture or Western culture, but I am, and I'm happy to admit it. A lot of independent filmmakers would look down their noses at their own pop influences, or at my pop influences. It's a cultural currency.

Causes:
Nontraditional Indian stories
Traditional Indian stories
Western literary culture
Television

Effect (topic sentence underlined): an artist influenced by diverse cultural forces

DEVELOPING AN ESSAY BY CAUSE-AND-EFFECT ANALYSIS
Getting Started

Assignments in almost any course or line of work ask for cause-and-effect analysis: What caused the Vietnam War? In the theory of sociobiology, what are the effects of altruism on the survival of the group? Why did costs exceed the budget last month? You can find your own subject for cause-and-effect analysis from your experiences, from observation of others, from your course work, or from your reading outside school. Anytime you find yourself wondering what happened or why or what if, you may be onto an appropriate subject.

Remember that your treatment of causes or effects or both must be thorough; thus your subject must be manageable within the constraints of time and space imposed on you. Broad subjects like those below must be narrowed to something whose complexities you can cover adequately.

BROAD SUBJECT	Causes of the increase in American industrial productivity
NARROWER SUBJECT	Causes of increasing productivity on one assembly line
BROAD SUBJECT	Effects of cigarette smoke
NARROWER SUBJECT	Effects of parents' secondhand smoke on small children

Whether your subject suggests a focus on causes or effects or both, list as many of them as you can from memory or from further reading. If the subject does not suggest a focus, then ask yourself questions to begin exploring it:

- Why did it happen?
- What contributed to it?
- What were or are its results?
- What might its consequences be?

One or more of these questions should lead you to a focus and, as you explore further, to a more complete list of ideas.

But you cannot stop with a simple list, for you must arrange the causes or effects in sequence and weigh their relative importance: Do the events sort out into a causal chain? Besides the immediate causes and effects, are there also less obvious, more remote ones? Besides the major causes or effects, are there also minor ones? At this stage, you may find that diagramming relationships helps you see them more clearly. The diagram on the next page illustrates the earlier example of the plant closing (see p. 298):

Though uncomplicated, the diagram does sort out the causes and effects and show their relationships and sequence.

While you are developing a clear picture of your subject, you should also be anticipating the expectations and needs of your readers. As with the other methods of essay development, consider especially what your readers already know about your subject and what they need to be told:

- Do readers require background information?
- Are they likely to be familiar with some of the causes or effects you are analyzing, or should you explain every one completely?
- Which causes or effects might readers already accept?
- Which ones might they disagree with? If, for instance, the plant closing affected many of your readers — putting them or their relatives out of work — they might blame the company's owners rather than economic forces beyond the owners' control. You would have to address these preconceptions and provide plenty of evidence for your own interpretation.

To help manage your ideas and information, try to develop a thesis sentence that states your subject, your perspective on it, and your purpose. The thesis sentence should reflect your judgments about the relative significance of possible causes or effects. For instance:

EXPLANATORY THESIS SENTENCE   Being caught in the middle of a family quarrel has affected not only my feelings about my family but also my relations with friends.

PERSUASIVE THESIS SENTENCE   Contrary to local opinion, the many people put out of work by the closing of Windsor Manufacturing were victims not of the owners' incompetence but of the nation's weak economy.

Organizing

The introduction to a cause-and-effect essay can pull readers in by describing the situation whose causes or effects you plan to analyze, such as the passage of a bill in the legislature or a town's high unemployment rate. The introduction may also provide background, such as a brief narrative of a family quarrel; or it may summarize the analysis of causes or effects that the essay disputes, such as the townspeople's blaming the owners for a plant's closing. If your thesis is not already apparent in the introduction, stating it explicitly can tell readers exactly what your purpose is and which causes or effects or both you plan to highlight. But if you anticipate that readers will oppose your thesis, you may want to delay stating it until the end of the essay, after you have provided the evidence to support it.

The arrangement of the body of the essay depends primarily on your material and your emphasis. If events unfold in a causal chain with each effect becoming the cause of another effect, and if stressing these links coincides with your purpose, then a simple chronological sequence will probably be clearest. But if events overlap and vary in significance, their organization will require more planning. Probably the most effective way to arrange either causes or effects is in order of increasing importance. Such an arrangement helps readers see which causes or effects you consider minor and which major, while it also reserves your most significant (and probably most detailed) point for last. The groups of minor or major events may then fit into a chronological framework.

To avoid being preoccupied with organization while you are drafting your essay, prepare some sort of outline before you start writing. The outline need not be detailed so long as you have written the details elsewhere or can retrieve them easily from your mind. But it should show all the causes or effects you want to discuss and the order in which you will cover them.

To conclude your essay, you may want to restate your thesis—or state it, if you deliberately withheld it for the end—so that readers are left with the point of your analysis. If your analysis is complex, readers may also benefit from a summary of the relationships you have identified. And depending on your purpose, you may want to specify why your analysis is significant, what use your readers can make of it, or what action you hope they will take.

Drafting

While drafting your essay, strive primarily for clarity—sharp details, strong examples, concrete explanations. To make readers see not only *what* you see but also *why* you see it, you can draw on just about any method of writing discussed in this book. For instance, you might narrate the effect of a situation on one person, analyze a process, or compare and contrast two interpretations of cause. Particularly if your thesis is debatable (like the earlier example asserting the owners' blamelessness for the plant's closing), you will need accurate, representative facts to back up your interpretation, and you may also need quotations from experts such as witnesses and scholars. If you do not support your assertions specifically, your readers will have no reason to believe them. (For more on evidence in persuasive writing, see pp. 332 and 339–40.)

Revising and Editing

While revising and editing your draft, consider the following questions and the box on the facing page to be sure your analysis is sound and clear.

- *Have you explained causes or effects clearly and specifically?* Readers will need to see the pattern of causes or effects—their sequence and relative importance. And readers will need facts, examples, and other evidence to understand and accept your analysis.
- *Have you demonstrated that causes are not merely coincidences?* Avoid the error of post hoc, of assuming that one event caused another just because it preceded the other. To be convincing, a claim that one event caused another must be supported with ample evidence.
- *Have you considered all the possible causes or effects?* Your analysis should go beyond what is most immediate or obvious so that you do not oversimplify the cause-and-effect relationships.

FOCUS ON CLARITY AND CONCISENESS

While drafting a cause-and-effect analysis, you may need to grope a bit to discover just what you think about the sequence and relative importance of reasons and consequences. As a result, your sentences may grope a bit, too, reflecting your initial confusion or your need to circle around your ideas in order to find them. The following draft passage reveals such difficulties:

> WORDY AND UNCLEAR   Employees often worry about suggestive comments from others. The employee may not only worry but feel the need to discuss the situation with coworkers. One thing that is an effect of sexual harassment, even verbal harassment, in the workplace is that productivity is lost. Plans also need to be made to figure out how to deal with future comments. Engaging in these activities is sure to take time and concentration from work.

Drafting this passage, the writer seems to have built up to the idea about lost productivity (third sentence) after providing support for it in the first two sentences. The fourth sentence then adds more support. And sentences 2–4 all show a writer working out his ideas: sentence subjects and verbs do not focus on the main actors and actions of the sentences, words repeat unnecessarily, and word groups run longer than needed for clarity.

These problems disappear from the edited version below, which moves the main ideas up front, uses subjects and verbs to state what the sentences are about, and cuts unneeded words.

> CONCISE AND CLEAR   Even verbal sexual harassment in the workplace causes a loss of productivity. Worrying about suggestive comments from others, discussing those comments with coworkers, planning how to deal with future comments—all these activities take time and concentration that a harassed employee could spend on work.

For more on editing for conciseness and clarity, see pages 47–51.

Your readers will expect you to present the relationships in all their complexity.

- *Have you represented the cause-and-effect relationships honestly?* Don't deliberately ignore or exaggerate causes or effects in a misguided effort to strengthen your essay. If a cause fails to support your thesis but still does not invalidate it, mention the cause and explain why you believe it to be unimportant. If a change you are proposing will have bad effects as well as good, mention the bad effects and explain how they are outweighed by the good. As long as your reasoning and evidence are sound, such admissions will not weaken your essay; on the contrary, readers will appreciate your fairness.

- *Have you used transitions to signal the sequence and relative importance of events?* Transitions between sentences can help you pinpoint causes or effects (*for this reason, as a result*), show the steps in a sequence (*first, second, third*), link events in time (*in the same month*), specify duration (*a year later*), and indicate the weights you assign events (*equally important, even more crucial*). (See also *transitions* in the Glossary.)

A NOTE ON THEMATIC CONNECTIONS

Analyzing our cultural identity often leads writers to ask what causes a particular identity or what its effects are. The authors in this chapter attempt to pinpoint how their own cultural makeup works in their lives. In a paragraph (p. 299), Amy Tan discusses the effects of the language spoken within immigrant families like her own. In another paragraph (p. 300), Sherman Alexie explains the influences— both Native American and Western—on his identity. In essays, Judith Ortiz Cofer (next page) and Aliza Kimhachandra (p. 313) discuss being on the receiving end of ethnic stereotypes, while Barbara Ehrenreich writes of having no specific "cultural baggage" (p. 319).

Prejudices are the refuge of those who cannot think for themselves.
—Comtesse Diane

Prejudice is a seeping, dark stain, I think, more difficult to fight than hatred—which is powerful and violent and somehow more honest.
—Josephine Lawrence

As surely as night follows day, our country will fail in its democracy because of race prejudice unless we root it out. —Pearl S. Buck

Journal Response   At one time or another, almost everyone has been the object of other people's stereotypes or prejudices—because of skin color, style of dress, activities, weight, or physical condition, among other possible factors. Write in your journal about a time when you felt or knew that assumptions were being made about you because of some outward characteristic.

Judith Ortiz Cofer

Judith Ortiz Cofer, who was born in Puerto Rico, is a writer and a teacher of literature and writing at the University of Georgia in Athens. Her works include The Latin Deli *(1993) and many other books of poems and stories. She has been anthologized in* The Best American Essays, The Norton Book of Women's Lives, The Pushcart Prize, *and the* O. Henry Prize Stories. *She received a PEN/Martha Albrand Special Citation in nonfiction for* Silent Dancing *(1990) as well as the Anisfield Wolf Book Award for* The Latin Deli. *She recently coedited an anthology of essays,* Sleeping with One Eye Open: Women Writers and the Art of Survival *(1999). Cofer has received fellowships from the National Endowment for the Arts and the Witter Bynner Foundation for poetry. Her most recent book is* Woman in Front of the Sun: On Becoming a Writer *(2000).*

Don't Misread My Signals

"Don't Misread My Signals" first appeared in Glamour *magazine. Stereotyped in her youth because of her Puerto Rican heritage, Ortiz knows well the damage that ethnicity can do.*

On a bus to London from Oxford University, where I was earning *1*
some graduate credits one summer, a young man, obviously fresh

from a pub, approached my seat. With both hands over his heart, he went down on his knees in the aisle and broke into an Irish tenor's rendition of "Maria" from *West Side Story*.[1] I was not amused. "Maria" had followed me to London, reminding me of a prime fact of my life: you can leave the island of Puerto Rico, master the English language, and travel as far as you can, but if you're a Latina, especially one who so clearly belongs to Rita Moreno's gene pool, the island travels with you.

Growing up in New Jersey and wanting most of all to belong, I   2
lived in two completely different worlds. My parents designed our life as a microcosm of their *casas*[2] on the island — we spoke Spanish, ate Puerto Rican food bought at the *bodega*[3] and practiced strict Catholicism complete with Sunday mass in Spanish.

I was kept under tight surveillance by my parents, since my virtue   3
and modesty were, by their cultural equation, the same as their honor. As teenagers, my friends and I were lectured constantly on how to behave as proper *señoritas*. But it was a conflicting message we received, since our Puerto Rican mothers also encouraged us to look and act like women by dressing us in clothes our Anglo schoolmates and their mothers found too "mature" and flashy. I often felt humiliated when I appeared at an American friend's birthday party wearing a dress more suitable for a semiformal. At Puerto Rican festivities, neither the music nor the colors we wore could be too loud.

I remember Career Day in high school, when our teachers told us   4
to come dressed as if for a job interview. That morning I agonized in front of my closet, trying to figure out what a "career girl" would wear, because the only model I had was Marlo Thomas[4] on TV. To me and my Puerto Rican girlfriends, dressing up meant wearing our mother's ornate jewelry and clothing.

At school that day, the teachers assailed us for wearing "every-   5
thing at once" — meaning too much jewelry and too many acces-

---

[1] *West Side Story*, a musical loosely based on Shakespeare's *Romeo and Juliet*, depicts the clash between white and Puerto Rican street gangs. Also in this paragraph, "Maria" is a song from the musical about one of the main characters, a Puerto Rican girl, and Rita Moreno (born 1931) played the role of another Puerto Rican in the movie version. [Editor's note.]

[2] Spanish, "houses." [Editor's note.]

[3] Spanish, a small grocery store. [Editor's note.]

[4] An American actress (born 1938), best known for her role as a modern, independent career woman on the late 1960s sitcom *That Girl*. [Editor's note.]

sories. And it was painfully obvious that the other students in their tailored skirts and silk blouses thought we were hopeless and vulgar. The way they looked at us was a taste of the cultural clash that awaited us in the real world, where prospective employers and men on the street would often misinterpret our tight skirts and bright colors as a come-on.

It is custom, not chromosomes, that leads us to choose scarlet   6 over pale pink. Our mothers had grown up on a tropical island where the natural environment was a riot of primary colors, where showing your skin was one way to keep cool as well as to look sexy. On the island, women felt free to dress and move provocatively since they were protected by the traditions and laws of a Spanish Catholic system of morality and machismo, the main rule of which was: *You may look at my sister, but if you touch her I will kill you.* The extended family and church structure provided them with a circle of safety on the island; if a man "wronged" a girl, everyone would close in to save her family honor.

Off-island, signals often get mixed. When a Puerto Rican girl   7 who is dressed in her idea of what is attractive meets a man from the mainstream culture who has been trained to react to certain types of clothing as a sexual signal, a clash is likely to take place. She is seen as a Hot Tamale, a sexual firebrand. I learned this lesson at my first formal dance when my date leaned over and painfully planted a sloppy, overeager kiss on my mouth. When I didn't respond with sufficient passion, he said in a resentful tone: "I thought you Latin girls were supposed to mature early." It was the first time I would feel like a fruit or vegetable—I was supposed to *ripen*, not just grow into womanhood like other girls.

These stereotypes, though rarer, still surface in my life. I recently   8 stayed at a classy metropolitan hotel. After having dinner with a friend, I was returning to my room when a middle-aged man in a tuxedo stepped directly into my path. With his champagne glass extended toward me, he exclaimed, "Evita!"[5]

Blocking my way, he bellowed the song "Don't Cry For Me,   9 Argentina." Playing to the gathering crowd, he began to sing loudly a ditty to the tune of "La Bamba"—except the lyrics were about a girl

[5] Eva de Peron (1919–52), known as "Evita," was the first lady of Argentina from 1946 to 1952. "Don't Cry for Me, Argentina" (next paragraph) is a song from *Evita*, a musical about her life. [Editor's note.]

named Maria whose exploits all rhymed with her name and gonorrhea.

I knew that this same man — probably a corporate executive,   10
even worldly by most standards — would never have regaled a white
woman with a dirty song in public. But to him, I was just a character
in his universe of "others," all cartoons.

Still, I am one of the lucky ones. There are thousands of Latinas   11
without the privilege of the education that my parents gave me. For
them every day is a struggle against the misconceptions perpetuated
by the myth of the Latina as a whore, domestic worker or criminal.

Rather than fight these pervasive stereotypes, I try to replace   12
them with a more interesting set of realities. I travel around the
United States reading from my books of poetry and my novel. With
the stories I tell, the dreams and fears I examine in my work, I try to
get my audience past the particulars of my skin color, my accent or
my clothes.

I once wrote a poem in which I called Latinas "God's brown   13
daughters." It is really a prayer, of sorts, for communication and respect. In it, Latin women pray "in Spanish to an Anglo God / with a
Jewish heritage," and they are "fervently hoping / that if not omnipotent, / at least He be bilingual."

Meaning

1. In paragraph 1 Cofer says, "you can leave the island of Puerto Rico,
   master the English language, and travel as far as you can, but if you're a
   Latina, especially one who so clearly belongs to Rita Moreno's gene
   pool, the island travels with you." How would you paraphrase this
   statement? What does it say about the enduring effect of stereotypes on
   Cofer's identity?
2. What explanations does Cofer offer for styles of dress on Puerto Rico?
   What does she mean when she states that "custom, not chromosomes,
   [. . .] leads us to choose scarlet over pale pink" (paragraph 6)? What reactions do such styles of dress often provoke outside of Puerto Rico?
3. In what way does the author regard herself as "lucky" (paragraph 11)?
   How does she attempt to combat stereotypes?
4. If any of the following words are new to you, try to guess their meanings
   from their context in Cofer's essay. Look up the words in a dictionary to
   check your guesses, and then use each word in a sentence or two of your
   own.

surveillance (3)   misinterpret (5)   regaled (10)
agonized (4)   chromosomes (6)   pervasive (12)
ornate (4)   mainstream (7)   fervently (13)
assailed (5)   gonorrhea (9)   omnipotent (13)

Purpose and Audience

1. What seems to be Cofer's primary purpose in this piece? Does she want to express her frustration at being the target of ethnic stereotyping, or does she want in some way to educate her readers? How can you tell?
2. The poem Cofer quotes in paragraph 13 contains a plea. How does this plea relate to the purpose of her essay?
3. To whom does Cofer seem to be writing here? Why do you think so?

Method and Structure

1. How well does cause-and-effect analysis suit Cofer's subject of the ethnic stereotyping to which she has been subjected? Does this method provide an effective means of achieving her purpose?
2. At the beginning and near the end of her essay, Cofer offers anecdotes about being sung to by strangers (paragraphs 1 and 8–10). How are the experiences similar and how are they different? Why do you think Cofer opens with the one rather than the other?
3. **Other Methods**   Aside from cause-and-effect analysis, what other method does Cofer use extensively to show the kinds of stereotyping she has suffered? Why does she use it?

Language

1. Cofer uses several Spanish words, such as *casas, bodega,* and *señoritas.* Why do you think she chooses to do so? What do the words add to the essay?
2. The Spanish word *maduro* means both "mature" and "ripe." How is this linguistic overlap reflected in Cofer's reaction to her date's comment at her first formal dance (paragraph 7)? Does it seem likely that a non-Spanish-speaking person would make the same connection? Why, or why not?

Writing Topics

1. **Journal to Essay**   In your journal entry (p. 307), you wrote about a time when you felt yourself to be stereotyped because of some outward characteristic. Now use your experience as the starting point for an

essay modeled loosely on Cofer's. What are the reasons for the appearance or behavior that draws out the prejudice of others? What are the effects of that prejudice on you and others like yourself? How do you, or might you, respond?

2. Cofer focuses on how the clothing and accessories worn by Latinas affect non-Latinos' views of them. More broadly, why does a person's clothing often affect others' opinions of that person? Are opinions formed on the basis of clothing generally fair or unfair? Does clothing serve a useful function in guiding our responses to others? For example, what if a person deliberately dresses to provoke a negative reaction? Should he or she be judged in the same light as someone whose religion requires seemingly strange clothing choices? Should clothing be judged at all? Considering the answers to these and other questions that may occur to you, write an essay that explains your idea of the role of clothing in the interaction of people.

3. **Cultural Considerations**   In a longer version of this essay, Cofer criticizes the communications media for offering images of Latin women mainly as "hot tamales," domestic workers, or criminals. Do you agree or disagree that the media often portray people, especially minorities, in a negative way? Write an essay exploring the media's role in perpetuating or undermining negative stereotypes.

4. **Connections**   Both Cofer and Noel Perrin, in "The Androgynous Man" (p. 287), close their essays by envisioning a God who is like them in some way. Perrin proposes that God, like himself, is balanced between masculine and feminine. Cofer prays for a God who, like herself, embraces ethnic diversity and understanding. What do these authors' wishes say about their common desire for greater diversity and tolerance? Write an essay comparing their visions.

Ethnic stereotypes are misshapen pearls, sometimes with a sandy grain of truth at their center, but they ignore complexity, change, and individuality.
—Anna Quindlen

I have a dream that my four little children will one day live in a nation where they will not be judged by the color of their skin but by the content of their character. —Martin Luther King Jr.

We all know that we are unique individuals, but we tend to see others as representatives of groups. —Deborah Tannen

Journal Response Write a short journal entry about stereotypes that you have observed or experienced in American society concerning ethnicity, age, social class, sexual preference, religion, or other attributes.

Aliza Kimhachandra

Aliza Kimhachandra was born in 1979 in Oklahoma and attends Boston College. When asked to identify herself in terms of nationality, she states that she's both American and Thai. Kimhachandra says that her essay "is about a cross between two ethnic cultures but that culture could also mean a post-office-work culture, a Boston College culture, a water polo or Gold's Gym culture, a string-quartet culture. Prejudice, discrimination, and hate may begin to diminish as we begin to realize that we all are the same, we are all multicultural." Kimhachandra currently resides in Newton, Massachusetts.

Banana

"Banana" was first published in Fresh Ink, *a collection of first-year writing by students at Boston College. The essay tackles the idea that an individual can be a synthesis of two different people, personalities, ethnicities, or races. According to Kimhachandra, America is made up of "bananas," whether or not each person's differences are visible.*

So you call me a banana. Well, maybe I am one. What's it to you 1 anyway? I didn't ask to be born one, but I was, and you will just have to accept me for what I am. A banana is a wonderful fruit.

My parents come from Thailand, a beautiful tropical country in   2
Southeast Asia. I was born in America, but I am still Thai at heart.
Actually, my yellow skin has been something of an asset. Attached to
my appearance is a long string of stereotypes: Asian girls are quiet
and obedient; they all play the piano; they are smart little robots that
do everything right; they are like computers, studying all the time and
storing information. There is not much creativity in these robots, but
they can make the grade and that's what's important. Throughout
primary and most of secondary school it was very easy for me to fall
into these stereotypes. All those things that parents, teachers, and administrators like. I was a very quiet student. The only time I spoke
was when I was sure what I was about to say was not stupid. This
was usually a correct answer to some math problem, which led everyone to believe I was a whiz. I never disrupted class. I always did what
I was told. I played the piano. I was the stereotypical Asian kid.

To add to my "yellowness," after years of being ignorant about   3
my Asian heritage, I became a self-made expert on Thai culture. In
high school, people would come to me and say, "You were born and
raised in America, how come you're so Thai? How do you know so
much about Thailand? And how come you can still speak Thai?"
Well, it's inevitable. When most of your life you've seen people with
round light eyes, light skin, and light hair, characteristics you don't
have, and then you take a trip and begin to see people with slanted
dark eyes, dark hair, and a tan complexion, characteristics you do
have, you have to question yourself. "Hey, self, why do you look like
those people when you speak and act like these people?" This question swallowed me up and I had to find the answer. In my search, I
ended up teaching myself to speak and read Thai and learning all I
could about Thai traditions and customs. It's really interesting how
much ethnicity affects a person's way of thinking. It's like a conscience. For example, if you ask an Asian what she needs to eat to become full, she would most likely respond by saying, "Rice." But if
you ask an Irish person the same question, wouldn't that person say,
"Potatoes"? Anyway, you understand what I mean.

My white part, under the yellow skin, is my American side. It's a   4
funny thing. I was kind of living a double life all through school.
While in school, it was more advantageous to act Asian, so that's
what I did. Outside school, in society, it was more advantageous to
act American. Outgoing and friendly, talkative, I became all these
outside the classroom. Friends from school have always found it
strange that my personality changes so much depending on whether I

am inside or outside class. It's just a matter of fitting in and assessing what kind of behavior is more advantageous in certain places. When I tell them this, they understand why I change, but it is still difficult for them to understand how I can be so American and also be so Thai. Well, everyone knows that America is made up of immigrants. In the area I live in now, there are many Americans of Italian descent. They have Western features, for the most part they speak with an American accent, and their families have been in America for generations. They don't question whether they are American or not and neither do their peers and colleagues; of course they are American. But if we look closer at these families, they are still very Italian. They eat a lot of pasta, spend hours preparing meat sauce from an old family recipe, abide by the Catholic Church. They are still very Italian but are also very American.

After a long period of thinking and trying to understand who I am — am I really able to be both Thai and American? am I more Thai or more American? — I realized that I really am both. A unique mixture of East and West. So I began to act like both. I took the bad aspects of the cultures, like female inferiority, and threw them away; then I picked up their good characteristics and meshed them together to make . . . well, me. Now I can be smart, loud, obedient yet daring, all the good stuff that is associated with being Asian and being American. The next thing I need to do is to try and get others to understand this about me.

Most of those people who say I am *so* Asian are white Americans. On the other hand, those who say I am *so* American are Asian. If my analysis is correct, this stems from the very human tendency of a group of similar people to notice more readily the differences in people who are not so similar to themselves. To the typical white American, who sees "American" acts every day and is immune to them, my Asian side is definitely different and they notice these differences. The same goes for the Asians. To them, I am very American because they notice the American things I do while they are immune to the Asian things. An example: If I bow to an elder in the Thai community, non-Thais will take more notice than Thais would. On the other hand, if I'm wearing a tank top and shorts, Thais will take more notice because for Thais dressing this way in public is improper. I think it's funny how neither group can accept me as both Asian *and* American. I guess it's just human nature to try to put things into specific categories. It's too bad, though, because it shows that people don't realize what America is — a wonderful nation enriched by the diversity of her people.

So I am a banana. Being a banana is not at all bad. There are many   7
advantages to being one. It is a unique fruit that has its own characteristics, way of growth, and way of presenting itself to the world. It is a
distinct member of the fruit family. It is sweet and satisfying. I love
being a banana. And have you ever noticed that after peeling back its
golden yellow skin, the ripe pulp of a banana is actually a shade of pale
yellow? A harmonious mixture of yellow and white together in a sweet,
wonderful fruit. It's a nice color, perfectly acceptable, but not many
people notice it. Here's my final question: If I am a banana, unique,
sweet, wonderful . . . what kind of fruit are you?

Meaning

1. In her first paragraph Kimhachandra asks a question and then offers a
   response. What is a *banana* in the context of this essay? How does
   Kimhachandra's introduction effectively summarize the main idea of her
   essay?
2. In paragraph 6 Kimhachandra refers to the "very human tendency of a
   group of similar people to notice more readily the differences in people
   who are not so similar to themselves." Does she condemn this tendency?
3. Based on their context in Kimhachandra's essay, try to guess the meanings of any of the following words. Test your guesses in a dictionary,
   and then try to use each word in a sentence or two of your own.

whiz (2)	advantageous (4)	immune (6)
heritage (3)	abide (4)	harmonious (7)
inevitable (3)		

Purpose and Audience

1. Do you believe that Kimhachandra writes mainly to convince others of
   her viewpoint or to articulate her feelings more clearly to herself? Make
   specific references to the text to support your opinion.
2. Whom is Kimhachandra addressing in the opening sentence? What do
   this sentence and the rest of the essay tell you about the author's conception of her audience?
3. In paragraph 7 Kimhachandra poses a final question to readers. What
   does this query reveal about both her purpose and her audience?

Method and Structure

1. Why might Kimhachandra rely on cause-and-effect analysis to develop
   her ideas? What are some causes of ethnic stereotypes, in her opinion?
   What is the effect of the human tendency to categorize others?

2. Why do you think Kimhachandra chooses to make so much of *banana,* a term often used as an ethnic slur? How does she use the symbol of a tropical fruit to combat the stereotypes she experiences?
3. **Other Methods** In addition to cause-and-effect analysis, Kimhachandra also relies on narration (Chapter 5) and example (Chapter 6). What does each of these other methods contribute to her essay?

Language

1. How would you describe the author's tone? Is she angry? optimistic? passionate? self-confident? hesitant? cheerful?
2. Kimhachandra begins her essay with "So." She also uses interjections such as "well" (paragraphs 3, 4, and 5) and "hey" (3). How would you characterize this language? What does it add to Kimhachandra's essay?

Writing Topics

1. **Journal to Essay** On the basis of your journal entry and your reaction to the quotations at the beginning of "Banana" (p. 313), expand your ideas about what Kimhachandra calls the "very human tendency" to pigeonhole those who are different from ourselves. Do you agree with Kimhachandra that this reaction is inevitable? At what point does stereotyping become harmful and destructive? Do you think that it is always harmful, or can it sometimes be beneficial? Write from a personal perspective, as Kimhachandra does, or from a broader societal perspective. If you choose the latter course, however, pin your meaning down with plenty of details and examples.
2. Kimhachandra writes about the effects of her dual identity as a Thai American. In addition to ethnic background, what other factors also make us who we are? In a cause-and-effect essay, explain how your age, socioeconomic background, religion, outward appearance, academic ability, or some other characteristic has helped to create your identity. If you were to choose a symbol—like Kimhachandra's banana—to represent yourself, what would that symbol be? Why?
3. **Cultural Considerations** As home for immigrants from scores of other countries, the United States thrusts together people from almost every imaginable ethnic background. Write an essay in which you consider the challenges of living in such a diverse society. What are some sources of friction? What are some advantages? To what extent should we recognize each other's differences, and to what extent should we ignore them? Use examples from your own experiences, observations, and reading.

4. **Connections**   Aliza Kimhachandra has at times felt herself to have too much ethnic identity. Barbara Ehrenreich, in contrast, has at times felt herself to have too little ethnic identity ("Cultural Baggage," opposite). Compare and contrast these two writers' attitudes toward the advantages and disadvantages of a distinct ethnic identity.

Culture may even be described simply as that which makes life worth living.
—T. S. Eliot

Growing up, I came up with this name: I'm a Cablinasian (Caucasian, Afro-American, Native American, Thai, and Chinese).   —Tiger Woods

Traditions are the guideposts driven deep into our subconscious minds.
—Ellen Goodman

Journal Response How does your religious, ethnic, or racial background influence your everyday life? Write a short journal entry to explore the answer to this question.

Barbara Ehrenreich

Barbara Ehrenreich was born in 1941 in Butte, Montana. She graduated from Reed College, took a Ph.D. from Rockefeller University, and taught for a while at the State University of New York. Her feature articles, reviews, and essays have appeared in a wide range of publications, including the New York Times Magazine, *the* Washington Post Magazine, *the* Wall Street Journal, Esquire, The Atlantic, Harper's, The New Republic, Social Policy, Vogue, *and* Z Magazine. *She is currently a contributing writer at* The Nation. *Ehrenreich's books include* The Sexual Politics of Sickness *(1973),* Fear of Falling: The Inner Life of the Middle Class *(1989),* The Worst Years of Our Lives *(1990),* The Snarling Citizen *(1995), and* Nickel and Dimed *(2001).*

Cultural Baggage

After struggling to identify her "ethnic genes," Ehrenreich looks to the spirit of her parents, whose unofficial motto was "new things [are] better than old." This essay from The Snarling Citizen *presents an unorthodox understanding of cultural heritage: a celebration of lineage free from the shackles of "poverty, superstition, and grief."*

An acquaintance was telling me about the joys of rediscovering her   1
ethnic and religious heritage. "I know exactly what my ancestors
were doing 2,000 years ago," she said, eyes gleaming with enthusi-

asm, "and *I can do the same things now.*" Then she leaned forward and inquired politely, "And what is your ethnic background, if I may ask?"

"None," I said, that being the first word in line to get out of my   2
mouth. Well, not "none," I backtracked. Scottish, English, Irish—that was something, I supposed. Too much Irish to qualify as a WASP; too much of the hated English to warrant a "Kiss Me, I'm Irish" button; plus there are a number of dead ends in the family tree due to adoptions, missing records, failing memories and the like. I was blushing by this time. Did "none" mean I was rejecting my heritage out of Anglo-Celtic self-hate? Or was I revealing a hidden ethnic chauvinism in which the Britannically derived served as a kind of neutral standard compared with the ethnic "others"?

Throughout the 60s and 70s, I watched one group after another—   3
African-Americans, Latinos, Native Americans—stand up and proudly reclaim their roots while I just sank back ever deeper into my seat. All this excitement over ethnicity stemmed, I uneasily sensed, from a past in which *their* ancestors had been trampled upon by *my* ancestors, or at least by people who looked very much like them. In addition, it had begun to seem almost un-American not to have some sort of hyphen at hand, linking one to more venerable times and locales.

But the truth is, I was raised with none. We'd eaten ethnic foods   4
in my childhood home, but these were all borrowed, like the pasties, or Cornish meat pies, my father had picked up from his fellow miners in Butte, Montana. If my mother had one rule, it was militant ecumenism in all matters of food and experience. "Try new things," she would say, meaning anything from sweetbreads to clams, with an emphasis on the "new."

As a child, I briefly nourished a craving for tradition and roots. I im-   5
mersed myself in the works of Sir Walter Scott.[1] I pretended to believe that the bagpipe was a musical instrument. I was fascinated to learn from a grandmother that we were descended from certain Highland clans and longed for a pleated skirt in one of their distinctive tartans.

But in *Ivanhoe,* it was the dark-eyed "Jewess" Rebecca I identi-   6
fied with, not the flaxen-haired bimbo Rowena. As for clans: Why

---

[1]Scott (1771–1832) was a Scottish poet and novelist. His novel *Ivanhoe* (next paragraph) is a historical romance set in medieval times. The Jewish Rebecca falls in love with the Christian Ivanhoe, but it is Lady Rowena, the upper-class Saxon, who wins Ivanhoe's love. [Editor's note.]

not call them "tribes," those bands of half-clad peasants and warriors whose idea of cuisine was stuffed sheep gut washed down with whisky? And then there was the sting of Disraeli's[2] remark—which I came across in my early teens—to the effect that his ancestors had been leading orderly, literate lives when my ancestors were still rampaging through the Highlands daubing themselves with blue paint.

Motherhood put the screws on me, ethnicity-wise. I had hoped 7 that by marrying a man of Eastern European–Jewish ancestry I would acquire for my descendants the ethnic genes that my own forebears so sadly lacked. At one point, I even subjected the children to a seder[3] of my own design, including a little talk about the flight from Egypt and its relevance to modern social issues. But the kids insisted on buttering their matzohs and snickering through my talk. "Give me a break, Mom," the older one said. "You don't even believe in God."

After the tiny pagans had been put to bed, I sat down to brood 8 over Elijah's wine.[4] What had I been thinking? The kids knew that their Jewish grandparents were secular folks who didn't hold seders themselves. And if ethnicity eluded me, how could I expect it to take root in my children, who are not only Scottish-English-Irish, but Hungarian-Polish-Russian to boot?

But, then, on the fumes of Manischewitz,[5] a great insight took 9 form in my mind. It was true, as the kids said, that I didn't "believe in God." But this could be taken as something very different from an accusation—a reminder of a genuine heritage. My parents had not believed in God either, nor had my grandparents or any other progenitors going back to the great-great level. They had become disillusioned with Christianity generations ago—just as, on the in-law side, my children's other ancestors had shaken off their Orthodox Judaism. This insight did not exactly furnish me with an "identity," but it was at least something to work with: we are the kind of people, I realized—whatever our distant ancestors' religions—who do *not* believe, who do not carry on traditions, who do not do things just because someone has done them before.

[2] Benjamin Disraeli (1804–81), British statesman, writer, and prime minister, was of Jewish descent. [Editor's note.]

[3] A Jewish ceremonial meal, eaten on the first or second day of Passover, that celebrates the release of the Jews from captivity in Egypt. [Editor's note.]

[4] A special cup of wine placed on the Seder table as an offering to the Hebrew prophet Elijah. [Editor's note.]

[5] The brand name of a kosher wine often served during Passover. [Editor's note.]

The epiphany went on: I recalled that my mother never intro- 10
duced a procedure for cooking or cleaning by telling me, "Grandma
did it this way." What did Grandma know, living in the days before
vacuum cleaners and disposable toilet mops? In my parents' general
view, new things were better than old, and the very fact that some ritual had been performed in the past was a good reason for abandoning it now. Because what was the past, as our forebears knew it?
Nothing but poverty, superstition and grief. "Think for yourself,"
Dad used to say. "Always ask why."

In fact, this may have been the ideal cultural heritage for my par- 11
ticular ethnic strain — bounced as it was from the Highlands of Scot-
land across the sea, out to the Rockies, down into the mines and
finally spewed out into high-tech, suburban America. What better
philosophy, for a race of migrants, than "Think for yourself"? What
better maxim, for people whose whole world was rudely inverted
every thirty years or so, than "Try new things"?

The more tradition-minded, the newly enthusiastic celebrants of 12
Purim and Kwanzaa and Solstice,[6] may see little point to survival if the
survivors carry no cultural freight — religion, for example, or ethnic
tradition. To which I would say that skepticism, curiosity and wide-
eyed ecumenical tolerance are also worthy elements of the human tradition and are at least as old as such notions as "Serbian" or "Croat-
ian," "Scottish" or "Jewish." I make no claims for my personal line of
progenitors except that they remained loyal to the values that may have
induced all of our ancestors, long, long ago, to climb down from the
trees and make their way into the open plains.

A few weeks ago, I cleared my throat and asked the children, 13
now mostly grown and fearsomely smart, whether they felt any stir-
rings of ethnic or religious identity, etc., which might have been,
ahem, insufficiently nourished at home. "None," they said, adding
firmly, "and the world would be a better place if nobody else did,
either." My chest swelled with pride, as would my mother's, to know
that the race of "none" marches on.

Meaning

1. What personal heritage does Ehrenreich embrace? How does she feel
   this heritage was passed down to her?

[6]Purim is a Jewish festival also known as the Feast of Lots. Kwanzaa is a holiday
that celebrates the cultural heritage of African Americans. Solstice, occurring on the
shortest day of the year, is an ancient pagan celebration welcoming the return of the
sun. [Editor's note.]

2. At the end of paragraph 2, Ehrenreich asks herself whether, by claiming no ethnic background, she was "revealing a hidden ethnic chauvinism in which the Britannically derived served as a kind of neutral standard compared with the ethnic 'others.'" What does she mean? Why might this make her feel guilty?

3. In what ways did Ehrenreich attempt to assert an ethnic identity for herself? Why did her efforts fail?

4. If any of the words below are new to you, try to guess their meanings from their context in Ehrenreich's essay. Check your guesses in a dictionary, and then use each word in a sentence or two of your own.

chauvinism (2)	pagans (8)	skepticism (12)
venerable (3)	secular (8)	ecumenical (12)
ecumenism (4)	eluded (8)	progenitors (12)
daubing (6)	epiphany (10)	fearsomely (13)

Purpose and Audience

1. Ehrenreich's thesis does not become clear until paragraphs 12 and 13. What is her thesis?

2. What seems to be Ehrenreich's main purpose in this essay? To defend her lack of ethnic identity? To persuade her readers that there are traditions more important than ethnic traditions? To explore the evolution of her own sense of tradition and cultural identity? Something else? Why do you think so?

3. Is Ehrenreich writing primarily for those with a strong ethnic identity, for those—like herself—without one, or for both? How can you tell? What other assumptions does she seem to make about her audience?

Method and Structure

1. What are the two main cause-and-effect relationships that Ehrenreich explores in this essay? How are these central to her purpose for writing?

2. Ehrenreich opens and closes her essay with two anecdotes. How is the dialogue in these anecdotes connected?

3. Ehrenreich poses a number of questions (for example, in paragraphs 2, 8, 10, 11, and 13). Why are such questions particularly appropriate in this essay?

4. **Other Methods** In paragraphs 3 and 12, Ehrenreich brings in comparison and contrast (Chapter 10). What are her subjects in each case? What point does comparison and contrast help her make?

Language

1. How would you describe Ehrenreich's tone in this essay? Is it consistent throughout?

2. Why does Ehrenreich italicize the words "I can do the same things now" when quoting her friend in paragraph 1? Does this phrase have a larger point in the essay?
3. Why does Ehrenreich link "Purim and Kwanzaa and Solstice" in paragraph 12? What is her point?
4. In her final sentence Ehrenreich refers to "the race of 'none.'" Why does she use the word "race" in this context?

Writing Topics

1. **Journal to Essay**   In your journal entry (p. 319), you considered the effect of your ethnic or religious heritage on your everyday experiences. Now develop your ideas into an essay in which you evaluate the importance you assign to any outward symbols of your heritage: food, music, holidays, customs, religious services, clothing, and the like. For example, do such signs serve to strengthen your cultural identity? If you don't have such signs, how important is their absence?
2. Only by implication (for example, her reference to Serbs and Croats in paragraph 12) does Ehrenreich suggest the potentially negative consequences of ethnic pride and religious zeal. In an essay, consider when people's cultural identity can be a source of conflict, even violence. Is there any way such conflicts can be avoided or resolved? You may wish to think globally about this issue, but be sure to bring your essay down to earth by focusing primarily on what you've experienced or witnessed closer to home.
3. **Cultural Considerations**   The United States is a country of immigrants, and each group has made an indelible mark on American identity. For example, consider just foods: salsa recently outsold ketchup, tacos are to be found everywhere, and cappuccino and sushi are now everyday food items for many Americans who have no Italian or Japanese heritage. Write an essay about the effects of immigration on your daily life: the food you consume, the music you listen to, the dress styles you prefer, and so forth. Include personal examples to bring your ideas to life.
4. **Connections**   Like Ehrenreich, Langston Hughes, in "Salvation" (p. 97), tells of an epiphany in his life. In his case, he painfully comes to terms with the fact that he will have to make his own decisions in life, even when that means going against what others would have him do or think. Ehrenreich, in contrast, is not devastated but rather reassured when she remembers her father's advice to think for herself. Write an essay in which you describe the difficulties each author faced, and summarize their reactions. How do you account for the differences in the reactions of Ehrenreich and Hughes?

Writing with the Method
Cause-and-Effect Analysis

Choose one of the following questions, or any other question they suggest, and answer it in an essay developed by analyzing causes or effects. The question you decide on should concern a topic you care about so that your analysis of causes or effects is a means of communicating an idea, not an end in itself.

PEOPLE AND THEIR BEHAVIOR

1. Why is a past or present politician, athlete, police officer, or fire fighter considered a hero?
2. Why did one couple you know marry or divorce?
3. What does a sound body contribute to a sound mind?
4. Why is a particular friend or relative always getting into trouble?
5. Why do people root for the underdog?
6. How does a person's alcohol or drug dependency affect others in his or her family?

WORK

7. At what age should a person start working for pay, and why?
8. What effects do you expect your education to have on your choice of career and your performance in it?
9. Why would a man or woman enter a field that has traditionally been filled by the opposite sex, such as nursing or engineering?
10. What effect has the job market had on you and your friends?

ART AND ENTERTAINMENT

11. Why do teenagers like rock music?
12. Why have art museums become so popular?
13. What makes a professional sports team succeed in a new city?
14. Why is (or was) a particular television show or movie so popular?

CONTEMPORARY ISSUES

15. Why does the United States spend so much money on defense?
16. What are the possible effects of rising college tuitions?
17. How can a long period of involuntary unemployment affect a person?
18. Why is a college education important?

19. Why do marriages between teenagers fail more often than marriages between people in other age groups?
20. What are the possible effects of widespread adult illiteracy on American society?
21. Why might someone resort to a public act of violence, such as bombing a building?

Writing About the Theme
Exploring the Effects of Cultural Identity

1. In discussing their own cultural backgrounds, the writers represented in this chapter touch on several broader models of cultural influence in contemporary U.S. society. Which of the most common models — such as the melting pot, the salad bowl, or the cultural mosaic — most resembles the environment in which you live? What are the cultural influences that have had an impact on your own neighborhood or community?

2. All the authors represented in this chapter are acutely aware of their ethnic identities. Write an essay describing your own cultural, ethnic, or racial identity, distinguishing the influences that have made you the person you are today.

3. Although the writers represented in this chapter focus on a common subject, their tones vary widely, from humorous to angry to introspective. Choose the two authors that seem most different in tone, and analyze how their chosen tones clarify their points. Is one author's tone more effective than the other's? Why? (For more on tone, see pp. 41–42.)

Chapter 13

ARGUMENT AND PERSUASION

Debating Current Issues

USING THE METHOD

Since we argue all the time—with relatives, with friends, with the auto mechanic or the shop clerk—a chapter devoted to argument and persuasion may at first seem unnecessary. But arguing with an auto mechanic over the cost of repairs is quite a different process from arguing with readers over a complex issue. In both cases we are trying to find common ground with our audience, perhaps to change its views or even to compel it to act as we wish. But the mechanic is in front of us; we can shift our tactics in response to his or her gestures, expressions, and words. The reader, in contrast, is "out there"; we have to anticipate those gestures, expressions, and words in the way we structure the argument, the kinds of evidence we use to support it, even the way we conceive of the subject.

A great many assertions that are worth making are debatable at some level—whether over the facts on which the assertions are based or over the values they imply. Two witnesses to an accident cannot

328

agree on what they saw; two scientists cannot agree on what an experiment shows; two economists cannot agree on what measures will reduce unemployment; two doctors cannot agree on what constitutes life or death. Making an effective case for our opinions requires upholding certain responsibilities and attending to several established techniques of argumentation, most of them dating back to ancient Greece.

Technically, argument and persuasion are two different processes:

- **Argument** appeals mainly to an audience's sense of reason in order to negotiate a common understanding or to win agreement with a claim. It is the method of a columnist who defends a president's foreign policy on the grounds of economics and defense strategy.
- **Persuasion** appeals mainly to an audience's feelings and values in order to compel some action, or at least to win support for an action. It is the method of a mayoral candidate who urges voters to support her because she is sensitive to the poor.

But argument and persuasion so often mingle that we will use the one term *argument* to mean a deliberate appeal to an audience's reason and emotions in order to create compromise, win agreement, or compel action.

The Elements of Argument

All arguments share certain elements:

- The core of the argument is an **assertion** or **proposition,** a debatable claim about the subject. Generally, you express this assertion as your thesis statement. It may defend or attack a position, suggest a solution to a problem, recommend a change in policy, or challenge a value or belief. Here are a few examples:

  > The college should give first priority for on-campus jobs to students who need financial aid.

  > School prayer has been rightly declared unconstitutional and should not be reinstituted in any form.

  > Smokers who wish to poison themselves should be allowed to do so, but not in any place where their smoke will poison others.

- You break down the central assertion into subclaims, each one supported by evidence.

- You raise significant opposing arguments and dispense with them, again with the support of evidence.
- You organize the parts of the argument into a clear, logical structure that pushes steadily toward the conclusion.

You may draw on classification, comparison, or any other rhetorical method to develop the entire argument or to introduce evidence or strengthen your conclusion. For instance, in a paper arguing for raising a college's standards of admission, you might contrast the existing standards with the proposed standards, analyze a process for raising the standards over a period of years, and predict the effects of the new standards on future students' preparedness for college work.

Appeals to Readers

In arguing you are appealing to readers: you want them to listen to what you have to say, judge your words fairly, and, as much as they can, agree with you. Most arguments combine three kinds of appeals to readers: ethical, emotional, and rational.

Ethical Appeal

The **ethical appeal** is often not explicit in an argument, yet it pervades the whole. It is the sense you convey of your expertise and character, projected by the reasonableness of the argument, by the use of evidence, and by tone. A rational argument shows readers that you are thinking logically and fairly (see pp. 332–34). Strong evidence establishes your credibility (see pp. 332, 339–40). And a sincere, reasonable tone demonstrates your balance and goodwill (see p. 343).

Emotional Appeal

The **emotional appeal** in argument aims directly for readers' hearts — for the complex of beliefs, values, and feelings deeply embedded in all of us. We are just as often motivated by these ingrained ideas and emotions as by our intellects. Even scientists, who stress the rational interpretation of facts above all else, are sometimes influenced in their interpretations by emotions deriving from, say, competition with other scientists. And the willingness of a nation's citizens to go to war may result more from their fear and pride than from their reasoned considerations of risks and gains. An emotional appeal in argument attempts to tap such feelings for any of several reasons:

- To heighten the responsiveness of readers
- To inspire readers to new beliefs
- To compel readers to act
- To assure readers that their values remain unchallenged

An emotional appeal may be explicit, as when an argument against capital punishment appeals to readers' religious values by citing the Bible's Sixth Commandment, "Thou shalt not kill." But an emotional appeal may also be less obvious, because individual words may have connotations that elicit emotional responses from readers. For instance, one writer may characterize an environmental group as "a well-organized team representing diverse interests," while another may call the same group "a hodgepodge of nature lovers and irresponsible businesspeople." The first appeals to readers' preference for order and balance, the second to readers' fear of extremism and disdain for unsound business practices. (See pp. 52 and 343 for more on connotation.)

The use of emotional appeals requires care:

- The appeal must be directed at the audience's actual beliefs and feelings.
- The appeal must be presented dispassionately enough so that readers have no reason to doubt your fairness in the rest of the argument.
- The appeal must be appropriate to the subject and to the argument. For instance, in arguing against a pay raise for city councilors, you might be tempted to appeal to readers' resentment and distrust of wealthy people by pointing out that two of the councilors are rich enough to work for nothing. But such an appeal would divert attention from the issue of whether the pay raise is justified for all councilors on the basis of the work they do and the city's ability to pay the extra cost.

Carefully used, emotional appeals have great force, particularly when they contribute to an argument based largely on sound reasoning and evidence. The appropriate mix of emotion and reason in a given essay is entirely dependent on the subject, your purpose, and the audience. Emotional appeals are out of place in most arguments in the natural and social sciences, where rational interpretations of factual evidence are all that will convince readers of the truth of an assertion. But emotional appeals may be essential when you want an audience to support or take an action, for emotion is a stronger motivator than reason.

Rational Appeal

A **rational appeal** is one that, as the name implies, addresses the rational faculties of readers—their capacity to reason logically about a problem. You establish the truth of a proposition or claim by moving through a series of related subclaims, each supported by evidence. In doing so, you follow processes of reasoning that are natural to all of us and thus are expected by readers. These processes are induction and deduction.

Inductive reasoning moves from the particular to the general, from evidence to a generalization or conclusion about the evidence. It is a process we begin learning in infancy and use daily throughout our lives: a child burns herself the three times she touches a stove, so she concludes that stoves burn; we have liked four movies directed by Oliver Stone, so we form the generalization that Oliver Stone makes good movies. Inductive reasoning is also very common in argument: you might offer facts showing that chronic patients in the state's mental hospitals receive only drugs as treatment, and then you conclude that the state's hospitals rely exclusively on drugs to treat chronic patients.

The movement from particular to general is called an **inductive leap** because you must make something of a jump to conclude that what is true of some instances (the chronic patients whose records were available) is also true of all other instances in the class (the rest of the chronic patients). In an ideal world we could perhaps avoid the inductive leap by pinning down every conceivable instance, but in the real world such thoroughness is usually impractical and often impossible. Instead, we gather enough evidence to make our generalizations probable.

The evidence for induction may be of several kinds:

- Facts: statistics or other hard data that are verifiable or, failing that, attested to by reliable sources (for instance, the number of drug doses per chronic patient, derived from hospital records).
- The opinions of recognized experts on the subject, opinions that are themselves conclusions based on research and observation (for instance, the testimony of an experienced hospital doctor).
- Examples illustrating the evidence (for instance, the treatment history of one patient).

A sound inductive generalization can form the basis for the second reasoning process, **deductive reasoning.** Working from the general to the particular, you start with such a generalization and apply it to a new situation in order to draw a conclusion about that situation. Like induction, deduction is a process we use constantly to order our experience. The child who learns from three experiences that all stoves burn then sees a new stove and concludes that this stove also will burn. The child's thought process can be written in the form of a **syllogism,** a three-step outline of deductive reasoning:

> All stoves burn me.
> This is a stove.
> Therefore, this stove will burn me.

The first statement, the generalization derived from induction, is called the **major premise.** The second statement, a more specific assertion about some element of the major premise, is called the **minor premise.** And the third statement, an assertion of the logical connection between premises, is called the **conclusion.** The following syllogism takes the earlier example about mental hospitals one step further:

> MAJOR PREMISE   The state hospitals' treatment of chronic patients relies exclusively on drugs.
>
> MINOR PREMISE   Drugs do not cure chronic patients.
>
> CONCLUSION   Therefore, the state hospitals' treatment of chronic patients will not cure them.

Unlike an inductive conclusion, which requires a leap, the deductive conclusion derives necessarily from the premises: as long as the reasoning process is valid and the premises are accepted as true, then the conclusion must also be true. To be valid, the reasoning must conform to the process outlined above. The following syllogism is *not* valid, even though the premises are true:

> All radicals want to change the system.
> Georgia Allport wants to change the system.
> Therefore, Georgia Allport is a radical.

The flaw in this syllogism is that not *only* radicals want to change the system, so Allport does not *necessarily* fall within the class of radicals just because she wants to change the system. The conclusion, then, is invalid.

A syllogism can be valid without being true if either of the premises is untrue. For example:

> All people who want political change are radicals.
> Georgia Allport wants political change.
> Therefore, Georgia Allport is a radical.

The conclusion here is valid because Allport falls within the class of people who want political change. But the conclusion is untrue because the major premise is untrue. As commonly defined, a radical seeks extreme change, often by revolutionary means. But other forms and means of change are also possible; Allport, for instance, may be interested in improving the delivery of services to the poor and in achieving passage of tougher environmental-protection laws — both political changes, to be sure, but neither radical.

In arguments, syllogisms are rarely spelled out as neatly as in these examples. Sometimes the order of the statements is reversed, as in this sentence paraphrasing a Supreme Court decision:

> The state may not imprison a man just because he is too poor to pay a fine; the only justification for imprisonment is a certain danger to society, and poverty does not constitute certain danger.

The buried syllogism can be stated thus:

> MAJOR PREMISE   The state may imprison only those who are a certain danger to society.

> MINOR PREMISE   A man who is too poor to pay a fine is not a certain danger to society.

> CONCLUSION   Therefore, the state cannot imprison a man just because he is too poor to pay a fine.

Often, one of a syllogism's premises or even its conclusion is implied but not expressed. Each of the following sentences omits one part of the same syllogism:

> All five students cheated, so they should be expelled. [Implied major premise: cheaters should be expelled.]

> Cheaters should be punished by expulsion, so all five students should be expelled. [Implied minor premise: all five students cheated.]

> Cheaters should be punished by expulsion, and all five students cheated. [Implied conclusion: all five students should be expelled.]

Fallacies

Inappropriate emotional appeals and flaws in reasoning—called **fallacies**—can trap you as you construct an argument. Watch out for the following, which your readers will find if you don't:

- **Hasty generalization:** an inductive conclusion that leaps to include *all* instances when at best only *some* instances provide any evidence. Hasty generalizations form some of our worst stereotypes:

  > Physically challenged people are mentally challenged, too.
  > African Americans are good athletes.
  > Italian Americans are volatile.

- **Oversimplification:** an inductive conclusion that ignores complexities in the evidence that, if heeded, would weaken the conclusion or suggest an entirely different one. For example:

  > The newspaper folded because it couldn't compete with television.

  Although television may have taken some business from the paper, hundreds of other papers continue to thrive; thus television could not be the only cause of the paper's failure.

- **Begging the question:** assuming a conclusion in the statement of a premise, and thus begging readers to accept the conclusion—the question—before it is proved. For example:

  > We can trust the president not to neglect the needy, because he is a compassionate man.

  This sentence asserts in a circular fashion that the president is not uncompassionate because he is compassionate. He may indeed be compassionate, but this is the question that needs addressing.

- **Ignoring the question:** introducing an issue or consideration that shifts the argument away from the real issue. Offering an emotional appeal as a premise in a logical argument is a form of ignoring the question. The following sentence, for instance, appeals to pity, not to logic:

  > The mayor was badly used by people he loved and trusted, so we should not blame him for the corruption in his administration.

- **Ad hominem** (Latin for "to the man"): a form of ignoring the question by attacking the opponents instead of the opponents' arguments. For example:

  > O'Brien is married to a convict, so her proposals for prison reform should not be taken seriously.

- **Either-or:** requiring that readers choose between two interpretations or actions when in fact the choices are more numerous.

  > Either we imprison all drug users, or we will become their prisoners.

  The factors contributing to drug addiction, and the choices for
  dealing with it, are obviously more complex than this statement
  suggests. Not all either-or arguments are invalid, for sometimes
  the alternatives encompass all the possibilities. But when they do
  not, the argument is false.
- **Non sequitur** (Latin for "it does not follow"): a conclusion derived illogically or erroneously from stated or implied premises.
  For instance:

  > Young children are too immature to engage in sex, so they should not
  > be taught about it.

  This sentence implies one of two meanings, both of them ques-
  tionable: only the sexually active can learn anything about sex,
  or teaching young children about sex will cause them to engage
  in it.
- **Post hoc** (from the Latin *post hoc, ergo propter hoc,* "after this,
  therefore because of this"): assuming that because one thing preceded another, it must have caused the other. For example:

  > After the town banned smoking in closed public places, the incidence
  > of vandalism went up.

  Many things may have caused the rise in vandalism, including improved weather and a climbing unemployment rate. It does not
  follow that the ban on smoking, and that alone, caused the rise.

ANALYZING ARGUMENT AND
PERSUASION IN PARAGRAPHS

David Lindorff (born 1949) is a free-lance journalist who has written
extensively about the death penalty. The following paragraph is
adapted from "The Death Penalty's Other Victims," an article Lindorff wrote for the online magazine *Salon* in 2001. The paragraph offers an inductive argument.

A major and controversial element of the death-
penalty system is being largely ignored: the right of
prosecutors and judges to eliminate, "for cause,"
any potential jurors who say they might not be will-

ing or able to vote for death during the penalty phase of a murder trial. Whatever one might think about the death penalty itself, the trouble with screening out death-penalty skeptics—a process known as "death-qualifying" the jury—is that it does a lot more than simply eliminate jurors opposed to capital punishment. It makes for juries that tend to be white, male, and significantly more likely to convict the person accused of the crime in the first place. In a 1968 landmark study, Hans Zeisel found that death-qualifying juries led to an 80 percent increase in the conviction rate. In a 1994 study Craig Haney, Aida Hurtado, and Luis Vega reported that while minorities accounted for 18.5% of the people in California jury pools they examined, they represented 26.3 percent of those excluded from jury panels through the death-qualifying process. And a North Carolina jury study conducted in 1982 found an even greater disparity, with 55.2 percent of black potential jurors being excluded during the death-penalty qualifying process, in contrast to 20.7 percent of whites. Studies also indicate that women tend to be excluded, since they are also more likely to oppose the death penalty.

The generalization: death-qualifying creates juries that are more white, male, and likely to convict

Evidence: Increase in convictions

Exclusion of minorities

Exclusion of women

Rush Limbaugh (born 1951) is a nationally syndicated radio talk-show host known for his outspoken conservative views. The following paragraph, from Limbaugh's book *The Way Things Ought to Be* (1992), uses examples to make a deductive argument against distributing condoms in schools.

Advocates of condom distribution say that kids are going to have sex, that try as we might we can't stop them. Therefore they need protection. Hence, condoms. Well, hold on a minute. Just whose notion is it that "kids are going to do it anyway, you can't stop them"? Why limit the application of that brilliant logic to sexual activity? Let's just admit that kids are going to do drugs and distribute safe, untainted drugs every morning in homeroom. Kids are going to smoke, too, we can't stop them, so let's

Major premise: the argument that "kids are going to do it anyway" assumes that sexual behavior must be catered to because it can't be stopped

Minor premise: any argument is ridiculous that assumes harmful behavior must be catered to because it can't be stopped

provide packs of low-tar cigarettes to the students for their after-sex smoke. Kids are going to get guns and shoot them, you can't stop them, so let's make sure that teachers have bullet-proof vests. I mean, come on! If we are really concerned about safe sex, why stop at condoms? Let's convert study halls to Safe Sex Centers where students can go to actually have sex on nice double beds with clean sheets under the watchful and approving eye of the school nurse, who will be on hand to demonstrate, along with the principal, just how to use a condom. Or even better: if kids are going to have sex, let's put disease-free hookers in these Safe Sex Centers. Hey, if safe sex is the objective, why compromise our standards?

Conclusion: "kids are going to do it anyway" is a ridiculous argument

DEVELOPING AN ARGUMENTATIVE AND PERSUASIVE ESSAY

Getting Started

You will have many chances to write arguments, from defending or opposing a policy such as progressive taxation in an economics course to justifying a new procedure at work to persuading a company to refund your money for a bad product. To choose a subject for an argumentative essay, consider a behavior or policy that irks you, an opinion you want to defend, a change you would like to see implemented, a way to solve a problem. The subject you pick should meet certain criteria:

- It should be something you have some knowledge of from your own experience or observations, from class discussions, or from reading, although you may need to do further research as well.
- It should be limited to a topic you can treat thoroughly in the space and time available to you—for instance, the quality of computer instruction at your school rather than in the whole nation.
- It should be something that you feel strongly about so that you can make a convincing case. (However, it's best to avoid subjects that you cannot view with some objectivity, seeing the opposite side as well as your own; otherwise, you may not be open to

flaws in your argument, and you may not be able to represent the opposition fairly.)

With your subject in hand, you should develop a tentative thesis. Since the thesis is essentially a conclusion from evidence, you may have to do some preliminary reading to be sure the evidence exists. This step is especially important with an issue like welfare cheating or tax advantages for the wealthy that we all tend to have opinions about whether we know the facts or not. But don't feel you have to prove your thesis at this early stage; fixing it too firmly may make you unwilling to reshape it if further evidence, your audience, or the structure of your argument so demands.

Stating your thesis in a preliminary thesis sentence can help you form your idea. Make this sentence as clear and specific as possible. Don't resort to a vague generality or a nondebatable statement of fact. Instead, state the precise opinion you want readers to accept or the precise action you want them to take or support. For instance:

VAGUE   Computer instruction is important.

NONDEBATABLE   The school's investment in computer instruction is less than the average investment of the nation's colleges and universities.

PRECISE   Money designated for new dormitories and athletic facilities should be diverted to constructing computer facilities and hiring first-rate computer faculty.

VAGUE   Cloning research is promising.

NONDEBATABLE   Scientists have been experimenting with cloning procedures for many years.

PRECISE   Those who oppose cloning research should consider the potentially valuable applications of the research for human health and development.

Once you have framed a tentative thesis sentence, the next step is to begin gathering evidence in earnest. You should consult as broad a range of sources as necessary to uncover the facts and opinions supporting not only your view but also any opposing views. Though it may be tempting to ignore your opposition in the hope that readers know nothing of it, it is dishonest and probably futile to do so. Acknowledging and, whenever possible, refuting significant opposing views will enhance your credibility with readers. If you find that some counterarguments damage your own argument too greatly, then you will have to revise your thesis.

Where to seek evidence depends on the nature of your thesis.

- For a thesis derived from your own experiences and observations, such as a recommendation that all students work part-time for the education if not for the money, gathering evidence will be primarily a matter of searching your own thoughts and also uncovering opposing views, perhaps by consulting others.
- Some arguments derived from personal experience can also be strengthened by the judicious use of facts and opinions from other sources. An essay arguing in favor of vegetarianism, for instance, could mix the benefits you have felt with those demonstrated by scientific data.
- Nonpersonal and controversial subjects require the evidence of other sources. Though you might strongly favor or oppose a massive federal investment in solar-energy research, your opinions would count little if they were not supported with facts and the opinions of experts.

As you generate or collect evidence, it should suggest the reasons that will support the claim of your thesis — essentially the minor arguments that bolster the main argument. In an essay favoring federal investment in solar-energy research, for instance, the minor arguments might include the need for solar power, the feasibility of its widespread use, and its cost and safety compared with the cost and safety of other energy sources. It is in developing these minor arguments that you are most likely to use induction and deduction consciously — generalizing from specifics or applying generalizations to new information. Thus the minor arguments provide the entry points for your evidence, and together they should encompass all the relevant evidence you find.

As we have already seen, knowledge of readers' needs and expectations is absolutely crucial in argument. In explanatory writing, detail and clarity alone may accomplish your purpose; but you cannot hope to move readers in a certain direction unless you have some idea of where they stand. You need a sense of their background in your subject, of course. But even more, you need a good idea of their values and beliefs, their attitudes toward your subject — in short, their willingness to be convinced by your argument. In a composition class, your readers will probably be your instructor and your classmates, a small but diverse group. A good target when you are addressing a diverse audience is the reader who is neutral or mildly biased one way or the other toward your thesis. This person you can hope to influence as long as your argument is reasonable, your evidence is thorough and convincing, your treatment of opposing views is fair, and your appeals to readers' emotions are appropriate to your purpose, your subject, and especially your readers' values and feelings.

Organizing

Once you have formulated your thesis, gathered reasons and the evidence to support them, and evaluated these against the needs and expectations of your audience, you should plan how you will arrange your argument. The introduction to your essay should draw readers into your framework, making them see how the subject affects them and predisposing them to consider your argument. Sometimes, a forthright approach works best, but an eye-opening anecdote or quotation can also be effective. Your thesis sentence may end your introduction. But if you think readers will not even entertain your thesis until they have seen some or all of your evidence, then withhold your thesis for later.

The main part of the essay consists of your minor arguments or reasons and your evidence for them. Unless the minor arguments form a chain, with each growing out of the one before, their order should be determined by their potential effects on readers. In general, it is most effective to arrange the reasons in order of increasing importance or strength so as to finish powerfully. But to engage readers in the argument from the start, try to begin with a reason that they will find compelling or that they already know and accept; that way, the weaker reasons will be sandwiched between a strong beginning and an even stronger ending.

The views opposing yours can be raised and dispensed with wherever it seems most appropriate to do so. If a counterargument pertains to just one of your minor arguments, then dispose of it at that point. But if the counterarguments are more basic, pertaining to your whole thesis, you should dispose of them either after the introduction or shortly before the conclusion. Use the former strategy if the opposition is particularly strong and you fear that readers will be disinclined to listen unless you address their concerns first. Use the latter strategy when the counterarguments are generally weak or easily dispensed with once you've presented your case.

In the conclusion to your essay, you may summarize the main point of your argument and state your thesis for the first time, if you have saved it for the end, or restate it from your introduction. An effective quotation, an appropriate emotional appeal, or a call for support or action can often provide a strong finish to an argument.

Drafting

While you are drafting the essay, work to make your reasoning clear by showing how each bit of evidence relates to the reason or minor argument being discussed, and how each minor argument relates to the main argument contained in the thesis. In working through the reasons and evidence, you may find it helpful to state each reason as the first sentence in a paragraph and then support it in the following sentences. If this scheme seems too rigid or creates overlong paragraphs, you can always make changes after you have got the draft down on paper. Draw on a range of methods to clarify your points. For instance, define specialized terms or those you use in a special sense, compare and contrast one policy or piece of evidence with another, or carefully analyze causes or effects.

Revising and Editing

When your draft is complete, use the following questions and the box opposite to guide your revision and editing.

- *Is your thesis debatable, precise, and clear?* Readers must know what you are trying to convince them of, at least by the end of the essay if not up front.
- *Is your argument unified?* Does each minor claim support the thesis? Do all opinions, facts, and examples provide evidence for a minor claim? In behalf of your readers, question every sentence you have written to be sure it contributes to the point you are making and to the argument as a whole.
- *Is the structure of your argument clear and compelling?* Readers should be able to follow easily, seeing when and why you move from one idea to the next.
- *Is the evidence specific, representative, and adequate?* Facts, examples, and expert opinions should be well detailed, should fairly represent the available information, and should be sufficient to support your claim.
- *Have you slipped into any logical fallacies?* Detecting fallacies in your own work can be difficult, but your readers will find them if you don't. Look for the following fallacies discussed earlier (pp. 335–36): hasty generalization, oversimplification, begging the question, ignoring the question, ad hominem, either-or, non sequitur, and post hoc. (All of these are also listed in the Glossary under *fallacies*.)

FOCUS ON TONE

Readers are most likely to be persuaded by an argument when they sense a writer who is reasonable, trustworthy, and sincere. A rational appeal, strong evidence, and acknowledgment of opposing views do much to convey these attributes, but so does tone, the attitude implied by choice of words and sentence structures.

Generally, you should try for a tone of moderation in your view of your subject and respectfulness and goodwill toward readers and opponents.

- State opinions and facts calmly:

    OVEREXCITED   One clueless administrator was quoted in the newspaper as saying she thought many students who claim learning disabilities are faking their difficulties to obtain special treatment! Has she never heard of dyslexia, attention deficit disorders, and other well-established disabilities?

    CALM   Particularly worrisome was one administrator's statement, quoted in the newspaper, that many students who claim learning disabilities may be "faking" their difficulties to obtain special treatment.

- Replace arrogance with deference and sarcasm with plain speaking:

    ARROGANT   I happen to know that many students would rather party or just bury their heads in the sand than get involved in a serious, worthy campaign against the school's unjust learning-disabled policies.

    DEFERENTIAL   Time pressures and lack of information about the issues may be what prevents students from joining the campaign against the school's unjust learning-disabled policies.

    SARCASTIC   Of course, the administration knows even without meeting students what is best for every one of them.

    PLAIN SPEAKING   The administration should agree to meet with each learning-disabled student to learn about his or her needs.

- Choose words whose connotations convey reasonableness rather than anger, hostility, or another negative emotion:

    HOSTILE   The administration *coerced* some students into dropping their lawsuits. [*Coerced* implies the use of threats or even violence.]

    REASONABLE   The administration *convinced* some students to drop their lawsuits. [*Convinced* implies the use of reason.]

See pages 41–42 for more on tone and page 52 for more on connotation.

A NOTE ON THEMATIC CONNECTIONS

Argument and persuasion is generally the method of choice for presenting an opinion or proposal on a controversial issue. In a paragraph (p. 336), David Lindorff takes a stand against screening out certain jurors in death-penalty cases. Rush Limbaugh, in another paragraph (p. 337), attacks an argument favoring condom distribution in schools. Bill Bryson's essay (opposite), argues for laws and behavior that will protect the environment. Jeremy Steben's essay (p. 352) takes an unusual tack to criticize police activity in his town. And Charles Krauthammer's essay (p. 359) takes a strong stand against cloning.

Waste not, want not.   — Proverb

Reduce, recycle, reuse.   — Slogan

I am I plus my surroundings, and if I do not preserve the latter, I do not preserve myself.
                                            —José Ortega y Gasset

Journal Response   In a journal entry, comment on one example of material or energy waste, such as plastic shopping bags, disposable razors, or gas-guzzling cars. Where do you observe the waste happening? What causes it? Is it a significant problem? Should, or can, anything be done about it?

Bill Bryson

Bill Bryson was born in Des Moines, Iowa, in 1951. After attending Drake University, he spent almost twenty years in England as a journalist, writing for the Times *and the* Independent, *among other publications. His books, largely perceptive takes on language or humorous accounts of culture clash, include* Mother Tongue: English and How It Got That Way *(1990),* Made in America *(1996),* Notes from a Small Island *(1995),* A Walk in the Woods *(1998), and* I'm a Stranger Here Myself *(1999). Most recently, Bryson published the travel memoir* In a Sunburned Country *(2000), about his trek through the Australian outback, and wrote a tribute to his father, baseball critic Bill Bryson, which appeared in* The New Yorker. *He lives in Hanover, New Hampshire, with his wife and four children.*

The Waste Generation

Returning to the United States after living nearly twenty years in England, Bryson discovered many amusing differences between Americans and Europeans, reported in I'm a Stranger Here Myself. *One difference that he found not amusing is Americans' waste of natural resources. Though somewhat dated by its references to the Clinton administration, the essay is nonetheless a fresh indictment of our habits.*

One of the most arresting statistics that I have seen in a good while is   1
that 5 percent of all the energy used in the United States is consumed
by computers that have been left on all night.

I can't confirm this personally, but I can certainly tell you that on 2 numerous occasions I have glanced out hotel-room windows late at night, in a variety of cities, and been struck by the fact that lots of lights in lots of office buildings are still burning, and that computer screens are indeed flickering.

Why don't we turn these things off? For the same reason, I sup- 3 pose, that so many people leave their car engines running when they pop into a friend's house, or keep lights blazing in unoccupied rooms, or have the central heating cranked up to a level that would scandalize a Finnish sauna housekeeper—because, in short, electricity, gasoline, and other energy sources are so relatively cheap, and have been for so long, that it doesn't occur to behave otherwise.

Why, after all, go through the irksome annoyance of waiting 4 twenty seconds for your computer to warm up each morning when you can have it at your immediate beck by leaving it on all night?

We are terribly—no, we are ludicrously—wasteful of resources 5 in this country. The average American uses twice as much energy to get through life as the average European. With just 5 percent of the world's population, we consume 20 percent of its resources. These are not statistics to be proud of.

In 1992 at the Earth Summit in Rio de Janeiro, the United States, 6 along with other developed nations, agreed to reduce the emission of greenhouse gases to 1990 levels by 2000. This wasn't a promise to think about it. It was a promise to do it.

In the event, greenhouse emissions in the United States have con- 7 tinued relentlessly to rise—by 8 percent overall since the Rio summit, by 3.4 percent in 1996 alone. In short, we haven't done what we promised. We haven't tried to do it. We haven't even pretended to try to do it. Frankly, I'm not sure that we are even capable of trying to pretend to try to do it.

Consider this: in 1992, Congress decreed that before the end of 8 the decade half of all government vehicles should be able to run on alternative fuels. To comply with this directive, the Postal Service bought ten thousand new trucks and, at a cost of $4,000 each, modified them to run on ethanol as well as gasoline. In May 1998, the first of 350 such trucks ordered for the New York City area began to be delivered. Unfortunately, none of these vehicles is ever likely to use ethanol for the simple reason that the nearest ethanol station is in Indianapolis. When asked by a reporter for the *New York Times* whether anyone anywhere at any level of government had any intention of doing anything about this, the answer was no. Meanwhile, the

Postal Service, along with all other federal agencies, will continue to spend $4,000 a pop of taxpayers' money modifying trucks to run on a fuel on which almost none of them will ever run.

What the administration *has* done in terms of greenhouse emis- 9 sions is introduce a set of voluntary compliance standards that industries are entirely free to ignore if they wish, and mostly of course they so wish. Now President Clinton wants another fifteen or sixteen years before rolling back emissions to 1990 levels.

Perhaps I am misreading the national mood, but it is hard to find 10 anyone who seems much exercised about this. Increasingly there is even a kind of antagonism to the idea of conservation, particularly if there is a cost attached. A recent survey of twenty-seven thousand people around the globe by a Canadian group called Environics International found that in virtually every advanced nation people were willing to sacrifice at least a small measure of economic growth for cleaner air and a healthier environment. The one exception: the United States. It seems madness to think that a society would rate marginal economic growth above a livable earth, but there you are. I had always assumed that the reason to build a bigger economy was to make the world a better place. In fact, it appears, the reason to build a bigger economy is, well, to build a bigger economy.

Even President Clinton's cautiously inventive proposals to trans- 11 fer the problem to a successor four terms down the road have met with fervent opposition. A coalition of industrialists and other interested parties called the Global Climate Information Project has raised $13 million to fight pretty much any initiative that gets in the way of their smokestacks. It has been running national radio ads grimly warning that if the president's new energy plans are implemented, gasoline prices could go up by fifty cents a gallon.

Never mind that that figure is probably inflated. Never mind that 12 even if it were true we would still be paying but a fraction for gasoline what people in other rich nations pay. Never mind that it would bring benefits that everyone could enjoy. Never mind any of that. Mention an increase in gas prices for any purpose at all and—however small the amount, however sound the reason—most people will instinctively resist.

What is saddest about all this is that a good part of these goals to 13 cut greenhouse emissions could be met without any cost at all if we merely modified our extravagance. It has been estimated that the nation as a whole wastes about $300 billion of energy a year. We are not talking here about energy that could be saved by investing in new technologies. We are talking about energy that could be saved just by switching things off or turning things down.

Take hot water. Nearly every household in Europe has a timer   14
device on its hot water system. Since people clearly don't need hot water when they are at work or fast asleep, there isn't any need to keep the tank heated, so the system shuts down. Here in America I don't know how to switch off my hot water tank. I don't know that it is possible. There is piping hot water in our house twenty-four hours a day, even when we are far away on vacation. Doesn't seem to make much sense.

According to *U.S. News & World Report,* the United States must   15
maintain the equivalent of five nuclear power plants just to power equipment and appliances that are on but not being used—lights burning in rooms that are unoccupied, computers left on when people go to lunch or home for the night, all those mute, wall-mounted TVs that flicker unwatched in the corners of bars.

In England, we had something called an off-peak energy plan.   16
The idea was to encourage users to shift some of their electricity consumption to nighttime hours, thus spreading demand. So we bought timer devices and ran our washing machine, dryer, and dishwasher in the middle of the night and were rewarded for this small inconvenience with big savings on the electricity consumed during those hours. I would be pleased to continue the practice now, if only some utility would offer it to me.

I am not suggesting that the British are outstandingly virtuous   17
with regard to conservation—in some areas like recycling and insulation their behavior is nothing to write home about—merely that these are simple ideas that could be easily embraced here.

It would be really nice, of course, to see a wholesale change in di-   18
rection. I would dearly love, for instance, to be able to take a train to Boston. Every time I travel to Boston now, I have either to drive myself or sit in a cramped minibus with up to nine other hapless souls for two and a half hours. How nice it would be to speed across the New England landscape in the club car of a nicely appointed train, like Cary Grant and Eva Marie Saint in an Alfred Hitchcock movie. Once, not so long ago, it was possible to travel all over New England by train. According to a body called the Conservation Law Foundation, the whole of the rail system in northern New England could be restored for $500 million. That's a lot of money, of course, but consider this: as I write, Burlington, Vermont, is spending $100 million on a single twelve-mile loop road.

I don't know how worrying global warming is. No one does. I   19
don't know how much we are imperiling our futures by being so singularly casual in our consumption. But I can tell you this. Last year I
spent a good deal of time hiking the Appalachian Trail. In Virginia,
where the trail runs through Shenandoah National Park, it was still
possible when I was a teenager to see Washington, D.C., seventy-five
miles away, on clear days. Now, in even the most favorable conditions, visibility is less than half that. In hot, smoggy weather, it can be
as little as two miles.

The forest that covers the Appalachian Mountains is one of the   20
richest and loveliest on Earth. A single valley in the Great Smoky
Mountains National Park can contain more species of native trees
than the whole of western Europe. A lot of those trees are in trouble.
The stress of dealing with acid rain and other airborne pollutants
leaves them helplessly vulnerable to diseases and pests. Oaks, hick-
ories, and maples are dying in unsettling numbers. The flowering
dogwood—one of the most beautiful trees in the American South,
and once one of the most abundant—is on the brink of extinction.
The American hemlock seems poised to follow.

This may be only a modest prelude. If global temperatures rise by   21
four degrees Centigrade over the next half century, as some scientists
confidently predict, then all of the trees of Shenandoah National Park
and the Smokies, and for hundreds of miles beyond, will die. In two
generations one of the last great forests of the temperate world will
turn into featureless grassland.

I think that's worth turning off a few computers for, don't you?   22

Meaning

1. What is Bryson's main idea, and where do you find it in the essay?
2. What reasons does Bryson give for our wastefulness? What examples
   does he provide for this kind of behavior?
3. Why is Bryson so alarmed about the broken promises of our government? Whom else does he blame for the environmental problems that
   we now face?
4. If you are unsure of any of the following words used by Bryson, try to
   determine their meanings from their context in the essay. Check their
   meanings in a dictionary to test your guesses. Then use each word in a
   sentence or two of your own.

arresting (1)	ludicrously (5)	fervent (11)
flickering (2)	emission (6)	imperiling (19)

scandalize (3)   relentlessly (7)   prelude (21)
irksome (4)   ethanol (8)   featureless (21)
beck (4)   exercised (10)

Purpose and Audience

1. What seems to be Bryson's purpose in writing this essay? Is he writing mainly to complain or to influence government decisions or to influence individuals' behavior? What evidence from the text supports your answer?
2. The problem of wasteful habits is huge and, as Bryson himself suggests, not easy to solve. What effect do you think Bryson expects to have on his audience? How does this relate to the purpose of his essay?
3. Who do you think is the author's target audience? How does Bryson engage these readers' support?

Method and Structure

1. What kind of reasoning—inductive or deductive—does Bryson's argument mainly rely on? What kinds of evidence does the author provide? Is one kind of evidence more convincing than the others? Why, or why not?
2. Bryson's interpretation of the problem of waste is sometimes quite personal. Does this personal approach contribute to or detract from the essay? Why?
3. **Other Methods** Bryson supports his argument with other methods, such as description (Chapter 4), narration (Chapter 5), and example (Chapter 6). Locate one instance of each method. What does each contribute to the essay?

Language

1. What is the effect of Bryson's expressions of uncertainty, such as "Perhaps I am misreading the national mood" (paragraph 10) and "I don't know how worrying global warming is. [. . .] I don't know how much we are imperiling our futures by being so singularly casual in our consumption" (19)? Are these expressions sincere, do you think? What purpose, or purposes, do they serve?
2. Bryson wrote this essay largely in the first person, either singular (*I*) or plural (*we*). What does this choice accomplish? How would the essay have been different if Bryson had avoided the first person altogether?

Writing Topics

1. **Journal to Essay**   Take off from the comments you made in your journal entry (p. 345) to write an essay about protection of the environment. Do you regard waste and pollution as critical problems? Do you believe that the government is taking adequate steps to protect the environment? Do you believe that the actions of individuals can make a difference? Your essay may but need not be an argument: that is, you could explain your answer to any of these questions or argue a specific point. Either way, use examples and details to support your ideas.

2. Using the library or the Internet, research an environmental organization such as Friends of the Earth or Greenpeace. In an essay summarize the global vision the organization outlines in its mission statement, which may include goals met to date as well as plans for the future. Then discuss whether you agree with the organization's assessment of the current environmental situation, its proposed solutions, and its methods for achieving those solutions. (You may need to narrow this discussion to a particular environmental problem.)

3. **Cultural Considerations**   Bryson makes the point that the United States is more wasteful than other countries are: "With just 5 percent of the world's population, we consume 20 percent of its resources" (paragraph 5). Write an essay that defends or argues against the relative resource consumption of the United States. Do geography, cultural ideals, product output, or other characteristics somehow make the United States more needful or deserving of resources than other nations? In formulating your answer, consider also how a person from another country might respond—a resident of, say, Italy or China or South Africa.

4. **Connections**   Both Bryson and Jeremy Steben, in "Small Town, Quiet Town, Safe Town" (next page), write about behavior they clearly disapprove of: wasting resources in Bryson's case, infringing on civil rights in Steben's. Their approaches and tones are quite different, though, with Bryson's being more straightforward than Steben's. Write an essay in which you consider the advantages and disadvantages of each approach. What if Bryson had written like Steben, or vice versa?

The end must justify the means.
— Matthew Prior

The right of the people to be secure in their persons, houses, papers, and effects, against unreasonable searches and seizures, shall not be violated, and no warrants shall issue but upon probable cause [. . .].
— Fourth Amendment of the U.S. Constitution

Every society gets the kind of criminal it deserves. What is equally true is that every community gets the kind of law enforcement it insists on.
— Robert Kennedy

Journal Response Write about a recent time when you were aware of law enforcement in your community—perhaps a noteworthy arrest, a controversy involving police methods, a report of rising or falling crime, even a personal experience. What did you read, hear, or experience, and what did you think about it?

Jeremy Steben

Jeremy Steben was born in 1981 and grew up in Avon, Connecticut. He studied for two years at Boston College and is currently taking time off from school to marshal in aircraft at Nantucket Memorial Airport and to instruct Alpine skiing in Vermont. His interests include reading, collecting comic books, sailing, and skiing.

Small Town, Quiet Town, Safe Town

Steben wrote the following essay for his freshman writing course at Boston College in 2000. The police in his suburban hometown had been sued for pulling over drivers not because of wrongdoing but just because of the driver's or the car's appearance. The question is whether such police behavior unacceptably violates civil liberties or constitutes a reasonable price for public safety. To get Steben's answer, pay careful attention to his tone.

The streets of my town can be dangerous places. I know; I drive them all the time. On the surface my town is a quiet, upscale little suburb in Connecticut, with the occasional cow pasture and golf course lend-

1

ing a sense of serenity and simplicity. But underneath the sugarcoated topping lies a not-so-sweet reality. Criminal elements travel our streets at night, while good citizens sleep, or boldly prowl our avenues in the glare of daylight. Thankfully, our streets are patrolled by a valiant police force that takes up the thankless task of stamping out crime with a vigor and enthusiasm that are to be commended. These dauntless men and women are the only bastion of defense against the darkness that constantly threatens to boil over and consume our fair community. These unsung heroes should be extolled and held up as an example to police forces all over the nation. One might presume that most officers patrol the streets regularly, setting speed traps and staying alert for any sign of traffic infractions or other criminal activity. However, my town's officers are far more proactive in their duties. They dislike waiting until they actually observe a crime being committed. Our officers have learned to be on the lookout for various indications ("clues," if you will) that action may be required. Occasionally these leads may prove false, but only diligent pursuit of them guarantees that order is maintained, and the innocent parties involved are only mildly inconvenienced.

For instance, our officers are quite aware of the problem of teenagers. It's common knowledge that teenagers have a tendency to be up to no good. Now, I happen to be a member of this group, and by no means do I suggest that we all engage in such things, but enough of us do that teenagers warrant special attention by the police. Especially on weekend nights, or when there are more than one of us in a car, we can count on a watchful eye being turned on us. Police pull us over regularly to ensure that there is nothing illegal going on. Officers rely on their instincts and observation when determining which cars to pull over. Should some smart aleck demand a specific reason for being stopped, our officers placate him by saying that he was driving "erratically." This could mean that a tire touched the median or the white strip or that the driver jerked the wheel a little too sharply on the last turn, but it lets the officer get on with the investigation unimpeded.

But knowing which cars to target is only half of proper law enforcement; a thorough officer doesn't stop there. Once the cars have been stopped, the officer must determine whether he has discovered a crime. Unfortunately this can be a difficult task. Our constitutional protection from unwarranted search and seizure is, sadly, often abused by criminals, and the laws regulating when and how an officer can conduct a search are numerous and cloying. Thankfully, over years of experience, our police have developed a system by which they can easily search any car that they feel is suspicious, and rarely do they concern themselves over such bothersome things as constitutional rights.

The first thing that a young or minority driver will notice upon   *4* being stopped by an officer is the demeanor of the officer. The brisk and abrasive bearing, which seems to say, "I know you're guilty of *something*, and I'm going to find out *exactly* what," is of course intended to scare criminals, make them nervous, and make it easier for the officer to do his job. I appreciate this because it establishes the proper relationship between the officer and me right off the bat. The appropriate pressure is applied at once as the officer attempts to ascertain whether any illegal substances have been consumed. "So, you boys been doing some drinking tonight?" This question is then repeated several times throughout the ensuing conversation in slightly varied forms, such as "So, what, you guys have a few beers tonight?" or "So, you been partying, having a little fun?" This is just in case the driver forgot that he *had* in fact been drinking and accidentally answered "no" the first time. After five minutes of this the driver begins to think maybe he *did* have a few beers that night, even if he didn't. This interrogation gives the officer time to shine his flashlight all through the interior of the car in a visual examination.

What happens next depends on what the officer sees and, to   *5* some extent, on the driver's reaction. For instance, if the driver turns around in his seat for any reason, perhaps to speak to somebody in the back seat, the following exchange is likely to occur:

> "Hey! What did you just throw back there?" the officer might say.
> "What? Nothing, I was just saying..." would be the stammered reply.
> "Step out of the vehicle. We're going to search it."

Suspicious clues like air fresheners hanging from the rearview mirror can also provide a reason to search, as they may be intended to cover up the scent of alcohol or marijuana. Even a twig can help officers do their job:

> "What's that on your floor? It looks like a stem."
> "It's just a twig."
> "I think it's a stem. Please exit the vehicle."

If all else fails, the officer can always claim the car smells like alcohol or marijuana or simply that the driver appears high or slightly drunk.

In this way officers can feel free to pursue their suspicions and ensure that no crime is being committed.

Teenagers and minorities are not the only "problem" groups that are habitually targeted. Drivers of vehicles that do not look expensive, are not well kept, or are particularly old must be investigated. In a town full of Grand Cherokees and Mercedes, such cars tend to be a bit out of place. The police are consistent about checking these vehicles, as my friend Ellie can personally attest. When she received her license she was given a car that looked, to put it kindly, like a piece of junk. Driving a car that was dented in many places, rusting in spots, and with several panels caved in, it was no wonder that within a few months she had been pulled over no less than fifteen times. The only reason this impressive number stopped growing was that eventually Ellie had been pulled over at least once by every patrolman on the force and it was established that she did indeed belong in town. She expressed a slight annoyance at all the trouble, but I assured her that it was absolutely necessary to our town's continued safety, and besides, she got to know several officers much better than she might have.

Diligent, dogged, and thorough, our officers are doing the best they can. It is truly a pity that not everyone sees their efforts for the blessings they are. The recent lawsuits against our maligned department have brought our town to the attention of the entire state of Connecticut. The fact that we have been portrayed with infamy rather than respect in the papers is truly a wrong. I don't see what all the fuss is about. The plaintiffs claim that the police stop cars based on the looks of the car and the driver and that cars traveling out of or into Hartford are flagged for inspection. But as I stated above, certain seemingly superficial clues do indeed indicate suspicious persons and motives, and paying attention to such details is an important part of law enforcement. Strangely, the lawsuits don't mention police victimizing minors, although the police pay just as much special attention to the age of the driver as they do to these other factors. Whenever some indignant teenager complains about his treatment by the police, adults just shrug, especially if he is particularly scruffy looking. "What do you expect?" is the common reply. Indeed, what can you expect if you're a member of a group commonly associated with criminal activity? And what's more, if you further differentiate yourself from proper citizens by being unkempt, you can't help but draw suspicion.

If police treated everybody the same they would be hampered in their ability to fight crime. I accept my position and realize that to safeguard the greater good I must occasionally give up a few constitutional rights, a sacrifice that I make gladly. In fact, I think it rather petty that some individuals seek to shirk this shared civic responsibility. I can only hope that these lawsuits have a fleeting impact on the methods of our police. In the future our officers must feel free to enforce the law as they see fit, and if their methods circumvent a few of our civil liberties, well, that's the price that we must pay for living in a quiet, safe town.

Meaning

1. What is the main point of Steben's essay? How far along were you when you realized the irony of his approach? (See *irony* in the Glossary if you need a definition.) What clues in the first paragraph hint at this approach?
2. What, exactly, does Steben believe the police do wrong? Whom do they victimize, and how?
3. How does Steben explain police officers' justification for their actions? Does he believe their methods are at all justified?
4. If you are unsure of the meanings of any of the following words, try to guess them from their context in Steben's essay. Look up the words in a dictionary to see if your guesses were right, and then practice using each word in a sentence or two of your own.

upscale (1)	unimpeded (2)	plaintiffs (7)
bastion (1)	cloying (3)	hampered (8)
extolled (1)	demeanor (4)	petty (8)
proactive (1)	dogged (7)	shirk (8)
diligent (1)	infamy (7)	circumvent (8)
placate (2)		

Purpose and Audience

1. Why do you believe Steben wrote this essay? To make fun of the police? To express his indignation? To argue for or against something? (If so, what?) For some other purpose?
2. Whom do you believe Steben imagined as his primary readers? Teenagers, minorities, and the poor—the groups he says that are habitually targeted by the police? The "good citizens" (paragraph 1) whom the police are protecting? The police, of whom he is so critical? Support your answer with specific examples from the text.

Method and Structure

1. Steben's irony requires that he say the opposite of what he means, and in doing so he sometimes turns the principles of argument on end. For instance, can you find examples of some of the fallacies listed on pages 335–36? How do they support Steben's purpose?
2. How effective do you find Steben's choice to present his argument indirectly, cloaked in a counterargument? Your answer may depend on many factors, such as how confusing, amusing, offensive, or powerful you find the essay.
3. **Other Methods**   In paragraphs 2–5 Steben uses process analysis (Chapter 9) to detail police methods. What does this lengthy passage contribute to the essay?

Language

1. Steben's language is quite formal, with phrases such as "One might presume" (paragraph 1) and "by no means do I suggest" (2). Some of the language mimics oldsters speaking of youngsters, such as teenagers who are "up to no good" and the "smart aleck" teen (2). Some of the language even mimics a speech by a city mayor who is handing out awards to police officers — phrases such as "These dauntless men and women" (1). Why do you think Steben chose this formal style? How effective is it?
2. Why does Steben quote dialogue in paragraphs 4 and 5? What function or functions do these exchanges play?

Writing Topics

1. **Journal to Essay**   Starting from your journal entry (p. 352), write an essay about the state of law enforcement in your community, as you see it. You could focus on a particular incident involving the police or on more general patterns of action illustrated with examples. Do the police do their jobs effectively and fairly? Do they contribute to easing or to increasing tensions among groups of people? Do some groups support the police while others don't?
2. Choose a social or other kind of problem you care about — it could be the difficulty of obtaining health insurance, overcrowding in public schools, violence in the media, child neglect, or anything else. Describe the problem as you understand it, particularly how it affects people. Then discuss your solution to the problem or some part of it. Be sure at least to acknowledge opposing views. You may choose to write ironically, as Steben does, or straightforwardly.

3. **Cultural Considerations**   Steben refers to the "constitutional protection from unwarranted search and seizure" (paragraph 3) — a reference to the Fourth Amendment of the United States Constitution, quoted before the essay (p. 352). The United States is noteworthy among nations for the protections it affords citizens and others who might be suspected or accused of crime. In some other countries, for instance, law-enforcement officers may use almost any means deemed necessary to obtain evidence against a suspected wrongdoer, whereas in the United States not only the Constitution but also federal, state, and local laws tightly restrict when and how evidence may be gathered. Still, many in the United States are concerned that individual rights are not protected enough or that the protections are not equally enforced. Do you think the U.S. system achieves an appropriate balance between fairness to individuals and effectiveness in deterring or stopping crime, or does it lean one way or the other? Write an essay stating your opinion and supporting it with examples from your experience, observations, and reading. If you are familiar with individual rights and law-enforcement procedures in another country, you may want to use comparison and contrast (Chapter 10) to help make your point.

4. **Connections**   Steben writes about the experience of being falsely accused just because he is young. In contrast, Annie Dillard, in "The Chase" (p. 108), narrates an incident in which she was rightly accused of playing a childish prank. Although the incidents described by these authors differ greatly, both Steben and Dillard are subject to adults' negative attitudes about young people. Write an essay in which you outline adult society's attitudes toward young people, both just and unjust, using evidence from Steben's and Dillard's essays and from your own experience and observations.

Once again, we seem to have a situation where technology is out ahead of ethics.
— Timothy Backous

We ought not to permit a cottage industry in the God business.
— John Marchi

[In creating human clones without heads and thus without consciousness], nobody's natural rights are being compromised. No natural fetuses are being killed, nor will thinking slaves be made. We would instead be making machines like toasters, incredibly useful machines such as hearts and lungs that will save lives. Is that morally wrong?
— Kenneth Hamner

Journal Response   The announcement in 1997 that scientists had created a sheep named Dolly sparked a continuing public controversy over the ethics of cloning: copying the genetic makeup of an individual to produce one or more genetically identical individuals. In a journal entry, explore what you know about cloning and what you think about the ethics of it.

Charles Krauthammer

Born in 1950 in New York City, Charles Krauthammer was raised in Montreal, Canada, and attended McGill University (B.A., 1970), Oxford University, and Harvard Medical School (M.D., 1975). He worked as a psychiatrist at Massachusetts General Hospital until 1978 and then left medicine to serve as a science adviser to President Jimmy Carter and a speechwriter for Vice President Walter Mondale. Turning to journalism in 1981, Krauthammer wrote for The New Republic *and in 1985 began a weekly column for the* Washington Post *and a monthly column for* Time *magazine. In 1987 he won the Pulitzer Prize for distinguished commentary.* Cutting Edges, *a collection of his essays, was published in 1985. He lives in Washington, D.C.*

Of Headless Mice . . . and Men

To Krauthammer, the cloning of human beings would be nothing more than vanity, nothing less than "high-tech barbarity." This essay was published in Time *in 1998.*

Last year Dolly the cloned sheep was received with wonder, titters and some vague apprehension. Last week the announcement by a

1

Chicago physicist that he is assembling a team to produce the first human clone occasioned yet another wave of Brave New World anxiety. But the scariest news of all—and largely overlooked—comes from two obscure labs, at the University of Texas and at the University of Bath. During the past four years, one group created headless mice; the other, headless tadpoles.

For sheer Frankenstein wattage, the purposeful creation of these 2 animal monsters has no equal. Take the mice. Researchers found the gene that tells the embryo to produce the head. They deleted it. They did this in a thousand mice embryos, four of which were born. I use the term loosely. Having no way to breathe, the mice died instantly.

Why then create them? The Texas researchers want to learn how 3 genes determine embryo development. But you don't have to be a genius to see the true utility of manufacturing headless creatures: for their organs—fully formed, perfectly useful, ripe for plundering.

Why should you be panicked? Because humans are next. "It 4 would almost certainly be possible to produce human bodies without a forebrain," Princeton biologist Lee Silver told the London *Sunday Times.* "These human bodies without any semblance of consciousness would not be considered persons, and thus it would be perfectly legal to keep them 'alive' as a future source of organs."

"Alive." Never have a pair of quotation marks loomed so ominously. Take the mouse-frog technology, apply it to humans, combine it with cloning, and you are become a god: with a single cell taken from, say, your finger, you produce a headless replica of yourself, a mutant twin, arguably lifeless, that becomes your own personal, precisely tissue-matched organ farm.

There are, of course, technical hurdles along the way. Suppressing 6 the equivalent "head" gene in man. Incubating tiny infant organs to grow into larger ones that adults could use. And creating artificial wombs (as per Aldous Huxley),[1] given that it might be difficult to recruit sane women to carry headless fetuses to their birth/death.

It won't be long, however, before these technical barriers are 7 breached. The ethical barriers are already cracking. Lewis Wolpert,

[1] Aldous Huxley (1894–1963) was an English novelist and essayist. His novel *Brave New World* (1932) offers a dark satire of a technological society in which human embryos are developed in bottles. (Krauthammer refers to the title of the book in his opening paragraph.) [Editor's note.]

professor of biology at University College, London, finds producing headless humans "personally distasteful" but, given the shortage of organs, does not think distaste is sufficient reason not to go ahead with something that would save lives. And Professor Silver not only sees "nothing wrong, philosophically or rationally," with producing headless humans for organ harvesting, he wants to convince a skeptical public that it is perfectly O.K.

When prominent scientists are prepared to acquiesce in—or indeed encourage—the deliberate creation of deformed and dying quasi-human life, you know we are facing a bioethical abyss. Human beings are ends, not means. There is no grosser corruption of biotechnology than creating a human mutant and disemboweling it at our pleasure for spare parts.   8

The prospect of headless human clones should put the whole debate about "normal" cloning in a new light. Normal cloning is less a treatment for infertility than a treatment for vanity. It is a way to produce an exact genetic replica of yourself that will walk the earth years after you're gone.   9

But there is a problem with a clone. It is not really you. It is but a twin, a perfect John Doe Jr., but still a junior. With its own independent consciousness, it is, alas, just a facsimile of you.   10

The headless clone solves the facsimile problem. It is a gateway to the ultimate vanity: immortality. If you create a real clone, you cannot transfer your consciousness into it to truly live on. But if you create a headless clone of just your body, you have created a ready source of replacement parts to keep you—your consciousness—going indefinitely.   11

Which is why one form of cloning will inevitably lead to the other. Cloning is the technology of narcissism, and nothing satisfies narcissism like immortality. Headlessness will be cloning's crowning achievement.   12

The time to put a stop to this is now. Dolly moved President Clinton to create a commission that recommended a temporary ban on human cloning. But with physicist Richard Seed threatening to clone humans, and with headless animals already here, we are past the time for toothless commissions and meaningless bans.   13

Clinton banned federal funding of human-cloning research, of which there is none anyway. He then proposed a five-year ban on cloning. This is not enough. Congress should ban human cloning now. Totally. And regarding one particular form, it should be dra-   14 conian: the deliberate creation of headless humans must be made a crime, indeed a capital crime. If we flinch in the face of this high-tech barbarity, we'll deserve to live in the hell it heralds.

Meaning

1. In what two separate statements does Krauthammer most forcefully state his position on the issue of cloning?
2. Does Krauthammer see any benefit to cloning? What is his objection to the use of clones for replacement body parts?
3. Some of the following words may be new to you. Try to guess their meanings from the context of Krauthammer's essay. Test your guesses in a dictionary, and then use each new word in a sentence or two of your own.

wattage (2)	breached (7)	facsimile (10)
plundering (3)	acquiesce (8)	narcissism (12)
semblance (4)	quasi- (8)	draconian (14)
ominously (5)	abyss (8)	capital (14)
suppressing (6)	mutant (8)	heralds (14)
incubating (6)	disemboweling (8)	

Purpose and Audience

1. Krauthammer makes his purpose quite clear in the last paragraph: he wants Congress to ban human cloning immediately and entirely. Can an essay like this one, published in a magazine with a circulation in the millions, have an effect on national legislation? What would the intermediary steps have to be?
2. Who would Krauthammer's ideal readers be? Geneticists? Members of Congress? Average Joes and Janes?

Method and Structure

1. Is Krauthammer's appeal mostly emotional or mostly rational? How so?
2. Which part of the essay is more explanatory than argumentative? Is this part entirely objective? Why, or why not?
3. How does Krauthammer present his opponents' side of the issue? What is the effect of the quotations from Lee Silver and Lewis Wolpert in paragraphs 4 and 7?
4. **Other Methods** In paragraphs 9–11, Krauthammer uses comparison and contrast (Chapter 10) to distinguish headless clones from so-called

normal clones. What are the "advantages" of headless clones? How does this comparison further Krauthammer's anticloning argument?

Language

1. How would you describe Krauthammer's attitude toward his subject? What is the tone of the last paragraph?
2. What is the effect of "Because humans are next" (paragraph 4)?
3. What is the difference between "acquiescing in" and "encouraging" something (paragraph 8)?

Writing Topics

1. **Journal to Essay** Reread the quotations on page 359 and the journal entry you wrote before reading Krauthammer's essay. Develop your ideas into an essay that explains and supports your opinion about cloning human beings. Should research into potentially beneficial techniques, such as creating organs, be encouraged, discouraged, or banned entirely? What are the ethical issues, as you see them? How can they be resolved?
2. Find five or six articles on the subject of cloning, either in the periodicals collection at the library or on the World Wide Web. (The cloning of Dolly the sheep was announced in early 1997, and a great many articles appeared in that year and the next.) From these articles, list the actual and potential uses of cloning: Krauthammer mentions only two (to treat infertility and to replace body parts), but there are many other possibilities. Write a classification essay in which you sort the various uses of cloning into categories of your choosing—for example, "frivolous," "useful," and "dangerous." Be sure to explain the reasons for your categories and the uses you assign to each.
3. Until recently, cloning was a topic for science fiction. Find a novel or film that takes cloning, or something like cloning, as its subject. (For novels, you might consider Aldous Huxley's *Brave New World*, mentioned by Krauthammer, or Fay Weldon's *The Cloning of Joanna May*. Films touching on this subject include *Gattaca, Planet of the Apes*, and *Artificial Intelligence*.) Write an essay comparing and contrasting the novel's or film's attitudes toward cloning with the views of Krauthammer. Are the hopes and fears the same? Has science fiction become reality?
4. **Cultural Considerations** As Krauthammer's essay indicates, cloning is an issue that raises questions about basic human values: What makes us human? Is it ethical to tamper with our genetic coding? How far should we go in trying to cure human diseases or repair human bodies? To a great extent, the answers to such questions depend on one's moral framework—one's religious beliefs or philosophy of life. Write an essay of personal response to Krauthammer's essay, explaining how your

moral framework colors or dictates your views. It may help you get started to consider Krauthammer's assertion that "[h]uman beings are ends, not means" (paragraph 8).

5. **Connections**   Krauthammer and Bill Bryson, in "The Waste Generation" (p. 345), both impart a sense of urgency about their subjects, but their approaches are as different as their last lines: Krauthammer's "If we flinch in the face of this high-tech barbarity, we'll deserve to live in the hell it heralds" (paragraph 14) versus Bryson's "In two generations one of the last great forests of the temperate world will turn into featureless grassland. I think that's worth turning off a few computers for, don't you?" (21–22). What do these lines and others like them reveal about each author's attitude toward his subject and his readers? Are both approaches equally effective, or not? Why?

Writing with the Method
Argument and Persuasion

Choose one of the following statements, or any other statement they suggest, and support *or* refute it in an argumentative essay. The statement you decide on should concern a topic you care about so that argument is a means of convincing readers to accept an idea, not an end in itself.

MEDIA

1. Pornographic magazines and films should be banned.
2. Violence and sex should be prohibited from television.
3. Advertisements for consumer products (or political candidates) should be recognized as serving useful purposes.
4. Recordings of popular music should be specially labeled if their lyrics contain violent or sexual references.

SPORTS

5. Professional athletes should not be allowed to compete in the Olympics.
6. Professional athletes are overpaid for their work.
7. The school's costly athletic programs should be eliminated in favor of improving the academic curriculum.

HEALTH AND TECHNOLOGY

8. People should have the right to choose when to die without interference from the government or medical community.
9. Private automobiles should be restricted in cities.
10. Laboratory experiments on dogs, cats, and primates should be banned.
11. Smoking should be banned in all public places, including outdoors in congested places.

EDUCATION

12. Students caught in any form of academic cheating should be expelled.
13. Students should not be granted high-school diplomas until they can demonstrate reasonable competence in writing and mathematics.
14. Like high-school textbooks, college textbooks should be purchased by the school and loaned to students for the duration of a course.

SOCIAL AND POLITICAL ISSUES

15. The elderly are entitled to unlimited free medical care.
16. Private institutions should have the right to make rules that would be unconstitutional outside those institutions.
17. Children should be able to sue their parents for negligence or abuse.
18. A citizen should be able to buy and keep a handgun for protection without having to register it.
19. When they turn eighteen, adopted children should have free access to information about their birth parents.

Writing About the Theme
Debating Current Issues

1. Both Rush Limbaugh (p. 337) and Jeremy Steben (p. 352) adopt a sarcastic tone in arguing about issues. Write an essay in which you analyze their strategy and consider the effectiveness of such an approach. Do you believe that most readers are entertained or angered by this kind of writing? Does it communicate an argument effectively? Have you encountered other writing about social issues that relies on this technique?

2. All the writers represented in this chapter address social issues that have implications both for individuals and for policymakers. Choose another social issue that affects you on a personal level and that you believe the government needs to take a more active role in. Describe the issue in detail, outline the controversy surrounding it, and explain what steps should be taken to address it.

3. The topics chosen by the writers in this chapter—miscarriage of justice, lack of appropriate sex education, misuse of the environment, police profiling, and cloning—all could prove troubling in the future. Select the topic that you think is the most important for society to focus on. Predict the outcome, twenty or thirty years from now, if steps are not taken to adequately address this issue. Describe the best way to deal with the controversy surrounding the problem you have chosen.

Chapter 14

COMBINING
METHODS
OF DEVELOPMENT

Articulating a Vision

Though each essay in the preceding chapters illustrates one overall method of development, all the essays also illustrate other methods at the level of passages or paragraphs. (Follow-up questions labeled "Other Methods" highlight these varied strategies.) In fact, an essay is rarely developed by a single method alone. Even when you are purposefully comparing or classifying, you may also describe, narrate, define, or employ other methods. And often you may use no dominant method at all but select whatever methods you need, in whatever sequence, to achieve your purpose.

Combining methods usually adds texture and substance to an essay, for the methods provide different approaches to a subject, different ways to introduce the details and other evidence needed to interest and convince readers. Sometimes the appropriate methods may suggest themselves, but at other times it can help to explore them deliberately. The introductory discussion of the writing process shows how a set of questions derived from the methods of development can aid such a deliberate search (see pp. 23–27). Say you are writing a paper on owls. Right off several methods suggest themselves: a classification of kinds of owls, a description of each kind of owl, a process analysis of an owl's life cycle or hunting behavior. But you want your paper to go beyond the facts to convey your fascination with owls. Running through the list of questions, you find that "What is the story in the subject?" suggests a narrative of your first encounter with a barn owl, when your own awe and fear recalled the owl's reputation for wisdom and bad luck. Other questions then lead you further along this path: for instance, "How can the subject be illustrated?" calls forth examples of myths and superstitions involving owls; and "Why did the subject happen?" leads you to consider why people see owls as symbols and omens. In the course of asking the questions, you have moved from a straightforward look at owls to a more imaginative and complex examination of their meaning and significance for human beings.

The more you use the methods of development—alone or in combination—the more comfortable you will be with them and the better they will serve you. The two essays in this chapter illustrate how the methods may be combined in any way the author chooses to express ideas and achieve a purpose. (Brief annotations accompany each essay to point out some of the methods.) Both essays demonstrate how much the authors gain from having a battery of techniques and strategies to employ at will.

A NOTE ON THEMATIC CONNECTIONS

The authors of the essays in this chapter combine methods of development to articulate, or spell out, a vision of a future in which a person's race can no longer impede his or her freedom and opportunity. In a 1963 speech that has become a classic of American prose, Martin Luther King Jr. gives voice to the frustrations and aspirations of African Americans (next page). And in an essay written for his college newspaper, Brian Kaufman considers how communication by computer could make American society race-blind (p. 376).

——— Martin Luther King Jr. ———

Born in 1929 in Atlanta, Georgia, the son of a Baptist minister, Martin Luther King Jr. was a revered and powerful leader of the African American civil rights movement during the 1950s and 1960s. He was ordained in his father's church before he was twenty and went on to earn degrees at More-house College (B.A. in 1948), Crozer Theological Seminary (B.D. in 1951), and Boston University (Ph.D. in 1955). In 1955 and 1956, while he was pastor of a church in Montgomery, Alabama, King attracted national attention to the plight of Southern blacks by leading a boycott that succeeded in deseg-regating the city's buses. He was elected the first president of the Southern Christian Leadership Conference and continued to organize demonstrations for equal rights in other cities. By the early 1960s his efforts had helped raise the national consciousness so that the landmark Civil Rights Act of 1964 and Voting Rights Act of 1965 could be passed by Congress. In 1964 King was awarded the Nobel Peace Prize. When leading sit-ins, boycotts, and marches, King always insisted on nonviolent resistance "because our end is a commu-nity at peace with itself." But his nonviolence often met with violent opposi-tion. Over the years he was jailed, stoned, and stabbed. His house in Mont-gomery was bombed. And on April 4, 1968, at a motel in Memphis, Tennessee, he was assassinated. He was not yet forty years old.

I Have a Dream

On August 28, 1963, one hundred years after Abraham Lincoln's Emancipa-tion Proclamation had freed the slaves, 200,000 black and white Americans marched on Washington, D.C., to demand equal rights for blacks. It was the largest crowd ever to assemble in the capital in behalf of a cause, and the high point of the day was this speech delivered by King on the steps of the Lincoln Memorial. Always an eloquent and inspirational speaker, King succeeded in giving hope to the oppressed and opening the eyes of many oppressors.

King's speech is an argument: a persuasive appeal for racial justice. It is especially notable for its use of repetition and parallelism, two devices com-mon to inspirational speech. (See pp. 37 and 50.) But King also uses several of the methods of development discussed in this book, such as narrative, ex-ample, and cause-and-effect analysis. He uses description to convey the situa-tion and feelings of African Americans, relying heavily on figures of speech to make these qualities concrete. Some (but not all) of these descriptive figures are noted. (See the discussion of figures of speech on pp. 53–54.)

Five score years ago, a great American, in whose symbolic *1*
shadow we stand, signed the Emancipation Proclamation.
This momentous decree came as a great beacon light of
hope to millions of Negro slaves who had been seared in *Description*
the flames of withering injustice. It came as a joyous day-
break to end the long night of captivity.

But one hundred years later, we must face the tragic *2*
fact that the Negro is still not free. One hundred years *Narration*
later, the life of the Negro is still sadly crippled by the
manacles of segregation and the chains of discrimination.
One hundred years later, the Negro lives on a lonely is- *Description*
land of poverty in the midst of a vast ocean of material
prosperity. One hundred years later, the Negro is still lan-
guishing in the corners of American society and finds himself an exile in his own land. So we have come here today
to dramatize an appalling condition.

In a sense we have come to our nation's capital to *3*
cash a check. When the architects of our republic wrote
the magnificent words of the Constitution and the Decla-
ration of Independence, they were signing a promissory
note to which every American was to fall heir. This note
was a promise that all men—yes, black men as well as
white men—would be guaranteed the unalienable rights *Comparison*
of life, liberty, and the pursuit of happiness.

It is obvious today that America has defaulted on this *4*
promissory note insofar as her citizens of color are concerned. Instead of honoring this sacred obligation, America has given the Negro people a bad check, a check which
has come back marked "insufficient funds." But we refuse
to believe that there are insufficient funds in the great
vaults of opportunity of this nation. So we have come to
cash this check—a check that will give us upon demand
the riches of freedom and the security of justice. We have
also come to this hallowed spot to remind America of the
fierce urgency of *now*. This is no time to engage in the luxury of cooling off or to take the tranquilizing drugs of
gradualism. *Now* is the time to make real the promises of *Description*
Democracy. *Now* is the time to rise from the dark and
desolate valley of segregation to the sunlit path of racial
justice. *Now* is the time to open the doors of opportunity
to all of God's children. *Now* is the time to lift our nation

from the quicksands of racial injustice to the solid rock of brotherhood.

It would be fatal for the nation to overlook the urgency of the moment and to underestimate the determination of the Negro. This sweltering summer of the Negro's legitimate discontent will not pass until there is an invigorating autumn of freedom and equality; 1963 is not an end, but a beginning. Those who hope that the Negro needed to blow off steam and will now be content will have a rude awakening if the nation returns to business as usual. There will be neither rest nor tranquility in America until the Negro is granted his citizenship rights. The whirlwinds of revolt will continue to shake the foundations of our nation until the bright day of justice emerges.

Cause and effect

But there is something that I must say to my people who stand on the warm threshold which leads into the palace of justice. In the process of gaining our rightful place we must not be guilty of wrongful deeds. Let us not seek to satisfy our thirst for freedom by drinking from the cup of bitterness and hatred. We must forever conduct our struggle on the high plane of dignity and discipline. We must not allow our creative protest to degenerate into physical violence. Again and again we must rise to the majestic heights of meeting physical force with soul force. The marvelous new militancy which has engulfed the Negro community must not lead us to a distrust of all white people, for many of our white brothers, as evidenced by their presence here today, have come to realize that their destiny is tied up with our destiny and their freedom is inextricably bound to our freedom. We cannot walk alone.

Example and comparison

And as we walk, we must make the pledge that we shall march ahead. We cannot turn back. There are those who are asking the devotees of civil rights, "When will you be satisfied?" We can never be satisfied as long as the Negro is the victim of the unspeakable horrors of police brutality. We can never be satisfied as long as our bodies, heavy with the fatigue of travel, cannot gain lodging in the motels of the highways and the hotels of the cities. We cannot be satisfied as long as the Negro's basic mobility is from a smaller ghetto to a larger one. We can never be satisfied as long as a Negro in Mississippi cannot vote and a

Example and cause and effect

Negro in New York believes he has nothing for which to vote. No, no, we are not satisfied, and we will not be satisfied until justice rolls down like waters and righteousness like a mighty stream.

Example and cause and effect

I am not unmindful that some of you have come here out of great trials and tribulations. Some of you have come fresh from narrow jail cells. Some of you have come from areas where your quest for freedom left you battered by the storms of persecution and staggered by the winds of police brutality. You have been the veterans of creative suffering. Continue to work with the faith that unearned suffering is redemptive.

8

Description

Go back to Mississippi, go back to Alabama, go back to South Carolina, go back to Georgia, go back to Louisiana, go back to the slums and ghettos of our northern cities, knowing that somehow this situation can and will be changed. Let us not wallow in the valley of despair.

Example

9

I say to you today, my friends, that in spite of the difficulties and frustrations of the moment I still have a dream. It is a dream deeply rooted in the American dream.

10

I have a dream that one day this nation will rise up and live out the true meaning of its creed: "We hold these truths to be self-evident, that all men are created equal."

11

I have a dream that one day on the red hills of Georgia the sons of former slaves and the sons of former slave-owners will be able to sit down together at the table of brotherhood.

12

I have a dream that one day even the state of Mississippi, a desert state sweltering with the heat of injustice and oppression, will be transformed into an oasis of freedom and justice.

13

Description

I have a dream that my four little children will one day live in a nation where they will not be judged by the color of their skin but by the content of their character.

14

Example

I have a dream today.

15

I have a dream that one day the state of Alabama, whose governor's lips are presently dripping with the words of interposition and nullification, will be transformed into a situation where little black boys and black girls will be able to join hands with little white boys and white girls and walk together as sisters and brothers.

16

I have a dream today.   17

I have a dream that one day every valley shall be   18
exalted, every hill and mountain shall be made low, the
rough places will be made plain, and the crooked places
will be made straight, and the glory of the Lord shall be
revealed, and all flesh shall see it together.[1]

This is our hope. This is the faith with which I return to   19
the South. With this faith we will be able to hew out of the
mountain of despair a stone of hope. With this faith we will
be able to transform the jangling discords of our nation into
a beautiful symphony of brotherhood. With this faith we   *Cause and*
will be able to work together, to pray together, to struggle   *effect*
together, to go to jail together, to stand up for freedom together, knowing that we will be free one day.

This will be the day when all of God's children will be   20
able to sing with new meaning

> My country, 'tis of thee,
> Sweet land of liberty,
>   Of thee I sing:
> Land where my fathers died,
> Land of the pilgrims' pride,
> From every mountainside,
>   Let freedom ring.

So let freedom ring from the prodigious hilltops of   21
New Hampshire. Let freedom ring from the mighty mountains of New York. Let freedom ring from the heightening
Alleghenies of Pennsylvania. Let freedom ring from the
snowcapped Rockies of Colorado. Let freedom ring from   *Example*
the curvaceous peaks of California.

But not only that. Let freedom ring from Stone Moun-   22
tain of Georgia. Let freedom ring from Lookout Mountain of Tennessee. Let freedom ring from every hill and
molehill of Mississippi. From every mountainside, let freedom ring.

When we let freedom ring, when we let it ring from   23
every village and every hamlet, from every state and every
city, we will be able to speed up that day when all of

---

[1] This paragraph alludes to the Bible, Isaiah 40:4–5. [Editor's note.]

God's children, black men and white men, Jews and Gentiles, Protestants and Catholics, will be able to join hands and sing in the words of the old Negro spiritual, "Free at last! Free at last! Thank God almighty, we are free at last!"

Brian Kaufman

Brian Kaufman was born in 1952 in Cleveland, Ohio, and grew up in Berea, a nearby suburb. He moved to Fort Collins, Colorado, during high school. He attended Colorado State University, "resuming," he says, "an education that I abandoned twenty-five years ago" and graduating wih a degree in English literature. Kaufman cooks for a living and in his free time lifts weights, plays blues guitar, and enjoys the company of his wife and three children. He also writes fiction and has published a historical novel, The Breach *(2002).*

Can Technology Make Us Colorblind?

Many writers have predicted bold changes in our lives and society resulting from communication by computer. Kaufman foresees an especially positive change, the achievement of the vision articulated by Martin Luther King Jr. in "I Have a Dream." This essay appeared in 1998 in the Collegian, *Colorado State's student newspaper.*

My wife plays in computer chat rooms. Recently, she told me about a twenty-nine-year-old artist, single, who turned out to be a forty-five-year-old married salesman. I had a hard time mustering the proper amount of sympathetic outrage. "You don't ever really know who you're talking to," she complained.

Narration and example

Exactly. The Internet lets us go beyond ordinary role-play, to the extent that we can ignore the limitations of who and what we are. Chat rooms are a testing ground for the lives you've never led. Men can go online as women and discover what it's like to be (virtually) drooled on by every slob with whom they come in contact. Women can go online as men and find out how clever they have to be—as in trained-dog-through-hoops clever—in order to attract attention.

Cause and effect

Example

Most chat programs have picture access, but the user decides what snapshot to scan. Heavy people can be thin, angry people can put on a smile, and old people can be

young again. Nor is the potential for identity-liberation *Example*
limited to chat-room conversation.

Time magazine estimates that within the decade, over 4
half of the jobs in the United States will be done at home.
With so many people doing their primary commercial *Cause and*
work over a keyboard and monitor, we have a chance to *effect*
do something no other culture has done. Simply put, we
can go colorblind.

In his landmark "I Have a Dream" speech, Dr. Mar- 5
tin Luther King Jr. wished for a day when children will
"live in a nation where they will not be judged by the
color of their skin but by the content of their character."

Thanks to technology and a changing workplace, that 6
day no longer seems impossible. Without a visual label,
how can we continue to discriminate on a consistent basis? If we don't know what the people at the other end of
the terminal look like, how can we judge them on the *Cause and*
basis of their appearance? *effect*

Yet at the moment when technology offers a chance 7
at an old dream, we seem to wish to separate and alien-
ate. Most people (you know, Toyota's "everyday people")
don't believe in what used to be called "melting pot"
equality. In the 90s, personal identities are based on differences and similarities are viewed with suspicion, as if
every shared moment is a potential shackle.

Even the form our language takes becomes a separat- 8
ist's battleground. For example, one side of the ebonics
controversy[1] is the contention that ebonics is a legitimate, *Example*
rule-driven language in its own right and, as such, is a le- *and division*
gitimate primary language and genuine voice for black *or analysis*
America. (This line of reasoning is discrete from a second
argument that educational approaches that attend properly to vernacular dialects, comparing and contrasting

---

[1] *Ebonics* is a name given to the African American vernacular (or everyday language), generally considered a dialect of English with a distinct grammar, vocabulary,
and pronunciation. In late 1996 the school board of Oakland, California, decided to
recognize ebonics as a language whose speakers can use help learning to translate between ebonics and standard English. The school board's decision ignited a nationwide
debate. [Editor's note.]

rather than ignoring the vernacular, are more successful in teaching commercial English.)

I respect these arguments, but in the context of our new technology, I can't help wondering if ebonics amounts to a lingual uniform. Does our sense of self depend on providing language clues to our genetic heritage through the one medium that shields visual clues? We have a common language of commerce and a technology with the potential for a certain kind of equality. Must we sacrifice this opportunity in the name of personal identity through collective identifications?

9

Cause and effect

I am not arguing that ebonics is the sole impediment to freedom on the information highway. I am arguing that it is a symptom of an America that has splintered, perhaps irreparably.

10

It may be that we no longer share King's dream of transforming "the jangling discords of our nation into a beautiful symphony of brotherhood." Perhaps I am being nostalgic for a romantic vision with no relevance to today's world. King's importance may lie in the symbol, not the substance, of his discourse.

11

Or maybe the change is already underway, like it or not. Watch any politician speak on television. His or her cadence is cued by a TelePrompTer. The width of the screen dictates sentence breaks.

12

Example

The fact is that technology alters communication. Perhaps the computer and its blind-eye monitor have already become too large a part of our lives to avoid the influence. In the near future, the way we do business may drag us, kicking and screaming, into King's dream.

13

Cause and effect

Glossary

abstract and concrete words An **abstract** word refers to an idea, quality, attitude, or state that we cannot perceive with our senses: *democracy, generosity, love, grief*. It conveys a general concept or impression. A **concrete** word, in contrast, refers to an object, person, place, or state that we can perceive with our senses: *lawnmower, teacher, Chicago, moaning*. Concrete words make writing specific and vivid. See also pp. 52–53, p. 65, and *general and specific words*.

allusion A brief reference to a real or fictitious person, place, object, or event. An allusion can convey considerable meaning with few words, as when a writer describes a movie as "potentially this decade's *Star Wars*" to imply both that the movie is a space adventure and that it may be a blockbuster. But to be effective, the allusion must refer to something readers know well.

analysis (also called **division**) The method of development in which a subject is separated into its elements or parts and then reassembled into a new whole. See Chapter 7 on division or analysis, p. 146.

anecdote A brief narrative that recounts an episode from a person's experience. See, for instance, McCuistion, paragraph 1, page 282. See also Chapter 5 on narration, p. 88.

argument The form of writing that appeals to readers' reason and emotions in order to win agreement with a claim or to compel some action. This definition encompasses both argument in a narrower sense—the appeal to reason to win agreement—and persuasion—the appeal to emotion to compel action. See Chapter 13 on argument and persuasion, p. 328.

assertion A debatable claim about a subject; the central idea of an argument.

audience A writer's audience is the group of readers for whom a particular work is intended. To communicate effectively, the writer should estimate readers' knowledge of the subject, their interests in it, and their biases toward it and should then consider these needs and expectations in choosing what to say and how to say it. For further discussion of audience, see pp. 2, 12–13, 20.

body The part of an essay that develops the main idea. See also pp. 27–28.

cause-and-effect analysis The method of development in which occurrences are divided into their elements to find what made an event happen (its causes) and what the consequences were (its effects). See Chapter 12 on cause-and-effect analysis, p. 296.

chronological order   A pattern of organization in which events are arranged as they occurred over time, earliest to latest. Narratives usually follow a chronological order; see Chapter 5, p. 88.

classification   The method of development in which the members of a group are sorted into classes or subgroups according to shared characteristics. See Chapter 8 on classification, p. 173.

cliché   An expression that has become tired from overuse and that therefore deadens rather than enlivens writing. Examples: *in over their heads, turn over a new leaf, march to a different drummer, as heavy as lead, as clear as a bell.* See also p. 54.

climactic order   A pattern of organization in which elements—words, sentences, examples, ideas—are arranged in order of increasing importance or drama. See also p. 40.

coherence   The quality of effective writing that comes from clear, logical connections among all the parts, so that the reader can follow the writer's thought process without difficulty. See also pp. 37–40 and 238–39.

colloquial language   The language of conversation, including contractions (*don't, can't*) and informal words and expressions (*hot* for new or popular, *boss* for employer, *ad* for advertisement, *get away with it, flunk the exam*). Most dictionaries label such words and expressions *colloquial* or *informal.* Colloquial language is inappropriate when the writing situation demands precision and formality, as a college term paper or a business report usually does. But in other situations it can be used selectively to relax a piece of writing and reduce the distance between writer and reader. (See, for instance, Hughes, p. 97.) See also *diction.*

comparison and contrast   The method of development in which the similarities and differences between subjects are examined. Comparison examines similarities and contrast examines differences, but the two are generally used together. See Chapter 10 on comparison and contrast, p. 230.

conclusions   The endings of written works—the sentences that bring the writing to a close. A conclusion provides readers with a sense of completion, with a sense that the writer has finished. Sometimes the final point in the body of an essay may accomplish this purpose, especially if it is very important or dramatic (for instance, see Winik, p. 189). But usually a separate conclusion is needed to achieve completion. It may be a single sentence or several paragraphs, depending on the length and complexity of the piece of writing. And it may include one of the following, or a combination, depending on your subject and purpose:

- A summary of the main points of the essay (see Visser, pp. 167–68)
- A statement of the main idea of the essay, if it has not been stated before (see Klass, p. 139), or a restatement of the main idea incorporating information from the body of the essay (see Nadler, p. 255)

- A comment on the significance or implications of the subject (see Woiwode, p. 75, Dillard, p. 112).
- A call for reflection, support, or action (see Sadiq, p. 162; McCuistion, p. 284; Bryson, p. 349; Krauthammer, p. 362).
- A prediction for the future (see King, pp. 374–75)
- An example, anecdote, question, or quotation that reinforces the point of the essay (see Brady, p. 278; Kimhachandra, p. 316; Ehrenreich, p. 322)

Excluded from this list are several endings that should be avoided because they tend to weaken the overall effect of an essay: (1) an example, fact, or quotation that pertains to only part of the essay; (2) an apology for your ideas, for the quality of the writing, or for omissions; (3) an attempt to enhance the significance of the essay by overgeneralizing from its ideas and evidence; (4) a new idea that requires the support of an entirely different essay.

concrete words   See *abstract and concrete words.*

connotation and denotation   A word's **denotation** is its literal meaning: *famous* denotes the quality of being well known. A word's **connotations** are the associations or suggestions that go beyond its literal meaning: *notorious* denotes fame but also connotes sensational, even unfavorable, recognition. See also pp. 51–52.

contrast   See *comparison and contrast.*

critical reading   Reading that looks beneath the surface of a work, seeking to uncover both its substance and the writer's interpretation of the substance.

deductive reasoning   The method of reasoning that moves from the general to the specific. See Chapter 13 on argument and persuasion, especially pp. 333–34.

definition   An explanation of the meaning of a word. An extended definition may serve as the primary method of developing an essay. See Chapter 11 on definition, p. 267.

denotation   See *connotation and denotation.*

description   The form of writing that conveys the perceptions of the senses — sight, hearing, smell, taste, touch — to make a person, place, object, or state of mind vivid and concrete. See Chapter 4 on description, p. 59.

diction   The choice of words you make to achieve a purpose and make meaning clear. Effective diction conveys your meaning exactly, emphatically, and concisely, and it is appropriate to your intentions and audience. **Standard English,** the written language of educated native speakers, is expected in all writing for college, business and the professions, and publication. The vocabulary of standard English is large and varied, encompassing, for instance, both *comestibles* and *food* for edible things, both *paroxysm* and *fit* for a sudden seizure. In some writing situations, standard English may also include words and expressions typical of conversation (see *colloquial language*). But it excludes other levels of diction that only certain groups understand or find acceptable. Most dictionaries label expressions at these levels as follows:

- **Nonstandard:** words spoken among particular social groups, such as *ain't, them guys, hisself,* and *nowheres.*
- **Slang:** words that are usually short-lived and that may not be understood by all readers, such as *tanked* for drunk, *bread* for money, and *honcho* for one in charge.
- **Regional** or **dialect:** words spoken in a particular region but not in the country as a whole, such as *poke* for a sack or bag, *holler* for a hollow or small valley.
- **Obsolete:** words that have passed out of use, such as *cleam* for smear.

See also *connotation and denotation* and *style.*

division or analysis   See *analysis.*

dominant impression   The central ideal or feeling conveyed by a description of a person, place, object, or state of mind. See Chapter 4 on description, especially p. 60.

effect   See *cause-and-effect analysis.*

emotional appeal   In argumentative and persuasive writing, the appeal to readers' values, beliefs, or feelings in order to win agreement or compel action. See pp. 330–32.

essay   A prose composition on a single nonfictional topic or idea. An essay usually reflects the personal experiences and opinions of the writer.

ethical appeal   In argumentative and persuasive writing, the sense of the writer's expertise and character projected by the reasonableness of the argument, the use and quality of evidence, and tone. See p. 330.

evidence   The details, examples, facts, statistics, or expert opinions that support any general statement or claim. See pp. 332 and 339–40 on the use of evidence in argumentative writing.

example   An instance or representative of a general group or an abstract concept or quality. One or more examples may serve as the primary method of developing an essay. See Chapter 6 on example, p. 118.

exposition   The form of writing that explains or informs. Most of the essays in this book are primarily expository, and some essays whose primary purpose is self-expression or persuasion employ exposition to clarify ideas.

fallacies   Flaws in reasoning that weaken or invalidate an argument. Some of the most common fallacies are listed below (the page numbers refer to further discussion in the text).

- **Oversimplification,** overlooking or ignoring inconsistencies or complexities in evidence: *If the United States banned immigration, our unemployment problems would be solved* (pp. 239, 335).
- **Hasty generalization,** leaping to a conclusion on the basis of inadequate or unrepresentative evidence: *Every one of the twelve students*

polled supports the change in the grading system, so the administration should implement it (p. 335).

- **Begging the question,** assuming the truth of a conclusion that has not been proved: *Acid rain does not do serious damage, so it is not a serious problem* (p. 335).
- **Ignoring the question,** shifting the argument away from the real issue: *A fine, churchgoing man like Charles Harold would make an excellent mayor* (p. 335).
- **Ad hominem** ("to the man") **argument,** attacking an opponent instead of the opponent's argument: *She is just a student, so we need not listen to her criticisms of foreign policy* (p. 335).
- **Either-or,** presenting only two alternatives when the choices are more numerous: *If you want to do well in college, you have to cheat a little* (p. 336).
- **Non sequitur** ("It does not follow"), deriving a wrong or illogical conclusion from stated premises: *Because students are actually in school, they should be the ones to determine our educational policies* (p. 336).
- **Post hoc** (from *post hoc, ergo propter hoc,* "after this, therefore because of this"), assuming that one thing caused another simply because it preceded the other: *Two students left school in the week after the new policies were announced, proving that the policies will eventually cause a reduction in enrollments* (pp. 298, 336).

figures of speech   Expressions that imply meanings beyond or different from their literal meanings in order to achieve vividness or force. See pp. 53–54 for discussion and examples of specific figures.

formal style   See *style.*

freewriting   A technique for discovering ideas for writing: writing for a fixed amount of time without stopping to reread or edit. See pp. 22–23.

general and specific words   A **general** word refers to a group or class: *car, mood, book.* A **specific** word refers to a particular member of a group or class: *Toyota, irritation, dictionary.* Usually, the more specific a word is, the more interesting and informative it will be for readers. See also pp. 52–53, p. 65, and *abstract and concrete words.*

generalization   A statement about a group or a class derived from knowledge of some or all of its members: for instance, *Dolphins can be trained to count* or *Television news rarely penetrates beneath the headlines.* The more instances the generalization is based on, the more accurate it is likely to be. A generalization is the result of inductive reasoning; see p. 332.

hasty generalization   See *fallacies.*

hyperbole   Deliberate overstatement or exaggeration: *The desk provided an acre of work surface.* See also p. 54. (The opposite of hyperbole is understatement, discussed under *irony.*)

image   A verbal representation of sensory experience—that is, of something seen, heard, felt, tasted, or smelled. Images may be literal: *Snow stuck to her eyelashes; The red car sped past us.* Or they may be figures of speech: *Her eyelashes were snowy feathers; The car rocketed past us like a red missile.* (See pp. 53–54.) Through images, a writer touches the readers' experiences, thus sharpening meaning and adding immediacy. See also *abstract and concrete words.*

inductive reasoning   The method of reasoning that moves from the particular to the general. See Chapter 13 on argument and persuasion, especially p. 332.

informal style   See *style.*

introductions   The openings of written works, the sentences that set the stage for what follows. An introduction to an essay identifies and restricts the subject while establishing your attitude toward it. Accomplishing these purposes may require anything from a single sentence to several paragraphs, depending on your purpose and how much readers need to know before they can begin to grasp the ideas in the essay. The introduction often includes a thesis sentence stating the main idea of the essay (see pp. 18–19). To set up the thesis sentence, or as a substitute for it, any of the following openings, or a combination, may be effective:

- Background on the subject that establishes a time or place or that provides essential information (see Rember, p. 102; Voccola, p. 209; Gould, p. 181; McClain, p. 258; Krauthammer, p. 360)
- An anecdote or other reference to the writer's experience that forecasts or illustrates the main idea or that explains what prompted the essay (see Dillard, p. 108; Brady, p. 276; Kaufman, p. 376)
- An explanation of the significance of the subject (see Cofer, p. 307)
- An outline of the situation or problem that the essay will address, perhaps using interesting facts or statistics (see Sadiq, p. 160; Zimring, p. 192; King, p. 370)
- A statement or quotation of an opinion that the writer will modify or disagree with (see Steben, p. 352)
- An example, quotation, or question that reinforces the main idea (see Klass, pp. 136; Kimhachandra, p. 313)

A good introduction does not mislead readers by exaggerating the significance of the subject or the essay, and it does not bore readers by saying more than is necessary. In addition, a good introduction avoids three openings that are always clumsy: (1) beginning with *The purpose of this essay is . . .* or something similar; (2) referring to the title of the essay in the first sentence, as in *This is not as hard as it looks* or *This is a serious problem;* and (3) starting too broadly or vaguely, as in *Ever since humans walked upright . . .* or *In today's world. . . .*

irony   In writing, irony is the use of words to suggest a meaning different from their literal meaning. Steben's "Small Town, Quiet Town, Safe

Town" presents an ironic statement relying on reversal: he says the opposite of what he really means (pp. 352–56). But irony can also derive from understatement (saying less than is meant) or hyperbole (exaggeration). Irony can be witty, teasing, biting, or cruel. At its most humorless and heavily contemptuous, it becomes **sarcasm**: *Thanks a lot for telling Dad we stayed out all night; that was really bright of you.*

metaphor A figure of speech that compares two unlike things by saying that one is the other: *Bright circles of ebony, her eyes smiled back at me.* See also p. 54.

narration The form of writing that tells a story, relating a sequence of events. See Chapter 5 on narration, p. 88.

nonstandard English See *diction.*

oversimplification See *fallacies.*

paragraph A group of related sentences, set off by an initial indentation, that develops an idea. By breaking continuous text into units, paragraphing helps the writer manage ideas and helps the reader follow those ideas. Each paragraph makes a distinct contribution to the main idea governing the entire piece of writing. The idea of the paragraph itself is often stated in a topic sentence (see pp. 35–36), and it is supported with sentences containing specific details, examples, and reasons. Like the larger piece of writing to which it contributes, the paragraph should be unified, coherent, and well developed. For examples of successful paragraphs, see the paragraph analyses in the introduction to each method of development (Chapters 4–13). See also pp. 35–36 and 274–75 (unity), 37–38 and 238–39 (coherence), and 40–41 and 179 (development).

parallelism The use of similar grammatical form for ideas of equal importance. Parallelism occurs within sentences: *The doctor recommends swimming, bicycling, or walking.* It also occurs among sentences: *Strumming her guitar, she made listeners feel her anger. Singing lines, she made listeners believe her pain.* See also p. 50.

personification A figure of speech that gives human qualities to things or abstractions: *The bright day smirked at my bad mood.* See also p. 54.

persuasion See *argument.*

point of view The position of the writer in relation to the subject. In description, point of view depends on the writer's physical and psychological relation to the subject (see pp. 60–61). In narration, point of view depends on the writer's place in the story and on his or her relation to it in time (see pp. 89–90). More broadly, point of view can also mean the writer's particular mental stance or attitude. For instance, an employee and employer might have different points of view toward the employee's absenteeism or the employer's sick-leave policies.

premise The generalization or assumption on which an argument is based. See *syllogism.*

process analysis   The method of development in which a sequence of actions with a specified result is divided into its component steps. See Chapter 9 on process analysis, p. 201.

pronoun   A word that refers to a noun or other pronoun: *Six days after King picked up his Nobel Peace Prize in Norway, he was jailed in Alabama.* The personal pronouns (the most common) are *I, you, he, she, it, we,* and *they.* See also pp. 37–38 (pronouns and coherence), 61 and 89–90 (pronouns and point of view), and 207 (consistency in pronouns).

proposition   A debatable claim about a subject; the central idea of an argument.

purpose   The reason for writing, the goal the writer wants to achieve. The purpose may be primarily to explain the subject so that readers understand it or see it in a new light; to convince readers to accept or reject an opinion or to take a certain action; to entertain readers with a humorous or exciting story; or to express the thoughts and emotions triggered by a revealing or instructive experience. The writer's purpose overlaps the main idea—the particular point being made about the subject. In effective writing, the two together direct and control every choice the writer makes. See also p. 18 and *thesis* and *unity.*

rational appeal   In argumentative and persuasive writing, the appeal to readers' rational faculties—to their ability to reason logically—in order to win agreement or compel action. See pp. 332–34.

repetition and restatement   The careful use of the same words or close parallels to clarify meaning and tie sentences together. See also pp. 37–38 and 238.

revision   The stage of the writing process devoted to "re-seeing" a draft, divided into fundamental changes in content and structure (revision) and more superficial changes in grammar, word choice, and the like (editing). See Chapter 3, pp. 33–58.

rhetoric   The art of using words effectively to communicate with an audience, or the study of that art. To the ancient Greeks, rhetoric was the art of the *rhetor*—orator, or public speaker—and included the art of persuasion. Later the word shifted to mean elegant language, and a version of that meaning persists in today's occasional use of *rhetoric* to mean pretentious or hollow language, as in *Their argument was mere rhetoric.*

sarcasm   See *irony.*

satire   The combination of wit and criticism to mock or condemn human foolishness or evil. The intent of satire is to arouse readers to contempt or action, and thus it differs from comedy, which seeks simply to amuse. Much satire relies on irony—saying one thing but meaning another (see *irony*).

simile   A figure of speech that equates two unlike things using *like* or *as*: *The crowd was restless, like bees in a hive.* See also p. 53.

slang   See *diction.*

spatial organization   A pattern of organization that views an object, scene, or person by paralleling the way we normally scan things—for instance, top to bottom or near to far. See also pp. 39 and 64.

specific words   See *general and specific words.*

Standard English   See *diction.*

style   The *way* something is said, as opposed to *what* is said. Style results primarily from a writer's characteristic word choices and sentence structures. A person's writing style, like his or her voice or manner of speaking, is distinctive. Style can also be viewed more broadly as ranging from formal to informal. A very formal style adheres strictly to the conventions of Standard English (see *diction*); tends toward long sentences with sophisticated structures; and relies on learned words, such as *malodorous* and *psychopathic.* A very informal style, in contrast, is more conversational (see *colloquial language*); tends toward short, uncomplicated sentences; and relies on words typical of casual speech, such as *smelly* or *crazy.* Among the writers represented in this book, King (p. 370) writes quite formally, Hughes (p. 97) quite informally. The formality of style may often be modified to suit a particular audience or occasion: a college term paper, for instance, demands a more formal style than an essay narrating a personal experience. See also *tone.*

syllogism   The basic form of deductive reasoning, in which a conclusion derives necessarily from proven or accepted premises. For example: *The roof always leaks when it rains* (the major premise). *It is raining* (the minor premise). *Therefore, the roof will leak* (the conclusion). See Chapter 13 on argument and persuasion, especially pp. 333–34.

symbol   A person, place, or thing that represents an abstract quality or concept. A red heart symbolizes love; the Golden Gate Bridge symbolizes San Francisco's dramatic beauty; a cross symbolizes Christianity.

thesis   The main idea of a piece of writing, to which all other ideas and details relate. The main idea is often stated in a **thesis sentence** (or sentences), which asserts something about the subject and conveys the writer's purpose. The thesis sentence is often included near the beginning of an essay. Even when the writer does not state the main idea and purpose, however, they govern all the ideas and details in the essay. See also pp. 17–18, p. 35, and *unity.*

tone   The attitude toward the subject, and sometimes toward the audience and the writer's own self, expressed in choice of words and sentence structures as well as in what is said. Tone in writing is similar to tone of voice in speaking, from warm to serious, amused to angry, joyful to sorrowful, sympathetic to contemptuous. For examples of strong tone in writing, see Woiwode (p. 72), Steben (p. 352), McClain (p. 258), Brady (p. 276), and King (p. 370). See also pp. 41–42 and 343.

transitions   Links between sentences and paragraphs that relate ideas and thus contribute to clarity and smoothness. Transitions may be sentences

beginning paragraphs or brief paragraphs that shift the focus or introduce new ideas. They may also be words and phrases that signal and
specify relationships. Some of these words and phrases—by no means
all—are listed below:

- **Space:** above, below, beyond, farther away, here, nearby, opposite,
there, to the right
- **Time:** afterward, at last, earlier, later, meanwhile, simultaneously,
soon, then
- **Illustration:** for example, for instance, specifically, that is
- **Comparison:** also, in the same way, likewise, similarly
- **Contrast:** but, even so, however, in contrast, on the contrary, still, yet
- **Addition or repetition:** again, also, finally, furthermore, in addition,
moreover, next, that is
- **Cause or effect:** as a result, consequently, equally important, hence,
then, therefore, thus
- **Summary or conclusion:** all in all, in brief, in conclusion, in short, in
summary, therefore, thus
- **Intensification:** indeed, in fact, of course, truly

understatement See *irony*.

unity The quality of effective writing that occurs when all the parts relate
to the main idea and contribute to the writer's purpose. See also pp.
35–37 and 274–75.

Index of
Authors and Titles

Guide to the Elements of Writing

The Compact Reader offers advice on writing from the general, such as organizing and revising, to the particular, such as tightening sentences and choosing words. Consult the page numbers here for answers to questions you may have about the elements of writing.